ARAB
versus
EUROPEAN

ARAB
versus
EUROPEAN

DIPLOMACY AND WAR
IN NINETEENTH-CENTURY
EAST CENTRAL AFRICA

NORMAN ROBERT BENNETT

 AFRICANA PUBLISHING COMPANY
a division of
Holmes & Meier
New York   London

First published in the United States of America 1986 by
Africana Publishing Company, a division of
Holmes & Meier Publishers, Inc.
30 Irving Place
New York, N.Y. 10003

Great Britain:
Holmes & Meier Publishers, Ltd.
Hillview House
One Hallswelle Parade
London NW11 ODL, England

Book design by Ellen Foos

Library of Congress Cataloging in Publication Data

Bennett, Norman Robert, 1932-
  Arab versus European.

  Bibliography: p.
  Includes index.
  1. Africa, East—History—To 1886. 2. Zanzibar—
History—To 1890. 3. Arabs—Africa, East—History—19th
century. 4. Arabs—Tanzania—Zanzibar—History—19th
century. 5. Oman—History. I. Title.
DT431.B46 1986   967   84-15686
ISBN 0-8419-0861-3

Manufactured in the United States of America

To the memory of
Al Castagno,
a good friend who
left us too soon

Contents

CONTENTS

Acknowledgments

THIS STUDY BEGAN when I had the good fortune to hold a Ford Foundation Africa Training Grant. Additional help over the years generously came from the African Studies Center of Boston University. A legion of individuals—far too many to name—assisted me in one way or another while I conducted research in Africa, Europe, and the United States. My warmest thanks go to them all. Special thanks go to Roland Oliver; his sage advice at a particularly difficult moment encouraged me to continue with my planned researches. Jeanne Penvenne, as always, did all that was necessary to help in the writing of this work while we lived in Parede, Maputo, and Nantucket.

Nantucket

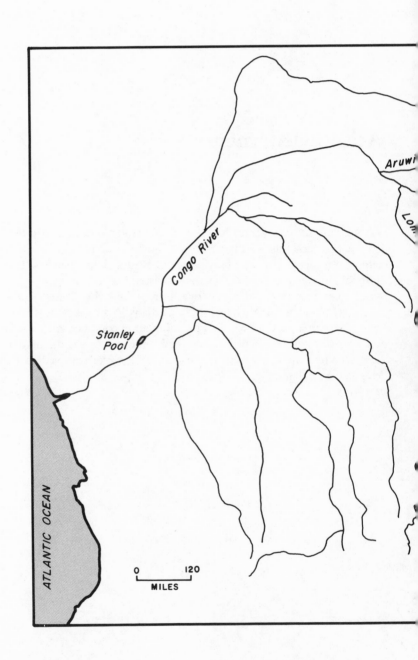

Aruwi

Lom

Congo River

Stanley
Pool

ATLANTIC OCEAN

0   120
MILES

BUGANDA

Lake Victoria

NGWE
ASONGO

NYAMWIZI

UJIJI

TABORA

*Lake
Tanganyika*

GOGO

MOMBASA

PEMBA

SŌDANI

ZANZIBAR

BAGAMOYO

DAR ES
SALAAM

ZARAMU

INDIAN OCEAN

KILWE
KIVINJE

KARONGA

MIKINDANI

Lake Nyasa

Introduction

> I once overheard an intelligent Mohammedan explaining
> to his following that only those Europeans who had
> failed elsewhere came out to these parts.
>
> —*W. P. Johnson*

DURING THE SECOND half of the nineteenth century the followers of two
major world religions met in intense competition for the mastery of East
Central Africa's lands and peoples. One group, representing the Islamic
world, by the nineteenth century had been present for over a millennium
on that stretch of the East African littoral extending from the Somali
territories in the north to the lightly administered Portuguese possessions
south of Cape Delgado. And even centuries before the birth of Muhammad venturesome traders from southwest Asia had utilized the regular
monsoon winds of the western Indian Ocean to visit Africa's eastern coast.
Over these many centuries occurred a slow but continuous intermingling
of southwest Asian and eastern African peoples, the two regions maintaining an enduring relationship that made the East African littoral often more
responsive to influences originating in the broader Indian Ocean world
than to developments in its own hinterland. The contacts between conti-
nents persisted, even intensified, during the destructive sixteenth- and
seventeenth-century Portuguese domination. The Arabs of Uman in 1650
reconquered the important southeast Arabian port of Muscat, becoming
the champions of an aggressive Islamic offensive against the Portuguese.
The Muslims of East Africa quickly sought aid, the Umani from 1652
responding by a series of attacks culminating in the 1698 capture of
Mombasa. The Umani, under the BuSaidi dynasty from the 1740s, remained and exercised a precarious overlordship upon many of the city
states, the great distance between Arabia and East Africa allowing others
to win effective independence from their erstwhile allies. Mombasa, ruled
by the Umani Mazrui clan, became the leading opponent of the Muscat-

based Arabs, safeguarding its freedom through a wise policy of cooperation with African inhabitants of the city and environs.

By the first decade of the nineteenth century, commencing with the long
reign of the dominant BuSaidi sovereign Said bin Sultan (1804–1856),
the Umani increasingly intervened in the affairs of the coast; in the process
they developed a flourishing political and commercial entity centered
upon the fertile offshore island of Zanzibar. The links between East Africa
and Arabia endured even after the British-enforced political separation of
Zanzibar and Muscat in 1861. Traders continued to follow the monsoons;
in 1929, for example, 118 dhows arrived in Zanzibar from the ports of the
Persian Gulf and Arabia. As late as 1946 Pemba Arab Said bin Ali el
Mugheiri maintained that the relations between Uman and Zanzibar were
"like that of a mother and her child."[1]

In East Africa the result of these centuries of relationships was an Islamic civilization composed of heterogeneous ethnic groups. Tracing origins to Arabian, Persian, and African sources, its members followed an
interpretation of Islam that incorporated African beliefs while they spoke
Swahili, a Bantu language with significant borrowing from Arabic.[2] The
Ibadhi Arabs of Uman, although few in number, were the dominant
element in east coast society. The Umani reigned supreme in political and
social life, the minor doctrinal differences separating Sunni and Ibadhi
approaches resulting in few serious societal frictions. The same tolerance
generally was extended to other creeds, whether held by indigenous Africans, Indians, or the later arrivals from Europe and the United States. In a
typical observation British traveler William Palgrave in the 1860s noted of
Muscat's Indian residents: "Toleration is here the word, and religious
belief or practices are neither asked nor interfered with." French missionary Anton Horner concurred for Zanzibar, enthusiastically praising the
"unlimited liberty which everyone enjoyed." Twentieth-century British
administrator Harold Ingrams added: "Of all men I know the Ibadhi is the
least bigoted in religion."[3] The natural skepticism greeting such evaluations was expressed when a British missionary explained the treatment of
Christians in Zanzibar as a political issue, the consequence of British
support for the BuSaidi dynasty. "Indeed," said Charles New, "it may be
said that the present throne has been established by English power. The
present Sultan owes his all to England." But the frequent examples of
good feeling mentioned by Zanzibar's Christian residents require more
than a political explanation. In a most telling instance, missionary Arthur
West simply recounted that on the dedication day of the foundation stone
of Zanzibar's Anglican cathedral "Abd er Bahman [sic], the Ismam [sic] of
the mosque close by, had in the morning brought flowers and green
plants, and set them along our path . . ."[4] There were, of course, strict
limitations to the Christians' freedom of action. Proselytization among

Zanzibar's Muslims was forbidden, and the Arab government of the island enforced the traditional ban within Islam against apostasy *(ridda)*.[5] The Christians avoided controversy by confining their efforts largely toward immediate conversion to newly arrived Africans, although one missionary society during the 1870s felt confident enough of Arab goodwill to begin setting up in its press an anti-Muslim tract in the Swahili language and in Arabic script.[6]

The heterogeneous nature of east coast civilization was increased by the relative lack of ethnic bigotry held by Umani Arabs.[7] In their Arabian homeland, long a major receiving center for African slaves, racial admixture was a common occurrence: Palgrave estimated individuals of African ancestry comprised about one-third of Muscat's population.[8] Some Umani Muslims, of course, shared the racist beliefs present in both the contemporary Islamic and Christian worlds. An aristocratic female Arab of Zanzibar, for example, expressed a bigotry common to other slave-owning societies when explaining the lot of Africans: "Oh God made them to be slaves. Why [else] were they made different from us?"[9] But, since the children of marriages, along with many offspring from less formal arrangements, were incorporated into their father's families, Umani individuals at all levels of society possessed African ancestors. Said bin Sultan's favorite son Hilal (d. 1851), described by a British consul as "the most shrewd and energetic of all the Imam's sons," had an Ethiopian mother; so did another son, Barghash, the energetic ruler of Zanzibar from 1870 to 1888.[10] The most famous of all Zanzibar Arabs, Hamid bin Muhammed, better known as Tippu Tip, had African ancestors, while Said bin Sultan's secretary, the influential Ahmad bin Hamis, was described by one visitor "as black as the ace of spades."[11] In less prominent walks of Zanzibar life persons of Arab and African ancestry participated together in many occupations, poor Arabs from the Hadramawt, for instance, working at menial tasks until they saved enough resources either to rise in local society or to return to enjoy a better life in their homeland.[12]

More importantly, many Africans shared the beliefs and values of Umani-directed society; their numbers included the Swahili-speaking populations of Zanzibar, Pemba, and the African coastlands, peoples long incorporated into the Muslim world. Other African Muslims had origins in all regions of East Central Africa, representing groups either coming to Islam by free choice or by the brutal circumstances of a slave trade tearing them from the culture of their birth. In both instances Africans adopted many Islamic beliefs and practices, themselves making the conscious decision to become Muslim. Nonetheless, Europeans commonly argued that Arabs had minimal interest in bringing their religion to Africans. "So much has been said about Arab proselytism," observed David Livingstone at the beginning of his last African journey, "that it was with interest enquiries were made about their success in converting the Makonde . . . Here as elsewhere no attempt to teach had been made. Some Arabs asserted that it would be useless for the Makonde had no idea of a Deity."[13] Muhammad bin Khalfan, the prominent Lake Tanganyika Arab, reputedly went even further, justifying his harsh treatment of Africans on the grounds that "these heathen had no soul and were only beasts."[14] Therefore, concluded Livingstone, "in all their long intercourse with the tribes on the mainland, not one attempt has ever been made to propagate the Mahometan faith . . . [The Arabs] have propagated syphilis and the domestic bug alone."[15] In more recent scholarship J. Spencer Trimingham lends his weighty authority to the view that Arabs made little special effort to disseminate Islam.[16]

Yet instances of Arabs teaching Africans the precepts of Islam are just as common as contrary examples. When Walter Hutley in central Tanzania definitively asserted, "I have never heard or met with a Muslim missionary," he doubtless was remarking on the absence among Muslims of salaried professionals like himself. As elsewhere, the teaching of Islam in East Central Africa was the result of the labors of individual believers, the great majority traders, who passed over to Africans personal comprehension of their faith. "Almost every Arab and half-caste Arab trader in these parts (and they are numerous)," lamented a companion of Hutley's, "are zealous propagators of Islamism. They neglect no opportunity, by persuasion and by force of arms (especially the latter) to accomplish their object."[17] John Speke in 1861 observed followers of Musa Mzuri of Unyanyembe endeavoring to convert Africans, while in 1884 W. P. Johnson of the Universities' Mission stated: "I have passed large caravans amongst which were conspicuous the teacher with his alphabet-board, and sometimes large bundles of the Koran."[18] Many visitors to interior settlements discovered Muslim teachers, mosques, and other indications of a vigorous religious life, a White Father remarking concerning an arrival in a Yao village during Ramadan that "one could believe himself in Istanbul or at the least in Zanzibar."[19] The ubiquitousness and influence of Muslims certainly explains many of the vigorous denunciations made by competing Europeans. "One meets many—too many—of these traders, fellows in long white shirts and small close-fitting skull caps," complained one missionary, another morosely explaining that "everybody looks up to them implicitly [even though] . . . they are utterly ignorant and only represent the lowest vilest side of Arab civilization." In short, acknowledged Livingstone, after learning more about the Arab impact upon Africans of the interior, "the Arabs are imitated in everything."[20]

The usual European understanding of the character of individual Muslims intent upon spreading their faith, or of the depth of the African convert's commitment to Islam, requires little serious comment. The

European rivals of the Arabs normally denigrated the beliefs of new followers of Islam. Missionary R. S. Hynde typically characterized some Yao Muslims as "Black Arabs," individuals "who have been at the coast and picked up a little Swahili and a little Mohammedan varnish." The relatively well-educated Johnson agreed. "Islam here," he opined, "has little in common with real Islam. Coast slaves or underlings are always passing . . . These coast villains flatter and cheat the few really free men about, and teach themselves to call themselves WaIslamu and each new caravan brings more of these men, whom the natives very vaguely distinguish from Arabs."[21] "The best taught," concluded Edward Steere, "learn very little, and seldom understand what they learn."[22] Nonetheless, the Arabs, often not long present in the interior before the arrival of the first Europeans, gained thousands of converts all over East Central Africa. They did not bring to the region the European sense of mission into a heathen darkness; instead they generally accepted Africans as they found them, relegating these nonbelievers to that inferior place in society reserved for non-Muslims. Even if some Arabs took little personal initiative in making converts, they did not discourage Africans from seeking to understand the truths claimed by Islam. Many new individual African believers doubtless lacked the knowledge of the learned representatives of Islam resident in Zanzibar, but then so did most of the Arabs who traveled into the interior. The Africans believed they were Muslims, the essential step in any personal religious experience. The Yao turned increasingly to Islam from the 1870s; in Buganda, in 1876, hundreds of Africans died for possessing Muslim beliefs.[23]

In all East Central Africa only the vital assistance of the African Muslims of the coast and interior made possible Arab penetration of the continent and the concomitant creation of an Arab state centered on Zanzibar, exercising forms of control over vast inland regions. It must be emphasized when discussing this process that most Muslims had not arrived in interior locations to spread their religion, by active or passive means, until well into the nineteenth century. Commentators upon Islam in East Central Africa generally stress that the religion did not flourish until after the European conquest, advancing such reasons as the *pax Europica* or African reactions to the racially restricted congregations of their conquerors.[24] Just as important, however, was the indispensable groundwork, fundamental to any conversion process, laid by the pioneer Muslims of the nineteenth century. Unfortunately for these individuals the flowerings of their endeavors followed Arab defeats by the various Christian European powers.

The racial perceptions of nineteenth-century Europeans usually led to the drawing of a series of sharp distinctions among members of the diverse East Central African Muslim community, the fundamental division being the supposedly separate racial categories of Arab and African. Many observers, then and later, had difficulty accepting the wisdom of Aidan Southall's sage counsel: "We must . . . remember that races are constructs of the observer and do not exist empirically."[25] The light-complexioned Arab, however grudgingly, was recognized by Europeans as a fellow member of a superior racial group. But his commitment to Islam and participation in the slave trade certainly convinced European contemporaries that the Arab resided in an inferior niche in the scale of human evolution. Thus American consul Andrew Ward could characterize Said bin Sultan as similar to "the whole Arab people . . . crafty, deceitful, faithless and only operated upon by the display of physical power."[26] Nevertheless, the Arab occupied a much higher status than the African. To Samuel Baker, for example, "Central Africa is peopled by a hopeless race of savages, for whom there is no prospect of civilization."[27] Consequently, from the time of the earliest modern visitors, most Europeans believed that the Arabs of East Central Africa, so often possessing both Arabian and African ancestors, were a very inferior people. "The half-caste Arab is degenerate in body and mind," explained Richard F. Burton. "The third generation becomes as truly negroid as the inner heathen." Consul Christopher P. Rigby reasoned that if "the prosperity of the Zanzibar dominions . . . [depended] on these degenerate Arabs, it might well be despaired of," adding elsewhere "I look upon the Arabs of Zanzibar as the very vilest race I have ever met."[28]

Other visitors used this reasoning to blame most of the excesses accompanying the hunt for and sale of, human merchandise upon Afro-Arab and African associates of the Arabs. Livingstone, apparently forgetting what he once had scorned as "the stupid prejudice against colour," excused Arabs for such actions and assigned guilt to "those vile half-castes that swarm about every caravan." Frederick D. Lugard, with his usual nicety of expression, concurred: "Your slave-raider is more usually a mongrel—the son of some poor slave girl by the fortieth cousin of a half-caste Arab." He added: "Very many pure-bred Arabs [are] most gentlemanly fellows."[29] The "pure-bred Arabs," usually prominent Muslims with lighter skin coloring, often received favorable descriptions from Europeans. "I think the experience of the generality of travellers," said missionary Alexander Mackay, "is that the Muscat Arab in the interior of Africa is a gentleman whom it is a pleasure to meet among the surrounding barbarism." Another missionary, Alfred Swann, praised Muhammad bin Khalfan: "He was a pure Arab—quiet in manner, cultured and courteous, always a gentleman in his dealings with us." Congo State official J. Troup similarly was impressed with the demeanor of Rashid bin Muhammad. "One was struck with the perfect manners of this well-bred Arab," Troup wrote, adding that "he was the handsomest Arab I ever saw, a tall, well-built young man, a thoroughbred Arab, of light complexion scarcely more than olive, with sparkling eyes, a well-formed nose, and small mouth, altogether very delicate features."[30] This unfounded attitude, as often as not made ridiculous by the European's lack of knowledge of his Arab companion's supposed ancestry, unfortunately has lingered on until the present;[31] it has been maintained only by ignoring the ethnic realities of the East Central African Muslim world where, for example, a dhow captain could be described, without other comment, as "quite black but an Arab I fancy from his manner and carriage."[32] To counter their racial confusion Europeans propounded additional explanations to distinguish the "better class" of followers of the Prophet from the "Moslem Nigger," or ordinary African Muslim;[33] thus they resolved to their satisfaction the differences in behavior, puzzling to their ingrained beliefs concerning individuals possessing darker skin coloring, among the Muslims encountered. The bewildered Verney L. Cameron, after meeting Tippu Tip, observed: "He was a good-looking man and the greatest dandy I had seen amongst the traders. And not withstanding his being perfectly black, he was a thorough Arab, for curiously enough the admixture of negro blood had not rendered him less of an Arab in his ideas and manners."[34]

The effort to draw racial boundaries among the Arabs of nineteenth-century East Central Africa ludicrously exposes the fallacies of thought based upon variously perceived racial distinctions. The Europeans hopelessly confused the ethnic status of Arabs and Africans they encountered. Lugard, for instance, described Yao leader Mponda as "a semi-Arab chief," while a British consul was impressed enough by another Yao leader, Makanjira Nakanjire, to picture him as "a bright, intelligent man . . . [who] might easily be taken for a pure-bred Arab." As the last statement indicates, a chief factor in establishing an individual's origins was the personal evaluation of the European. If the individuals aided a European, as often did Abdullah and Shaykh bin Nasibu of Unyanyembe, they became to Cameron and Adolphe Burdo "fine Arab gentlemen." But to German traveler Paul Reichard, following many differences, Abdullah, because of his mixed Arab and African ancestry, was a perfect example of the treacherous-by-nature Afro-Arab.[35] The untenable distinctions applied to the Muslims of East Central Africa should be ignored. The designation *Arab* is a cultural term encompassing disparate members of the Islamic world; many Egyptians, Sudanese, Algerians, and others, after all, remain part of the Arab world even without Arab ancestry.[36] Regrettably, the racial considerations of the past have survived in East Central African historiography, thus causing, without the unfortunate derogatory connotations of an earlier era, the making of unnecessary distinctions among Arabs of varying skin coloration.[37] The tendency to classify believers in Islam by analytically considering, in terms of some absolute standard, their knowledge and comprehension of Muslim tenets is equally unrewarding and

ignores thereby the diversity within unity characterizing the far-flung
Muslim world. The first Zanzibari I encountered, the possessor of a very
dark skin, spoke very little Arabic; nonetheless, he regarded himself as an
Arab. His nineteenth-century ancestors thought the same. In this study
the designation *Arab* includes all Muslim individuals who thought of
themselves as Arabs and who participated in the political, economic, and
cultural system centering upon Zanzibar.

Of course the Arabs of East Central Africa of the last quarter of the
twentieth century, due to the changing thought currents of recent times,
are now often classified by their governments, or themselves, as Africans.
The changing of ethnic identities, a characteristic of Zanzibar society
throughout most of the nineteenth and twentieth centuries, has been
discovered in numerous African regions.[38] Many of the participants in the
Muslim movements described in this study, whatever their ethnic background, thought of themselves as Arabs, striving, like most men, for
acceptance as members of the ruling class of their society, an aspiration
incorporated in the Swahili word *ustaarabu,* to be like an Arab, meaning
to be civilized. "These better circumstanced dress in resemblance to the
Arabs," said one nineteenth-century visitor to Zanzibar, "whose captivat-
ing manners and customs, all classes of the Suahelians imitate as far as the
condition in life of each will allow." "People here," explained Steere in a
revealing aside, "are mostly ashamed of their own tongue and proud of
their very small modicum of Arabic."[39]

The ranks of Muslims naturally included many Africans not recognized
as, perhaps not even aspiring to be, Arabs. Often described as Zanzibari,
these Africans came from all areas of East Central Africa. Many had been
brought as slaves to the coast, there finding new lives as members of its
Muslim society, later often returning to the interior as members, either
free or slave, of Arab expeditions. These individuals, the backbone of Arab
ranks, proudly accepted their place in the Zanzibar system; many doubtless shared the feelings of a Banda man of similar status: becoming a slave,
he recounted, "happened once, and all was soon over. Then you were
given a home, food, clothes, etc., and above all a *gun;* you were a man."
Thus, copying many Arab and European commanders, Belgian Francis
Dhanis could without confusion describe his followers as "my Zanzibaris,
natives of Maniema."[40]

Differences certainly were present among the many members of the vast
and variegated community of Muslims. The Umani, for instance, appeared
to outsiders as overly convinced of their own superiority. "They think
themselves," said missionary F. T. Haig, "the finest race on the face of the
earth, and their manner, while perfectly polite, is the natural expression of
this feeling." John Kirk maintained that Majid bin Said, Zanzibar's ruler
from 1856 to 1870, "still hankers after a good name among the people of

Oman, whom he looks on, and with justice, as a race superior to their descendants, the Arabs of Zanzibar." The attitude was shared by many Europeans, Cameron asserting, "the Omân Arabs are far superior to those of Zanzibar or rather of the coast . . ." In the far interior, missionary E. C. Gordon noted that there were differences among natives of the Arabian peninsula, describing "natives of Sheher, reckoned Arabs also but despised by the more pure Arabs." And many Europeans commented upon what they saw as proof that some Arabs regarded darker-skinned Muslims as inferior. British naval officer Joseph Nourse early in the century judged that one individual, "being of the Negro cast . . . could never be seated on the same mat with the Governor [of Zanzibar], or an Arab of consequence." Missionary Kerr Cross on Lake Malawi maintained that "true Arabs spurn M'loze and his party and refuse to call them Arabs, and say they are little better than the natives," while French traveler E. Trivier even asserted some Arabs regarded Tippu Tip with disfavor.[41] If so, in view of existing power realities, such individuals expressed their opinions in private. Many Arabs, certainly realizing the racial attitudes of European visitors, may even have overemphasized their own views. And, since most information concerning Arab views of others in East Central Africa comes from European sources, how can we be sure what most Arabs really thought? Any differences, whether real or alleged, among the ranks of Muslims will be noted in this study only if having some effect upon the course of Arab conduct.

Opposed to the Arabs were the representatives of European civilization entering East Central Africa in steadily increasing numbers during the nineteenth century. Before the 1870s the two groups by and large coexisted peacefully; most Europeans confined their activities to Zanzibar and the coastal regions, residing and laboring as consuls, explorers, missionaries, and traders. These men, mostly citizens of Britain, France, German Hansa cities, and the United States, very few accompanied by their families, had minimal influence upon the lives of Arabs or Africans. The consuls did have an important role in political life; the British representatives, because of an alliance of convenience between their nation and the BuSaidi, secured dominant influence through supporting the Arab dynasty against its rivals in return for assistance in limiting the slave trade of the western Indian Ocean. The few early explorers whose published accounts made the East Central African interior known to the European and American public, had virtually no immediate local impact. The missionaries, restricted to Zanzibar and a few coastal locations, similarly were more important for the foundations provided for later European arrivals. The traders, because of the commercial policies of the Arab state, resided in Zanzibar. Not until the 1870s did the activities of the Europeans become more intrusive, their interference in East Central African affairs progressively enlarging until, from 1885, their governments began the conquest of the peoples looking to Zanzibar for political and commercial direction.

Virtually all Europeans, whether representing governments or private organizations, regarded Arabs as opponents hindering achievement of their varying secular and religious goals. To French priest Léonce Bridoux the "work [of the Arabs] is that of destruction, and all their efforts tend to diminish, if not to destroy, ours, the work of edification." Thus, reasoned Anglican cleric West, "the best remedy I can see is the destruction of Mahomedanism which means the extinction of the Arabs . . . but this would be a severe remedy." But perhaps not too severe a remedy, many Europeans sharing German officer Hermann von Wissmann's conviction that the Arabs were the "enemy of mankind."[42] The few individuals regarded by contemporaries as favoring Arabs generally did so either for reasons of government policy, as the British consuls in Zanzibar, or because they considered Arabs as useful intermediaries in the process of achieving European cultural, political, and economic domination over the African majority. Belgian trader Arthur Hodister, for example, a man with many Arab friends, thought of the Arab as "a natural intermediary between the native and the whites" in the era before Europeans dominated Africa.[43]

Among missionaries there were several opinions. The well-known views of Isaac Taylor drew some support: he thought Islam, "though quite unfitted for the higher races . . . eminently adapted to be a civilizing and elevating religion for barbarous tribes." Others simply conceded that any Christian progress in East Central Africa was impossible without some Arab support. Lake Tanganyika missionary Edward Hore concluded: "It is a great mistake to suppose that the cure for the slave trade or the means to help the natives to peace and civilization is to be achieved by driving out the Arab and Wangwana traders and settlements. With very few exceptions in the territories of exceptional chiefs the reverse is the case and these small traders and settlements form the only oasis of peace and prosperity to the natives and are a cementing power to keep society together." The value of assistance from prominent Arabs also was recognized. "Tippu Tib [sic] is the only one of his class who shows signs of overcoming prejudice and joining with Europeans to open up roads for commerce . . . ," judged Hore, "and I do think it would be quite possible for a prudent European government to obtain his help for the improvement of Africa."[44] But when crises occurred, the supposedly pro-Arab individuals—even if responsibility for the troubles did not rest with Arabs—always sided with their fellow Europeans. Belgian Jerome Becker, for example, regarded as the European closest to Tippu Tip, though blaming the onset of hostilities in the Congo in 1892 on his countrymen, nonetheless favored an Arab defeat.[45]

By the mid-1880s, when Europeans were prepared to use force against Arabs, they had propounded for the Western world an enduring characterization of their opponents. "The Arabs . . . without exception," charged Emin Pasha, "are thieves or beggars, [and] must be removed or sent back to their native land without any chance of ever returning."[46] The interpretation grew from the long period of mistrust between Christianity and Islam. From the European Middle Ages onward, stressed Norman Daniel, "the frontier that divided the mental attitudes of Christians and Muslims was emphatically defined and crossed only with the greatest difficulty."[47] The nineteenth century added the racist underpinnings discussed above, plus the important fact that Arabs and Africans were members of societies accepting as integral parts of their culture the ownership of, and commerce in, human beings at a moment in history when Europeans had evolved a near universal belief in the evils of slavery and the slave trade. The Europeans came to East Central Africa possessing the fiery zeal for beliefs often held by recent converts to a new cause. Forgotten was the circumstance of their own society only recently ceasing to transport millions of Africans across the Atlantic to the Americas, even later abolishing the status of slavery in European overseas territories. The Arabs became the "slave trading Arabs"—even usually careful scholars scarcely could speak of them thereafter without the qualifying epithet[48]—while virtually all other aspects of their civilization were disregarded.

The newcomers to East Central Africa were sincere in their beliefs. Most of them, after all, previously never had experienced directly the horrors common to slave-based societies, although the tolerated societal ills of their own European homelands often were outrageous enough to make some observers question the sincerity of the denunciations made of the faults of other cultures. It was obvious to many individuals that not only Arabs were involved in the slave trade, that all nations represented in Zanzibar, regardless of the strength of their denunciations, profited from supplying Arabs with the merchandise necessary for human purchases. "Seldom has a slave-vessel been taken by our cruisers," explained John Kirk, "that did not more or less affect some of the European and American houses here, as it rendered some Arab or other unable to meet his obligations when due." But, concluded Kirk, "I fear that neither an Indian, nor a German, or American, will ask what is done by the purchaser or the borrower with goods taken up so long as money is paid when due."[49]

The blind spots of nineteenth-century Europeans are understandable: Livingstone could believe that "it is on the Anglo-American race that the hopes of the world for liberty and progress rest."[50] Participants in a historical process usually are not aware of the underlying currents motivating their behavior. But the attitudes of the nineteenth century have persisted, frequently surfacing in contemporary scholarly endeavors.

There should be little need to reaffirm that slavery was an abominable institution, Arabs, like all slave-owning peoples, perpetrating unspeakable indignities upon other human beings.[51] When Western historians discuss the past of their own societies, European and American participation in slavery and the slave trade is not emphasized over all other aspects of activity. Simón Bolívar or Thomas Jefferson, noted rulers of slave societies, receive analytical praise or blame for specific actions; their responsibilities toward slavery or the slave trade, when mentioned at all, are measured against the backdrop of their times. As David Brion Davis commented: "Jefferson's record on slavery can only be judged by the values of his contemporaries and by the consistency between his own professed beliefs and actions. One needs to remember that he was a man burdened by many conflicting fears, roles, and responsibilities."[52] British social historian E. P. Thompson's apt comment that "men must be judged in their own context,"[53] is as valid for Arabs as for any other people.

Nonetheless, Arabs have not received this treatment. Attitudes have remained virtually unchanged since the nineteenth century. "Islam has never brought forth anything; it can only destroy," intoned French priest Charmetant. Lord Salisbury expressed it most succinctly during the late 1880s: the Arabs opposing the British on Lake Malawi were "the scum of humanity . . . This terrible army of wickedness."[54] To scholars of our century the Muslims of East Central Africa remained equally damned. One of the principal twentieth-century historians of the region, Reginald Coupland, concluded: "Throughout all the centuries since first they colonised the coast, the Arabs had never attempted to administer the country of exploit its natural resources (except ivory and human beings) at any distance from their seaboard towns or inland settlements. They had done no good to the people of East Africa. Indeed, as Livingstone often said, they had done nothing but harm." To succeeding scholars the Muslims of East Central Africa above all remain the "Swahili slave-traders . . . and their followers"; Tippu Tip and Rumaliza are remembered principally as "the two great slaving partners."[55] Clearly, most Europeans, from the nineteenth century onward, were convinced that Arabs were practitioners of a way of life making their defeat a desirable outcome of the confrontation in East Central Africa.

Furthermore, the generally accepted viewpoint regarding Arabs has colored the entire analysis of the period of open conflict between Arab and European. The ordinary standards for evaluation of historical evidence no longer seem to apply, the often unfounded accusations of Europeans against their rivals being accepted as fact. A parallel may be drawn with the history of Carthage where, explained B. H. Warmington, scholars "must rely largely on the information provided by the Greek and Roman enemies of Carthage." As Norman Daniel observed of Christians and Muslims,

"The human capacity to believe what one wishes of one's enemies is without bounds."[56] The movement against the Arabs, with its heavy Christian component, became a crusade against the slave trade, its proponents rekindling the embers of the persisting rivalry between Muslim and Christian; their views differed but little from those expressed centuries earlier by Fra Fidenzio of Padua: "and if there were no other cause but this, it would be the duty of Christians to fight against them, and to cleanse the earth."[57] Most contemporary European participants naturally did not realize the apt linking of their crusade in the Arab mind with the excesses committed in the name of Christianity following the eleventh-century call of Pope Urban II for action against the Muslim occupiers of the Christian Holy Land.[58]

The ensuing hostilities of the nineteenth-century crusade were recounted by the participants and their supporters as a form of inspiring epic wherein a few determined and resolute Europeans fought to rescue Africans from the oppressive clutches of evil slave traders. The story of the fighting between Arabs and Europeans for control of regions around the northern shores of Lake Malawi, for example, said Lugard's biographer Margery Perham, "read like the classic schoolboy's adventure story," with Lugard "struggling with wholly inadequate forces and weapons . . . to save the missionaries and the weaker tribes from the slave-raiders and their tribal allies." She does not sound much different from Lugard. The war, he contended, "reads like a page of fiction . . . [with] six white men holding their own against an army of Arabs, utterly cut off from assistance, voluntarily remaining rather than haul down the British flag, slowly firing their last rounds of ammunition one by one!" Echoing the foregoing opinions, Roland Oliver, describing the same struggle, declared: "The little Livingstonia Company, with the aid only of private subscriptions, in two years fought the Arabs to a standstill."[59] But with equal validity one could contend that a few Arabs, with African allies, fought the British-backed company to a standstill.

The characterizations of European and Arab leaders during the Lake Malawi hostilities are typical of other struggles of the 1880s and 1890s in East Central Africa. The initial commander of British forces, L. Monteith Fotheringham, was "a man of very strong character and upright disposition, severe occasionally with the natives in maintaining the laws that he laid down for the maintenance of order, but of great bravery, and absolutely just in his dealings." Mlozi bin Diwani, the head of the Arab community, however, although recognized as "a man of great qualities, indominable will, and insatiable ambition," was at heart "a wily chief and sly diplomat."[60] To increase the excitement of the confrontations, commentators on Arab-European wars invariably charge that Muslims possessed seemingly overwhelming numbers matched against the smaller

European-commanded forces. The fact that in many struggles, like the one involving Mlozi, Fotheringham, and Lugard, the Arabs and Europeans, who were not supported by their distant governments and who each depended upon the aid of African allies, met with roughly equal forces, is characteristically ignored. In a typical example a British historian of the Congo claimed, on the eve of the final conflict in that territory between Arab and European, that the numerical strength of the former was potentially 100,000 men while the latter had only about 4,000 regular troops.[61] Strangely ignored is the reality that both competing parties were few in numbers, each relying upon African allies to do most of the fighting. Equally ignored by writers following in this tradition is the significant truth that Europeans, representatives of the most technically advanced civilization of their era, usually had access to superior military resources, paid for by the contributions of thousands of European Christians or by their own governments, while Arabs, supported by neither an organized missionary force nor any technically advanced government, fought largely without access to outside assistance. The Arabs resisted Europeans as staunchly as they did, not because of the frequently claimed "Islamic fanaticism,"[62] but because of their own determination, backed by the vital support of African allies.

The failure of many historians to escape interpretations inculcated by accepted myths of the past possibly might be excusable if the course of events had evolved differently in East Central Africa. But the same Europeans who came to the region, sincerely appalled at the losses of life caused by the slave trade, after defeating the Arabs went on to subject Africans to their rule, justifying in the cause of the advancement of their civilization the heavy loss of life entailed by this conquest. To describe the Muslim advance from Zanzibar, as, in the words of two determined defenders of European colonial rule, "part of a great blood-stained drive"[63] is sensible only if similar treatment is given to the equally harsh European conquest and administration. A Belgian officer in 1892 reported that Ujiji Arab Nassur bin Khalfan had questioned whether it was a crime to kill an African[64]—unfortunately later many Europeans shared his attitude. The stress by contemporaries on the suppression of the slave trade and slavery as the reason for conquest no longer is supportable. Horace Waller's judgment that "ours has been, and is, an expenditure in men and money for purely philanthropic purposes"[65] must be recognized merely as the emotion of a participant. Even the conclusions of such sound historians as D. A. Low—"it would not be going too far to say that a fear for the revival of the slave trade was the most important single factor in persuading British public opinion to insist on the retention of Uganda"[66]—must be reexamined. The attitude toward slavery and the slave trade was equivocal among Europeans. The Congo Independent State, for instance, was a prime purchaser of slaves; Consul Charles Euan Smith, after one State recruiting venture in Zanzibar, charged that it "bids fair to become in this way one of the largest employers of slave labour in the world."[67] And once Europeans had defeated Arabs and Africans and established colonial governments, the abolition of slavery, possibly disrupting their new economic concerns, suddenly became much less urgent. The institution of slavery in the European territories of East Central Africa persisted in one form or another until into the twentieth century, while the succeeding forms of forced labor often seemed to Africans a continuation of slavery under another name.[68]

It quickly became apparent that the new rulers, allegedly rescuing Africans from the ravages of the slave trade, had, unlike the Arabs, after imposing their own controls, restricted their subjects through racist-inspired ideologies and policies to an inferior place in colonial society, at the same moment brutally denigrating many facets of indigenous African culture. The many instances of psychic and physical repression of Africans during the years of European rule are too familiar to require extended comment here. Only individuals sharing the myopic vision of the determined defenders of the colonial experience can regard the defeat of the Arabs as a clear advance toward a better way of life for the region's Africans.[69] "Ah! yes, we miss the Arabs," said, in 1902, one African from the western shore of Lake Tanganyika. A prime reason for the attitude was expressed by another African: "At least the BaNgwana left us our beliefs, but the white man even wants to steal them from us."[70]

The Europeans of the nineteenth century were convinced they fought against Arabs in the name of humanity; similarly many twentieth-century Americans believed they struggled in Vietnam to preserve Western democracy. In each case we can acknowledge the sincerity of contemporary interpretation, but as historians it is our duty to go beyond the depictions of events provided by participants. This conclusion, of course, is a commonplace. Nevertheless, the past interpretations of the rivalry between Arab and European in East Central Africa warrant its reiteration.

FIRST CONTACTS

c. 1800 to the 1870s

1 Zanzibar and Its Sultans

> . . . even on the shores of the Lake Tanganyika six hundred miles inland [said Burton of Majid], the natives composed songs in his praise, as the great and just prince dwelling on the sea shore.
>
> —*Christopher P. Rigby*

THE MODERN MOVEMENT into East Central Africa by Arabs based upon the East African littoral was tied intimately to the rise of the island entrepot of Zanzibar, a development that began during the second half of the eighteenth century.[1] The major turning point in the evolution of relationships between Umani and Africans followed Said bin Sultan's accession, the young and talented Arab presiding over a process wedding Arabians and Africans into a dynamic political, economic, and cultural entity influencing a major part of the African continent. Realizing Zanzibar's potentialities Said harnessed developments under way before his arrival—the introduction of clove trees, the penetration of the continent in search of slaves and ivory, the arrival of Indian, European, and American traders—to make Zanzibar both "the gate to Equatorial Africa" and "the great meeting place of India, Arabia and Africa."[2]

The British, their Indian empire the dominant power in the western Indian Ocean since the latter third of the eighteenth century, maintained, because of Muscat's strategic location in relation to India, careful surveillance of Uman's affairs. Their newfound devotion to the suppression of the slave trade gave the British an additional reason for upholding a connection with the ruler of a state increasingly involved in East Central Africa. Said, understanding the necessity of the continuing approval and support of the powerful British, concluded, despite the obvious antagonism of his subjects,[3] the Moresby Treaty of 1822 restricting the trade in slaves from his African dominions. Since, in Said's relatively unstructured state, all significant governmental activity required his physical presence, the Arab ruler's ever longer residences in Zanzibar caused an initially reluctant British Indian administration to sanction from 1841 the stationing there of an agent representing both Indian and metropolitan governments. Henceforth most decisions made by Zanzibar's BuSaidi sovereigns had to pass the watchful scrutiny of resident British consuls. To guarantee continuation of a political friendship protecting him from potential and actual enemies, Said signed additional agreements in 1839, 1845, and 1850 further limiting the slave trade. The ties to the British aroused fierce resentment and opposition among Said's followers; Atkins Hamerton, first British consul, explained that the 1850 concession allowing the British the right to pursue suspected slavers onto the southern coastal region's shores had brought the Arab leader "the contempt and hatred of all his people, even to the members of his own family."[4] Realizing the dangers of hindering the attainment of British goals through excessive application of antislave trade policies, Hamerton refrained from pushing Said into a stance too far removed from his subject's opinions. "It is not best to agitate this slave question in Zanzibar as the natives do not understand it," he once informed a skeptical American listener.[5]

Ever more closely linked to his powerful ally, Said and his successors, well aware of the dangers of any unsettling differences, persisted in a relationship which, until the mid-1880s, excellently served BuSaidi needs. The resulting correlation of interests between Arab and British governments can cause misunderstanding of the actual relationship, characterizing the Arab ruler as "the puppet sultan," while describing Zanzibar as "an unofficial protectorate of Britain,"[6] both clearly overstated interpretations. The sultans naturally deferred to British might, especially in slave-trade matters, but Britain, little interested for much of the nineteenth century in most aspects of Arab policy, left Zanzibar's rulers considerable opportunity to profit from their ally's preference for continuation of a stable administration. The sultans, by surrendering freedom in one sphere, considerably strengthened their general authority over not always obedient subjects. In the words of a Swahili proverb: "An unbeliever that is of use to you is better than a Moslem that is of no use to you."[7]

"The Sultan himself is the government," concluded American merchant Charles Ward in a simplified yet essentially accurate description of Zanzibar's political structure. Under the Umani system the ruler represented one of his region's clans, with rival clans constantly standing prepared to take advantage for their own interests of any weakness among the ruling group. The fiercely individualistic Umani regarded the titular head of their state as a necessary figure, particularly for dealings with foreign peoples and nations; he was a first among a group of equals, designated since pre-Islamic times only as *sayyid*.[8] Some rulers of Uman had been called *imam*, but Said never took the religious title, although nineteenth-century observers, followed by succeeding generations of historians,[9] continually used that appellation. Other foreign visitors called Said and his successors *sultan,* too encompassing a term for their Umani subjects, yet one which came increasingly into use.[10] It has been adopted for this volume.

In Zanzibar, with its relatively small Arab community, Said possessed a more secure position than in Uman, although the presence of some Umani clans, especially the long-resident al Harthi, required constant attention. The indigenous inhabitants of Zanzibar and Pemba—the Hadimu, Tumbatu, and Pemba—quickly came to terms with the Arab ruler, thereafter offering no significant opposition to the BuSaidi. For the necessary decisions of state Said held council with trusted advisors, heads of Umani clans, *gadis* (judges), and the customs master, seeking a consensus of opinion for any major decision. Apart from slave-trade issues, where British determination made opposition both futile and dangerous, the sultan effectively was guided by these deliberations, the absence in the Arab state of any bureaucratic apparatus requiring, to make enforcement a reality, general acceptance of governmental regulations. The most important individual functionary serving the sultan was the customs master, aptly described by a later resident as "practically the Chancellor of the Exchequer,"[11] who from the 1820s was an Indian merchant who administered all functions relating to the import and export of merchandise, and secured the office through payment of an annual rent to the Arab ruler.[12] By 1856 Said yearly received the sum of $220,000 from the customs master. Added to the revenues coming from his extensive estates and from other sources, the sultan then had an annual income of about $500,000,[13] which provided the necessary resources for managing state affairs. The slave trade during the first half of the century averaged an estimated yearly import into Zanzibar and Pemba of from 10,000 to 15,000 individuals;[14] many later reexported, contributed a significant share of the revenues upon which the customs lease was based. Thus every slave-trade concession made by Said to the British potentially decreased state revenues, further strengthening the ties binding together BuSaidi and British.

State revenues, apart from expenditures for the sultan's large personal establishment, were spent to keep the inhabitants of the East African coast and Uman subordinate to BuSaidi rule. Important individuals, both Arab and African, received annual payments to help ensure loyalty; recipients included the Hadimu ruler, the head of the al Harthi,[15] and the leaders of coastal settlements who recognized the sultan's overlordship.[16] Hamerton described the payments—he called them bribes—as a basic prop for Said's rule.[17] But the payments were more than simple bribery; with an administration lacking a permanent salaried bureaucracy Said gained adherents, usually the already existing local leaders, to his Zanzibar-based economic and political system by compensating them, from the increased profits his policies brought, for any existing rights and privileges lost through accepting his rule.

When monetary inducements did not secure loyalty, the Zanzibar sovereign utilized his formidable navy, a force far outclassing the naval strength of any other indigenous polity of the western Indian Ocean. The sultan's army was a much less formidable force; during the 1840s it comprised about 400 regular troops, mostly Baluchi and Hadrami, poorly paid, equipped and trained, stationed along the coast at the more important settlements as a sign of Zanzibar's authority. Their number was augmented by perhaps an equal complement of irregular troops, drawn from various ethnic groups, as well as a few soldiers serving the customs master. For extraordinary situations Said summoned additional levies from both his Arabian and African dominions. By the 1860s the sultan's regular forces had risen to over 1,200 men.[18] The soldiers gained few notable triumphs; consequently Said sent them into battle only when all other means of resolving specific quarrels failed. The existence of the sultan's combined naval and land forces effectively served to maintain loyalty along the coast. There were limits to this loyalty, of course; the Arab ruler remained all too aware that excesses on the part of his officials might end in an unwanted interruption of commerce. In a typical example, from the reign of Barghash, an African was killed near Dar es Salaam during a minor dispute with the sultan's followers. When the aggrieved Africans did not secure justice, they simply boycotted the Arab settlement, completely disrupting trade.[19] Such occurrences were not the rule: after the taking of Mombasa only the stubborn leadership of the minor port of Siyu and the equally determined Mazrui rebel, Mbaruk bin Rashid, accepted the consequences of protracted resistance to Zanzibar's sovereign.

With the death of Said bin Sultan in 1856 the lack of fixed rules of succession, a common characteristic of Muslim political systems,[20] resulted in a dangerous quarrel among the deceased monarch's sons. Said had designated Majid as successor to his African dominions. Challenged both by rivals in Zanzibar (the al Harthi and Barghash) and in Uman (his brother Thuwayni), Majid drew upon the vitality of the polity created by his father and triumphantly emerged as Zanzibar's sultan. When Thuwayni threatened invasion, Majid prepared to defend the island, gathering 1,400 soldiers from coastal garrisons, augmenting their number by distributing about 20,000 firearms to free and slave inhabitants of the islands and nearby coast. Five vessels, carrying from two to forty-four guns, stood ready off Zanzibar's shore.[21] By an adroit manipulation of another legacy of Said bin Sultan, Majid avoided the dangers inherent in any battle. Convincing the British BuSaidi allies that both pro-French and pro-slave trade factions among Zanzibar's population were supporting his rivals, Majid secured assistance against Thuwayni and Barghash, and by October

1861, gained universal recognition as sovereign of the African dominions left him by Said. The British concluded the dispute by an 1861 decision recognizing a permanent division of the BuSaidi state into the independent polities of Zanzibar and Muscat.

The intervention guaranteed continued British predominance at the sultan's court. Majid's shaken financial structure left him even more dependent upon his ally. But the inherent prosperity of Zanzibar, based upon a steadily rising demand for its exports, allowed Majid to gain sufficient financial resources to meet his responsibilities. Just before his death the sultan's income was over $300,000,[22] a sum that allowed the support of about 1,500 Baluchi and Hadrami regular soldiers in the coastal settlements, their strength supplemented when necessary by an even greater number of irregulars. The Zanzibar fleet also grew, the sailing strength of the late 1850s being maintained while, by the middle of the 1860s, Majid increased its efficiency by adding steam-driven vessels.[23]

In the decade following Majid's British-supported victory the BuSaidi sovereign maintained generally amicable relations with his ally, accepting without significant resistance—or enthusiasm—several British initiatives to counter the still-growing commerce in slaves. From 1859 to 1872 the annual average number of individuals exported to southwest Asian ports ranged between 20,000 and 25,000.[24] Barghash's British-sanctioned return from an Indian exile in 1863 provided an additional inducement for Majid not antagonizing his ally. The British consuls reciprocated by infrequent interventions into the sultanate's internal affairs, clearly recognizing that Majid did all that appeared feasible, in view of his subjects' opinions, against the slave trade.[25] Consul Lewis Pelly was so sure of British influence that he once enthused to a compatriot: "Indeed the American Consul recently guessed at His Highness' feelings when he calculated to me that the Sultan would endeavor to go up my Flag-staff heels uppermost, if I should express the wish." Rigby had a sounder interpretation: "When he was in want of our assistance he would act very fairly, and do anything I wished, at other times, when he thought there was no danger of rebellion, he would not."[26]

British endeavors against the slave trade naturally at times created situations of great tension within the sultan's dominions. Along with the obvious growth of British influence at court, officers of the Royal Navy, while conducting their established task of patrolling East African waters in search of illegal slaves, began practices considered outrageous by Arabs and most Europeans and Americans residing in Zanzibar. Missionary Johann Krapf charged: "It is the indiscriminate destruction of property which enrages the natives against the English, not the suppression of the slave trade itself." To a French naval officer, the British actions simply were "true piracy."[27] The men active on slave patrols normally judged the guilt or innocence of Arab dhows shortly after the moment of capture and destroyed craft considered slavers without adequate measures to safeguard their crews' lives. "Such things could only happen on a coast like this," lamented American merchant and consul F. R. Webb, explaining that "a man's dhow is boarded, his papers when produced torn up, his valuable cargo taken out, his vessel then burned and with his crew he is landed destitute at the first port his captor enters."[28] The case of one captain, Mehemet Ali, indicates the scope of the problem. About 1859 the British seized Mehemet and other Arabs en route between Mombasa and Lamu. After taking their goods and destroying the dhow, they landed the group in distant Cape Town. Friendless in the strange city the Arabs eventually had to call on the representative of the Ottoman government for assistance.[29]

Since the British sailors involved in slave patrols usually possessed only an imperfect knowledge of Arabic or Swahili—Kirk said of one so-called interpreter, "He would have been of quite as much service off the Congo or Sierra Leone"—there were obvious grounds for misunderstandings, particularly since it remained legal to transport slaves between the sultan's East African ports.[30] The Arab sense of injustice was heightened by the naval men receiving bounties from their government for captured vessels and slaves, some abusing the regulation. "There was a vile custom among naval men here of swearing that their dhows were many times larger than they really were in order to increase the prize money," reported a disgusted Bishop Steere. After evaluating the usual conduct of the Royal Navy, an overcritical French officer repeated a stricture heard many times in Zanzibar: "The repression of the slave trade, for the commanders of English vessels, is nothing but a matter of money."[31] Beset by the complaints of his subjects, Majid sought relief from the British consul, the departure of the inflexible Rigby allowing resumption of rational discussion of matters of discord between Briton and Arab. New consul Pelly found that the navy's conduct endangered British interests, with Krapf even reporting threats of murdering Pelly in retaliation for the sailors' actions. Pelly suggested to his superiors the negotiation of a new treaty to require the bringing of captured dhows to Zanzibar for judgment. The advice went unheeded, the sailors continuing activities against innocent and guilty alike. Pelly's successor, R. L. Playfair, observing in East Africa and Arabia "a feeling of the most bitter animosity against the English," claimed consequently that "in few places was a Christian life safe beyond the immediate precincts of the Sultan's forts and such a feeling of insecurity was engendered that legitimate commerce languished and threatened to collapse."[32]

Finally, in 1868 a vice admiralty court was established in Zanzibar to judge the guilt of captured dhows, the navy, accepting Foreign Office pressure, agreeing, "if possible," to bring Arab vessels to port, promising "on no account to destroy a vessel without ample evidence of being illegally engaged in the Slave Traffic." And, if the dhow was destroyed, every effort was promised to return the crew to Zanzibar for questioning in court.[33]

The conduct of the British throughout this protracted affair was typical of much nineteenth-century European treatment of Arabs; the Europeans based their actions upon a supposed moral code that allowed the sanctioning of acts that appeared to Arabs as completely unjust. Even if blatant excesses were halted, as eventually happened in the seizing of dhows, no redress was provided to innocent owners, crewmen, or their families for losses of lives and property. To the Arabs such treatment was only another manifestation of a policy of aggression, cloaked under cover of the anti-slave trade movement. They reacted by occasionally harassing individual Europeans, such as missionaries, or, with surprizing infrequency, acts of violence against Britons.[34]

By the late 1860s the childless Majid was in declining health, with Barghash emerging as the leading candidate for the succession. Convincing the resident British representative to accept projected plans to limit further the slave trade, Barghash received immediate recognition as sultan when Majid died on 7 October 1870. After some troubled episodes during the first years of his reign, Barghash accepted the prevailing relationship with the British. Soon, taking Zanzibar's administration in hand, Barghash drew praise for efforts at reform. "Majid was a good man," said one merchant when reflecting on the new sultan, "but he did allow his favorites to rob the people in the name of the law shamefully." "I am glad to inform you," said an important Indian merchant to a Boston correspondent, "the practice of bribery and hush up money which was in vogue in Zanzibar is now entirely gone." Bishop Tozer concurred, adding significantly that British interests now "meet with the earliest *personal* attention" of the sultan.[35]

Facing upon accession the same financial situation that had plagued Majid, Barghash similarly began his reign heavily encumbered with debts, and costly expeditions to several mainland trouble spots further depleted available resources. The sultan's expenses overran revenues probably into 1873. Barghash's efforts to live within his means gained him, commented Steere, "the very bad reputation for an Arab of being mean and greedy." But thereafter the vitality of Zanzibar's still-expanding economy provided the resources—by the early 1880s Barghash's annual income was over $1,000,000—necessary for the major developments occurring in the sultanate during the remainder of his very active reign.[36]

2 Zanzibar, the Coast, and the Interior

BY THE 1840s Said bin Sultan claimed African dominions extending along the East African coast from Mogadishu to Cape Delgado, foreign powers connected with the region's affairs generally recognizing the claims of the Arab ruler and his descendants until the European partition of the sultanate began in 1885. To the south of the Somali Banadir[1] stretched a region, marked by several settlements located on offshore islands, dominated by the important regional center of Lamu. Accepting BuSaidi sovereignty since 1813, Lamu by the 1880s had a population estimated at 7,000. The sultan's *liwali* (representative), often a BuSaidi, was one of the most prestigious officeholders in the Zanzibari administration; his authority extended over nearby towns, including Pate and Siyu, although interference in their internal affairs normally was limited to customs matters. The commerce of the region, centered upon Lamu despite continuously unsettled political conditions in both hinterland and neighboring coastal areas, was important enough by the 1870s to draw a resident Indian community of about ninety. The products exported included grains, sesamun, hides, cattle, ivory, and, until the 1860s, Africans sold as slaves to European buyers.[2]

The Lamu region incorporated one of the most troublesome sections of the sultan's claimed littoral. The small center of Siyu, with a few local allies, consistently opposed Zanzibari authority. British officer Thomas Smee in 1811 found the locality "unfortunately distracted by cruel dissentions," a situation not changing until the BuSaidi finally imposed their writ during the 1860s.[3] But some trouble persisted. One leader, Ahmad bin Fumo Loti, called Simba, continued to defy Majid from his inland stronghold. Founding a new settlement at Witu and there providing a haven for slaves fleeing from owners, Simba became a major disturber of the sultan's peace. A Zanzibari expedition of November 1866 failed to dislodge allies of the Witu chieftan, but the continued pressure led Simba in 1867 to conclude a treaty of protection with an unofficial German visitor, Richard Brenner. The governments of that era, busily involved in European concerns, ignored the accord. So did the rulers of Zanzibar. Thereafter Simba retained freedom of action, at times even giving general recognition to the sultan by accepting subsidies; not until the 1880s did he become a major source of trouble for Zanzibar.[4] The constant unrest in the Lamu region, despite its unsettling influence upon local prosperity, never posed an important threat to the stability of Zanzibar's coastal dominions; the limited wealth available from the restricted northern hinterland did not attract serious rivals capable of exploiting the determined opposition to the BuSaidi.

Between Lamu and Mombasa several towns had close relationships with Zanzibar. The old settlement of Malindi, once the ally of the Portuguese, long in decline by the beginning of the nineteenth century, revived in importance after midcentury. In 1861 Majid sent settlers to found an agricultural establishment; payment of subsidies to the Oromo and the decreasing might of this formerly formidable people allowed the town, with its small garrison, to prosper through the cultivation and export of grains and sesame. By the 1870s Malindi possessed a *liwali*, customs agent, and an Indian community of about fifty, with a total population estimated between the 1860s and 1880s from 5,000 to 15,000. Not far from Malindi was Mambrui, a settlement created in 1865 to watch over the territories around the Sabaki River, which also served as a base for caravans venturing into Oromo country. The payment of an annual subsidy to the Oromo—between $300 and $450—allowed peaceful relations for commerce and the harvesting of orseille. Mambrui's population was estimated at 3,000 in the 1880s.[5] Further south along the coast was Takaungu, a center rising in importance from the 1830s following the arrival of Mazrui, fleeing the BuSaidi conquest of Mombasa. By the early 1870s Takaungu had a population of around 3,000. Takaungu's prosperity was based upon cultivation of millet and sesame and upon commerce in ivory and cattle with the Oromo and Mijikenda. Its Mazrui rulers, generally content to live at peace with Zanzibar, received subsidies from the sultans.[6]

The next stretch of the coast included settlements significantly contributing to Zanzibar's prosperity. Mombasa, Pangani, and several lesser towns served as major termini for trade corridors leading toward Kilimanjaro, Lake Victoria, and the northern regions of Kenya. The Mombasa area inhabitants, although hampered by a harsh hinterland, nonetheless sought out commercial opportunities; by the close of the eighteenth century Mijikenda groups journeyed to lands occupied by the Oromo, Kamba, and Chagga.[7] The traders from the Pangani area had a less dangerous and difficult hinterland to traverse on their route inland.[8] The nearby Shambaa state, one of the few highly centralized African polities in coastal territories, had a strong influence in the region. During the rule of Kimweri ye Nyumbai (c. 1815–1862) the Shambaa evolved a special relationship with Zanzibar and the inhabitants of Tanga and Pangani. The *diwani* of the towns received authorization for their rule from Kimweri, subsequently gaining the sultan's confirmation. Kimweri held political control, collecting tribute from his dependents, while Zanzibar dominated commercial life, gathering customs receipts and excluding the Shambaa from direct economic relations with the island. Both Said bin Sultan and Kimweri respected each other's position, the only significant change in relationships occurring following an 1852 offer by Kimweri of a site for a European mission station at Mt. Tongwe, behind Pangani, to Johann Krapf.[9] The sultan reacted by sending garrisons to Tongwe and nearby Chogwe within the year. Kimweri, in declining health and beset by problems with surrounding peoples, let the occupation pass unchallenged.[10]

Succession struggles after Kimweri's 1862 death shattered the cohesion of the already weakened state, the contending Shambaa rivals seeking outside allies to buttress their limited followings. In the continuing hostilities the joint Shambaa-Zanzibari arrangement concerning coast administration lapsed. One of Kimweri's sons, Semboja, with assistance from Zanzibar, became the most important Shambaa leader without, however, winning absolute predominance. The real winners were the Zanzibari and other intervenors, who profited by securing through trade or raiding large numbers of slaves drawn from the hapless citizens of the divided Shambaa state.[11] Most of the northern lands continued to be of little interest to Europeans until the 1880s; the few Arab traders active in the interior pursued careers largely free of the major conflicts that arose elsewhere in East Central Africa. The impact of the Arabs in the northern regions was minimal, and we will hear little of their doings in the remainder of this study. For the coast, however, the interior commercial activity meant prosperity. Mombasa, Zanzibar's early rival, by the mid-nineteenth century ranked behind Bagamoyo and Kilwa in economic importance; nonetheless it remained a principal coast emporium, despite Playfair's assertion that it displayed "the usual Arab characteristics of ruin, neglect and filth, in a striking degree." Annual ivory exports to Zanzibar and India by the 1870s were valued at $70,000. Because of the presence in its environs of Mazrui enemies of the BuSaidi, Mombasa was always closely regulated by Zanzibar. Its liwali, usually a BuSaidi, held one of the most prestigious appointments in the Zanzibari administration, commanding one of the sultan's largest garrisons, in the 1840s and 1850s numbering up to 400 soldiers. If the liwali did not obey orders, Mombasa's proximity to Zanzibar allowed the taking of effective disciplinary measures. In 1841 Said bin Sultan brought the liwali in chains to Zanzibar for upsetting local trade; in 1884 Barghash reacted similarly when his appointee misappropriated food sent to relieve a famine. Between the mid-1840s and the 1870s estimates for Mombasa's population ranged between 8,000 and 15,000, including an Indian community, in the mid-1870s, of 300. The leaders of the indigenous inhabitants, yearly visiting Zanzibar to mark their special relationship with the Arab sovereign, continued to regulate the port's internal affairs, leaving to the sultan's agents the task of protecting Zanzibar's economic and political interests.[12]

Despite the size of the sultan's garrison and the strength of his Mombasa allies, the BuSaidi rulers had great difficulty in safeguarding the town's environs; Iloikop raiders continually swept the inhabitants before them and seized their cattle. In 1855 missionary Johann Rebmann announced that the Iloikop had arrogantly informed the hapless Mijikenda after one raid: "Take good care of your cattle, not depriving the young ones of too much milk, so that we may find them in good condition at the time we shall come to fetch them." A force of Zanzibari soldiers and townsmen did endeavor to check an Iloikop incursion in January 1857. Feigning retreat the Iloikop suddenly turned on the sultan's men when they broke ranks seeking plunder, scattering the troops before withdrawing with most of the cattle of the Rabai. During February 1857 the Iloikop, raiding among the Giriama, once again defeated a force venturing forth from Mombasa. In 1861 Decken portrayed the Mijikenda lands in ruins, claiming there had not been a caravan departure for Kilimanjaro in seven years.[13] Similar raiding successes for the Iloikop occurred throughout the next two decades, lasting until rinderpest and other disasters broke their power.[14]

Pangani, its inhabitants by the 1880s numbering between 3,000 and 5,000, with an Indian community of thirty-four in 1873, drew upon nearby peoples for staffing large expeditions, which at times totaled over 1,000, for the distant interior. Ivory trader Kurt Toeppen and explorer Oscar Baumann praised Pangani porters, describing them as the best carriers of the entire Swahili coast, near equals of the universally esteemed Nyamwezi. Pangani gained a reputation for exporting the highest quality ivory. In the 1840s French official Loarer estimated annual ivory exports at 12,000 to 15,000 *frasila;* during the 1850s Burton reported 35,000 pounds arriving yearly, with some indication of local prosperity expressed in a $26,000 debt owed to an Indian for merchandise carried inland. During the 1870s and 1880s traveling conditions for caravans further improved, allowing the safe departure of smaller groups, the increasing number of ventures returning more ivory to the port. In the 1880s G. A.

Fischer estimated exports at 35,000 kilograms, while Höhnel stressed their steadily increasing value.[15] Pangani's growing commercial importance was matched during the 1870s by similar agricultural prosperity. Retired Zanzibari soldiers and other individuals established sugar cane plantations in the Pangani River valley, doubtless taking advantage of the numerous slaves reaching the town because of Shambaa civil discord.[16]

The principal trading routes from Zanzibar into East Central Africa, those utilized by the most important of the island's merchants, started from the central section of the sultan's coastal dominions, leading westward to Unyamwezi and beyond to territories bordering Lakes Tanganyika, Victoria, and Malawi. When the Congo regions added their abundant ivory to the stream already flowing to the Indian Ocean, it became a torrent. In the 1840s Krapf reported 6,000 tusks arriving yearly on the coast; by the 1870s Belgian officer Adolphe Burdo placed the number reaching Zanzibar at 22,000. The experienced Fischer during the 1880s listed Zanzibar's ivory exports at 200,000 kilograms, one quarter of all ivory exported from Africa.[17] Another indication of the extent of commerce along the busy central route was an estimate from reliable observers that 100,000 individuals passed Mpwapwa annually during the 1880s. Other Europeans at the same time calculated over 400,000 yearly passed through Ugogo.[18] Bagamoyo, located directly across the narrow channel separating Zanzibar from the continent, became the dominant port on the sultan's African coastline. Some of the nearby smaller centers, particularly Sadani, maintained a steady secondary prosperity.

Shirazi immigrants, there called Shomvi, settled around Bagamoyo before the eighteenth century, intermarrying with indigenous Zaramo and gradually emerging as the town's rulers. Bagamoyo was divided into several units, each under its own *jumbe* (chief); the Shomvi leaders regulated land use and dealt with outsiders. The Zaramo retained control of the surrounding countryside, receiving annual tribute from the Shomvi. The two groups cooperated in providing a stable setting for arriving and departing traders. Before the favorable economic changes of the 1860s Bagamoyo's population ranged between 3,000 and 5,000; during the 1870s it rose to over 10,000, a total often swelled by entry of interior caravans. The newcomers added their own ambience to the port, seeking and finding after their hard journey the pleasures available in what Eugen Krenzler called the "Eldorado, the little Paris of East Africa." Majid, reacting to the growth in importance of the coast opposite his capital, dispatched a military commander and small garrison to reside at Kaole, a little to the south of Bagamoyo. In addition to watching the commerce of the central ports, the commander intervened when possible to restrain any Zaramo of the hinterland more interested in plundering than in welcoming caravans. Later the flourishing Bagamoyo received its own military

resident. Both Zanzibari officials generally maintained satisfactory relationships with African leaders. The proximity of this section of the coast to
Zanzibar, allowing quick dispatch of reinforcements, effectively kept its
inhabitants well within the profitable constraints offered by easy access to
the sultan's markets.[19]

The activities of the coast dwellers opposite Zanzibar provide a prime
example of how local communities prospered because of participation in
the commerce between Zanzibar and the continent's interior. Traveling in
the dry season, ivory-bearing Africans arrived along the coast mostly in
July and August, and Indians of Zanzibar then sent over agents to join
coastal brethren and resident Africans in preparing a reception. Delegates
of the awaiting mechants hurried inland, greeting caravans emerging from
Ugogo, using gifts and cajolery in an attempt to draw them to their
establishments. The acceptance of a gift bound the arriving African; representatives of the sultan, as well as the Indians and coastal Africans, refused
to countenance new agreements. On reaching the contracted locality the
Africans, after paying entry fees, received food and lodging, their hosts
maintaining careful account of purchases during the long bargaining over
sale of their ivory. When disputes arose, the customs master, or another
agent of the sultan, stood ready to offer arbitration. If all went well, the
Africans concluded bargaining by the end of August; many desired then to
leave the coast to ensure a return for agricultural work in home areas
during the October and November rains. The ever-increasing numbers of
Africans, along with the many Arab commanded caravans, gave Zanzibari,
Indians, and coastal inhabitants ample opportunity for lucrative participation in the trade. Payments made to leaders of the coastal communities,
analagous to customs duties paid on merchandise entering European nations, provided vital revenue for the upkeep of leadership functions. As
long as Zanzibar's rulers did not interfere unduly with the amounts received there was little danger of major disturbances upsetting the functioning of the Zanzibari economic and political system.[20]

The sultan's southern coastline, extending to an uncertain boundary
with the Portuguese south of Cape Delgado, included the dominant port
of Kilwa and lesser centers such as Lindi. Lindi early fell under direction of
the Umani Barwani clan, whose leaders firmly controlled town life. After
the death of one ruler in the 1830s Zanzibari influence rose; Said bin
Sultan confirmed new Barwani leader Muhammad bin Issa as governor.
Later Majid sent a liwali to Lindi, but effective control of affairs remained
with the Barwani.[21] Kilwa, the principal slave-exporting port of the East
African mainland, was a key component of the Zanzibari state. Effectively
part of the BuSaidi sphere from the late eighteenth century, Kilwa maintained a local administration until Said bin Sultan, fearing supposed
French intrigue, intervened; the elders then agreed to the appointment of

a liwali and in return received an annual subsidy. The consistent demand for slaves brought prosperity: in the 1840s, for example, a French visitor estimated that forty caravans bringing up to 10,000 slaves yearly entered the town. With a population around 15,000 during the 1840s, probably including thousands of visiting Yao and Bisa caravan personnel, Kilwa supported a resident Indian community of over 150.[22] The sultans maintained a full of staff of officials, the liwali being supported by a garrison, a customs master with his own contingent of soldiers—in 1873 both groups totaled about 130—and a *qadi*. During the reigns of Majid and Barghash the power of the officials grew; yet, as elsewhere, indigenous leadership remained important, their consent required for all policy decisions affecting life in Kilwa. These "old coast families," in Kirk's description, in the early 1870s still received a $400 subsidy from the sultan, plus the usual percentage from duties paid by Africans arriving from the interior.[23]

Kilwa suffered from considerable unrest in its immediate hinterland during the 1860s and 1870s. In the 1840s Ngoni immigrants entered southern Tanzania, intermixing with local populations and eventually stimulating regional disorder threatening Kilwa. Raiding Africans known as Maviti—to Steere the name was "a sort of synonym for a highway robber"—their numbers including Gindo, Donde, and Yao following Ngoni tactics, were reported active around Kilwa in 1866. The raiders reappeared in 1868, perhaps summoned by Kilwa's African leadership as a result of quarrels with Zanzibari officials. About forty members of the Arab garrison, accompanied by 200 slaves, advanced to meet the invaders, quickly meeting defeat. The sultan immediately sent 600 reinforcements to protect Kilwa, but the Africans left the town alone. According to later testimony by Steere, "Some of the town's people were . . . sent out to treat with them, and they were sent back without an answer, and with their hands cut off." The troubled situation persisted into the mid-1870s; by 1873 visitors reported extensive desert regions behind Kilwa in the former homelands of the Gindo and Mwera, with the raiders selling many of these Africans to Kilwa slavers.[24]

By the beginning of the nineteenth century the growing demand for ivory in world markets had joined together the commercial networks of coast and interior. Venturesome Nyamwezi traders marched through Ugogo's harsh environment to the Indian Ocean shores; during the second decade of the century they became numerous enough to be noted by British observers in Zanzibar. Already aware of the route inland from Kilwa, Arabs had started exploiting the immediate hinterland of the central coast, encountering the pioneering Nyamwezi and following their caravan paths into the distant interior.[25] The ivory available along the central routes, praised by contemporary agents for its superior quality,[26] guaranteed the penetration continuing with ever-increasing vigor. One of the pioneer individuals in the movement, visiting the Nyamwezi of Uyowa, was Juma bin Rajab, the grandfather of Tippu Tip. By 1839 the contacts with the Nyamwezi became vital enough for Said bin Sultan to conduct pourparlers with Nyamwezi visitors concerning the security of the road to their lands.[27]

The numbers of travelers marching to and from the interior soon made necessary the establishment of permanent Arab settlements capable of supplying caravans with needed provisions, trade goods, and manpower. After crossing Ugogo, a demanding experience because of scarcity of food and water, plus the menancing attitude of its inhabitants, caravans needed to rebuild strength before continuing westward. The most receptive Nyamwezi state for the Arabs was Unyanyembe, which controlled the area around modern Tabora. About 1840 the first Arab settlers arrived; the most prominent members of the small community included Snay bin Amir, the Indian Musa Mzuri, Abdulla bin Salim, and Muhammad bin Juma. The latter, Tippu Tip's father, acted similarly to many Arabs throughout East Central Africa and strengthened his local position by marrying into the family of the African ruler. The Arabs first clustered at Kazeh, later a section of Tabora, creating by the 1860s the major Muslim entrepot between Lake Tanganyika and the Indian Ocean. Snay bin Amir, because of declining health more or less adopting Tabora as a permanent home, acted as "general agent" to satisfy arriving caravans' needs. The residents of the Arab community in their daily dealings with both Africans and passing Arabs acted according to their own particular interests; Said bin Sultan, content with the steady flow of ivory entering Zanzibar, did not see any reason for direct interference in Tabora's internal affairs.

Meanwhile Tabora throve, the expanding coastward commerce stimulating a host of existing local economic activities to bring additional wealth. The Nyamwezi, despite Arab competition, continued in the coastal trade; their many small caravans carried an important portion of interior goods reaching Zanzibar. A French missionary in the early 1880s noted that up to 20,000 Nyamwezi yearly visited the coast.[28] They joined other Africans, most previously having little use for ivory,[29] in more organized elephant hunting, modifying extant practices to benefit from Zanzibar's continuous demand. Some Africans formed independent hunting bands, often, whatever their origins, known as Makua after the ethnicity of the first hunters supposedly hired by Said bin Sultan. The hunters, very hardy individuals, seldom if ever went to the coast; they operated in interior lands by agreement with Arab buyers, received firearms and ammunition, and in return surrendered one tusk of each elephent killed, plus the right for the Arabs to bargain for the other. One of the best-known huntsmen was Matumera, so successful that in the 1860s he commanded an estimated 1,000 armed followers while living in the fashion of a wealthy Arab. By the early 1880s, however, with the decline of the central Tanzanian herds, Matumera lost his fortune and spent his old age as a dependent of more prosperous Arabs. Apart from professional hunters, Arabs often concluded less formal arrangements, simply striking ad hoc deals with indigenous Africans encountered during the search for ivory.[30]

The inland Arab communities, especially Tabora, gained significant numbers of new residents because of the Zanzibar succession struggles of the late 1850s; Majid's frustrated opponents, generally belonging to the al Harthi clan, fled an uncertain future. ". . . all the blackguards of Zanzibar are flocking to . . . [Tabora]," said Speke; "I hear the road is thronged with them." Other Arabs participated, the bothersome activity during the 1860s of British slave patrols causing changes in economic pursuits. The newcomers, many possessing substantial capital resources, added a valuable component to the Unyanyembe Arab community.[31] Tabora's general prosperity was apparent during Burton's stay, the explorer describing Musa Mzuri's residence as "almost a village, with lofty gates and . . . spacious courts, full of slaves and hangers on;" in 1861 James Grant estimated the Indian magnate had about 300 men, women, and children connected to the establishment.[32] Some Arabs, when elephants became scarcer, turned to other livelihoods, founding extensive agricultural and stock-raising concerns for supplying both their own following and passing caravans. Speke noticed the movement from commerce to agriculture between his 1856–1857 and 1861 stopovers and remarked during the latter that some Arabs "looked more like great farmers, with huge stalls of cattle attached to their houses." Other Arabs came to profit from specialized skills; Cameron in 1873 viewed a blacksmith's caravan en route to repair firearms in Tabora.[33] By the early 1870s, according to Henry M. Stanley, the settlement encompassed 1,000 houses with a population of 5,000 Arabs living "quite luxuriously" in residences surrounded by gardens and livestock. Livingstone, at the same time, numbered Arabs and their followers at 1,600.[34]

Not all, naturally, shared equally in commercial profit. "Unyamwezi abounds in . . . paupers, who hang on to some more fortunate friend," commented Burton, "in hopes of better luck, till their beards wax grey, and their infirm limbs refuse to carry them home!" Most men participating in caravans lacked the capital for organizing independent ventures and borrowed heavily from Zanzibar's Indian merchants. Many fell into permanent subordinate relationships with creditors, their debts too large ever to pay off. Others, failing in the search for ivory, feared to return to the coast and settled at Tabora and similar localities while striving to recoup their fortunes, meantime providing a useful manpower source for more successful Arabs. A typical example of the career of an inland Arab with fortunes fluctuating over the years is that of Muhammad bin Gharib, the sometime companion of Livingstone. In the mid-1880s the long-resident inland Arab had debts of almost thirty years' standing. Muhammad's creditors finally refused additional advances, but upon their learning the Arab had ivory on the way to the coast the ban soon was rescinded. As long as an individual Arab stayed active, whatever past failures, he almost always had the opportunity to secure new backing from Zanzibar perhaps leading to the winning of long-hoped-for financial success.[35]

The Nyamwezi political system offered both advantages and disadvantages to Arabs choosing Unyanyembe as home: the Arabs are "too strong to yield without fighting," perceptively observed Burton, "and are not strong enough to fight with success."[36] But the unstable Nyamwezi succession process, plus perpetual strife between Nyamwezi polities, presented Arabs opportunities for entering into local politics. The resident Arabs became as integrated into Unyanyembe's political life as they were in its economy and emerged as a locus of power theoretically subordinate to the *ntemi* (chief), yet formidable enough, at least into the 1880s, to play a role as *ntemi*makers.[37]

Before the interference with Zanzibar's commerce caused by the Unyanyembe strife, the sultans paid little heed to organizing inland Arab communities. When trade routes were endangered or blocked by Africans, a periodic occurrence, the Arab sovereign usually first dispatched diplomatic agents to resolve the difficulties peacefully. If this failed, and the recalcitrant Africans lived not too far distant from the coast, an armed expedition marched inland. In 1860 and 1861, for example, Zaramo leader Mazungera, long an Arab nemesis, interfered with caravans and threatened Indians residing near the littoral. Majid finally reacted, twice sending Sulayman bin Hamid after Mazungera. The first venture failed; during the second Sulayman burned around thirty villages, killing two of Mazungera's sons and driving the Zaramo chieftain from the route.[38] There are other examples. In 1862 Majid dispatched an agent to an unnamed region to open commerce "by amicable means"; in 1863–1864 a representative quieted Zigula dissidents through "politic distribution" of $10,000; in 1865 Khamis bin Khalfan traveled into Ugogo to quiet some differences. Each of the agents succeeded in his mission.[39]

Judging the Unyanyembe disturbances as beyond the range of Zanzibar's military resources, Majid nonetheless desired to end the disruption of the ivory trade, deciding, probably aided by the customs master's urgings, to send a resident agent. The recent augmentation of al Harthi residents probably gave additional stimulant. Said bin Salim al Lemki, former coastal liwali and companion of Burton and Speke, around 1862 became Zanzibar's first interior official. Lacking military support, Said was not envisioned as a predominant ruler of the Arab community. To Livingstone, a determined foe because of Said's role in the slave trade, the liwali, "though called a governor . . . [was] only a Banian trade agent."[40] Whether Said was more responsible to sultan or customs master is irrelevant: his mission was watching over Zanzibar's interests, utilizing the influence conferred by membership in the sultan's service to prevent commerce-severing outbursts. The principal source of the liwali's authority—knowledge that disobeying their sultan might cause seizure of personal and family property held in Zanzibar, plus direct action against their persons—was an effective counter to many Unyanyembe Arabs; the majority wished to end their lives as wealthy, respected members of the island's dominant class. The liwali's appointment answered the sultan's goals. Despite the lack of outward signs of Zanzibari influence, Said bin Salim's arrival, and the cessation of Nyamwezi dynastic strife with the installation of the compliant Mkasiwa, brought Unyanyembe's Arabs to the beginning of their period of greatest power.

Elsewhere, by the early 1870s, most Arab settlements were in initial stages of organization. Even in Unyanyembe the Arab position did not offer protection from dangers caused by rival Nyamwezi leaders. When Mirambo of close-by Urambo sought to displace Unyanyembe as predominant Nyamwezi trading state, the Arabs and their African allies could not defeat their formidable opponent. When military stalemate, accompanied by a major drop in ivory entering Zanzibar, resulted from the hostilities, Barghash, perhaps stimulated by the customs master,[41] opted for a dramatic response. Possibly drawing upon unemployed manpower available in Zanzibar because of the extensive destruction brought by the great hurricane of 1872, the sultan dispatched a strong expedition, numbering up to 3,000 men, to terminate the war. Its commander, Amir bin Sultan al Harthi, an experienced Arab just home from ten years' activity among the Nyamwezi, also was named to replace Said bin Salim as liwali, Barghash grasping the chance to remove a man once loyal to Majid. But Mirambo's tenacity, added to Arab weakness flowing from quarrels among their leaders, forced eventual withdrawal of Barghash's costly inland military venture. Such discord was not unusual among East Central Africa's Arabs, each chieftain usually being more interested in maintaining his personal position than in advancing the welfare of the larger Arab community. In this instance there even were rumors that Said bin Salim worked against his rivals by providing vital assistance to Mirambo. Amir bin Sultan, the powerful newcomer, was suspect to Unyanyembe's Arabs, Said and the leaders of the resident Arabs, Abdullah and Shaykh bin Nasibu, all denying effective cooperation against the supposed common enemy. Finally, Zanzibar's customs master apparently also asserted his weighty influence, opposing Said's dismissal, according to a British informant, since "he is his agent there."[42] Barghash accepted the lesson, never again intervening directly in any distant interior struggles between Arabs and Africans.

3 Early Arab-European Relations

> We do not go to the country of the Whites—why do they come to ours? I laugh moreover when the Whites say they wish only to observe our country! They will continue to observe and observe until nothing more remains for us.
>
> —*A Brava Somali*

BEFORE THE EUROPEAN imperialistic expansion of the 1880s into the sultans' territories, and especially before the quickening arrivals of representatives of private and governmental organizations during the preceding decade, there had been few European individuals at any one time resident or traveling in East Central Africa. Zanzibar possessed the principal European colony, but its size was very limited: in 1844 the European and American community numbered twenty-two, in 1879 ninety-one.[1] Missionaries came to the region as early as the 1840s, yet only a handful lived away from Zanzibar before the 1870s, these pioneers generally remaining too involved in surviving the rigors of climate and disease, and in influencing the people they resided among, to be much more than a passing irritant to Arabs of their neighborhoods. European explorers, seeking to make known the African interior's mysteries, either for personal gain, advancing knowledge, or spreading the perceived blessings of commerce and Christianity, also were busy from the 1840s. They too were few in number, until the 1870s perambulating from one location to another without in most instances leaving much memory of passage. A third category of European visitor, the trader or businessman, apart from Zanzibar's busy, profitable marketplace, similarly was little in evidence until the 1870s. The activities of each group will be considered as far as they relate to the interests of East Central Africa's Arabs.

The first professional, permanently resident missionaries since the Portuguese period arrived during the 1840s. British Church Missionary Society agent Johann Krapf, seeking a new route to the lands of the Oromo following unsatisfactory experiences in Ethiopia, decided to attempt to use the territories of Zanzibar's ruler. The sultan, a tolerant individual, nonetheless knew the dangerous implications of having a European reside in or pass through lands claimed by his government, the visitor doubtlessly communicating to the always interested British upon the trade in slaves. But he could not refuse: Said bin Sultan remained prisoner of his need for British support. Krapf was the agent of a British society, requesting and receiving Hamerton's intervention. Promising to avoid interfering in political matters on the journey to the north, Krapf easily received letters from the sultan to facilitate travel.[2] Krapf's failure to attain the Oromo and his subsequent decision to settle and evangelize near Mombasa are well known. Suffering the usual hardships endured by pioneer missionaries, Krapf, later joined by other missionaries, was left free by Arabs, apart from minor frictions, to preach and travel. He was not always welcomed—at Tanga, for example, Krapf once attempted to preach, "but the Mahomedans who were present made, for a time, a great noise, so that my voice could only be heard by a few hearers"[3]—but he was not harmed.

The missionaries learned the limits of Arab tolerance following an incident of the early 1850s involving Krapf, French consular staff, Arabs, and Shambaa. Krapf aroused Arab anger through planning mission stations in Shambaa territory and by bringing two Shambaa traders to Zanzibar in hopes of bypassing Arab merchants normally conducting commerce between the mainland and the island. Then in 1852 Krapf held conversations with French agents concerning the nature of the shared authority of Said bin Sultan and Kimweri in the Pangani-Tanga region. "In a moment of abandon," reported the French consul, Krapf spoke slightingly of Zanzibari mainland sway, concluding with a prediction of the collapse of the sultan's state after his death. When news of the indiscreet meeting spread, Krapf heatedly denied all political motivation for his opinions; the Arabs, already annoyed by his intervention in Shambaa matters, understandably suspected otherwise. The frustrated missionary shortly afterward left East Africa, the consequences of his discussion lingering to plague other proponents of the Christian message. Hamerton, angry at his erstwhile protégé's conduct, advised Krapf's companions to remain quiet until Arab irritation passed.[4]

The mission in any case was at a low point in its history, the failure of Krapf's schemes for creating a chain of missionary stations clear across the continent resulting in general disillusionment.[5] Johann Rebmann, mission leader after Krapf's departure, in 1854 spoke of abandoning his labors, discouragingly predicting little likelihood of future success, "disliked as we are by the Arab Government and misapprehended and disbelieved by the natives in general." The disheartened missionary also advanced the notion, of course making any mission progress virtually impossible, that full adherence for Africans to Christianity was "a moral impossibility." Nevertheless, Rebmann stayed on in East Africa, even while complaining as in 1854 when his station was in danger of attack by Africans that "there seems now no spot in E. A. where the missionary might boldly set his foot upon." Hamerton shared the view; fearing possible war following Said bin Sultan's death he advised Rebmann to abandon his post before mission enemies forced removal. Rebmann did leave for a time, returning however, to work as an isolated, uninfluential figure devoting himself to studying African languages.[6]

Arab unease over the presence of Christian missionaries in places not immediately under the sultan's notice, strengthened by the Krapf affair, persisted, hindering the establishment of other missions. In 1854 a mission vessel, the *Kandaze,* sailed into Zanzibar harbor, bringing members of the Hermannsburg society, a German Protestant group desirous of settling among the Oromo of the northern Kenya coast. They had traveled directly to Malindi, where they learned from German merchants of the sultan's standing orders prohibiting the reception of Europeans on the littoral; therefore they proceeded to Zanzibar to plead their case. Rebmann supported their arguments, but Khalid bin Said, acting governor during his father's absence, only awarded permission to go to Mombasa. When written approval did not follow Khalid's oral statement, Mombasa's governor blocked the missionaries from moving into the interior and advised them to relocate in Natal. Without hope of a change in attitude, the Hermannsburg party left for South Africa. Hamerton, who had been instructed to aid the Germans, blamed the failure on the legacy of Krapf. The Germans remained hopeful and reappeared in 1859, doubtless hoping for a better reception from the new sultan. But Majid only presented the Germans the opportunity of living in Zanzibar if they concentrated on education, not evangelization. "They declined," commented Rigby, "saying their Mission was merely to convert, not to educate." The Germans left Zanzibar, blaming Rigby, as did Rebmann, for not fully supporting their cause; they attributed his conduct to their nationality and to fears that the establishment of a Protestant mission implied granting similar rights to French Catholics, men the francophobe consul was determined to keep from Zanzibar.[7]

Majid's astute diplomacy, awarding the fervid Germans residence rights in Zanzibar and thus satisfying the British government, permitted the Arabs to escape the unwanted Christians. But the respite was temporary. French Roman Catholics from Réunion became interested in inaugurating work in Zanzibar, the Abbé Fava holding discussions with Majid during

1860. The sultan, accepting the opportunity to offset the dominant British position by welcoming citizens of their principal European rival, awarded Fava permission. The Catholics began work in December 1860. Recognizing the realities of life in Muslim Zanzibar, the Frenchmen, from 1862 members of the Holy Ghost Order, limited activities to education, pastoral work among the city's small Roman Catholic Goan community, and health care, opening the sultanate's first European-directed hospital. They gained thereby a very favorable niche in Arab opinion.[8] The fact that the missionaries, not bound by British laws, bought slave children, in their opinion rescuing them from captivity, only increased general Arab approbation.[9] The Holy Ghost priests naturally looked beyond the narrow confines of Muslim Zanzibar and by 1862 sought Majid's permission to expand to the mainland. The sultan, well satisfied with mission usefulness to his people, readily consented, later offering a location in his newly established Dar es Salaam settlement. After studying the coastline the priests instead decided upon Bagamoyo, hoping to profit from its strategic position on the principal inland caravan route, securing land in 1862; but, because of limited resources, they did not begin actual work until 1868. The continuing cordiality of the sultan made the Frenchmen, in all honesty, regard Majid's death as "a great loss for the mission."[10]

Rigby's unsuccessful efforts to block the French arrival inevitably caused a request by the consul for similar rights for British missionaries. Majid complied, awarding permission for settlement anywhere within his dominions; Rigby however retired from Zanzibar before any Britons expressed interest.[11] Meantime, during 1861 the British United Methodist Church Mission sought and received the backing of their government for opening an East African station; their ultimate aim was to work among the Oromo. Consul Lewis Pelly in early 1862 requested Majid's assistance for the Methodists, in addition pressing a complaint from Rebmann concerning the actions of Mombasa's liwali.

During the previous October the Arab had questioned Rebmann's right to a building already under construction and threatened its destruction, this despite the long-recognized standing of his mission. Pelly sailed to Mombasa, warning the liwali of the consequences of interference, then bringing the issue to Majid for a formal order upholding mission rights. Majid quickly consented, later recalling the offending official, at the same moment begging that similar rights not be awarded to other Europeans since, remembering Krapf, they had "occasioned much trouble." Pelly had to inform the sultan that the unpopular Krapf, leading British Methodists, was en route to Zanzibar. Unwilling to offend his British ally, Majid promptly dropped all opposition to Krapf, adroitly—if untruly—asserting that he feared only the French, promising to welcome Krapf with a "general letter of protection" to his subjects. The Methodists were received with open cordiality, Pelly suggesting they first locate in the vicinity of Zanzibar, where he could provide adequate protection. Possessing instructions awarding sole authority for determining the initial station's site, Krapf, recalling earlier experiences, agreed, thinking of Pangani and the nearby Shambaa state. But the succession struggles that followed Kimweri's death made mission work impossible. Krapf then brought his inexperienced companions to Mombasa, locating them among the Mijikenda of Ribe, where British protection was possible, and also where the missionaries were under the watchful eyes of the sultan's administration.

It was a long step from the Oromo goal. Thomas Wakefield, one of the original party, later ruefully remarked that only his ignorance caused acceptance of Krapf's decision. "I should think," he said, "a more *un*promising field than Ribe could scarcely be found." Krapf did not stay on; he returned to Europe after setting up the Methodists, leaving behind a very insignificant mission establishment. The original group, hard hit by illness, had melted, leaving only Wakefield, later joined by Charles New, to carry on work. Persisting at the unimportant station, the two determined men during the first decade of their presence caused very little disturbance for the Zanzibari state. To Kirk, in 1873, the mission was in a "languishing state." But Wakefield and New kept alive the Oromo dream, petitioning Majid for letters of introduction for a journey into their lands. The sultan, reported British consul Seward, "very cheerfully" complied, the letter, according to the missionaries, assuring "civility and kindness" wherever they traveled. A prime reason for good relations between Methodists and Arabs was demonstrated during the resolution of a minor fracas in 1867. After returning to Ribe from their northern venture, the Britons were visited by a Mijikenda, this individual, as was the custom, later suffering seizure by local Swahili for an unpaid debt. The missionaries, claiming the prisoner was their servant, sought his release; the liwali of Mombasa, reacting to the conflicting arguments advanced by Europeans and Swahili, retained the man in confinement. Wakefield and New, instead of attempting to force the affair, simply wrote respectfully to the sultan requesting a resolution; they agreed to accept any ruling made by Majid. The relationships with the Arabs continued in this course until the 1870s, when growth of nearby Church Missionary Society stations led to a new, unstable relationship.[12]

The Methodist departure for Ribe left the French missionaries supreme in Zanzibar, the British consuls considering the situation harmful to their nation's prestige. Opportunity for a British arrival came subsequent to the failure of the Universities' Mission to Central Africa, which had been checked by disease and African hostility along the Zambezi.[13] The two leading members of the society's African component, Bishop William Tozer and Edward Steere, then surveyed other alternatives. British consul

Playfair—who, according to a Methodist, was "very wishful that an English Mission should be established at Zanzibar . . . belong[ing] to the
Established Church of England"—wrote promising full cooperation.
Tozer, after receiving a strong Steere memorandum emphasizing the
importance of Zanzibar's role as hub of routes entering and leaving East
Central Africa and the utility of its British connections—"there cannot be
a shadow of doubt that Zanzibar is the key to the whole Eastern Coast"—
decided in favor of the island. Recognizing its Muslim character and remembering his society's primary intentions, Tozer vowed that "the main
work, which we hope to prosecute will be the carrying of Missions step by
step among the tribes of the interior." The mission party arrived in August
1864, concentrating initially upon building a firm island base. The newcomers mixed amicably with the Arabs—in one indication of the relationship a missionary observed: "We also pray for His Highness [the sultan]
every day"—with the French Catholics limiting their endeavors to actions
not offensive to Muslim susceptibilities. There was no friction with the
Catholics: "The French priests," explained Steere, "say there is room
enough for us all and are as pleasant as men can be." By the late 1860s the
British missionaries were ready for a mainland move and built a first
station at Magila among the Bondei.[14]

With their main energies given to commercial exploitation of East Central Africa's people and resources, the Arabs, whatever their personal feelings about missionaries, could remain uninvolved in strife as long as the
intruding Europeans contented themselves with undertakings appropriate
to their calling. Other Europeans, particularly those envisaging activities
that might displace Arabs from their position as intermediaries between
the rest of the world and the resources of the region, were far less welcome. Fortunately for the Arabs there was little to be concerned about
from potentially competing Europeans during the first three-quarters of
the nineteenth century; foreign entrepreneurial activity was almost entirely
confined to Zanzibar. Treaty arrangements with the nations represented in
the sultanate kept their vessels from visiting the coast opposite the island,
roughly the stretch between Tanga and Kilwa, while other sections of the
littoral drew few visitors apart from occasional brief residences by individuals left ashore to collect merchandise for passing trading vessels.[15] The
handful of more intimate contacts did nothing to endanger the Arab
position.

A few Europeans entered into concession arrangements with the sultans, offering technical knowledge in exchange for a hopefully mutually
profitable development of selected resources of the state. Since Zanzibar's
climate and soil seemed suitable for growing and processing sugar cane,
several groups of Europeans endeavored to establish the industry. During
the 1840s former Indian Naval officer R. Cogan, working in cooperation

with Said bin Sultan, proposed buying and freeing African slaves as labor-ers for a sugar-producing venture. A steam-driven mill operated for a time. But Hamerton negated the scheme, considering it a violation of treaty provisions forbidding sale of slaves to Europeans.[16] A Frenchman from Réunion, M. Classun, who arrived during the late 1840s leading a party of workers and their families, unhampered by treaty restrictions, began an operation similar to Cogan's. The experiment ended in failure when Clas-sun and others of his group succumbed to endemic island diseases.[17] In 1864 another former officer of the Indian navy, H. A. Fraser, representing London and Bombay interests, received 700 slaves from Majid, placing them "in a transition towards freedom" whereby, in practical terms, five years' labor was owed before freedom came. The British government al-lowed the subterfuge. Fraser began operations on a large estate in north-west Zanzibar, growing sugar cane as principal crop, also installing machinery for processing the cane and for crushing coconuts and other oleagenous crops. A rum still soon joined the other activities. But Fraser was unsuccessful, fleeing the island and leaving behind debts of about £80,000.[18] Other Europeans attempted agricultural experiments during the 1870s and 1880s, none finding success.[19] Among the many Arab and African clove planters of the sultanate there was only one European, the Frenchman Pierre Cotoni, resident in Zanzibar and Pemba from 1864 into the 1890s; he owned a Pemba estate.[20]

Since little was known until past mid-century of the lands behind the coast, other profit-seeking Europeans had limited opportunities in East Central Africa. An isolated example of a mining concession occurred in 1847 when two Liverpool men, E. D. Parker and George Cram, received permission from Said bin Sultan "for working certain mines in the Wanika country" near Mombasa. The sultan, however, accepting Hamerton's ad-vice, declined "working the mines . . . on equal terms of profit and loss, or to furnish native labour." Instead he was to receive one-half of the profits earned, additionally requiring work to begin within the year for the con-cession to remain valid. Nothing significant resulted from the agreement; the refusal of laborers probably ended the Liverpool speculators' interest.[21] By the 1850s the rigors of commercial competition in Zanzibar pushed some resident firms into extending operations to the mainland. The first arrivals were Frenchmen, representatives of the Marseille firm of Vidal frères, opening transactions in Lamu about 1853 in hopes of beating rivals in purchasing the oleagenous sesame plant. The move merely intensified competition; the Marseille firm of Rabaud and the Hamburg house of O'Swald by 1856 sent agents to the northern town. Although there were men from one firm or another busy at Lamu into the 1870s, the Euro-peans, located well away from the main centers of Arab economic activity, and involved with products of secondary importance, experienced few

significant problems with Arab authorities; the latter rather profited from
the increased commercial activity brought to Lamu. In addition, one
agent, Bonaventura Mas of the Vidal firm, was a welcome presence to
some Arabs; he openly exported slaves until official British and French
pressure forced his expulsion from the Zanzibar dominions.[22]

The arrival in East Central Africa of European explorers undoubtedly
should have been regarded by Arabs as a most serious threat to Zanzibar's
economic and political system. Their reports described in full detail the
excesses of the slave trade while stimulating commercial competitors
through accounts of Arab prosperity. Possessing no more foresight than
most humans, the Arabs did not offer general opposition, whether·open or
secret, to explorers seeking to explain their region's mysteries to the Western world. Perceiving little harm in the passage of a few Europeans, Arabs
instead welcomed the chance to gain from supplying the necessities of life
and travel. It was a remunerative business. German explorer von der
Decken reportedly spent £30,000 on his last expedition. Cameron quickly
exhausted Royal Geographical Society funds for an expedition to relieve
Livingstone, at one moment spending in Tabora about £2,000 for re-
stocking his caravan. The total costs of his trans-African venture were over
£12,000, Cameron's conduct becoming a byword for later visitors. Mackay, for one, during the 1870s lambasted Cameron: "By his lavish expenditure [he] has done incalculable harm to East African travellers.
Dollars he threw about like stones."[23] Similar conduct was not unusual.
French Catholics often ruefully noted that their Protestant counterparts
"spent fabulous sums" during their journeys; Mackay's organization, the
Church Missionary Society, acted much as the others. "We have got a bad
name at Zanzibar for extravagance for which doubtless there has been
some ground," admitted its directors.[24]

Other Arabs, less interested in profiting from Europeans, were equally
restrained in treatment of explorers, as with missionaries, because of the
permission to travel given by the sultan, or, judged Cameron, "what was
perhaps still more important," by Zanzibar's customs master.[25] The Zanzibari officials, of course, had little real choice; a refusal to award letters
adversely influenced relations with consuls representing the principal
European nations. It must be stressed, moreover, that many interior Arabs
welcomed the arrival of European visitors; their personal inclinations toward hospitality joined the often commonly shared delusion that both
Arabs and Europeans represented civilizations more evolved than those of
Africans. Many would have agreed with Hore's dictum: "Arabs certainly
help us somewhat to keep from a sort of 'in the bush' like want of civilisa-
tion." And even without feelings of cultural superiority, the appearance of
visitors provided pleasurable opportunity for discussing and learning of
the happenings in Zanzibar, Europe, and Asia. Travelers' accounts abound

in instances of hospitality. Stanley praised the "real, practical, noble courtesy, [and] munificent hospitality" received from the Unyanyembe Arabs. Cameron concurred: "Whenever I have come in contact with Arabs, I have found them most kind, courteous, and hospitable." Often the Arab reception went beyond mere welcome: "By native medicines and carriage," admitted Livingstone, Arabs "saved my life in my late severe illness in Marangu."[26] Thus, for the overwhelming number of explorers, Arab cooperation, whether personal or financial, contributed toward success for their ventures; occasionally it even ensured that the explorer returned alive to win the accolades bestowed by geographical societies, governments, and general public.

The modern exploration of East Central Africa began in the late 1840s with the journeys of Rebmann and Krapf, the missionaries who in 1848–1849 discovered the snow-capped mountains, Kilimanjaro and Kenya. Although providing fundamental stimulation for subsequent expeditions, the exploits of the two did not produce any immediate observable impact. Soon reinvolved in more direct missionary labors, Rebmann and Krapf forsook extensive traveling, while Krapf, through his misunderstandings with the Zanzibar authorities, gave a ready excuse for official Arab lack of enthusiasm for new European interior ventures. When, for instance, the Hanoverian Friedrich Bialloblotzky arrived in Zanzibar in 1849, hoping to head inland from Mombasa to the White Nile and Egypt, he was blocked by a skeptical Hamerton and by the sultan's hostility.[27]

Another early explorer did not fare so well, demonstrating by his unfortunate career the always present dangers of the calling. M. Maizan, a French naval officer, secured permission to conduct an expedition inland from Zanzibar.[28] On attaining the island in 1844, the young Frenchmen momentarily appeared to lose initiative, delaying in the Arab city while several times changing travel plans. Many Arabs were suspicious of the expedition. Maizan decided to follow the general direction of the trade route to Unyanyembe. Moreover, since its official Zanzibar representation did not begin until 1844, France did not appear as a very effective protector for an explorer. When Maizan finally left the island, commanding a relatively rich and unprotected caravan, disaster ensued: about 100 miles inland the French officer was killed at the instigation of a Zaramo leader. Charges circulated, "dark innuendoes concerning French ambition," averred Burton, leading to suspicions that Arabs or Indians of Zanzibar bore some responsibility for the death, although proof never emerged to verify accusations.[29] For some years the French government contended, with minimal success, to secure punishment of the murderers, even threatening to invade Said bin Sultan's dominions to search out the guilty. The Arab ruler, protesting that the offenders were not Zanzibari subjects and that Zaramo lands were outside his dominions, finally bowed; he dispatched several punitive expeditions inland, at last apprehending one individual held culpable of Maizan's death. His imprisonment in Zanzibar allowed France to drop its protests without further loss of prestige.[30] In the opinion of other Europeans, the Frenchman's murder was the most damaging of precedents, endangering, because of lack of effective French reaction, all future travelers.[31] The fears proved groundless, Maizan's fate standing as a rare instance of the tragic consequences of poorly preparing to penetrate the African mainland.

The next major explorers, their work marking the practical opening of the interior to Europeans, were two officers of the British Indian army, Richard F. Burton and John Hanning Speke, leaders of an expedition funded by the Royal Geographical Society and British government. Their goal was the discovery of the sources of the Nile through reaching the great lakes reported by missionaries Krapf, Rebmann, and Erhardt. The latter had constructed a map incorporating information, supplied by Arab and African travelers, portraying an extensive lake encompassing Lakes Malawi, Tanganyika, and Victoria. Landing in Zanzibar in 1856 Burton and Speke received the new sultan's blessings, his precarious political position making any other decision unthinkable, although Krapf's legacy prompted Majid, said Burton, to press Hamerton into swearing the expedition was commanded by a Briton "upon whose good-will . . . [the Arabs] could rely," and who did not intend to proselytize. Burton had intended to seek out Rebmann as a partner for the proposed journey, but Majid's attitude immediately ended the possibility.[32] With their Zanzibar preparations accomplished Burton and Speke marched along the well-traveled trading highway leading to Unyanyembe, from there continuing until they struck Lake Tanganyika at Ujiji in 1857. During the trek to the lake and back both men often were ill, relying upon the conduct of others, particularly their principal Arab subordinate, Said bin Salim al Lemki, for efficient direction of their caravan. During the return trip, while Burton camped at Tabora, Speke ventured to the southern shore of the lake he named for Queen Victoria. The two officers had not resolved the Nile problem; nevertheless, the colorful accounts of their discoveries ensured a continuation of European penetration.

The expedition was one of the high points of Arab and European cooperation during the years of European exploration in East Central Africa. Burton, a fluent speaker of Arabic and a visitor to the holy cities of Mecca and Medina, had the closest possible relationship with Arabs encountered along the route. Responding to his appreciation of their way of life, the East African Arabs furnished Burton with vital supplies and assistance. The long conversations conducted all during the course of the expedition provided the scholarly European with the information that made his rendition of the venture one of the major sources of the region's history.

Burton and Speke fell out while in Africa. On the return Speke out-maneuvered Burton to secure command of a fresh expedition designed to investigate his claim that Victoria was the Nile's source. Accompanied by James Grant, another Indian army officer, Speke returned inland along the usual Arab route, assisted as far as Unyanyembe by Said bin Salim; from the Nyamwezi state he marched to the lake, visiting the polities of Karagwe and Buganda, from the latter proceeding northward to Egypt. The Nile's course generally had been ascertained, but definite proof of Speke's assertions continued lacking, the gaps being filled in succeeding decades by other explorers. While less intimately involved with Arabs than Burton, Speke nevertheless depended much upon them for success in traveling from Zanzibar to Buganda. His accounts, especially of the flourishing, powerful states of Karagwe and Buganda, served as important stimulation for subsequent arrivals of Europeans in the lake region.

Only one of the early explorers challenged the patterns followed by his predecessors who, whatever their inner sentiments toward Arabs, usually reserved their expression until they returned to Europe. The Hanoverian baron, von der Decken, traveling under British protection, came to Zanzibar in 1869 to investigate the death of another German. Albrecht Roscher, a scholarly explorer, in 1859 left Majid's capital, visiting along the coast to the south before heading westward from Kilwa. He marched disguised as an Arab, and in Arab company. Falling prey to a serious illness, the hapless Roscher, as was the custom among Arabs, was left by his companions to recover—or not—in an African settlement near the northern end of Lake Malawi. Continuing the journey after regaining his health in March 1860, Roscher was murdered by Africans, apparently for his baggage. With the support of other Africans of the vicinity, the supposed guilty individuals were brought to Zanzibar in August 1860. After a trial they were executed, the judgment requiring much pressure on Rigby's part since Zanzibar's Arabs normally did not practice capital punishment.[33]

Von der Decken, hoping to discover Roscher's missing journals—they never were found—failed to reach the place of Roscher's death; Kilwa Arab Abdulla bin Said, his guide, refused to continue the march, with the baron's baggage subsequently being plundered. In view of the German's future conduct, his misfortunes were not surprising. Decken became a notorious opponent of the Arabs of East Central Africa, openly ridiculing Arab beliefs and demonstrating contempt for their persons while journeying amongst them. He refused to attend Protestant services in Zanzibar, for example, "because the bishop prayed for Sultan Majid, and he as a knight was bound to extirpate all Turks and infidels." By 1863 the bigoted baron accused Majid of hindering his explorations, this despite the assistance given by the sultan during his successful trips to Kilimanjaro. When preparing in 1865 to venture into the lands of the Somali, Decken felt compelled to protest to British representative Playfair about Majid's attitude, seeking the consul's help in gaining letters of passage. Charging Majid was "trying to throw all sort of impediments in my way as he has always done, [and] would perhaps refuse them to me," Playfair, cognizant of the German's past conduct, supported Majid, specifically countering: "He objects to your making your request in an unwonted manner." Unimpressed with Playfair's answer, Decken insisted that Majid was secretly acting against him. When the letters finally came, Decken sailed to the Banadir, this time entering a region where feelings of loyalty to the sultan, and fear of the British, no longer shielded boorish behavior. Leading his large expedition up the Juba, the German was openly contemptuous of the Somali, publicly refusing the proferred hand of one chieftain. Shortly thereafter the party was attacked, the baron and several others perishing as the expedition suffered nearly total destruction. The authorities in Zanzibar, powerless in affairs away from the Somali coast, and lacking any motivation for avenging the deaths since most Europeans blamed the tragedy on the baron's conduct, made little effort to retaliate for the loss.[34]

PEACEFUL COMPETITION

Early 1870s to 1885

4 Barghash and the Sultanate

> We have said for a long time that Said Barghash was chosen by Providence to found a great African kingdom which will stretch from the coast to the great lakes and beyond to the west.
>
> —*P. Armand*

WITH THE DECADE of the 1870s, relations between Arabs and Europeans began to undergo fundamental change, the European presence in East Central Africa becoming more intrusive, the result of increased British pressure against the slave trade and the first significant entry into the interior of citizens of several European nations. The new era was marked, both on the coast and throughout inland regions, by steady increase in the Zanzibar state's strength and coherence, but the growing European involvement in East Central Africa inevitably undermined the continuing evolution of the Arab political and economic system.

The British, by the early 1870s, had decided to end the continuing slave trade of the western Indian Ocean and dispatched an important imperial official, Bartle Frere, to Zanzibar to conclude a treaty prohibiting the still allowed transport of slaves between ports of the Zanzibar dominions. Barghash, determined not to bow to expected British demands until his subjects clearly understood the lack of alternative, waited for Frere with outward calmness. Rumors of plots against the sultan by slave owners fearing for the future abounded; Barghash guarded his palace by day and night against attack, withal demonstrating a courageous attitude by daily public riding. There also were unconfirmed rumors of rural revolts by Africans anticipating an end to slavery.[1]

When Frere landed in January 1873 Barghash maintained his attitude, forcing a British-imposed solution. The threat of a blockade compelled

Barghash to accept terms, the sultan's subjects recognizing surrender as unavoidable. The Treaty of 1873 prohibited sea transport of slaves and closed all public slave markets in Zanzibar, the measures enforced by increased British intervention in the sultan's dominions. With the treaty, Kirk, now evolving with Barghash an intimate working relationship that was to endure into the mid-1880s, advised the Foreign Office to act liberally toward the Arab ruler. "The past misunderstanding with England has almost lost him the Mombas districts," warned the consul. "The slave population are not under their masters as they were before and there are many signs of a rapid internal change that needs a strong government to direct it in proper channels."[2]

One of the first problems the Zanzibar administration had to overcome was the immediate opening of overland slave routes countering the effects of sea traffic closure. A land route previously had been in existence; Kirk noted in early 1871 that over 3,000 slaves had marched to Banadir ports for local use and transshipment to southwest Arabia.[3] The closing of markets in Kilwa and surrounding ports quickly threw the coast economic system out of balance: by July about 4,000 slaves without buyers were reported stranded in Kilwa alone. Kirk hoped the losses suffered might prevent new interior caravans from setting forth for the coast and predicted the land route to the north was too difficult for important traffic.[4] Closer investigations on the mainland by British agents quickly proved Kirk had been mistaken, Frederick Elton in particular discovered a busy trade in the vicinity of Dar es Salaam. According to a naval officer accompanying Elton, the Briton "was plainly told by Arabs who were conducting slaves to the coast that the Treaty of 1873 had been the best thing possible for the dealers, as they now saved the Customs dues and freight to the north, and that larger slave-hunting caravans are going up country this year than usual." Another officer heard a similar tale at Bagamoyo.[5]

Prideaux, temporarily replacing Kirk, at first impressed by Elton's figures—about 5,000 slaves during the December 1873–January 1874 period—described to the Foreign Office a trade of "unprecedented extent," with most slaves going to Pemba to replace losses from a recent smallpox epidemic. Prideaux brought the route to Barghash's attention, and the sultan correctly countered that the treaty made no reference to land trade, adding the time-honored response of Zanzibar's rulers when wishing to avoid action: the districts where slaves were passing were beyond his authority. Prideaux later reversed his support for Elton's figures, leading to arguments about the magnitude of the trade among various concerned Britons. Holmwood undertook its resolution, his investigations confirming a flourishing land traffic employing amounts of capital equal to those invested in the previous system. A French trader active around Lamu later gave rough support to some of Holmwood's findings, reporting an annual arrival of 10,000 slaves at Malindi. Kirk monitored the arguments while on leave in Britain, remarking that it was best to reserve judgment on numbers until the exhaustion of existing slave supplies; but he realistically noted the impossibility of ever completely cutting the land traffic and predicted any interference would inevitably lead to slavers developing new routes. The only suggestion the experienced consul advanced was the foundation of a freed-slave settlement somewhere along the route to counter the slave trade. Holmwood proposed a similar solution.[6]

During 1875 the flourishing trade in slaves continued, one naval officer sorrowfully concluding: "The Arabs have completely 'check-mated' us." Prideaux chronicled the steady arrival at Kilwa of large caravans from the Lake Malawi region; the slaves marched north, touching the coast opposite Zanzibar only near Pangani. Other Europeans reported large caravans passing close by Sadani. Consul Charles Euan Smith estimated that 1,000 slaves a month arrived in Pemba, while Kirk, after a Banadir visit, judged 10,000 slaves yearly crossed the Juba near Kismayu on their way into the lands of the Somali. Once back in Zanzibar, Kirk discussed the land route issue with Barghash, the sultan agreeing, if upheld by Britain, to take appropriate action. It remained unclear, however, just what could be done; Kirk maintained belief in the impossibility of immediately blocking the route effectively.[7] He seriously began coping with the ongoing trade in 1876 and by April resolved for himself the arguments concerning its extent. Using an estimate of the Kilwa trade, derived from H. Ward of H.M.S. *Thetis,* that the port received 1,500 slaves monthly, two-thirds of which ended up in Zanzibar and Pemba, Kirk made the annual import of the two islands' 12,000 slaves. From other information the consul concluded that 35,000 slaves yearly reached all coastal centers. He sought restrictive measures from the sultan, requesting from Barghash a total ban of the land trade in slaves. Committed to close cooperation with the British, Barghash readily agreed and issued two proclamations on April 18, 1876. Henceforth the sultan "prohibit[ed] all conveyance of slaves by land under any conditions" and also forbade "the arrival of slave caravans from the interior and the fitting out of slave caravans by our subjects."[8]

In Kilwa, scene of an 1873 demonstration against Frere that led to reprimands of the port's liwali and customs master,[9] the many individuals still dependent upon the slave trade gathered to protest the sultan's new regulations, informing the liwali, said Steere, that they had 3,000 men under arms and "if he put up the proclamation they would pull it down and they recommended him to get out of the way." The arrival of the *Thetis,* followed by Kirk and about 200 of the sultan's soldiers, prevented any outward resistance, and several of the unhappy leaders of the protest demonstration accompanied Kirk to Zanzibar as "half prisoners." Most of the soldiers remained to strengthen Barghash's garrison. While at Kilwa, Kirk warned the Indian community no longer to expect support for recovery of debts from men involved in slave trading. Confident of the proclamations' effect, because of Barghash's enforcement measures, Kirk concluded that a major step toward ending the slave trade had been accomplished, buttressing the opinion with reports received from Kilwa that slave caravans sent by Makanjira and other Yao chieftans were unable to find buyers for their human wares. Additional confirmation came from Bagamoyo, where Holmwood met Arabs heading inland to seek their fortunes in activities unrelated to the slave trade. Thus Kirk announced in October to British philanthropist and businessman William Mackinnon, soon to be involved in East African affairs, that the slave trade basically had ended; he awarded most of the credit to Barghash, even claiming that the sultan acted throughout largely on his own initiative.[10]

The slave trade, of course, had not ceased; Kirk, after his congratulatory flights of rhetoric, remained acutely aware of the need for maintaining steady pressure against the traffic. The Kilwa traders, despite the enforcement measures taken by Barghash and the British, persisted in determined resistance, forcing Holmwood to visit the port and Barghash to remove from office liwali Salim bin Abdulla for complicity in the opposition. The governor of Pangani similarly was recalled. Kirk, still convinced of the proclamations' effectiveness, blamed resistance on the desire to sell existing stocks of slaves and to an unfortunate reduction in British naval strength in East African waters.[11]

The normal inefficiency of Zanzibari military forces, with their Muslim leadership, in enforcing antislave-trade regulations motivated Kirk to convince Barghash of the usefulness of creating a Western-trained army commanded by a British officer. The Arab ruler agreed, doubtlessly realizing its advantages as a tool for enforcing authority in all sections of his coastal dominions. Kirk immediately requested the Foreign Office to provide arms and ammunition as a reward for Barghash's 1876 proclamations, not waiting, however, to organize the military innovation. Commanded by naval officer Lloyd Mathews and assisted by Arab and Comorian subordinates, the soldiers, "dressed in white canvas trousers, blue serge patrol jackets, red fez . . . and . . . European boots and stockings," soon caused a great stir in Zanzibar. There were 300 men in training in 1877 and 500 in the next year. The recruits came from many sources, some from the ranks of the sultan's slaves, others from private owners judging the monthly wage a good return. Additional levies came from captured slave dhows and government prisons, the sultan manipulating evening curfew regulations to increase the available pool. In a related scandal, the liwali of Dar es Salaam suffered imprisonment for selling some recruits placed temporarily in his charge. Nonetheless, the army grew, its strength augmented during

1878 by Salisbury's dispatch to Zanzibar of 500 Snider rifles, with bay-
onets and ammunition, along with seven guns for the sultan's new vessel.
By the start of the 1880s Mathews commanded 1,300 well-trained and
-equipped men, giving the sultan clear military superiority along the coast.
In addition the Arab ruler still maintained a force of irregular troops: at
the beginning of the decade they totaled about 1,400 men, commanded at
their own cost by Arabs of the sultanate. The irregular cavalry of the sultan
recently had been disbanded, but an artillery group of 200 Persians, under
Persian command, remained.[12] Barghash also increased Zanzibari naval
power, in the 1880s having about six steamers active in Indian Ocean
commerce, all available when needed for military purposes.[13]

  With the new army able to enforce Barghash's regulations, Kirk became
even more certain of slave trade decline. But many informed observers
disagreed. In 1877 Lake Malawi missionary Robert Laws reported
Makanjira so busily involved in slave-trade business that the building of
new dhows was necessary to handle transport across the lake. Other
nearby missionaries similarly recounted continuing slaving activities;
Johnson of the Universities' Mission in 1881 recorded that Mataka's
neighborhood "swarms with slave caravans conducted more or less by
coast agents," while Bishop Charles Smythies in 1884 observed the slave
trade going on "very briskly" between the lake and Indian Ocean. Many of
the arriving slaves escaped notice upon the coast because of an evolving
system shaped to meet the hindrances caused by the 1876 proclamations.
Caravans halted before entering coastal centers watched by agents of the
sultan or British; their leaders sold slaves to surrounding populations for
agricultural and other labor. Some slaves were held in bush camps; taught
the rudiments of Swahili, they passed thereafter not as recent immigrants
but as long-resident slaves. Other traders avoided the sultan's regulations
by exchanging slaves for rubber collected by coastal Africans, then entered
Kilwa or Lindi to sell the "legitimate" commodity so welcomed by slave
trade opponents.[14]

  Even with the undoubted risks involved, slaves still entered Zanzibar
and Pemba. The islands' public slave markets, despite the 1873 treaty,
continued operating into the 1890s. In 1874 Steere noticed slaves for sale
"within the courtyards of more than one of the Sultan's retainers," while
American whaleman Ferguson in 1881 visited an auction held in "a high-
walled enclosure [where one] . . . passed through a wooden gate into a
large hall with dirty benches around the walls. A platform about three feet
high with steps leading up to it stood in the middle of the room." Enforcement of the treaty provisions, in the face of universal Arab opposition on
islands where sale of slaves owned before the accord's conclusion remained
legal—allowing owners to conceal new slaves until they learned the speech
and manners of their new environment—was impossible. Thus the British

consular staff realistically avoided public comment on continual illegal activities.[15] Smythies' conclusion regarding the trade to Zanzibar covered the entire East African coast: "As long as slavery is an institution here slaves will be imported and sold." And, added British official C. S. Smith, the slavers, utilizing their "network of cross communications," would continue directing human cargoes to the most profitable markets.[16]

Kirk in succeeding years modified his opinions, concluding that the traffic had been restricted as far as possible under existing East Central African conditions. Yet it was a grudging modification, the proud Briton never liking to admit shortcomings in policies put into operation through his urgings. When Universities' Mission member Williams announced that 2,000 slaves arrived yearly in the vicinity of Lindi and Mkindani, most he judged staying in that region, Kirk accepted the information. But when fellow missionary Chauncey Maples claimed slaves still arrived in Kilwa and were publicly sold at Lindi, Kirk steadfastly denied the possibility of such open violations of the law. The concerned Foreign Office officials were satisfied with their consul's explanations, one observing in 1879: "All that we can do is prevent the export of slaves from the mainland. It is useless to expect that we can at once put a stop to the passage of slaves from the interior to the tribes on the coast who require them to cultivate the soil. The traffic from the interior is greatly reduced and we must be content with this for a time." During a temporary absence of Kirk from Zanzibar, his replacement, S. B. Miles, an experienced observer of the Arabian scene, took a less optimistic reading of available information; he figured that 55,220 slaves entered Zanzibar and Pemba from 1874 to 1882, averaging between 6,000 and 8,000 over the last eight years of the period, with 10,000 arriving during 1881. Kirk characteristically denied the validity of Miles's reckoning, affirmed that his figures should be halved, and heatedly countered Miles's judgment that Barghash did what was asked of him against the slave trade—and nothing else—by explaining that Miles and the sultan had not enjoyed good relations. In all, intoned the positive Kirk, the slave trade was "now reduced to the very smallest limits."[17]

But the data gathered from many individuals in different localities of the East Central African interior cannot be ignored. The slave trade continued at levels roughly equal to past years during the two decades following the 1873 treaty and supplied a principal source of resources for the Zanzibari state. The above discussion was required since some standard authorities on East Central Africa have accepted Kirk's optimistic statements as reality. Coupland concluded: "For twenty years before . . . [1899] the Slave Trade as a regular, seasonal, methodical, expanding business, constituting the main interest and livelihood of a certain class of Arabs and their dependents, financed on a big scale by Indian firms, had come to an end."[18]

Any questions concerning Barghash's role can be similarly resolved. The sultan naturally shared the feelings of most Arabs of his era, supporting their right, sanctioned by the interpreters of Islam, to engage in the slave trade. But he accepted the fact of British determination to end the trade and bowed to demands when necessary to maintain British backing. Many contemporaries recognized this fact, countenancing Barghash's attitude, despite Kirk's reading, as a matter of course. Maples, pointing out that Kirk had forced the 1876 proclamations on the sultan, explained: "The Sultan hates us all, Dr. Kirk included, cordially."[19]

But during these years increasing signs of the Zanzibar administration's improved authority were apparent. An episode in Mombasa demonstrates how Barghash, utilizing his British allies, kept an important center under firm control. Muhammad bin Abdullah bin Mbarak Bakashwain, previously long-time commander of the town's Hadrami garrison, and thus called the *akida* by contemporaries, had been elevated to liwali in 1872 as a reward for his conduct in the wars against Mbarak of Gazi. Barghash removed Muhammad from office in 1874, probably because he abused the governorship to advance personal interests. A new liwali was appointed, Muhammad returning to command the fort. The akida (commander), according to Prideaux "a man of considerable ability and force of character . . . [with] unlimited influence over the men under his command," was embittered at the demotion, immediately becoming embroiled in acrimonious dispute with an old antagonist, Mustapha, leader of Mombasa's Baluchi contingent. The quarrel endangered the peace of the town, leading Barghash in August to recall the akida to Zanzibar. The summons precipitated hostilities; Muhammad rallied his Hadrami followers to defeat the outnumbered Baluchi and imprison Mustapha. Barghash, acting with the caution usual to Zanzibar's sultans, attempted to negotiate, dispatching influential advisor Hamid bin Sulayman to the troubled town. The akida agreed to evacuate Mombasa if the British consul guaranteed the safety of his life, property, and followers. At this stage of the deliberations, according to the French consul, Barghash endeavored to keep the British out of the affair. The akida held firm to his demands, resisting renewed pressure imposed by another Barghash advisor, his father-in-law Muhammad Bakashmir. The agreement that ensued freed Mustapha while leaving the akida in command of Mombasa's fort. Barghash, working in his normally devious manner, doubtless hoped by the arrangement to defuse the quarrel's immediate disrupting effects, pushing to the future any possible punishment of Muhammad bin Abdullah. Still the principal figure in Mombasa, the akida, closely observed by his sultan, by November realized that Barghash was plotting to win away from him the men of the garrison.

During the remainder of 1874 matters simmered; Muhammad

strengthened his local standing while the sultan reinforced the troops loyal to the governor. In January 1875 crisis at last came; the akida withdrew into the fort, on the ninth sending men out to raid the town. By the twelfth the akida's soldiers had fired on the liwali's troops, an episode succeeded by three days of disorder during which Mombasa's African neighborhoods were plundered, large sections being destroyed by fire. Hostilities ceased when assistance for the liwali arrived from Takaungu, but the local population feared the newcomers almost as much as the men of Muhammad.

At the disorder's commencement Prideaux, concerned over the safety and property of Mombasa's Indian community, ordered a Royal Navy vessel to visit the town. The British found that the akida, striving to avert consular involvement, had left the Indians untouched. The liwali, customs officials, and other leading citizens talked with the naval officers, but Muhammad refused a meeting, obdurately remaining in the fort. When Prideaux learned the town had been partially burned, he hurried to Mombasa, accompanied by a strong British force, reporting that Barghash had requested assistance. The consul speedily decided only direct intervention could quiet the disorders, justifying the decision by asserting the akida planned to seize the custom house. Prideaux ordered Muhammad to surrender or face British attack; the Arab refused the demand. A brief bombardment of the fort demonstrated the hopelessness of successful resistance, the British, without loss to themselves, killing fifteen and wounding fifty defenders. The akida surrendered upon receiving promise of security for life and property; Prideaux also agreed to do his best to return the Arab and his men safely to Arabia. Barghash, never noted for mercy to defeated enemies, reportedly was much disappointed at the terms, but he naturally accepted Prideaux's resolution of the Mombasa confusion.[20]

The tangled sequence serves as a revealing example of the sultan's ability to contain serious outbursts among subordinates holding positions in important coastal towns. The militarily weak Arab ruler, effectively utilizing his ally's strength, speedily removed the unruly akida and restored, without losing authority to the intervening British, his control over Mombasa's administration. The British also were pleased with the opportunity to support their ally in the struggle against the slave trade; the chief naval officer concluded: "We have materially shown the Sultan of Zanzibar how anxious the British nation is to support his authority, and thereby to enable him to assist us in the difficult task we have undertaken."[21]

The career of Mbarak bin Rashid al Mazrui serves further to illustrate the change in Barghash's ability to control events. The son of Rashid bin Salim, Mombasa's last Mazrui ruler, Mbarak grew up to the south of their former bastion, in Gazi, where one branch of the clan had fled after Said bin Sultan's final occupation. Mbarak was first heard of around 1850 when he challenged his relative Rashid bin Khamis for control of Takaungu. He drove Rashid from the town, but Said bin Sultan's intervention forced Mbarak back to Gazi. In the mid-1860s Mbarak succeeded to the rule in Gazi and received from Majid a subsidy marking incorporation into the Zanzibari coastal system. But by the decade's end Mbarak, seeking to extend his influence, was quarreling with the sultan's Mombasa liwali. The friction caused Majid to cancel the subsidy, although the sultan's 1870 death temporarily halted the troubles.[22] Barghash restored the payment, but the improved relations did not long endure since Mbarak persisted in the determination to extend into Mombasa's environs, activities running counter to the sultan's simultaneous effort to enhance Zanzibari controls.

In December 1871 Kirk reported "a slight disturbance" near Mombasa, Barghash sending soldiers who failed to capture Mbarak.[23] Relations continued to deteriorate. The Mazrui leader, wounded in a skirmish, in March 1873, moved to an inland stronghold at Mwele, where he received succor from Mijikenda allies. Barghash's endeavors to defeat the rebel Arab failed; Mbarak even routed one expedition accompanied by field artillery.[24] Meanwhile Mbarak had written Kirk requesting British protection, the message sent through Methodist missionary Wakefield. The latter informed the Arab he perceived no difficulty in his becoming a British subject, although worriedly asking Kirk, "Was I right?" The consul, recalling Krapf and the Shambaa, did not think so and emphasized Barghash's probable angry reaction if he learned of the intervention. Although ready to offer any assistance in negotiations between sultan and rebel, Kirk rejected Mbarak's offer.[25] By the close of the year Barghash was ready for new action; at first he sent through Rashid bin Khamis a message to Mbarak "that he should either quietly occupy some port on the coast, or come and render submission at Zanzibar, or finally settle the quarrel by force of arms." Mbarak answered by asking permission to settle near Takaungu; Barghash refused and countered that the rebel should either reside at the latter port or come to Zanzibar, there to be treated with full honors. Doubtless remembering the fate of earlier Mazrui, Mbarak demurred. "Come and fight with me whenever you like," he taunted the sultan. The Mombasa garrison, joined by a strong Lamu contingent, attacked and drove the rebel into the bush where he soon was living, with a few followers, in destitution. By April 1874 Mbarak again sought terms, sending a son to negotiate in Zanzibar, where French Lamu merchant Henri Greffulhe aided the deliberations. Barghash consented to a peace allowing Mbarak's return to Gazi, a decision perhaps motivated by the possibility that the Mazrui chief, if left unsatisfied, might join forces with Simba.[26] Mbarak apparently remained quiet for the next few years; his son paid frequent visits to Zanzibar. An 1876 caller at Gazi discovered the

Arab presiding over a not very important settlement, its commerce drawing only one resident Indian trader.[27]

When Mbarak next threatened, Barghash had his new army ready. In February 1882 Mbarak attacked Vanga with a force estimated at from 1,000 to 3,000 men, including a large Iloikop contingent. Much booty was seized and taken to Gazi. Mbarak threatened the same fate for Tanga; Barghash reacted quickly by sending Mathews commanding 750 regular and a large number of irregular soldiers, with artillery, to the mainland. Hamid bin Sulayman, through gifts, simultaneously sought Mijikenda assistance, increasing the total contingent under Mathews's command to about 5,000. When the soldiers began arriving from Zanzibar, Mbarak first retreated to Vanga, later moved to Gazi and prepared a defense of the town, but after a brief skirmish he fled from his opponents' superior numbers to Mwele.[28] Mathews followed, beginning an eighteen-day seige while rejecting as insincere Mbarak's essays at negotiations. The sultan's general attempted to utilize Barghash's artillery, "but the rotten carriages of the Sultan's field pieces broke down at the first discharge." Barghash then sought and received from his British allies the use of rocket launchers. Over 1,000 men stormed Mwele on March 29, the courageous Mbarak, with a few adherents, fighting free to safety. About 400 supporters, including some of Mbarak's family and most of his possessions, were seized by the sultan's victorious army. A reward of $1,000, soon doubled, was posted for the defeated rebel's capture.[29]

Accompanied by only thirty or forty men, Mbarak fled into the hills near Rabai, where groups of Duruma and Rabai gave assistance. Mbarak's twenty-year-old son Ayub, the issue of a Mijikenda mother, was very prominent in the subsequent raiding. Barghash sent irregular troops, led by the liwali of Mombasa, after Mbarak, but they proved more interested in raiding Africans for slaves than in apprehending the Mazrui leader. With the stalemate persisting, negotiations once more commenced; Ayub traveled to Zanzibar for talks with the sultan. Barghash first suggested Mbarak might settle in Pemba, receiving an allowance from the state treasury, but, observed Miles, the Arab was "too wily to place himself in a position from whence he could have no escape." Barghash then offered a Takaungu residence, doing so because Mbarak was not on the best of terms with its liwali; the sultan hoped after a time, he explained to the British consul, there to seize Mbarak. Ayub returned to the mainland without any decision being made, and the negotiations continued with Mathews's coast arrival. Mbarak and Mathews, each surrounded by armed retainers, after several meetings completed an accord. In November Mbarak made an "unreserved surrender and submission to the Sultan's authority," agreeing to disband his troops and reside at Mtanganyko, near Takaungu, until Barghash allowed a return to Gazi. Mathews certainly guaranteed Mbarak's personal safety or he would not have accepted the terms. Barghash, supposedly disappointed that his general had not seized Mbarak when the opportunity came, accepted the agreement. Remaining quiet, Mbarak soon was permitted to go home to Gazi.[30] But neither rival was satisfied; frictions continued until the German incursion into East Africa altered coastal political conditions.

It is clear that Mbarak's constant involvement with the Zanzibar state did not seriously endanger the sultan's coastal hold. In reality the necessity of meeting the challenge of Mbarak led the sultan to augment the number of his agents, doing so, for example, at Vanga around 1882. And Barghash's continued ability to defeat Mbarak was a strong reason for other coastal inhabitants' remaining loyal to Zanzibar.[31] But the crafty Mazrui Arab, carefully watching events from Gazi while waiting for another opportunity to throw off BuSaidi control, persisted as a potential danger source as more Europeans became involved in the sultanate's affairs.

Pangani continued to prosper during these years, benefiting from both interior trade and the lasting unrest in territories of the once-united Shambaa. The port's ivory traders, despite occasional unsettling Iloikop incursions, persisted in the penetration of the northern regions.[32] Zanzibari influence among the Shambaa remained high. The able Semboja of Mazinde, depicted by New in 1874 as "a short, stooping, yellow, haggard, tame-looking fellow, not at all imposing or impressive at first sight," drew closer to Arab authorities during the struggles with rivals, often in the presence of visitors looking and acting like a Muslim. During one 1883 European call, for example, Semboja appeared in Muslim attire, flying the Zanzibari flag over his town. Although never converting to Islam, Semboja, by the time of the German incursion, counted himself, as did most other nearby rulers, under the broad hegemony of Barghash. The sultan thought the same. In 1884 Smythies received a letter from Barghash assuring that Semboja had no intention, as was feared, of interfering in mission affairs since "he is an ally of his and professes allegiance to him." J. P. Farler of the Universities' Mission from 1876 found himself involved in quarrels between Kibanga, Shambaa leader of the Bondei, and Semboja, the former once firmly asserting independence of Zanzibar. Kirk intervened in the affair, explaining that "such chiefs as Kibanga cannot exercise an independent power if opposed to the interests of the authority that commands the coast and that it is not necessary for Seyid Barghash to send out a single soldier to overawe them." Kibanga proved the assertion by an 1883 trip to Zanzibar to render homage to Barghash.[33]

The prolonged Shambaa strife benefited Pangani residents, allowing them to gain slaves for agricultural establishments. But the arrival of large numbers of new slaves led to unsettling conditions upon some plantations. After the 1873 treaty between Britain and Zanzibar at least two significant flights of captives occurred. In 1873 Barghash sent Muhammad bin Hamad with a large expedition, including cannon, to storm one of the runaway settlements located in neighboring Zigula territory. The soldiers, apparently fearing African tenacity, much to the disgust of their sultan returned to Zanzibar without engaging in battle, leaving the slave center to continue troubling Pangani's plantation owners.[34] Barghash's receptivity a few years later to Kirk's recommendations for a Western-trained army was the outgrowth of many such fiascos.

After the formation of the army, Pangani, along with other ports, discovered the dangers of opposing Zanzibar. In 1881 Kirk informed Barghash that Pangani's liwali was cooperating in smuggling slaves to Pemba, compelling the sultan to demonstrate fidelity to the 1876 proclamations. Mathews, first learning through spies of the Pangani offenders' identities, led his men there. Taking the residents by surprise he arrested the accused smugglers for trial in Zanzibar and removed the liwali. Thereafter Mathews, with Barghash's acquisition of a suitable steamer for coastal work, maintained close surveillance over Pangani and the rest of the littoral, that presence perhaps inspiring a later liwali of Pangani forcibly to seize some slavers. Farler noted that the action gained the official promotion to the governorship of Kilwa.[35]

A very intimate political relationship evolved during the 1870s between Barghash and the ruler of the small port of Sadani. In 1857 Burton gave Sadani a population of between 700 and 800, including only one Indian, and described its leader, Mwinyi Kambi Bori, whom unfortunately he did not meet, as "considered the bravest and . . . most powerful diwan or chief of the Mrima." Bori apparently concluded an arrangement with Said bin Sultan whereby he received assistance in return for incorporating Sadani into the Zanzibari economic system. Another ruler, Juma Mfumbi, or Mwekambi Juma, was depicted by Burton as a pioneer in the inland caravan trade and a commander, along with Bori, of one of Said's expeditions against the Zaramo following Maizan's murder. The British explorer also named Said bin Salim al Lemki as a former liwali of Sadani.[36] The town, although remaining small, grew more prosperous in later years; the increasing entry of ivory-bearing caravans led several more Indians to take up permanent residence.[37]

During Majid's rule Sadani's chieftain was Bwana Heri bin Juma. His influence extended well inland among the indigenous Zigula of the hinterland. Heri governed Sadani without the presence of a liwali, supporting a garrison from funds provided by the sultan.[38] My first reference to the Sadani leader, described in 1876 by one Briton as "a light-coloured Swahili with very good features, large eyes and intelligent, a roundish nose,"[39] dates from 1873, the result of the seizure in Sadani harbor of one of his dhows carrying an illegal slave. Heri was then absent in the interior; the inhabitants and British exchanged shots during the incident. The vessel was condemned in Zanzibar and returned to Sadani for burning. In 1875 Bwana Heri again ran afoul of a British slave patrol; another dhow suffered seizure and condemnation when a Zigula leader en route to Zanzibar in his company attempted to smuggle a slave onto the island. In both instances, wisely recognizing the futility of protest, Heri accepted without argument the British court's dictates. Kirk said of the first case: "From what I personally know of Bwana Heri, he is not a man to have allowed a collision to occur had he been present."[40]

With influence reaching inland through the Zigula as far as the Morogoro region, Bwana Heri, once the increased European entry was under way, became a well-known and respected figure; his readily proffered hospitality and assistance drew universal praise. "Bwana Heri's kindness is wonderful," typically commented missionary Roger Price. Abdallah bin Bwana Heri, his son, often in charge when Heri was elsewhere, garnered similar praise.[41] The exact nature of the Sadani chieftain's interior influence remains uncertain, but it was real, even though some European assertions that he was nominal sovereign of all Zigula clearly overstated his position. Nonetheless, because of Bwana Heri, Barghash confidently advanced claims to all Uzigula; Holmwood, after an 1881 venture along the path from Sadani to Mpwapwa, described territory where Heri possessed influence as "well under the Sultan's eye and . . . [he] has fair control over the petty chiefs and heads of villages along the route."[42] Around Morogoro, Bwana Heri enjoyed an important stance among the ruling descendents of Kisabengo, one of a group of fugitive Zigula slaves who escaped from Zanzibar early in the nineteenth century. Eventually attaining Kami territory, Kisabengo, unable to overcome resistance with his limited following, accepted aid from the powerful BuSaidi Arab, Sulayman bin Hamid. Then, defeating the Kami, Kisabengo founded Morogoro, thenceforth recognizing a special dependence upon Sulayman. Kisabengo's daughter Simbamweni succeeded her father in the 1860s, while a son, Kingo, later became a substantial local personage. Both retained the family ties to Zanzibar, even after Sulayman's 1873 death;[43] Bwana Heri then became more and more active as the sultan's representative. In 1878 Mackay encountered him en route to Morogoro to settle a disturbance between Simbamweni and an Arab caravan; in the same year Henry Cotterill, returning from Lake Malawi, met Morogoro's ruler on the way to the coast to secure support against a local rival. Simbamweni was accompanied by her husband, Mwana Gomera, but in later years this relationship soured; the chief in the early 1880s requested Barghash's arbitration for resolving the difficulties. Accompanied by Heri she visited Zanzibar for this end in 1884. In 1886 Simbamweni openly affirmed to French explorer Georges Révoil that Barghash was her sovereign.[44]

Bwani Heri, like other coastal chieftains, acted as independently as possible in internal matters, doing no more than was necessary to enforce Barghash's slave-trade regulations. According to Mackay the sultan in 1877 warned Heri, after his open abetting of passing slave caravans, that he was "under peril of his life" if abuses persisted. Thereafter he formally cooperated with concerned Europeans in measures against slavers.[45] Any other serious friction between Barghash and the Sadani leader seems unlikely. An attack on Sadani would have been a dangerous undertaking; the Iloikop, for example, in the beginning 1880s learned to their cost of the strength and cunning of its chieftain. Bwana Heri and the town's defenders, supposedly 1,000 strong, learned the Iloikop were marching toward Sadani, quickly evacuated women and children to dhows, and left the gates of the stockade open to the invaders. When the Iloikop entered, the defenders shot them down without mercy.[46]

By Barghash's reign, Bagamoyo, because of its ivory trade, surpassed all other ports, its population of around 10,000 growing several times over during the season of caravan arrivals. Very few slaves came to the coast with the ivory caravans; the British, from Rigby through Kirk, found the numbers of arrivals "trifling." Kirk in 1879 put the total for that year at 500.[47] Majid's recognition of Bagamoyo's importance to his state led during the 1860s to the stationing of a liwali and other staff, inevitably causing frictions with the indigenous leadership. To help control payments of entering caravans, a military post was created at the town's outskirts, which diminished the jumbes' share of revenues. Other quarrels arose over land questions.[48] Some protest also accompanied the Holy Ghost Mission establishment in 1868, although the sultan quieted these complaints without especial difficulty.[49] Barghash marked Bagamoyo's status by a state visit in 1872, the only sultan ever to call in the vital port.[50] During 1875 the long latent unrest among the jumbes broke forth, a reported 500 Zaramo gathering near the town; the crisis was further exacerbated by Barghash's failure—he then was visiting Europe—to continue payments given the jumbes in place of their lost rights. The French Catholics, fearing for the safety of the mission, called on their Zanzibar consul for assistance, the Frenchman and his British counterpart accompanying 500 of the sultan's troops to Bagamoyo. After minor skirmishing the Zaramo withdrew; the quarrel terminated following meetings between the Europeans, liwali Nassir bin Suliman, and the jumbes, with resumption of the delayed payments.[51]

There are other indications of the sultan's strengthened hold on the central portion of the coast. Even though Majid's effort to create a new center for the Zanzibar dominions at Dar es Salaam lapsed at his death, the erstwhile capital remained as a moderately busy secondary commercial and agricultural town.[52] The stationing of Zanzibari forces at both Bagamoyo and Dar es Salaam reconciled the once troublesome Zaramo to the passage of caravans, with punitive expeditions forming quickly whenever commerce was endangered.[53]

5 The Europeans

> You must have seen that both the Missionaries and Explorers by their operations will ere long raise questions which will cause a great deal of trouble and bother to you and the Sultan.
>
> —*Charles Gordon*

DAVID LIVINGSTONE'S EAST Central African career serves as a useful guidepost marking increased inland penetration by Europeans. When Livingstone first entered the region in 1856 while marching from the Angolan to Mozambique coasts, contacts between Arabs and Europeans were minimal, scarcely intensifying during the succeeding decade while he vainly endeavored to found a European missionary establishment in the Zambezi-Shire area. Livingstone then accepted the challenge of determining the still unknown ultimate Nile sources, arriving in Zanzibar in 1866 for his last African venture. During the famous subsequent series of journeys, lasting until Livingstone's death in 1873, the missionary explorer in his letters and notebooks provided, often simultaneously, ample proofs of the devastation accompanying Arab and African participants in the slave trade and of the welcome hospitality given by both. Livingstone's long absence in the interior, marked by periodic rumors of his death, led to the organization of several relief expeditions culminating in Stanley's dramatic 1871 meeting in Ujiji, all the efforts continually focusing European attention upon East Central Africa. The new interest both accompanied and stimulated British reevaluation of the western Indian Ocean antislave-trade campaign ending with the treaty forced upon Zanzibar in 1873. "I find that . . . [Barghash] and the chief Arabs," said Kirk unsurprisingly in March 1873, "have at present a considerable jealousy of English travellers, whom they accuse as the sole cause of our present action against their Slave Trade." The consul's comment was motivated by difficulties from the Arabs of Bagamoyo encountered by Cameron at the beginning of his search for Livingstone. Not yet recognizing the existence of fundamental hostility between Arab and European, Kirk merely advised Cameron not to intervene in local Arab or African disputes, "but to claim the neutrality of an Englishman and an explorer."[1] During the next decade this supposed neutrality forever disappeared. Following Livingstone's death, and Stanley's subsequent transcontinental expedition, the latter marked by an important visit to Buganda and the equally vital discovery of the course and outlet of the Congo, a host of Europeans—missionaries, government representatives, private commercial agents—entered the interior. Their ultimate goal was destruction of Arab economic, political, and cultural influence.

During the remainder of the period of Arab independence European explorers, increasingly the agents of governments or private organizations, continued to move through the interior. Some, such as Frenchman Michel-Alexandre Debaize, traveling during an 1878 effort to cross the continent with a massive amount of baggage, including an organ, surely stretched Arab credulity.[2] Nonetheless, although there were many complaints,[3] very few Europeans encountered serious hindrances blamable on Arabs. Barghash, despite suspicions of his actual intentions,[4] provided upon request the customary introductory letters, in most cases thus ensuring the explorer a much easier journey. G. A. Fischer, for example, in 1883 hoping to travel from the northern Tanzanian coast to Lake Victoria, received permission to march with two large Arab caravans heading in the same direction; Barghash ordered full cooperation with the European.[5] Many Arabs went beyond their sultan's recommendations, offering visiting Europeans the fullest hospitality. "They issue a challenge to Europe," later said Alfred Swann of Tippu Tip's followers, "to produce one traveller who can prove he received any other but fair treatment and lavish hospitality at their hands in Central Africa."[6] Often Europeans receiving Arab assistance never acknowledged this essential help in the self-centered writings which followed return to their homelands; later visitors to the Arabs even noted complaints about previous explorers not paying debts contracted during periods of need. Oskar Lenz, for instance, in 1886 mentioned complaints from the Congo Arab community concerning outstanding bills owed by Stanley and Wissmann.[7] After a time, however, the explorers naturally became of less consequence, the details of East Central Africa's hinterland becoming generally known. The main focus of relations between Arabs and Europeans shifted to missionary and other arrivals increasingly wishing to settle in areas under Arab influence.

The missionary societies already resident in East Central Africa at the time of Livingstone's death all endeavored during the 1870s to strengthen existing positions and extend operations. The Church Missionary Society at the beginning of the decade still supported Rebmann's unimportant

Rabai station, the nearly blind missionary steadfastly maintaining the self-defeating opinion that "the heathen are not yet ready to begin the New Testament doctrines."[8] Deciding to reinvigorate their work, the mission directors retired Rebmann, sending in his place W. Salter Price, an experienced missionary possessing a careful temperament. Arriving in Mombasa in November 1874 Price encountered many difficulties, including, he recorded, "suspicion and fear on the part of Govt. officials." "I am anxious," he vowed, "to do nothing calculated to give offense to the authorities," characteristically adding, "however unreasonable and annoying their requirements may be."[9] Price managed the transition to a more active mission stance with some skill, and when he lacked the power to do otherwise accepted setbacks gracefully. During 1875, for example, an important Mijikenda, thinking of converting to Christianity, visited the mission, a step causing Takaungu's Rashid bin Khamis, who previously had converted the African to Islam, to attack his home and seize his slaves. Price fruitlessly intervened, the Arab meantime, with an unappreciated sense of humor, informing the aggrieved African, "You are going to join the Christians, what need have you of slaves?" Price acted cautiously, leaving it to Kirk to stimulate the sultan into sending "preemptory letters" ordering the seized property—minus the slaves—restored.[10]

But relations soon became more complicated by a problem that plagued dealings between Arabs and missionaries until the early 1890s: the flight of slaves, legally owned under the laws of the Zanzibar sultanate, to the refuge offered by Christian mission stations. The situation was complicated further by the fact that everyday management of the stations' African residents from the beginning was largely left to Africans previously liberated from slavery. Some freed Africans, sent after their British capture to India, where they were educated in mission schools and accepted Christianity, returned to Africa in the mid-1860s to serve the Church Missionary Society. Known locally as Bombay Africans, the early arrivals, including two later prominent members of the community, William Jones and George David, both of Yao origin, worked for Rebmann at Rabai. Jones, understandably finding the difficult old missionary an unpleasant employer, left in 1867 for the Universities' Mission in Zanzibar, later returning to Rabai. As the changes of employer indicate, the Bombay Africans maintained a freedom of action, considering themselves fully capable of managing their own affairs whatever the contrary opinions of paternalistic or racist Europeans. Additional groups of Bombay Africans landed in 1873 to assist the new operations around Mombasa. About 150 entered mission service during this period; most enjoyed satisfactory relations with the perceptive, sympathetic Price, but often became at odds with other staff members who found themselves more at home with Africans less aware of their rights as fellow Christians. To J. Sparshott, in a typical reaction, they were "the very dregs of Society, a shame and a dishonour to Christianity."[11]

The African Christians nonetheless went about their tasks, in the process independently inaugurating a policy of receiving and harboring fugitive slaves. It became increasingly easy to offer shelter when, because of a British government decision, the Mombasa mission's African population grew significantly. The Zanzibar consular authorities by the beginning of the 1870s became dissatisfied with the existing system of disposal for slaves freed from Arab dhows by the British navy; Kirk charged the Africans sent to the British possessions of Aden and the Seychelles often were "treated worse than slaves."[12] A new policy awarding slaves to the care of the several missions operating in Zanzibar and along the coast quickly transformed the labors of the Mombasa missionaries. A new station, named after Bartle Frere and envisaged as similar to Freetown in Sierra Leone, opened on a 200-acre location about one mile from Mombasa. The African residents, over 250 coming at one time in 1875, most speaking languages unknown to the Europeans, strengthened the Bombay Christians' position; many of the latter originated from the same homelands as the former slaves. By 1876 the numbers at Freretown became so large that surplus Africans were sent to Rabai, where they received plots of land for cultivation. In such extensive settlements, with the most numerous ethnic groups living in separate quarters, Africans, both from the Bombay and freed factions, necessarily gained a commanding role in managing daily tasks and easily concealed fugitives from searching owners. The runaway slave phenomenon, a general occurrence that extended beyond mission stations, naturally stimulated Arab concern. As early as the 1830s Zigula slaves, after rising against their Zanzibar owners, had fled to the coast, creating among the Digo what Burton called "a kind of East African Liberia." By the 1870s independent communities of fugitives were present in many locations behind the coast.[13]

Around Mombasa, Arab and African slave owners, aroused at their losses while frustratingly prevented by armed Africans from recovering lost property, progressively engaged in an ongoing quarrel with the missionaries influencing Arab opinion in all East Central Africa. The Arabs, their misunderstanding of most aspects of European culture equaling European ignorance of Arab ways, saw only that British authorities allowed missionaries the apparent use of their lost slaves' labor. And, as the Mombasa mission's European members became involved in regulating their African charges' behavior, at times treating them as harshly as the more sadistic individuals within the Arab community did their slaves, the European assertion of the moral nature of their stance against the slave trade and slavery was hooted down in derision. The mission also stood on uncertain ground regarding the status of its African population; the British denied official protection, while as Christians they lacked civil rights within the Zanzibar polity.[14]

Regardless of the moral merits of receiving slaves, the missionaries had to remember the decision endangered both continuance of their work and personal safety of all Africans residing under their nominal supervision. No significant Arab or African owners' protest occurred before the beginning of 1876; the refugees until then probably amounted to only a few arrivals. But in May, Price learned, about 400 Mombasa citizens had gathered, angrily protesting to liwali Ali bin Nassur against the 1876 proclamations and the mission's harboring of runaways. An Arab delegation visited Price to complain directly, while a petition blaming the missionary went to the sultan. "For whereas he formerly turned away any slave that took refuge with him from his master," charged the Arabs, "now he harbours him and when they find a slave in irons they release him . . ." "These [mission] negroes are arrogant," concurred Ali bin Nassur, "finding themselves supported by the Missionaries and reckless as to consequences." The Christians, in this instance, escaped potential harm, the liwali visiting the mission and quieting the crowd. Still, the issue had been raised, compelling some form of official response. But Kirk, more concerned with slave trade problems, sidestepped a decision, blaming the 1876 proclamations for most of the Mombasa unrest.[15] The worried Price, however, proposed a far-reaching solution: "The recognition of our Colony as British soil under the protection of the British flag would no doubt be a great step towards the suppression of slavery in East Africa. As it is," Price explained, "the existence of our colony is now widely known, and the number of poor slaves who come to us for protection . . . is increasing. The decision as to one's duty . . . is often painfully embarrassing; the dictates of humanity say one thing, the miserable laws of the country another." The mission directors thus sought a vice-consular appointment for their chief Mombasa secular officer, his authority thereafter to be bolstered by frequent Royal Navy visits. The Foreign Office, justifiably suspicious of involvement with missionaries living in Muslim-dominated lands, rejected the proposal.[16]

The Mombasa missionaries' continuing notoriety led to an 1877 visit by Kirk; the consul concluded the Bombay and other Africans, some carrying arms, were not leading much of a Christian life. One armed African, for example, according to a Universities' Mission member, had "deliberately murdered" another African. With Price away in Europe, Kirk observed a "fatal divergence of opinion between the clerical and secular management of what should be a Christian mission in the first place and a freed-slave settlement in the second." And, concluded Kirk, "I learned to my dismay that there existed a want of discipline and subordination among the leading Christianized negroes far more dangerous than an Arab attack would have been to the welfare of the settlement." Lay superintendent William Russell heatedly rejected such charges, correctly recognizing the Bombay Africans as the "backbone of the colony."[17] Russell, however, had as little success as other Britons in making Africans obey the laws of the land concerning slavery. Realistically, it is doubtful whether the British staff ever seriously endeavored to curb African mission followers; J. Streeter, in 1880 involved in receiving slaves belonging to the surrounding Giriama, succinctly explained the missionary attitude: "With regard to the Giriama runaways, of course we know we ought not to go against the laws, but what this country wants is a law-breaker—then a law maker."[18]

Despite frequent denials of knowledge of the presence of slaves, the European mission directors, both in East Africa and Britain, were well aware of African Christian behavior. In 1878, for example, runaways located at nearby Jilore requested a missionary for their settlement. Learning there was no one available, the Africans, about 300 in number, asked permission to join the mission community. Streeter first talked of agreeing only if the Zanzibar authorities consented, but a few months later he noted, supposedly to avoid unnecessary complications, that nothing had been said. By November, Rabai was gaining new arrivals daily; Jones explained to the London directors that the slaves remained on mission property subject to the understanding that searching owners were free to enter, a rather disingenuous statement because of the armed African Christian presence.[19] The aroused Giriama threatened to attack the station, with the liwali offering support to the Giriama until his troops were needed elsewhere. The Africans on mission ground remained adamant, resolutely preparing a defense, while the Europeans, obviously not worrying over what they judged empty threats, refused to overrule their subordinates. The liwali complained to Barghash, the matter ending before Kirk since the sultan feared the consequences of actions against his powerful advisor's fellow nationals. Kirk curtly informed the missionaries that protection would not be forthcoming if harboring slaves brought a crisis, Europeans possessing "no legal power to detain runaway slaves against the will of their masters," and advised instead that the slaves be told to flee.[20]

Kirk nevertheless realized the necessity of ensuring peace, holding discussions with both liwali and missionaries. Following the talks, Streeter in July 1880 visited the Giriama to patch up differences, promising not to receive additional slaves from their community.[21] Despite the supposed settlement, slaves continually entered mission property; Kirk thus remained worried over the Mombasa Christians' attitude, warning the Foreign Office after a later visitation that "at Rabai there were about 200 [Africans], all well-armed with poisoned arrows or guns, ready to defend their companions without the order of a missionary." Therefore, despite denials by the European staff, owners seeking slaves often were mistreated when they attempted to enter mission property. Relations had so degenerated that at one instant during 1880 when the missionaries expected Arab attack, Streeter prepared a flag emblazoned with the word *uhuru* (freedom) to serve as a rallying call for all slaves. In another incident an armed Rabai patrol murdered an innocent passing Arab merely for plunder of his belongings. The guilty individuals were surrendered to the Arabs, but Muslim tempers remained inflamed. Kirk finally warned the missionaries they would face the sultan's army, not merely a Mombasa mob, if excesses ended in disorder. The admonition influenced the Church Missionary Society directors to intervene. "No slave escaping thither will be retained by the missionaries, save when the claims of humanity require it," they declaimed, "but they will either induce the slave to return to his master or inform the Wali of the event."[22] But incidents continued; Barghash in early 1881 protested persisting detentions of legally owned slaves and African Christians firing on one of his soldiers. The Foreign Office, desiring to end frictions between Arab and missionary, advised the sultan to increase his authority around Mombasa, thus ensuring that mission followers "not be tempted by motives of humanity to interfere in matters with which they should have no concern."[23]

While the missionaries, citing moral imperatives, persisted in disobeying Zanzibar's laws, their conduct toward African mission members brought on a scandal seriously compromising the Christian image in East Central Africa. The missionaries, falling prey to the problem of keeping Africans living under their authority obedient to European-created rules, decided to administer temporal punishments to individuals determined guilty of misconduct. As early as 1874 they informed London of instances of corporal punishment; Sparshott, for example, wrote about "on one or two occasions . . . [giving] a fellow a good stripe with a stick." Price queried Kirk about the legality of such punishment and learned there was no authority for so acting. Nonetheless, in 1876 Russell continued the trend, opening a prison to detain Africans held guilty of violating mission norms. After Streeter's arrival, a pattern of increased brutality was obvious; in 1878 he openly recounted punishment of an offender; "determined to make an example . . . [I] had him tied to a coco-nut tree and given 2 doz[en] with a hide whip." During 1879 another African received forty-five strokes. Other missionaries reported similar actions, simply recording the accepted policy of the Mombasa mission.[24] Eventually the missionaries went too far, seizing a suspected thief who implicated other Africans, not members of the mission community. Even though the individuals denied the charge, Streeter imposed five strokes—"which," he said, "is my well known rule"—to force confession. The liwali promptly complained to Kirk; the consul, reacting to the mistreatment of the sultan's subjects, reversed his "rule always to support and never interfere with . . . [internal mission] authority" and sent Holmwood to investigate Streeter's conduct. Holmwood forced a settlement, the sultan accepting compensation for the aggrieved Africans if the mission recalled Streeter; the unhappy, unrepentent missionary protested "The mission might as well be given up for he had found that the stick was the only thing that would make the native speak."

Then a new crisis erupted. African Christian T. Smith filed a complaint with Holmwood against the mission staff for mistreating and imprisoning African Christians. Carefully investigating the charges, the consular agent uncovered an outrageous series of excesses committed under Streeter's orders. One African woman had been stripped to the waist and flogged because of transgressing station rules against drunkenness. African men had been beaten for arriving home after evening curfew; one African endured sixty lashes, administered by three individuals, for another offense. Holmwood met Africans imprisoned directly after suffering beatings, without ever receiving medical treatment, and discovered several had sustained permanent harm. The surprised missionaries, offended at Holmwood's persistence, complained that, after seeing the marks of one beating, he "broke out and sternly rebuked Mr. Streeter in a most unbecoming manner before all the people." The outraged official later informed Streeter than an Arab in Zanzibar treating a slave as he did mission Africans would lose his property since "persons inflicting such injuries are unfit to be entrusted with the charge of human lives." Kirk, finding Streeter's conduct "revolting," upheld his subordinate's strictures. After much missionary bickering, all seeking to escape responsibility for the excesses, the British government, labeling the actions "unjustifiable and unwarrantable" but not desiring a scandal injurious to British prestige, let the matter pass with the recall of the offending members. Price returned to restore sanity to mission operations, discovering some cases of mistreatment "too bad almost to think about." Freretown and Rabai, with about 800 African inhabitants, presented admitted problems for maintaining European control, but Price, with his usual tact, again brought the community together.[25]

The fugitive slave problem was not a primary concern from 1882 to 1885, despite one impassioned protest by the sultan's liwali in 1882 against Price for tolerating law violations by his men. "They never cease to injure your people residing in this town," he told Barghash, "and seduce their slaves and entice them."[26] Some floggings also continued; missionary W. E. Taylor, a firm believer that Africans were children, not understanding reasonable direction, noted their being "inflicted with great care."[27] The missionaries, however, avoided further serious friction with the Zanzibar administration until after 1885.

Both the Holy Ghost and Methodist missions had few major encounters with Arabs during this period. The French Catholics, with Zanzibar and Bagamoyo stations at the beginning of the 1870s, shunned involvement with runaway slaves, either returning fugitives to owners or expelling them from mission property. They continued to respect Arab suscep-tibilities by avoiding open proselytizing in their Muslim towns.[28] The Methodists at Ribe carried on as a small, relatively unimportant operation, although in 1877 they opened a new post at Jomvu, a small Muslim town ten miles inland from Mombasa. But on attempting to purchase land the Methodists were checked. "The Sultan," explained Wakefield, "refused to acknowledge the right of any person to sell land within his dominions, asserting that it all belongs to the crown." With the point made, however, Barghash presented the property to the mission.[29] The Methodists at inter-vals accepted fugitive slaves, sharing in a small way the crises in Church Missionary Society posts. In 1872 the Methodists prudently advised a fugitive to flee before his owner arrived, but by the 1880s they advanced to a more active role. In 1880 Kirk found all the Jomvu missionaries armed, the station having "more the look of a military barrack than the teaching of Christianity." Consequently, when missionary R. Ramshaw endeavored to help Jomvu's inhabitants in difficulties connected with the runaway problem by writing Kirk for assistance, he received minimal sympathy. "He refused," said Ramshaw, "and very kindly advised me 'to devote myself to the ordinary occupation of a missionary.'" But when the governor of Mombasa in 1881 sought to remove an African convert and mission employee the consul intervened, blocking the action.[30]

The Universities' Mission, with stations at Zanzibar, and intermittently at Magila among the Bondei, entered the 1870s with feelings of dissatis-faction, shared by both missionaries and outsiders, concerning the soci-ety's progress toward its planned return into the interior. But important work had been accomplished in Zanzibar; the missionaries educated res-cued slaves provided by the sultan and British consulate. "In fact," said Kirk of Bishop Tozer, "we have made him the chief of a large village, and given him such a start as no mission ever had before."[31] Laboring through necessity with former slaves, not members of Zanzibar's Muslim society, the mission was left alone by Arabs, accomplishing fundamental work in providing new recruits for the Western-educated African group until then represented in East Africa almost entirely by Bombay Africans. The mis-sionaries had little alternative, since although the Zanzibar government allowed open preaching, it nonetheless reacted harshly if individual Mus-lims demonstrated interest in the Christian message. One Muslim, Abdul-lah bin Muhammad, was imprisoned after participating in Christian ceremonies, and died while still confined some three and one-half years later.[32] The dissatisfaction at mission progress ended when Steere, a man who possessed superior linguistic skills and a sound appreciation of Afri-can ways, became bishop.[33]

Despite the normally amicable relationships, one member of the Universities' Mission was killed by Arabs, the only such violent death occurring in East Central Africa before the troubled years that followed 1884.[34] In early 1874 Benjamin Hutley was hunting between Tanga and Pangani. While awaiting porters for supplies en route to Magila, he encountered an Arab slave caravan. The exact sequence of events remains hazy; an African companion claimed Hutley attempted to free the slaves. "Hutley said . . . he would speak to them, so he went up to them and the next thing that is certain," concluded Steere, "is that they left him on the ground with six or seven wounds about the head and throat." Returned to Zanzibar, always denying that he had provoked the Arabs, Hutley died on February 15. With his habitual perspective Steere recognized the possibility of Hutley's being at fault. "It is certain," the bishop commented, because of the British imposed 1873 treaty, "that the slavers are in a state of fierce excitement and the least mistake just now might lead to such an attack."

British representative Prideaux was more direct, concluding Hutley perished "through his injudicious interference with the proceedings of slave-dealers." Nevertheless, the consul, whatever the cause, had responsibility for determining official response to the killing, a task made most difficult by the disappearance of the Arabs. Prideaux did learn the Arabs certainly had not planned a confrontation, even changing their usual road when learning an English missionary was ahead. "Although I have reason to believe the real truth is known to several people, both on the coast and at Pemba," recorded Prideaux, "it would be as much as an Arab's life was worth to give the slightest information to the Sultan or myself." He suggested the Foreign Office levy a $5,000 fine on the general region of the encounter and on Pemba, where the slaves were heading, if the murderers were not surrendered. The Foreign Office reminded Prideaux the Arabs had to be punished for murder, not for slave trading, and authorized the fine only if he proved the guilty Arabs had been concealed by local Arabs or Africans. The guilty individuals never were apprehended.[35] The incident, clearly the outcome of the participants' spontaneous behavior, passed without causing further trouble, and stood as an isolated example of the consequence of unwise interference undertaken by an individual lacking sufficient strength to defend himself against the probable response to his action.

Apart from the Hutley tragedy the Universities' Mission, by honestly endeavoring to comply with Zanzibar's laws, ensured satisfactory relations with Arabs. When refugee slaves arrived at stations, haven was not provided without official sanction.[36] And, fearing repetition of excesses committed against Africans by missionaries exercising a secular role, Steere took a stand unmatched by other missionary leadership. Learning to his dismay during 1881 that Chauncey Maples, at the Masasi station, had beaten a young African, leaving him bound overnight in the open, to force a confession of responsibility for the pregnancy of a just-married mission woman, Steere instructed his subordinates never to use force to uncover suspected wrongdoing. Expulsion from the station, said Steere, was the only recourse for punishing misbehavior. Maples, by then in Britain, clearly disagreed, upholding disciplinary rights of missionaries either through "stripes and fines" or "stripes and imprisonment," avowing Africans renounced the right to protest once they accepted the security provided in missionary establishments.

While yet disturbed by Maples's conduct, Steere received a request from Farler at Magila for military help to resolve a local quarrel. He heatedly responded: "I will not fight or sanction fighting or intimidation in any form whatever. The Church had better remain unbuilt for a hundred years than any violence be done." Persisting determinedly to secure acceptance of his principles, Steere sought approval from the mission's London board, warning that actions similar to Maples's were dangerous precedents, "as all missionaries are sorely tempted to make themselves sovereign powers and unless I am strongly supported we shall have the Blantyre and Mombasa cases reenacted by our own men." The result was a code of behavior for the Universities' Mission including the following broad assertion: "Politically we have no rights at all, and can only live in the country by the permission or sufferance of the people we find there. There can therefore be no formal administration of justice, or claim to independence, or anything like making war. We must get such justice as we can, and if our position becomes intolerable we must choose between becoming martyrs and leaving the place . . ."[37] Unfortunately for Arabs and Africans, most missionaries arriving to work throughout East Central Africa during the last quarter of the nineteenth century took a different attitude toward responsibility to indigenous civil authorities. After Steere's death, even Universities' Mission men ignored the regulations; Farler, for example, in 1885 noted, "A lot of . . . people . . . presented for Confirmation have been brought to me for fornication and I have three now in prison for it."[38]

By the middle 1870s mission societies and other European organizations were poised to push inland; the groups already active in East Central Africa were joined by newcomers from Britain (the London Missionary Society, Free Church of Scotland Mission, Church of Scotland Mission) and France (the White Fathers). Also arriving were members of Belgian, French, and German sections of the International African Association, plus a handful of individual traders holding various European nationalities. For the first time interior Arabs, hitherto far removed from their sultan and his immediate European pressures, became neighbors of permanently residing Europeans. In the initial stages of the European incursion the Arabs had the capability to guarantee disaster for the militarily weak newcomers, but apart from frequent minor frictions Christians and Muslims lived in peace.

Everywhere in East Central Africa the nature of the Arab presence depended upon specific relationships worked out between the intrusive Muslims and indigenous inhabitants; each locality presented to incoming Europeans a different balance of power realities. In the Lake Malawi region, where Arabs clustered around the northern coast, leaving the south primarily to the Yao, the most important early Arab settlement grew on the western lakeshore at Nkhotakota, a settlement governed by a line of rulers known as jumbes. During the 1840s coastal Arab Salim bin Abdallah arrived leading a large, well-armed caravan. Salim secured an important position among the Cewa of Marimba, profiting from the ability to protect them from Ngoni raids. Seizing advantage of Nkhotakota's good harbor and strategic location on the route to the coast, Salim built a strong base, extending controls over neighboring Africans. By the 1880s the influence of the jumbes covered much of the southern half of Lake Malawi, reaching inland toward the Luangwa River; the mostly Cewa subject populations retained significant control of local affairs while paying tribute in ivory, slaves, and provisions.[39]

Salim died in the 1860s; his brother and successor Mwinyi Mguzo ruled until late 1877 and met some of the first Europeans traversing the lake. The jumbe ruled over a considerable settlement; E. D. Young estimated about 100 Arabs resident, while Elton judged Nkhotakota had several thousand inhabitants. More is known of the third jumbe, Pangani-born Mwinyi Kisutu, according to Harry Johnston "a fairly well educated Arab, able to read and write, and a man who had to a great extent studied the literature of his own country of origin." George Shepperson, principal biographer of the line, probably overstates the case when claiming Kisutu's reign "marks the transition to a complete representative of the Sultan on Lake Nyasa."[40] The resident Muslims, as in other Arab settlements, selected a leader according to their community's internal power realities; Zanzibar's distant sovereign then accepted the designated individual as regional representative. From that moment both Arab leaders paid as much heed to each other as their respective interests made necessary and the distances involved made feasible. Actual formal inclusion of the jumbe in the Zanzibar system apparently occurred around 1877; Kirk learned that Barghash "intends shortly to establish an officer duly empowered to exercise his authority" on Lake Malawi, the Arab possessing rights either to take corrective action against violators of the sultan's regulations or to recommend that the Zanzibar ruler retaliate by seizing property held in his coastal dominions. Not welcoming the Arab initiative, the Foreign Office informed Kirk to advise Barghash to avoid interventions "in places which are beyond his territory," hoping thereby to prevent arousing, because of its hazy claims, "the susceptibilities of the Portuguese government."[41] Despite the negative opinion, the jumbe continued to fly Zanzibar's flag and to serve as Barghash's representative. The sultan, for example, in 1886 provided Universities' Mission Bishop Smythies an introduction to Mwinyi Kisutu, "the Diwan of Nyassa." To Smythies this "genial, elderly man" was the "one governor on the Lake appointed by the Sultan of Zanzibar."[42]

Closely associated with Arabs in the coastal trade were the region's Yao leaders. The Yao entered the lands near the southern end of the lake beginning in the 1830s. The movement accelerated during the 1860s, firearms assisting such chieftains as Makanjira and Mponda in altering in their favor existing political and economic systems. One of the earliest of East Central African peoples to become interested in Islamic teachings, Yao were intimately connected with Arabs, many often residing in coastal centers, while Arabs commonly inhabited Yao towns.[43] Makanjira Nakanjire, in control of the eastern side of a major passage across the lake, had visited Zanzibar during his youth, appearing to a missionary visitor in 1886 as "quite a young man, handsomely dressed in Zanzibar style and surrounded with Arabs, one of whom did all the talking for him."[44] The Europeans, blinded by inherent convictions of African inferiority, often overemphasized the role of resident coastal Muslims; Maples, for instance, declared Makanjira "a very young man who appears to be entirely in the hands of the Swahili courtiers, who are at once his ministers and his masters."[45] In reality Arabs possessed a varying influence, depending upon the talents of particular individuals, frequently seeming more important than they were since general Arab familiarity with European customs brought them to the forefront when visitors appeared.

The first permanent European settlers around Lake Malawi were missionaries from the Free Church of Scotland. Because of the hostilities between the Yao and Livingstone and his Universities' Mission associates during the 1860s, the missionaries, led by E. D. Young and Robert Laws, bore precise instructions forbidding forceful interference in Arab and African affairs.[46] Nevertheless, Steere, then perfecting plans for returning his mission to the same region, expressed a general apprehension concerning the reappearance of Europeans in one of the interior's busiest slaving areas. "If the Scotch are going to fight the Arabs," he warned, "they will breed trouble for everybody."[47] Steere had cause to worry, the Scots seemingly holding to the letter of their instructions only because lack of power ruled otherwise. Reaching the lake's shores in October 1875 the Free Church men visited Mponda, a later arrival portraying the Yao as "a pleasant middle aged man with a quick jerky manner and apparently plenty of wits." Mponda presided over a busy town served by dhows transporting

cargo for passing caravans. With his permission the missionaries settled at
Cape Maclear, an isolated location away from main trade routes, remaining there until they could learn more of the surrounding countryside.

During their initial travels the expedition stopped at Nkhotakota, receiving a hospitable welcome from the jumbe, although Young remarked
that "the chief man, when my back was turned, asked our doctor quietly
what I intended doing with their dhows." Their exact status had to puzzle
the lakeside inhabitants. "We are a wonder and astonishment to all Arabs
and natives," exulted Young; "the former shake their heads, no doubt
thinking that their game is up." More to the point Laws, admitting the
sight of slaves in yokes "made my blood boil within me," noted "Mr.
Young wore his [Royal Navy] uniform cap on going ashore." Seeing a
presumed slave dhow when back on the lake, Young again put on the cap,
ran up a white ensign, and interfered with the vessel's course. "There were
no slaves aboard," commented Laws, "and so we were relieved of all
trouble in regard to further action." According to Young, the Arabs were
so upset at the European presence that slaves ceased crossing the lake for a
month.[48] "A small vessel similar to mine, with a dozen resolute Englishmen could paralyse the whole trade," concluded Young. "All that
would be required would be a few bales of calico and beads to buy up the
ivory. Then it would not pay the Arabs to march all round the lake for
slaves alone. Of course the dhows would have to be taken; but that could
be done with the greatest ease." Harry Henderson of the Church of Scotland, accompanying the Free Church expedition to scout the lake region
for his church, concurred: "I can see we must be prepared to trade a little,
so as to shove the Arabs out . . ." Not surprisingly Kirk in Zanzibar soon
learned from Arab sources that the missionaries had "commenced to stop
the Slave Trade that crosses the lake."[49] But the Free Church party did not
overstep orders. There were minor irritants, but Arabs and missionaries
lived in peace. The Church of Scotland party arrived in 1876, locating in
the south at Blantyre. They had few contacts with Arabs during succeeding years.[50]

Even though fully occupied with problems within their own ranks and
with African neighbors, both Scots establishments continued to be interested in replacing Arabs as traders. During 1876 Dr. James Stewart of the
Free Church urged opening a station store since the Arabs, once newness
of the Christian presence had worn off, were busy as usual buying slaves
and ivory, and in return supplying Africans with desired imports. "It is the
only counterpoise we have to Arab influence," explained Stewart. His
superiors, however, denied the request.[51] In 1877 Laws accompanied the
British consul in Mozambique, Frederick Elton, on visits to Makanjira and
Mwinyi Kisutu. The Europeans were welcomed at both settlements even
though Elton, while distributing copies of Barghash's 1876 proclama-

tions, spoke forcefully against participation in the slave trade. Less diplomatically, Elton informed Kisutu of the punishment of Kilwa's liwali for not obeying his sultan's orders; the unimpressed Arab replied curtly that the trade in slaves was "his means of making a living." During a subsequent stay Laws discovered Elton's forensics had made minimal impression on Nkhotakota's residents: "They seemed to regard . . . [Barghash's] proclamation as a good joke, so far as their immediate vicinity is concerned."[52] Still, the jumbe kept on generally satisfactory terms with missionaries; in 1878 he even promised, although later changing his mind, acceptance of a mission presence if its members agreed not to interfere in local affairs—including the slave trade.[53]

One individual accompanying Elton represented a type more dangerous in the long run to Arabs: men motivated by Livingstone's dreams of the beneficial joint effects of commerce and Christianity "whose minds," said Steere, "are full of the putting down of the slave trade."[54] The first significant practitioner of the commercial-missionary approach, Henry Cotterill, learned Livingstone's ideas were easier to discuss than achieve. "The operation of purchasing a tusk is . . . exceedingly tiresome and demands a vast amount of patience," Cotterill explained. "On an average each tusk took about six hours of haggling, and sometimes the bargain came to nothing till two or three days had been expended over it." Watching Cotterill procure a tusk for £14, missionary Stewart observed: "I would not recommend anyone to come here to purchase ivory at present, with a view of making a profitable business of it." Admitting lack of both resources and commercial experience, Cotterill still found other reasons for the unsatisfactory outcome of his venture, complaining that "it seems almost impossible to do anything where the Arabs are in power." The frustration over the Arabs' formidable position, joined with reaction to immediate observation of the slave trade, pushed Cotterill into considering a frontal attack on the Arab system. Surprisingly Kirk, although well aware of Cotterill's helplessness before the Arabs, consented. The London officials, knowing the dangers involved from incidents concerning individuals operating in distant lands where British retaliation was expensive and difficult, ruled otherwise, ordering Kirk to inform Cotterill he lacked legal sanction for seizing slaves. Once back in Britain, Cotterill, alleging the securing of enough ivory to cover his trip's costs, proclaimed the experiment a success, calling upon others possessing greater financial resources to undertake "in a businesslike fashion" the overcoming of Arab competition.[55]

The virtually unanimous opinion that peaceful displacement of Arabs was impossible as long as they fulfilled a vital commercial role led in June 1878 to the founding of a missionary-related commercial organization to work around Lake Malawi. The African Lakes Company, directed by

Frederick and John Moir, initially sought to free limited mission personnel from the time-consuming diversions of commercial pursuits. Possessing very limited financial backing, and hampered by high costs of transport that then made almost all local products unprofitable, the new organization wisely refrained from challenging Arab middlemen, instead dealing directly with them for ivory. But the Arabs, and their African partners, fully posted on the prevailing Zanzibar prices, where related slave sales brought additional profitable return, refused lesser company offers. An extra handicap to the company was a self-imposed prohibition on selling firearms and gunpowder. Company managers later claimed the regulation was violated only in exceptional circumstances, although many observers thought otherwise.[56] After a difficult initial period, when exchange of presents represented the only trade and when most ivory came from European hunters, the company at last won a limited place in the commerce of the lake region, successfully purchasing ivory from both Arabs and Africans.[57]

From the last months of 1879, Arab and European traders increasingly came into contact around Lake Malawi's northwest corner. The Ngonde and other nearby Africans, politically organized into several small independent states, were prosperous agriculturalists possessing abundant cattle herds: Harry Johnston described the land as "a veritable African Arcadia." Most important to the traders were the Ngonde of Karonga, ruled by the Kyungu and occupying an excellent location near the principal trade routes connecting coast and interior.[58] Drawn to Karonga in the endless search for ivory, both Arabs and Europeans also sought control over the routes where they passed. The Arabs, from the Senga region to the northeast, searched for better paths to the coast and increased contacts with Arabs already active between Lakes Tanganyika and Malawi. Impressed by the attractive Ngonde lands, perhaps profiting from the usual loosening of the Ngonde political framework following a ruler's death, or from usefulness as a potential ally against the Ngoni, the Arabs received permission to settle, developing an initial base on a strategic location that allowed control over routes leading to Lake Malawi, the Senga, and southern Lake Tanganyika. By about 1886 the leader of the resident Arab community was a coastman, Mlozi bin Diwani, an associate of Senga Arab Salim bin Nasir. Other important individuals, each with a separate village, included Kopa Kopa bin Barabara and Msalama bin Ali. The Arabs lived amicably with their African neighbors, trading more with nearby groups than the self-sufficient Ngonde.[59]

Ironically, the virtually simultaneous arrival of African Lakes Company agents was an important reason for the Arab settlement's growth. The British traders, as dependent upon ivory for survival as Arabs, in the search for elephants entered Ngonde territory, welcomed by the Africans as a means of controlling the incursions of the too numerous animals. Elephant hunting quickly became profitable; in one day F. Moir killed five, and by 1881 he had sixty to his credit. Clearly, Karonga, with its hospitable African population, abundant sources of ivory, and an adequate steamer anchorage, was a natural location for a company station; L. Monteith Fotheringham set up a post in June 1884. Quickly becoming a financial success, the Karonga base proved very popular with Arabs. Individuals came from as far away as the Senga and Tanganyika communities, benefiting from the company's water route to the coast for both sale of ivory and purchase of needed imports. Reacting to the growing commerce, other Arabs already resident nearby increased their establishments, overcoming the apparent earlier Ngonde opposition to an Arab presence nearer their settlements.[60]

Karonga's inhabitants thus joined the path already followed by Arabs and Africans at Tabora, Ujiji, and other interior commercial centers. But there was a major difference. Karonga had present both European and Arab traders. In other centers Arabs arrived first, henceforth resolutely defending their position against intruding European competitors. The growth in importance of economic activity at Karonga, as at all similar settlements, included significant potentialities for disorder in the life of the indigenous community. The Ngonde profited from the more intense Arab and European involvement through consequent general immunity from raiding, but the frequent entries and departures of caravans with retinues of often unruly and ill-disciplined men, usually bearing arms, inevitably led to friction. No problem-settling mechanism similar to that at Ujiji[61] took form in Karonga, perhaps due to the looser structure of Ngonde political organization, although certainly much of the explanation was in the simultaneous arrival of Europeans and Arabs at a time when tensions resulting from increasing European pressure on East Central Africa's peoples did not allow an opportunity for the slow, and often troublesome, adjustment between culture groups which had taken place elsewhere. Trade continued to flourish, even while the local political and security system remained fluid; Arabs continually visited Karonga to trade ivory, straining the always limited company resources, often enduring long delays when awaiting suitable payment. Other Arabs, not dealing directly in Karonga's market, visited the company post for minor commerce while their slave caravans passed on to the nearby Deep Bay Lake crossing.[62] By 1887 the African Lakes Company, in addition to Karonga, reported eleven trading bases on Lake Malawi, employing twenty-five Europeans and a much larger African staff, in that year shipping 40,815 pounds of ivory to the coast. One visiting Briton proudly asserted that this busy commerce "acted as a check on the slave trade," while a modern historian, looking over the first eight years of operations, similarly postulated the company was "remarkably successful in driving the Arabs from the Nyasa region . . ."[63] The reality was different: both Arabs and Africans continued operations unhindered by the European presence.

Meantime, the Universities' Mission at last was ready to return inland, Steere deciding to follow an overland route beginning at the sultan's southern port of Lindi. During the 1870s Lindi was controlled by Abdullah bin Amir al Barwani, a wealthy Arab regarded as "local Elder of the Arabs throughout the district," Steere adding that Abdullah was "sort of a king at Lindi." The sultan's liwali, Ahmad bin Abdullah al Hussani, serving since Majid's reign, clearly held second rank. Presiding over "an old decaying fort," the governor, recounted Steere, was "an old Arab soldier . . . [who] seems to have no power at all outside the fort." Abdullah bin Amir jealously guarded his established rights over conduct of Lindi's affairs; in 1875 he thereby drew Barghash's ire by collecting duties from Indians in defiance of regulations. Despite the sultan's protests the Arab continued the exactions, in 1880 even seizing the property of a hapless Indian. After the 1876 proclamations Lindi became an important cog in the overland slave transport system. When the liwali attempted to follow his sultan's orders against the continuing trade, Abdullah went his own way, all attempts at discipline failing.[64]

Abdullah bin Amir and the Lindi Arabs accepted without open opposition the Universities' Mission decision to use their port, although Steere charged that they delayed for two months his caravan recruiting. In September 1875 Steere led the first caravan to Lake Malawi, from necessity abandoning settlement plans because of his European companions' illness. Finally, in 1880, W. P. Johnson began work among the Yao at Mataka Nyenje's center, in his opinion "the biggest town inland anywhere of this part of the interior of Africa . . . necessarily a point where all the slave caravans to the coast pass, and other traders pass who come from far." Nyenje, described by the missionary as speaking fluent Swahili and as "quite the coast man in his dress," had spent time in Zanzibar, the result of capture and sale to Arabs, while his identity was unknown, by men of Makanjira. Taking the name of Muhammad bin Matumbula, Nyenje converted to Islam, returning to the interior when ransomed by his people. Some of the Muslims in the chieftain's entourage—Arab traders, teachers, and scribes—necessarily were disturbed at the arrival of a British missionary destined to be in frequent communication with fellow nationals in Zanzibar. Johnson charged that Abdullah bin Amir wrote Mataka suggesting his expulsion, but the Yao refused, perhaps motivated by the missionary's potential usefulness against his enemies' incursions. Other Muslims, whether due to tolerance, indifference, or the desire for profit, accepted Johnson's presence without protest.[65]

Practicing Steere's dictums concerning noninterference in African secu-

lar affairs, Johnson lived in relative harmony with the Yao until undermined by a British naval officer's unwonted intervention against a caravan
commanded by Mataka's men. C. E. Foot, not far from Lindi, as one
missionary apparently unimpressed with Barghash's 1876 proclamations
lamented, "took it upon himself to interfere with the lawful course of
traffic in the country." Both slaves and slavers fled, leaving Foot in possession of the caravan's ivory. Kirk castigated the officer's intervention as "a
blunder and worse [since] it failed, so far from taking slaves he lost one of
his men taken by the caravan people," admitting to the apprehensive
Universities' Mission that "all irregular and indefensible actions such as
this lead to complications and little good."[66] Complications indeed occurred. Johnson, returning from a temporary absence, discovered his residence and possessions destroyed; the Yao not unnaturally, albeit wrongly,
decided the missionary was a spy reporting to Foot. Although he was left
unharmed, Mataka's coolness and the open distrust of the people forced
Johnson to abandon the station. The dejected missionary, safely attaining
Zanzibar in November 1881, proposed that Barghash take some action
against Mataka, possibly seizing one of his numerous coast-arriving caravans. Consul Miles brought official pressure, requesting at the very least
compensation for Johnson's lost belongings. Barghash formally complied,
ordering the liwali of Kilwa to dispatch a "suitable person" to remonstrate
with Nyenje, warning the Yao that "traders are constantly going to his
place and if he acts in this manner he will be ruined." Nothing more was
heard of the affair, a not unexpected result since Miles learned Kilwa
traders had participated in inducing Mataka to expel Johnson.[67] The Universities' Mission later reestablished in the Lake Malawi region, in 1886
creating a post on Likoma island, a location largely free of significant Arab
contact.

The busy missionary and commercial activity of British subjects around
Lake Malawi inevitably drew their government's attention. The missionary societies desired appointment of one of their group as consul, but the
Foreign Office refused; in 1883 instead it selected naval officer C. E. Foot
as first resident European consul for the East Central African interior.
Foot received pro forma instructions that his primary task was to stop the
slave trade, this general directive effectively mitigated by other orders
forbidding use of force in ways possibly endangering his life or those of
British subjects. The consul rather was instructed to work through persuasion to spread legitimate commerce. The Foreign Office, fully aware of
dangers endemic in the sending of officials into distant places far from
effective supervision, had done its best to prevent any expensive and unwanted involvement in the African interior.[68] Some assistance came from
Barghash, however; Kirk persuaded the sultan to write his subjects residing around the lake, plus indigenous leaders "with which H. H. is in

friendly relations," to render succor when possible, the joint list including Mwinyi Kisutu, Makanjira, and Mataka.[69]

Reaching his district in January 1884, Foot acted as a powerless gatherer of information concerning the slave trade and other aspects of local political and economic life. Not satisfied with his limited role, the former pursuer of Arab dhows and caravans itched to take direct action against slavers; by March he requested that a small contingent of Royal Navy men be placed under his control.[70] Foot died in August 1884 before learning London's unfavorable answer; his successor, Albert Hawes, received similar instructions, with the addition of permission to warn Arabs involved in slaving that they ran risk of seizure by Zanzibar's authorities on return to the coast. It was an empty threat; the sultan acted only when particularly abhorrent behavior compelled the British consul to apply major pressure. Hawes, in his district from October 1885, assisted by Vice-Consul V. Goodrich, followed Foot's pattern, reporting about slaving and related activities; both officials claimed by the end of 1885 that slave trading was significantly more intense than in preceding years. Hawes, not appearing unusually concerned with the northern part of the lake territory, the scene of African Lakes Company and Arab activity, nevertheless did suggest appointment of a vice-consul for the region; the Foreign Office rejected the request.[71]

By 1885, despite an accelerating tempo of Arab and European involvement in territories surrounding Lake Malawi, relations between the two intrusive groups appeared stable, a situation probably due more to Arab tolerance than to European conduct; the Arabs did not react to the few minor challenges to their interests. The leaders of the Arab community accepted the Europeans and profited from facilities offered by the African Lakes Company, generally ignoring the still limited missionary presence. Barghash had every reason for satisfaction with the extent of his influence in the lands stretching inland from the southern ports of his dominions to the shores of Lake Malawi and beyond. Mwinyi Kisutu at Nkhotakota and Mlozi at Karonga, along with a host of minor traders, flew Zanzibar's red flag, giving their sultan all the fealty required in the continuing flow of ivory and slaves. Africans, even those away from intense Arab contact, also gave Barghash suitable acknowledgement.

One striking indication of the sultan's influence occurred in Kilwa's unsettled hinterland, a region still suffering from endemic unrest following the arrival of the Ngoni and allied peoples. In 1875 the Magwangwara were active around Kilwa, entering into agreement with the Kilwans to drive off the Maviti; they received a reported $400 for acting, then settled down to act similarly to the departed Maviti. They threatened to attack Kilwa in 1875, but were bought off by the town's authorities.[72] In 1878 an agent of Barghash, Bakiri, possessing much influence among the Makua, apparently sent into the hinterland to investigate a rumored coal deposit, endeavored to end the enduring warfare, gathering together representatives of Yao, Makua, and Maviti to discuss peaceful resolution of rivalries. H. Clark of the Universities' Mission assisted in the deliberations. The outcome was an agreement among Africans to forbear hostilities, instead referring disputes to the sultan for resolution. The Africans additionally promised to hoist the Zanzibari flag in a few selected localities and to cooperate in building a proposed road leading inland from the coast. The truce, despite a troubled period following the imprisonment and death of Bakiri in Zanzibar following supposed intrigues, seemingly was maintained for the next few years.[73] There, of course, was no possibility for Barghash to intervene in this distant region, whatever influence he possessed over its inhabitants coming from recognition given as ruler of East Central Africa's pervasive Arab system.

6 The Central Route

MOST EUROPEANS SEEKING the East Central African interior followed the principal trade routes leading initially to Tabora, thus inevitably intermixing themselves into affairs held vital for the continuing prosperity of Barghash's state. In Tabora, where almost all caravans halted before marching to more distant goals, the costly failure of the intervention against Mirambo caused Barghash and his customs master to lose confidence in liwali Said bin Salim. A reported Arab community debt in 1873 of £57,000 to an important Zanzibar Indian merchant perhaps increased displeasure at Said's stewardship.[1] Power within the Arab community passed in early 1878 from Said bin Salim to two brothers, Shaykh and Abdullah bin Nasibu, both, as the result of long, active interior careers, holding considerable prestige among Arabs. Shaykh bin Nasibu had served as representative of his sultan on missions to Karagwe and Buganda; in 1871 Stanley named Shaykh and Said bin Salim as "the two chief dignitaries of Unyanyembe." Shaykh's "power had in the past been very great," Tippu Tip later observed, "greater than the Wali, who couldn't do a thing without his sanction." Abdullah bin Nasibu, known as Kisessa (the valiant), long had been recognized for martial exploits; Burton, for one, in 1856 described the doings of this "stout fellow" while raiding in retaliation for losses suffered by another Arab caravan.[2] In late 1876 Abdullah returned from Zanzibar to Tabora with Barghash's backing, probably intending action against Said bin Salim; the liwali in 1877 admitted to Europeans his fears of the sultan's interference.[3]

In February 1878 the Nasibu faction, allied with Nyamwezi ruler Isike, drove Said from Unyanyembe. The most likely immediate cause of the coup was Said's relationship with Mirambo, especially his continuing effort to terminate the ongoing hostilities between the Urambo warrior and the majority of Tabora's Arabs. Abdullah bin Nasibu, a determined foe of

Mirambo, continued the sporadic fighting after the leadership change.[4] Said bin Salim found refuge in nearby Uyuwi, living in "genteel poverty" for the remaining few years of his life while conducting fruitless intrigues for his return to Tabora. From the Uyuwi haven Said also sought European aid, convincing several visitors that his plight stemmed from "assistance he has honestly given to the English," one Briton requesting Kirk's intervention in favor of the deposed Arab. But all Said's machinations proved futile; Mirambo denied Said, useful as a diplomatic counter, permission to leave Uyuwi. The aging Arab, "a man driven to despair," said Arthur Copplestone, died at Uyuwi in December 1879.[5]

The two Nasibus henceforth presided in Tabora, with Abdullah officiating as liwali. Many arriving Europeans benefited from their assistance; Joseph Thomson regarded "the governor and his brother . . . [as] a pair of glorious old gentlemen . . . [who] have taken me under their wing entirely." Walter Hutley, because of Shaykh's advice to visitors, thought he "deserves to be styled Professor of Philosophy to travellers in Central Africa." As always, such statements were highly personal; Mackay, after some difficulties, dismissed Abdullah as "a low half-caste slaver, and true blackguard."[6] But Barghash's renewed displeasure led to another change in Arab community leadership. The sultan's motivation is unclear, although there were many matters of friction between the Arab ruler and the Nasibus: Abdullah's role in an otherwise unknown plot by an Arab faction supporting Barghash's brother Ali, debts so extensive the liwali "dare[d] not show his face at the coast," interference with a sultan's caravan destined for Buganda, and claims resulting from the Segère affair.[7] Leaving Shaykh acting as liwali, Abdullah confidently returned to the coast, perhaps influenced by an attempt on his life in Tabora or by threats against family property in Zanzibar. After a year's stay in Zanzibar, Abdullah began the return journey during 1882, dying suddenly a few days from the coast. It was rumored that Barghash had had him poisoned, a suspicion apparently confirmed a few months later by Shaykh bin Nasibu's equally sudden death immediately following the Tabora arrival of a coastal caravan.[8] Barghash did not appoint a successor to the Nasibus, leaving the Tabora community to arrange its own affairs,[9] although in 1883 he had offered the position to Tippu Tip and his brother.

By the 1830s the Arab vanguard had reached the great lake just west of the divide from which Africa's inland waters flowed toward the Atlantic Ocean.[10] Lake Tanganyika, of great depth and frequently subject to harsh storms, but not over twenty miles wide, was a formidable though not impassible barrier to the Arabs. Their Indian Ocean maritime technology easily adapted to local circumstances; alliance with indigenous lakeshore inhabitants further simplified the problem. As in Unyanyembe, a local center quickly developed to serve the needs of Africans and Arabs; the Jiji, one of the divisions of the Ha peoples, grasped the opportunity for economic advancement brought by the coast caravans. By the 1840s several Arabs had chosen the port of Ujiji as principal place of residence, others crossing to the western lake shore on the way to more distant goals. The eventual leader of the Arab community, Mwinyi Kheri bin Mwenyi Mkuu al Ghasani of Pangani, was among the early arrivals. Muhammad bin Salim al Nabahani, one of the first Arabs to cross Tanganyika, returned to Ujiji during the late 1860s, rivaling Mwinyi Kheri for a time, his 1876 death leaving the Pangani Muslim supreme. Kheri, by the early1880s described as "a man of about sixty, with graying hair, regular features, but an extremely black complexion," standing "thick and fat and respectable and decent,"[11] built a position through alliance with the Ha ruler. Accepting African authority, confining themselves largely to commercial affairs, the Arabs gained a very secure niche in Jiji society; Kheri and a few peers in reality became integral components in local life, even gaining a role in selecting a new Ha ruler.

By the period of changes that occurred with the arrival of permanent European residents, the distant lake port—its population in the early 1880s estimated at 5,000[12]—had become an important cog in Zanzibar's commercial system; one missionary recalled walking "over tusks of ivory scattered about . . . representing thousands of pounds." The Arabs and Jiji, evolving a balanced, well-functioning system of mutual advantage, achieved a stable relationship seldom attained in other inland centers. The frequent arrival of coastal and Congo caravans continually injected large numbers of unruly, armed Arabs and Africans into Ujiji. "There is constantly something or other occurring in the daily market here between the Arabs' slaves and the Wajiji," commented Hutley, "and the former being assisted by guns generally gain the day. It is no uncommon thing for an Arab to muster all his slaves together and send them to attack an Jiji village because he has sustained some fancied wrong . . ." Nonetheless, as Stanley noticed earlier, Arab and African acted jointly to curb outbursts "because it is perfectly understood by both parties that many monied interests would be injured if open hostilities were commenced." There were a few important crises—in 1880 when the Arabs, briefly, were asked to leave, and in 1881 when Tippu Tip's large caravan caused serious difficulties—but they passed, the Arabs and Africans maintaining their relationship intact.[13]

A second important caravan path from Unyanyembe led northward toward Lake Victoria and its surrounding regions; merchandise from the Indian Ocean littoral, most likely passed through several intermediaries along a network of well-established, interconnecting local routes, reaching Buganda during the latter years of the eighteenth century. By the 1840s the first Arab adventurers had pushed as far as the lake region, a few—Isa bin Husayn, Ahmad bin Ibrahim al Ameri, Saim, Snay bin Amir—encouraged by gifts and assistance from the dynamic *kabaka* (ruler), Suna (c.1825–1856), venturing into Buganda. The distances involved were so great, and the risks so heavy, that only a handful of Arabs attempted the journey during Suna's lifetime, especially since the kabaka carefully restricted the beginning commerce, prohibiting commoners from purchasing or wearing the cloth brought by Arabs.[14] Some of the Muslim newcomers, anticipating later practices, aided the kabaka in warfare; Saim participated in a campaign against the Soga, while others, notably Baluchi Isa bin Husayn, a former soldier of Said bin Sultan heavily in debt to coastal merchants, settled permanently in Buganda, receiving in return for services landed wealth and position.[15]

Suna's successor, Mutesa I (1856–1884), one of East Central Africa's most important nineteenth-century rulers, had at first, like most kabakas, to establish authority over the competing political factions within the state, barring Arab traders from entering Buganda until he emerged, by 1860, as unqualified master. Resolving to utilize coastal commerce for strengthening Buganda, Mutesa placed the Muslims under firm state control while striving to establish his country as the terminus—not a mere way station on a road leading elsewhere—of trade routes beginning in Zanzibar.[16] The growing intercourse with Arabs was based primarily upon ivory, with slaves holding a decidedly secondary role. The Ganda, usually desirous of increasing the size of their own households, absorbed most captives; the kabaka and his most important subordinates gained the largest share. Overall commerce remained limited for some years; Mutesa continued Suna's restrictions until, by 1866, the more frequent entry of traders stimulated repeal.[17]

The particular nature of the Ganda polity, developing under Mutesa's efficient leadership into one of the most politically centralized states of all Africa, made the Arab role very different from what it was in other inland locations. When Arabs entered the Ganda capital, either brought across the lake for a price by Ganda canoes, or escorted through Ganda territory by state agents, the traders visited the kabaka to mark acceptance of Ganda supremacy, presenting appropriate gifts to the ruler and principal court figures. In return the newcomers received quarters in a designated section of the capital. After deliberations concerning the amount and value of merchandise brought, the Ganda leader and his officials decided how much to purchase for state requirements, then settling into a long bargaining process to determine terms of exchange; the necessity of drawing future Arab caravans kept the outcome mutually acceptable. Once official business was accomplished, Mutesa and his chief assistants dealt for their personal needs; any remaining items became available for the general public. The entire process extended over several months, sometimes even

longer; during the interval the Arab merchants, each provided with Ganda
agents for protection and supervision, resided in their assigned quarters.
Speke, visiting Mutesa in 1863, was unimpressed with the Arab quarter,
finding "a lot of dirty huts," the Arabs supposedly admitting "that from
fear they had always complied with the manners of the court." As the trade
continued, some Arabs, most agents of Tabora merchants, remained in
Buganda, working within the perimeters of the regulated Ganda system to
collect ivory for entering caravans.[18]

The Arab presence, however strictly regulated, had major importance
for the development of Islam in East Central Africa; Mutesa became one
of the few sovereigns to acquire an intense personal interest in the monotheistic message of his visitors. Possessing a lively intellect allied to a
healthy sense of curiosity for matters new to his experience, Mutesa early
was drawn to the religious doctrines and practices brought by Arabs.
Without relinquishing belief in the Ganda religion, the monarch began to
observe the requirements of Ramadan, learned the Arabic language, and
pored over the meaning of the Qur'an. And, once the kabaka began to be
involved with Islam's tenets, his subjects, obeying their ruler's peremptory
commands, joined in the process, giving the Muslim greeting and displaying other outward characteristics of the foreign faith. According to two
Ganda Christians, "Many who would not learn were then seized, called
infidels and killed. Then every married man fixed up a stone in his yard to
pray at, and every chief built a mosque, and a great many people became
readers, but were not circumcised, and all the chiefs learned that faith."
Extensive comprehension of Islamic beliefs, of course, was limited at first
to a very few Ganda but, nonetheless, a fundamental turning, an opening
of society to outside influences, was under way.[19] And, since Mutesa was
above all a practical ruler, from 1868 Ganda agents and caravans were en
route to increase contacts with the Muslim sultan of Zanzibar.[20]

The flirtation with Islam during the decade after 1865 did not result in
Mutesa's conversion, even though some observers judged that outcome
certain. The later dominant Protestant Ganda leader, Apolo Kagwa, simply stated that his kabaka was a "Mohammedan convert."[21] Nevertheless,
Mutesa stopped short of becoming a Muslim, the hold of the Ganda
religion which placed the ruler in the center of its belief system remaining
central to his thinking. Some compromise between the two faiths might
have transpired, as so often happened in the interaction between Islam and
indigenous religions in all parts of the world, if Mutesa outwardly accepted Islam while retaining some of his original beliefs. But the Ganda
ruler steadfastly refused circumcision: according to Ganda practice the
kabaka had to be physically perfect. Still, during the years of his interest in
Islam, the Arabs, especially their more articulate and learned members—
notably the long resident Ahmad bin Ibrahim—were very close to Mutesa,

the kabaka utilizing what he found most valuable in their knowledge and merchandise to increase Buganda's power and prestige. There were naturally reasons apart from interest in Islam's message motivating Mutesa's desire for intimate relationships with Arabs from the Zanzibar dominions. During this period the Egyptian push toward the headwaters of the Nile resulted in intervention in neighboring Bunyoro and the sending to Buganda of ambassadors. The obvious threat from the north provided sound reasons for increasing Ganda contacts with the principal monarch on the East Central African scene, the Sultan of Zanzibar. Mutesa, however, was not accustomed to dealing with a sovereign relatively unimpressed with Ganda power, and sought increased trade without offering any concessions to the sultan. Consequently, Mutesa's wishes for more formal ties between Zanzibar and Buganda proved fruitless.[22]

The presence of the followers of Islam led to complications unforeseen by Mutesa. The centralized Ganda state structure required Arab residence in the capital; the more important members of the Muslim community acted similarly to leading indigenous residents. The Arabs had abundant opportunity to discuss religious beliefs with individual Ganda, especially youths sent from all parts of the country to receive an education in the workings of the state while serving as pages to principal Ganda leaders. Many of the youths, losing conviction in the efficacy of traditional beliefs, proved unusually receptive to the teachings of Islam; their acceptance of the new creed caused a questioning of many heretofore integrally held Ganda norms. Some pages, openly becoming critical of a kabaka not complying with many Islamic precepts, introduced a new outlook into existing political conduct.

The aroused Mutesa, around 1875, struck at the dissidents, a sudden and bloody persecution ending with the death around the capital of about seventy Ganda Muslims. Perhaps an additional thousand were slain elsewhere in the kingdom, with a few hundred managing to flee to safety among Arabs. Mutesa in August 1876 "complained of the Arabs of Zanzibar, who troubled him with their fanaticism," but they did not suffer during the persecution. Neither did Mutesa surrender his personal interest in Islam; he continued to worship in the capital's mosque. Nonetheless, the progress of Islam, despite its adherents' devotion, for the moment was checked. And at this dangerous time the religion of the Arabs had to face the determined competition of arriving European missionaries.[23]

The members of the Tabora, Ujiji, and many smaller Muslim inland communities, whatever their relationships with African neighbors, generally offered European arrivals a guarded welcome. The Europeans, in turn—despite the common attitude represented by Stanley's advice to one group of missionaries, stressing the "extreme importance of not placing confidence, beyond what is absolutely necessary, in the Arabs, nor of taking them into your confidence in regard to plans,"[24]—naturally sought Arab assistance. Among missionaries even Alexander Mackay, a resolute foe of Arabs, by mid-1878 was employing Rashid bin Ali, son-in-law of Said bin Salim, as leader of supply caravans, the Arab continuing in missionary service for several years. Another Arab working for Europeans, Sefu bin Rashid, gave the International African Association loyal support, even acting as commander of Karema when Europeans were absent. Sefu feared such conduct might endanger his life, but he suffered no major difficulties from other Arabs.[25] In general, the help given by Arabs to passing and resident Europeans greatly eased the hardships faced along the central route by newcomers to East Central Africa.

Significant inland movement of Europeans began in the mid-1870s, several groups simultaneously undertaking ventures. All encountered the same problem, the difficulty of moving by human carriers large amounts of baggage over the narrow and winding paths leading inland.[26] Among the expeditions was a Church Missionary venture for Karagwe and Buganda, the result of Stanley's 1875 letter.[27] Because of the great distances involved, the society envisaged cooperating with the London Missionary Society in establishing a series of stations along the caravan road to Lakes Victoria and Tanganyika. Following Cameron's advice, the initial goal was the important carrefour of Mpwapwa, a place where caravan paths from Bagamoyo and the central coast converged. Full of enthusiasm for the future, expedition commander G. Shergold Smith began the westward march in September 1876, proudly proclaiming, "I feel convinced that no expedition ever started so well found in everything luxurious as we are."[28] During the first week in August the advance party reached Mpwapwa, where Shergold Smith and the others received a hospitable welcome from the resident Zanzibari community and indigenous Gogo, and secured a location for later construction of a mission residence. Inhabited mostly by Gogo, but including representatives of several other ethnic groups, Mpwapwa was more a series of residential clusters than one large agglomeration; its population was estimated at 1,500.[29] The main missionary party continued on toward Victoria, leaving Mpwapwa's development for the future.

During this initial stage of European activity there occurred one of the earliest challenges to Barghash's claimed rights in the interior. Trouble came when Mackay shot at and wounded four porters who were fleeing his caravan because of a dispute with Africans who protested passage through newly planted crops. Summoned by Kirk to Zanzibar to stand trial, Mackay instead pushed inland, denying the sultan's authority and leaving behind an unsettled affair that eventually threatened continuation of the Buganda mission.[30]

In 1878 Dr. E. J. Baxter, J. Last, and J. Henry, lay members of the society, began a permanent settlement at Mpwapwa; their orders envisaged creation of a self-supporting station serving both as proselytizing center for surrounding regions and a link in the line of bases leading inland. The first party, accompanied by about thirty African Christians from the Mombasa and Universities' missions, arrived in May; their welcome, now that a European presence was a certainty, was a little less hospitable than expected. The Africans, returning the funds advanced as payment for cooperation, denied the use of land supposedly agreed upon for a building site. Since the lost location overlooked the caravan route, providing a vantage point for observing all passing Arabs, the Britons blamed the resident Muslims.[31] If there was Arab opposition, it was of minor consequence; the missionaries speedily secured another plot, then became fully involved in problems of their own making, African and European Christians commencing arguments that caused withdrawal of most Africans in early 1879. Other African Christians arrived shortly thereafter; this time by a carefully worked out agreement they received their own residences and gardens, plus the promise of payment for mission labor. Last happily foresaw creation of a vigorous Christian village, but the dream quickly disappeared when fresh quarrels at once commenced. Fearing an armed uprising, the Europeans secured help from their Muslim Zanzibari followers, disarming the African Christians. The Africans left Mpwapwa, permanently ending hopes for a Christian settlement.[32] The Europeans additionally encountered hindrances in resolving questions with indigenous Africans, Last lamenting in frustrated description of the uncentralized local political structure: "Everyone does that which seems right in his own eyes."[33]

Under Baxter's direction the missionaries, motivated by hatred of the slave trade, quickly decided on taking action against Arabs. Relying upon the protection of the powerful British Zanzibar consulate, Baxter and his associates from April 1879 began to note names of Arabs leading slave caravans, sending the information to Kirk for forwarding to the sultan for their punishment as violators of the 1876 proclamations. Thus challenged, the sultan imprisoned some offending Arabs, members of the community operating in regions south of Lake Tanganyika. Once this news was known, Arab caravans hurried past Mpwapwa, taking paths out of the Europeans' sight. Other Arabs, before visiting the settlement, removed telltale signs, such as chains, from captives. Not content with reporting, Baxter further affronted Arabs, making the mission a haven for slaves fleeing from passing caravans. When aroused owners came seeking their property, Baxter, while denying all possibility of forceful resistance, announced that the British flag brought freedom to slaves who, if they accepted station rules, were free to remain in residence. Most owners, fearing Baxter might report them to Zanzibar as slave traders, did not even visit the mission.

By June 1879 Baxter, enthusiastic over the results of his campaign, mused about having the sultan appoint a Briton to serve as secular head of the growing refugee community. If the proposal actually was made, it was not accepted. The conduct of the defenseless missionaries almost ended in disaster when one aggrieved Arab challenged them for harboring his slaves. A few of Sayf bin Suliman's slaves fled their master's Mpwapwa camp, securing the usual welcome from Baxter. Judging that the missionaries were appropriating his property, Sayf, an important resident of a nearby Arab community, began gathering forces and announced he would attack unless the slaves were restored. Passing International African Association members prepared to assist the Britons, but all danger ceased when the fugitives, apparently not regarding the station as a safe refuge, fled into the countryside; the Arabs abandoned their martial stance to pursue and apprehend the slaves. French Association representative Bloyet from close-by Kondoa reported similar instances; the experiences converted Sayf into a firm opponent of the British.

The Church Missionary Society directors, remembering the problems caused by runaways at Mombasa, naturally were worried, and sought Kirk's interpretation of the legality of Baxter's conduct. The consul did not oppose the Mpwapwa Briton's doings since coastward traffic in slaves was illegal, although he noted the missionaries, until stopped by his orders, had harbored escaping domestic slaves legally owned by Arabs. Trusting to his prestige to restrain Arab attack, Kirk minimized the possibility of trouble at Mpwapwa, his certainty increased by a forthcoming expedition led by General Mathews ordered to build a fortified post not far from the mission.[34]

The tensions around Mpwapwa persisted into the 1880s, forty fugitives, for instance, arriving in June 1881 and twenty-six in August. The Africans never were promised protection, but their position appeared secure enough; the support of Mpwapwa's inhabitants, whose slaves were not harbored, and the backing of Kirk discouraged any overly aggressive Arabs.[35]

By May 1882 the Mpwapwa complex represented the largest group of Europeans residing in inland East Central Africa, including the first two European women. Henrietta Cole bore the first European child born in the interior. Both women died, Mrs. Last in March, Mrs. Cole in July 1883.[36] The mission apparently gained important support in October 1880 when Mathews, with a contingent of Barghash's army, founded a military base at Mamboya. But once the general returned to the coast, the garrison began preying upon the local population, one missionary grumbled that "the soldiers are about the most lawless set of men the country can produce."[37] If, in the end, the behavior of Baxter and his colleagues did not lead to any significant confrontations between Arab and European, the missionary conduct did send waves throughout East Central Africa; Europeans on Lakes Tanganyika and Victoria recorded problems with Arabs exacerbated by the Mpwapwa situation.[38] It was not coincidental that Mpwapwa was the only interior British missionary station destroyed by Arabs during the hostilities against the Germans during the late 1880s.

With its important location, Ujiji became an early inland goal. The London Missionary Society expedition reached Lake Tanganyika during August 1878. Arabs and Africans offered a friendly reception, although suspicions of the strangers' motives caused long delays before the missionaries secured a permanent home. Mission leader Edward Hore had doubts concerning the suitability of a town where he observed "only Arabs, Wangwana, and their hangers on," but a settlement was made. Mwinyi Kheri, protecting his position, kept the missionaries from direct contacts with the Ha leadership.[39] The unwanted European entry helped precipitate changes in the loosely structured relations between Zanzibar and Ujiji. The missionaries, frustrated despite possession of the usual letters from Barghash and Kirk, attempted to influence the Zanzibar authorities to exert pressure on the Ujiji Muslims. The reiterated requests raised an interesting situation for Barghash since Mwenyi Kheri ruled without confirmation from Zanzibar. Hore, discussing with Kirk the need for a British agent on Tanganyika, also spoke of the selection of "a properly appointed Governor" for Ujiji. Kirk concurred, warning Barghash "that if this is not done we shall conclude that the Sultan has no authority in these regions and no rights to be respected by us." Recognizing his limited inland authority, yet realizing the need to reply to the importunate Europeans, Barghash proceeded carefully, writing to the Ujiji Arabs, at the same time ordering Abdullah bin Nasibu to dispatch an agent empowered to confirm Mwenyi Kheri and his associates in office, "for they are the elders," if they recognized Zanzibar's sovereignty. If not, the liwali should appoint other leaders. When in December 1880 Hore met Abdullah, the Arab promised obedience to Barghash's commands, although earlier in 1879 he had admitted to another missionary his inability to interfere in Ujiji, a town not subject to his sultan.[40]

Meanwhile Hore opened discussions with Kirk concerning the missionary role toward the slave trade. Even though Arabs had moved most transactions away from the normal missionary haunts, Hore remained dissatisfied. "I itch to take more energetic measures than prudence perhaps and at any rate my missionary work would justify," he burst out, wondering whether "the Missionary marine departments on Nyanza, Tanganyika and Nyassa [might] be rendered effective for the seizure . . . of slaves either afloat or ashore?" Thus Hore volunteered to become a consular agent; Kirk, however, rejected formal ties because of the impossibility of protecting so distant an official. But Kirk acquiesced regarding the usefulness of some connection, the Foreign Office assenting that Hore serve "as . . . official means of communication with Ujiji." The discussion perforce ended when the mission directors refused to sanction involvement with the British government. Hore and his colleagues nonetheless continued communicating with the Zanzibar consuls, providing much information on Arab doings. Not surprisingly one missionary later admitted "it is . . . deeply rooted in the minds of these Arabs that we are emissaries of the British government."[41] Still, the missionaries managed to avoid direct conflicts with Arabs, joining in their prayers, as a sign of loyalty to the sultan's authority, the names of Barghash and Victoria.[42]

Roman Catholics, not content to leave East Central Africa to Protestant and secular organizations, joined the procession of new arrivals. French Cardinal Charles Lavigerie secured papal permission for his recently formed White Fathers to enter the competition for African souls.[43] The French missionaries landed in Zanzibar in June 1878, preparing a large caravan destined for Lakes Tanganyika and Victoria. Attaining Tabora, the White Fathers benefited from the good Arab impression of the French Holy Ghost priests; expedition leader Livinhac easily borrowed 50,000 francs, while Shaykh bin Nasibu aided the fathers in founding a mission. The Arabs, knowing that Frenchmen bought young Africans for their establishments, anticipated profiting from their presence. The priests purchased a residence from International African Association agent Théodore van den Heuvel, then returned to Zanzibar, inaugurating the education of Africans gained from Arabs in August 1881. The dealings between Arabs and White Fathers continued amicably through 1884. Nyamwezi ruler Isike, the recipient of frequent gifts, reacted in similar friendly fashion.[44]

Meantime the French expedition continued the march, dividing into separate columns for Tanganyika and Victoria. The group commanded by T. Deniaud, an experienced missionary, entered Ujiji in January 1879. Judging Muslim-dominated Ujiji an unsuitable headquarters—the British Protestant presence increasing Catholic distaste—the Frenchmen decided to make the town merely a base on the way to other stations.[45] With Mwinyi Kheri's help the fathers explored the lake region, in July building at Rumonge on the Rundi coast. But the White Fathers' slave-purchasing policy brought a quarrel with surrounding Africans when one slave fled the post; the aroused missionaries, when their neighbors refused his return, in retaliation seized some African cattle. As the Africans gathered in force, Deniaud decided a show of strength was required and advanced with an armed party. The unwise step precipitated hostilities, taking the lives of Deniaud and other missionaries; the shaken survivors evacuated Rumonge. Arabs had not been involved in the fracas, yet, in a typical reaction, Lavigerie in Europe immediately blamed the deaths on Muslims opposing Christian endeavors against slavery. Mwinyi Kheri, reacting to previous frictions with Rumonge's inhabitants, attacked the settlement, killing its chief and seizing much booty, then suggesting that the White Fathers reopen the station, promising protection against local Africans. The offer, understandably, was refused. Prior to the disaster the French priests, again with Arab assistance, in 1880 had opened another mission at Massanze, a region of small villages on the coast opposite Ujiji, the new location serving as headquarters after Deniaud's death.[46]

Relations continued satisfactory with the Ujiji Arabs; in 1883 Mwinyi Kheri supported negotiations leading to expansion of mission work at Massanze. Kheri's easy tolerance of Catholics was demonstrated in one episode recounted by *Père* Charbonnier: the Arab, when talking of religion, explained to a Muslim audience his opinion of the Frenchmen, saying "simply that we prayed as he did, that we recognized God as he did, but that we differed *a little* in religion." There was good reason for the amicable behavior; the White Fathers continually emphasized that their nation, unlike the British, had no interest in forcefully terminating the Arab trade in slaves. The priests also remained profitable associates for the Arabs, from 1879 to 1891 purchasing about 3,000 slaves. As *Père* Josset remarked, "One can say without exaggeration: so many redeemed slaves, so many converts." The Frenchmen occupied a Ujiji base from September 1882 to May 1884, but only as a contact point for their lakeside missions and as a market for slaves.[47] Mwinyi Kheri meantime, perhaps apprehensive that the deaths at Rumonge might be attributed to him, responded to Barghash's message, hoisted the sultan's flag, and acted henceforth as his liwali for Ujiji and the northern lake region.[48]

An important turning point for Buganda's Arab community came during Stanley's 1874–1877 crossing of Africa, the same journey having similar lasting consequences for the Congo Arabs. During conversations between the explorer and Mutesa, the kabaka, as always interested in anything new, particularly if it might benefit his kingdom, expressed the desire to learn more about the Europeans' religion. The persisting Egyptian threat was one of several factors making representatives of new foreign powers, especially men from states possessing advanced technological knowledge, wanted by Mutesa. Stanley dispatched his well-known letter of 14 March 1875 challenging British missionaries to work in the territories bordering Lake Victoria;[49] the Church Missionary Society answered the summons. The first Protestant missionaries, George Wilson and Mackay, entered Buganda in 1877, resolutely disposed to counter the seeming strength of the resident Arabs. Interminable bickering began, the Arabs, according to Wilson, spreading "the most abominable lies about us and about the English in general, representing us as a greedy, grasping nation, who only travel to such countries . . . for the purpose of conquering and annexing them." The Britons accepted, probably even anticipated, the Muslim arguments; Mackay avowed in November 1878 his willingness to utilize every opportunity "to put to confusion the pretentions of the Arabs."[50] The Muslims, many of them not literate, all of them merchants not formally trained as missionaries, probably preferred, as members of the generally tolerant community of East Coast believers, to avoid open conflict with Europeans. Faced, however, with the often outrageous European interpretations of Islam's meaning, the Arabs, led initially by Khamis bin Khalfan, an agent of Said bin Salim, and Masudi bin Suliman, a well-established resident serving the kabaka, endeavored to counter the verbal attacks.[51]

The European offensive had other, more dangerous nuances; the missionaries, like their Lake Malawi brethren, realized destruction of the firm Arab position meant replacing their rivals in the commercial functions so valuable to Mutesa. Wilson relatively quickly recommended the utilization of European Christian traders, informing Mutesa that the Arabs charged excessive rates for services, by November thinking the arguments had convinced the ruler to expell the Muslims if others were available as replacements. Thus Wilson advised his London superiors to place Christian traders under the aegis of the Buganda mission, contending that, with Mutesa's support, the possiblity existed of both supplanting the Muslims and keeping out other perhaps not so Christian European traders. Mackay kept the argument before Mutesa, emphasizing as part of the determined battle against Islam the supposed defects engendered by mixed Arab and African ancestry. Mutesa, not loath to utilize Christian and Muslim tensions for his own purposes, confessed to the missionaries a mistrust of the commercially useful Arabs; Mackay quickly offered to send for "an honest Christian trader."[52]

In December Mackay pushed the campaign a step further, condemning before Mutesa's court an incoming Arab seeking to exchange firearms and cloth for ivory and slaves. The missionary charged that the Arabs, while proclaiming Barghash as their sultan, openly violated his orders forbidding participation in the slave trade. Mutesa responded by declaring the slave trade ended in Buganda, following with a decree instituting the death penalty for transgressors of the new regulation. Mackay was skeptical about the monarch's zeal—perhaps he knew Mutesa had made similar promises to Egyptian officer E. L. de Bellefonds in May 1875—but nonetheless was gratified at the seeming success in influencing Mutesa's conduct.[53]

The verbal warfare continued into 1879; Mutesa, probably attempting to make the Arabs unsure of their standing, in January queried the missionaries about banishing Muslims from Buganda. When missionary reinforcements came, Mutesa once again pressured the Arabs, according to C. W. Pearson accepting the European introductory gifts, then turning to the Arabs and intoning "they never gave him such presents, and that for a small portion of such cloth they demanded a frasilah of ivory." The hapless Muslims, defenseless before comparisons with the noncommercial missionaries, had to feel threatened. They had good reason to think so. Following missionary advice, Mutesa requested Kirk to arrange for a European trader to visit Buganda. Kirk passed the message to British merchant Archibald Smith, who offered to be Mutesa's Zanzibar agent, supplying firearms and other commodities in return for ivory. But the proffer was abortive; Smith failed to secure transport for moving merchandise between Buganda and Zanzibar. The attack on the Arabs' commercial position went no further; the Church Missionary Society directors decided that involvement in business affairs was improper for missionaries.[54]

European and Arab squabbling at Mutesa's capital intensified during 1878 when the White Fathers arrived. The two European groups, their religious differences exacerbated by nationalistic rivalry, soon commenced intra-Christian bickering; the British advocates of Christ's message, in a reaction typical of both parties, agonized over the "question which is our worst enemy at court, Arab or Jesuit."[55] The astute Mutesa allowed the countercharges, realizing the usefulness of competition for his favor among Europeans and Arabs. During 1879, feeling the need for outside support, the kabaka approached the French with an unexpected proposal, requesting alliance with their government. Lacking authority for concluding any agreement, the priests forwarded the message to Paris. Throughout the long wait for an answer the Frenchmen, without much surprise, saw a drop in the Ganda monarch's friendship. Nonetheless, even when the priests relayed their government's refusal, Mutesa continued on friendly terms with the French missionaries. During the same period the White Fathers enjoyed relatively satisfactory relations with Arabs, Père Lourdel reasoning that the hostile stance of their British competitors was a main factor in the Arab attitude.[56]

Mutesa's open encouragement of Christian and Muslim rivalry, often staged in open court where only his consent let the arguing continue, was a normal reaction in a society where so much depended upon gaining the ruler's will. Sharp changes in the kabaka's attitude performed a useful function for the supposedly capricious Mutesa, aiding his never-ending task of containing all the fissaparous tendencies of the Ganda system, persistent stimulation of rivals increasing their willingness to do things to win the ruler's favor. But by 1880 it was apparent that Mutesa had not won all he had originally hoped for from the Europeans: they, after all, were not government agents. The Europeans, the British in particular, suffered from having talked too loosely about what they, or allied traders, might do to strengthen the Ganda state. The British status declined even more in March 1880 when a letter from Kirk arrived defining proper relationships between missionary societies and the British government. The statement, in very direct terms, of their private character probably was stimulated by Mackay's behavior toward Africans while en route to Buganda, plus his subsequent refusal to stand trial for assault in Zanzibar. The messenger bearing the communication increased the drama of presentation, affirming it was not to be opened in Mackay's presence; the Arabs seized the opportunity to stress his past deeds and the likelihood of his reverting to type while in Buganda. The arguments of the consular messengers, coastal Muslims, and the Arabs very nearly, in one missionary's opinion, resulted in Mackay being returned in chains to Zanzibar.[57] Mutesa took no action, leaving resolution of the problem to the British. The accompanying swing away from Europeans perhaps explains Mutesa's new turning toward the Muslims: in July the kabaka marked the shift by declaring Islam the state religion, building a small mosque near his residence, and attending daily prayer, all without interfering with individual freedom of worship.[58] It is quite possible, of course, that Mutesa acted without regard to Europeans, turning to Islam, as he had in the past, when in need of its spiritual message.

The Protestant mission meanwhile was rent by personal differences, the fault largely due to Mackay's intemperate behavior toward his fellow workers. The society directors, seeking an end to dissension, attempted to recall Mackay, dispatching to Buganda Philip O'Flaherty, an experienced missionary with some knowledge of Arabic.[59] O'Flaherty, an unstable extrovert bursting with zeal to work against Muslims and anyone else opposing him, reached Buganda in March 1881, finding Christian-Muslim relations much the same as during the past year. As elsewhere within the area influenced by Zanzibar, the Arabs did not present a united front to Europeans. Among active opponents were Hashid bin Surur (known as Khambi Mbaya), Masudi bin Sulayman, and Idi; more friendly Arabs included Khamis bin Khalfan, Said bin Hajid, and Said Muhammad.[60] But O'Flaherty wasted little time in judging the many Muslims in Buganda, openly challenging all at Mutesa's court. Hashid bin Surur, the most vocal of the Arabs, was dismissed as "a mean low bred ignorant servant of a British subject." By April the exultant missionary considered Arabs "at a discount"; they were temporarily expelled from Mutesa's presence because of his success in explaining the meaning of the Qur'an.

Mutesa certainly did not share O'Flaherty's partisan nonsense—Hashid

bin Surur, for example, had treated Mutesa for an illness during February—but he did not oppose the denigration of the Arabs. A good reason
for the attitude was the fact, reported by O'Flaherty without connection to
his supposed success, of the Ganda monarch's extensive debts to Arab
merchants. Often kept waiting for a year or longer for ivory, the Arabs
doubtless often reminded Mutesa of outstanding claims, naturally rousing
his irritation.[61] Hashid bin Surur, so said O'Flaherty, was "thrashed by the
palace pages and turned outside the gate," the incident perhaps sparked by
the Arab's approaching return to the coast, an event certainly calling for a
settling of accounts. But then the balance once more lurched back to the
Arabs, possibly assisted by O'Flaherty's unwise boasting of conquering
Buganda with one hundred armed followers and rumors that the Catholics
were training men for military action. By July the Muslims closed ranks,
gaining additional strength from the August entry of new caravans. The
arriving Arabs included the powerful and influential Sulayman bin Zuhayr
commanding a caravan bringing six hundred firearms among its loads. The
Arab also brought Mutesa a letter supposedly sent by Barghash: when
interpreted by Masudi bin Sulayman, it called for expulsion of all Britons
from Buganda. Little attention probably was awarded the unlikely missive; Mutesa's desire to work out satisfactory rates for Arab merchandise
explained his turn in attitude.[62]

During most of 1882 the differences between Arabs and Europeans
moderated, verbal competition breaking forth sporadically without seriously damaging existing relations. The French priests, reacting against the
many hindrances facing their labors, evacuated Buganda later in the year,
moving across Victoria to Sukuma territory at Bukumbi. The White
Fathers did not return until 1885, although Ganda Catholics kept up
adherence to the new faith during the French absence.[63]

In 1883, following general patterns in East Central Africa, tensions
heightened between Arab and European. Led by Masudi bin Sulayman,
the holder of an important Ganda subchieftaincy, the Arabs accused the
missionaries of seeking the overthrow of existing Ganda social, political,
and military customs—as, of course, in the long run they were—without
inaugurating any major setback for the Britons.[64]

In 1884 the rivalry at the Ganda capital intensified, O'Flaherty announcing, although there is no evidence to verify the claim, the arrival of a "great
Mwalimu or Professor of Moslem divinity," plus other teachers, to oppose
the Christians. The discussions at court continued animated, Masudi bin
Sulayman persisting as prime proponent of the Muslim viewpoint.[65]

Mutesa's death in October 1884 closed an important era, marking a
change to a period when the ruler of Buganda no longer dominated the
perimeters of the relationship between Christians and Muslims, whether
foreign or indigenous, within his state. Mutesa, during his almost thirty-

year reign, had encouraged the entry and residence of both competing world religions, studying, at times with intense interest, their monotheistic and moral dogmas. But he never lost sight of his position as political ruler of a flourishing African state, guiding Buganda to become the dominating power of the Lake Victoria region. Thus he remained equally interested in the secular knowledge outsiders brought to Buganda, learning what he could, and welcoming, in the case of some Muslims, their ingress into the ranks of the Ganda hierarchy. The same treatment would have been awarded European Christians if the missionaries had accepted Mutesa's offers.[66] Nonetheless, despite Mutesa's overwhelming political motivation, encouragement of the presence of Muslim and Christian visitors began a far-reaching revolution in the thinking of an important segment of the population, the young men training at the capital for future roles in state service. It is essential to remember that the young Ganda persisted in studying foreign religions while unedifying bickering continued between Arab and European. In opening their minds to Islam and Christianity the youths passed beyond the existing constraints of the accepted political order, thus preparing the way for the dramatic events of 1888.

The Holy Ghost fathers, cut off from the deep interior by the White Fathers, reacted to Protestant incursions by undertaking a modest expansion into not too distant areas. Between 1877 and 1885 the Frenchmen opened stations among the Ngulu, Zigula, and Luguru at Mhonda, Mandera, Morogoro, and Tununguo.[67] Even though the missionaries chose most of the new locations because of the absence of Arab settlers, relations with the Zanzibar administration, especially Bwana Heri of Sadani, remained harmonious. During the 1880s Heri became a well-known figure along the route to the interior, often acting to demonstrate his and Barghash's authority. In 1881, for example, the Holy Ghost priests encountered hostility at Mhonda, repulsing an attack on the station. Since the affair continued unsettled, the Frenchmen sought Barghash's aid, the sultan immediately sending Heri, accompanied by a few hundred men, to Mhonda. The Sadani ruler quickly settled the dispute, taking some of the local population back to Zanzibar as hostages. At Morogoro, the reception of fleeing slaves by the Mpwapwa British missionaries caused initial opposition to the Catholics, but knowledge of the nationality difference, and communications from Zanzibar, ended the problem.[68] The Frenchmen encountered little significant opposition from Arabs until after 1885.

The International African Association, a supposedly international body created for humanitarian and scientific purposes in Africa, but in reality a concern directed by Belgium's Leopold II for furthering private dreams for African empire, organized the most important nonmissionary effort of the late 1870s.[69] Recognizing Arab utility in achieving his goals, Leopold initially ordered avoidance of overt friction with Muslims.[70] The members of the first Association expedition disembarked in Zanzibar at the end of 1877, receiving, said the French consul, a cool welcome, Barghash lacking a clear perception of the organization's nature. In addition, Zanzibar's customary diplomatic usage required a treaty prior to the landing of expeditions.[71] Still, the diplomatic realities of the era did not permit open opposition. After initial personnel problems the Association caravan, led by Ernest Cambier, left for the interior in June 1878, ultimately aiming for Lake Tanganyika and the principal Congo Arab centers. At Tabora, Cambier received a communication from Stanley, then in Leopold's employ on the lower Congo River, warning against involvement in Arab political quarrels and advising a settlement at Karema on Tanganyika's eastern shore.[72] In Unyamwezi, Cambier, delayed by inadvertent involvement in feuding between Mirambo and the Tabora Arabs, profited from the assistance of the Nasibu brothers. After a difficult march Cambier attained the lake in August 1879, finding at Karema, about 150 miles south of Ujiji, a village of 250 Africans in a location well off the region's main trade routes. Karema became principal base for the Association, the terminus of three succeeding expeditions. All, though destined for the Congo, failed to advance much beyond Karema.[73] During this time Barghash harbored suspicions of Leopold's officers, in June 1880 apparently informing Abdullah bin Nasibu that "no time should be lost in hoisting our flag in the district where the settlement has been made." The reality of Karema's isolated location, however, left it free of Arab interference.[74]

The second Association venture, commanded by Emile Popelin, in October 1879 established a minor station at Tabora, leaving Dr. Théodore van den Heuvel behind as resident. The isolated European, his principal function to arrange supplies for Karema, lived amicably among Arabs and Africans, his only problem related to delays in concluding the concession for a residence. The Belgian's medical knowledge made him a valued member of the community, the Nyamwezi even utilizing Heuvel as arbitrator for disputes. Wearied of living without European companionship, Heuvel left Tabora in August 1881, his replacement, Jêrome Becker, continuing the existing satisfactory relationships with Arabs.[75]

The next Association expedition, commanded by Guillaume Ramaeckers and accompanied by several other European groups, marched inland in 1880. Their passage was blocked near Mdaburu by a war between Barghash's agent Mwinyi Mtwana and an indigenous leader, the Belgian captain intervening to help award victory to the Arab. It was the only instance of the newly arriving Europeans acting to extend Barghash's authority.[76] Instructed to strengthen Karema, Ramaeckers worked to this goal by purchasing Africans supposedly given freedom after the transaction. The Africans actually were bound to the station, subject to harsh treatment, including the death penalty, for not obeying their new master's dictates. Ramaeckers further improved Association authority when, following the death of the local ruler, he received from the African population the right to confirm a successor, promising in return support against their enemies.[77] The Belgian died at his post in March 1882. Emile Storms, commander of the fourth Association expedition, took charge, finding about sixty soldiers, plus over one hundred other Africans, in the Karema station. He opened another post at Mpala, on the western shore of Tanganyika, in March 1883. Like his predecessors, Storms lacked the support required for further penetration into the Congo.[78]

Earlier, at Tabora, Becker had inaugurated, in September 1881, interesting discussions with Tippu Tip, then returning from the Congo to Zanzibar. The Belgian, destined to become one of Tippu Tip's closest European associates, proposed accompanying the Arab to the Congo. Nothing came of the discussion, but the matter was pursued once again in August 1882 when Storms encountered Tippu Tip in Tabora. The Belgian claimed the Arab agreed to sell his ivory to Association representatives in the Congo, apparently wishing to avoid payment of large debts in Zanzibar. Tippu Tip probably was not serious in the negotiation, merely saying what the young European wanted to hear. In Zanzibar he informed the sultan and others of the talks, thus stimulating already present suspicions against the Association. Since scarcity of resources then precluded sending an expedition from Zanzibar to the Congo, Leopold's men never had the opportunity to test the validity of Tippu Tip's supposed promises.[79]

According to the International African Association's charter, national branches remained free to create separate divisions of the greater organization. The British, uninterested in working within a multinational society whose aims they suspected, quickly withdrew from possible participation. "Amateur co-operation," boasted Elton, "is not necessary."[80] The French and Germans, however, increased the numbers of Association expeditions by forming national committees to support independent African ventures. The French began organizing as early as October 1876, eventually perfecting plans for establishing two stations, one in the Congo region, the other in the sphere of the sultan of Zanzibar. Financial backing came from individual Frenchmen, their government, and Leopold II, the latter, caught in the farce of the Association's international nature, thus contributing to a group sending Savorgnan de Brazza to hamper Stanley's advance along the Congo. The expedition destined for East Africa was entrusted to Captain Bloyet, a forty-year-old merchant seaman. Carefully prepared for the African adventure by a special course of study with experienced explorers, Bloyet headed for Zanzibar in May 1880, intending to found a station in the region of modern Kilossa. Taking advantage of the newly organized European-Indian commerical enterprise represented in the interior by Emile Segère, the French Association entrusted to it the travel plans and initial establishment of their agent.[81]

Bloyet arrived at Kondoa, a small settlement located in the thickly populated, fertile lowlands of the Mukondokwe Valley. Not far distant were the residences of Sayf bin Suliman and Said bin Umar al Nabahani, two prominent, long-established Arabs trading with the Irangi region and elsewhere.[82] Suffering from an illness contracted on the journey, Bloyet in February 1881 entered Kondoa in poor condition. The Arabs were hostile to the planned station. Sayf bin Said, one of the wealthiest Arabs residing between Tabora and the coast, remembering his troubles with the British Mpwapwa missionaries, led the opposition, but, with backing from other Arabs of the vicinity, Bloyet was allowed a provisional installation. Through additional negotiations with Arabs and Africans, the Frenchman won permanent approval, both groups, observing Bloyet's few followers, even aiding in building his house.[83]

Once settled, Bloyet enjoyed comfortable relations with Arabs and Africans, both Sayf bin Suliman and Said bin Umar becoming friendly enough, once they realized the European's disinterest in commercial matters, to intervene when necessary to protect the Frenchman and his group. There are unclear references to differences with some coastmen, the issue apparently resolved by letters from Barghash sent on the request of the French consul. By 1881 the station was secure enough for Mme Bloyet to join her husband, the couple for the next few years living a busy life, frequently traveling for mapmaking and to gather materials for French museums while leaving the post in the care of Africans. The only unfavorable report concerning Bloyet came from Mpwapwa; Baxter claimed from second-hand information that the Frenchman had purchased slaves, his subsequent harsh treatment causing their flight from Kondoa. With clear exaggeration, Baxter added that Bloyet's conduct had frightened all other Africans from visiting. As we have seen, it was common practice for Frenchmen to buy slaves; whatever the truth of Baxter's tales, the events described certainly did not harm Bloyet's reputation with Arabs.[84]

The Kondoa station, without a political future after Peters's treaties,[85] and with the French Association's intense involvement in the Congo, was terminated in 1885. Bloyet, realizing the choice was likely, had arranged for a provisional transfer to the Holy Ghost Mission. But Kondoa's future as a missionary center was blighted by a two-year drought that caused the nearby river to run dry; the station, occupied by only a few African Christian families, became merely a small outpost of the Holy Ghost Longa mission. Bloyet meantime returned to France, receiving the gold medal of the Paris Geographical Society for the results of his topographical work around Kondoa.[86]

The Germans, then beginning their interest in overseas expansion, also formed a national committee of the International African Association, from April 1878 planning a German post in Africa. Deciding on the Nyamwezi region, the committee received financial assistance from Leopold and the German government. Commanded by D. von Schöler, the expedition arrived in Zanzibar in 1880: its other members were E. Kaiser, biologist Richard Böhm, and Paul Reichard. The latter, a young manufacturer motivated by commercial reasons, paid his own expenses and developed into one of the more perceptive contemporary observers of the East Central African scene. With assistance from the Segère transport concern, the German party, in company with Ramaeckers' caravan, left Zanzibar in July. Entering Tabora in October the Germans discovered their original goal blocked by raiding from Nyamwezi war leader Nyungu ya Mawe. After conferring with Arabs and others in Tabora the Germans selected instead the Nyamwezi state of Ugunda, southwest of Unyanyembe near the Ngombe River. While in Tabora the Germans purchased a few slaves, requiring the supposedly liberated Africans to labor at their planned station. Schöler left when the initial building was completed. When the Germans settled at Kakoma in Ugunda, Böhm charged the outwardly friendly Tabora Arabs with intriguing to prevent their establishment. If so, the Nyamwezi ignored Arab advice. Ugunda ruler Mlimangombe, residing at Igonda, a short distance away, approved of the newcomers, remaining in amicable contact until his July 1881 death. His successor, Dishia, threatened by rivals backed by Shaykh bin Nasibu and Isike, sought a German alliance; the Association men concluded an agreement to support her in return for the promise of important influence in conduct of state policy. The Arabs and their Nyamwezi allies, although unhappy at interference in one of their spheres of concern, accepted the arrangement.

Not content in their isolated location, the Germans soon thought of traveling to more distant lands, particularly to Lake Mweru, but their plans were disrupted by a fire that destroyed much of their property—and Böhm's notes—and by the death of the Kaiser. Böhm and Reichard eventually marched to Karema, there assisting Storms in combat against nearby Africans. While Böhm recovered from wounds suffered in the action, Reichard helped in founding Mpala. The two Germans continued on into the Congo, Böhm dying in March 1884. Reichard ended the expedition in Katanga. The last survivor of the German Association returned to Zanzibar, ending a five-year-and-seven-month stay in the interior, the longest residence of any Association member. Reichard brought with him claims to Ugunda, but the evolving German position in East Africa did not require the treaties.[87] To the Arabs, the French and German Association branches had been of minimal consequence, neither group posing the slightest danger to their regional interests.

The final group of Europeans, limited to a few venturesome private traders intending to compete as buyers of ivory for transport to Zanzibar, directly threatened the Arabs. The traders, the only open, immediate challengers of the Arab system, but lacking the capability to defend themselves, had little chance of displacing the entrenched Arabs and their African allies. During the period before the mid-1880s, the Arabs simply made conditions too dangerous for the European competitors, not finding direct action necessary.

The first serious rival of the Arabs was Swiss adventurer Philippe Broyon. Traveling inland during the mid-1870s Broyon ranged as far as central Tanzania, establishing a special relationship with Mirambo. When missionaries and others appeared, Broyon grasped the opportunity for profit, exulting that a new era, one removing commerce from Arab hands, was underway. A quarrel with Mirambo concerning ivory brought to Zanzibar saved the Arabs the trouble of acting. Compelled to flee Unyamwezi, the Swiss trader finished his East African career on a coastal plantation.[88] The most important of the early European commercial undertakings was organized by Frenchman Emile Segère and Indian entrepeneur Sewa Hajji,[89] with some backing from influential Marseille merchant Alfred Rabaud, also a sometime confidant of Leopold II. By 1880 Segère and Sewa Hajji perfected a plan for transporting merchandise inland, at their company's risk, from a Zanzibar headquarters. They intended to recruit a permanent staff of carriers to avoid the delays encountered at Zanzibar, while inland founding comptoirs initially at Tabora and later in Ujiji and Buganda for storing goods for sale to needy travelers. The purchaser could arrange for later payment in Zanzibar. The new company actively sought business, Rabaud and Segère visiting the directors of the Church Missionary Society to promote their services, also successfully securing contracts with the Belgian and French divisions of the International African Association. In East Africa, however, the company encountered resistance, the British, as always, regarding with suspicion foreign competitors for influence in the sultan's dominions.[90]

Sègère headed for Tabora in 1880, accompanying the Ramaeckers caravan, impressing his marching companions by a knowledge of Swahili and popularity with Africans, the latter the consequence of medical skills. Reaching his goal in October, Segère purchased a building for his abundant supply of good cloth, beginning a search for ivory. Later he extended operations beyond Unyanyembe to at least the neighboring Nyamwezi states of Uyuwi and Urambo. By February 1881 opposition began surfacing, the Frenchman quickly finding Tabora untenable, the leading Arabs, along with ntemi Isike, threatening death unless he left immediately. The Arab motives were clear, Isike joining because of Segère's foolhardy gunpowder sales to Mirambo. Segère additionally roused Isike's suspicions by concluding blood brotherhood with his brother Swetu; the ntemi even claimed Segère intended poisoning him. Given only twenty-four hours to evacuate Tabora, Segère fled, abandoning his merchandise. Since most Europeans regarded Isike as an Arab puppet, blame for the expulsion went to the Nasibu brothers, Isike escaping major criticism. The French consul quickly sought redress from Barghash for his countryman's losses, but Segère apparently never received compensation from the Arabs. Considering his defenseless stance while in Tabora, Segère was fortunate to escape unharmed, even succeeding in sending one large ivory consignment to the coast before the final debacle. Facing intense opposition from the Arabs of Zanzibar and the interior, Segère never had any realistic expectation of success, even if he had pursued a more careful policy toward Unyanyembe's Arab and African leadership.[91]

7 The Congo

The Arabs in fact are very fond of their Manyema, which
they compare to a Paradise.

—*Francis Dhanis*

IN THE CONTINUING search for new ivory-supplying lands Arab trader-
adventurers before midcentury pushed beyond Lake Tanganyika into regions now within Zambia and Zaire.[1] With one group of coastmen was a
youth destined to become the most famous of the interior Arabs, Hamid
bin Muhammad al Murjebi, better known as Tippu Tip. Born on Zanzibar
about 1840 Tippu Tip followed the example of many of his generation,
participating in caravan trade while in his early teens.[2] Soon entering the
long-distance trade, the young Arab journeyed, probably during the late
1850s or 1860s, to the territories grouped around Lake Tanganyika's
southern end, marching into Luba country before returning to the East
African coast. In 1867, after some lesser trips, the now-experienced
traveler regained the lake region, becoming involved in conflict with
Tabwa ruler Nsama III Chipili Chipioka. Adopting a tactic that served
him well during his subsequent career, Tippu Tip increased his strength
through judiciously allying with a nearby African ruler. The combined
Arab and African force defeated Nsama, securing the victors a rich booty.[3]

Growing more confident of his organizing abilities, Tippu Tip during
1869–1870 reentered the lands beyond Tanganyika, this time leading a
caravan 4,000 strong. Reaching the territory, on the Lomami River, of
Kusu leader Kassongo Rushie, and supposedly recognized as kin of the
ruler, a decision more likely due to his firearms and knowledge of the
outside world, Tippu Tip quickly built a strong military following among
his new subjects, raiding extensively between the Lomami and Lualaba
rivers. The transition undergone by the young Arab, from a wandering
trader to a locally based ruler, joined to roughly similar happenings experienced by other Arabs to the north, marked the inauguration of the most

important commercial and political component of the Zanzibar-focused system of East Central Africa.

During the same general period other adventurers from the Indian Ocean littoral had followed the well-traveled Ujiji route, probing westward from the lake. The beginning of the process was evident as early as Burton's 1857 Ujiji arrival, when his subordinate Said bin Salim complained that in the busy port "dhows or boats are very scarce . . ."[4] The Arabs discovered one of Africa's richest ivory-producing territories, lands inhabited by peoples not especially valuing ivory and organized in weak political systems not providing effective forms of resistance to invaders. Moreover, the Africans had little knowledge of firearms; "the Manyema," said Livingstone in 1870, "flee in terror at the reports of guns and no danger is incurred in catching their children, wives, and goats." According to Stanley, Tippu Tip in 1876 boasted that in Manyema "slaves cost nothing, they only require to be gathered."[5]

Whatever the initial behavior, Arabs soon reverted to their usual practices, forming alliances with local Africans while establishing permanent bases for exploiting the eastern Congo's resources. The most influential among pioneer Arab settlers was Muhammad Dugumbi from Sadani, whose activities from the early 1860s centered around the Lualaba town of Nyangwe, destined to become one of the principal Arab commercial and residential centers. In 1874 Stanley vitriolically described Dugumbi as "a half-caste, a vulgar, coarse-minded old man of probably seventy years of age, with a negro nose and a negroid mind . . . ignorant of everything but the art of collecting ivory."[6]

Another leading individual was Abed bin Salum al Khaduri. Roughly the same age as Dugumbi, Abed appeared to Stanley as "a tall, thin old man, white-bearded, patriarchial in aspect, narrow-minded, rather peevish and quick to take offense, a thorough believer in witchcraft and a fervid Muslim."[7] Other important individuals included Dugumbi's principal subordinate, Mwinyi Mtagamoyo bin Sultani Waksine, a native of Whindi better known as Mwinyi Moharra. In his midforties in 1874 Moharra succeeded the old Arab at his death, remaining in Nyangwe to become during the last decades of the century one of East Central Africa's most powerful Arabs. When Abed bin Salum died in the late 1880s, Moharra and representatives of Tippu Tip increased their influence, his son Said ben Abedi, a youth of about twenty, proving unable to withstand the combined opposition.[8]

Moharra gained a formidable reputation for cruelty. His repute first reached the outside world as perpetrator of the 1869 massacre of Africans at the Nyangwe market so graphically described by Livingstone. "He is brave, no doubt, but he is a man whose heart is as big as the end of my little finger," said Tippu Tip.[9] A final member of the Nyangwe leadership was Said bin Habib al Afifi, an Arab famous for crossing the continent, from Zanzibar to Angola and back, during the 1840s and 1850s. Much less is known of Said's doings in the Congo, since he avoided European company whenever possible, but he nevertheless continued until his 1889 death as one of its foremost Arabs.[10]

Important Arabs residing outside Nyangwe included other pioneer arrivals Juma bin Salim, known as Juma Merikani, and Hamid bin Ali. Pictured by Cameron as "a fine, portly Arab with a slight dash of the tarbrush," Juma, owning several residences, one near Nyangwe, became a permanent Congo resident, normally returning eastward only as far as Ujiji to exchange ivory for Zanzibar merchandise.[11] Hamid bin Ali, better known as Kibonge, originated in the Comoro Islands. He and Abed bin Salum had entered the Congo together. Hamid, after rising to the control of Kirundu, on the right bank of the river above Stanley Falls, became an influential individual among the secondary Arab leadership.[12]

The early years of activity were extremely profitable for the newcomers operating in a region as yet little known to the larger Arab community. Even the astute Kirk, monitoring the news in the Zanzibar nerve center of East Central Africa, in 1871 had to admit ignorance of what appeared "to be a rather new and special line of trade;" he concluded later that the distant Congo commerce was left to "the most desperate characters," those Arabs operating from Ujiji who seldom returned to Zanzibar. To explain his ignorance Kirk added, with a touch of contemporary racism, "no true Arab has yet passed that way," copying many later commentators on Congo affairs by covering a lack of hard information with tales of its peoples' supposed cannibalistic practices.[13] Information of the rich region inevitably quickly spread among Arabs and Europeans. In typical statements Livingstone in 1871 commented that "ivory is like grass," with "door-posts and house-pillars . . . made of ivory," while Cameron a few years later described Arabs securing tusks "irrespective of weight, for an old knife, a copper bracelet, or any other useless thing which might take the fancy of the natives."[14] The growing amounts of ivory reaching Zanzibar verified the Congo's repute. By 1869, for example, Muhammad Dugumbi brought to Ujiji a caravan carrying a reputed 18,000 pounds of ivory. Other caravans matched Dugumbi's; in 1871 Ujiji received one bearing 35,000 pounds.[15] Such prospects for profit flashed along East Central African trade networks, causing "a sort of California gold-fever at Ujiji" and other places where Arabs and Africans met to exchange wares and information. The reputation persisted, missionary Hore in 1878 proclaiming that "Manyuema is just now the Ujijians Ophir." Proof of the assertion was the continuing arrival of large Congo caravans: 2,400 men serving Tippu Tip entered Ujiji in 1878 and 1,500 in Said bin Habib's employ in 1880.[16]

Neither Tippu Tip nor the Nyangwe Arabs knew of each other's presence until 1874, when some men from Nyangwe quarreled with an African ally of Tippu Tip. The latter promptly marched to Nyangwe, where
Dugumbi and other Arabs bowed to the reality of Tippu Tip's superior
military might and commanding personality, and in the future regarded
him as their regional overlord. "From then on Tippu Tib was no longer a
simple trader," concluded Jan Vansina, "he was organizing a state."[17]
Tippu Tip, however, did not unduly interfere with other Arabs, in return
for a general recognition leaving them to manage their own affairs. All
Arabs, after all, were beginning occupation and exploitation of an immense territory; Tippu Tip lacked the resources, even if he had the desire,
to regulate closely the daily doings of the widely separated establishments
of the Congo Arabs. The wiser course of allowing each group to operate in
an area recognized as its own, under the broad cover of Tippu Tip's
authority, permitted every Arab to work for a prosperity benefiting the
entire community. The system, buttressed by the essential tactic of allying
through marriage or other means with local African leadership, persisted
until the end of the Arab era.

By the mid-1870s Tippu Tip in the lands stretching between the
Lomami and Lualaba possessed the authority to appoint or confirm indigenous political leaders and also exercised rights in elephant hunting and
raiding. Other economic activity centered upon Arab plantations where
coastal cultigens were grown along with local crops; some Arabs, because
of its high agricultural potential, even called Nyangwe the "New Bengal."
Tippu Tip moved his principal residence to Kasongo in about 1875,
setting the town on a path of development to the largest of all Arab centers
in the East Central African interior. Associated henceforth with Tippu Tip
at Kasongo was one of his relatives, Muhammad bin Said bin Hamadi al
Murjebi, called Bwana Nzige. Pictured in 1887 by a British observer as "a
tall, light-coloured Arab with a long beard, the most benevolent and
pious-looking old gentleman," Nzige might have been much richer but for
giving his ivory to less fortunate Arabs. Always a loyal subordinate, Nzige
remained Tippu Tip's principal lieutenant until the downfall of the Arab
regime.[18]

Not content to rest satisfied with exploiting existing domains, Tippu
Tip continued on the move, leading or dispatching expeditions into new
regions. It was a dangerous, exciting, and prosperous way of life, one
which by 1883 brought the Arabs as far down the Congo River as the
mouth of the Aruwimi, leading around 1880 to the building of an Arab
camp at Stanley Falls to serve as principal staging base for additional
moves to the north and west. Other Arab activity occurred in the regions
of the upper Lomami where one of Tippu Tip's important subordinates
rose to a position of much power. Ngongo Lutete, a Tetala or Songye by

birth, had been captured by Arabs when a youth and distinguished himself in their service by martial abilities. Freed from bondage he continued to rise through Arab ranks until he became, said S. L. Hinde, "chief slave and ivory hunter" of Tippu Tip. During the 1880s Ngongo led the largest section of his Arab master's armed followers. "I had never seen a slave with obedience like his," observed Tippu Tip; "everything he got he brought in."[19] Thus by the end of the decade of the 1870s the Congo region, virtually unknown to men from the coast two decades previously, was a vital component of the Zanzibar system. The focus for most of the Congo commerce was Ujiji. The lakeside town drew Africans as well as Arabs. Individual Manyema often came on their own initiative to work for local merchants and planters. "The great Wamanuema immigration still continues . . . ," Hore reported in 1880; "the great ambition of a Manyuema man is to possess a gun for which he will labour or carry loads for five or six months."[20]

What sort of man was Tippu Tip, the primary personality among Congo Arabs? When in 1876 Stanley met Tippu Tip, then beginning his period of dominance, he saw "a tall, blackbearded man, of negroid complexion, in the prime of life, straight and quick in his movements, a picture of energy and strength . . . His *tout-ensemble* was that of an Arab gentleman in very comfortable circumstances." This Arab of commanding mien, reported T. H. Parke, "standing . . . nearly six feet, with bright intelligent black eyes, and displaying manners of imperial dignity and courtesy," much to the confusion of race-conscious Europeans, had, said A. van Gele, "features of the purest negroid type: flat nose, projecting cheek bones, deep black complexion, superb teeth."[21] The Arab had "a nervous twitching of the eyes," which, according to some acquaintances, accounted for the sobriquet Tippu Tip. The latter himself explained the name came from the victory over Nsama: Africans had said "this man's guns went 'tiptip,' in a manner too terrible to listen to."[22] In conversation with Europeans Tippu Tip invariably demonstrated the courteous manners of the East Central African Arab. In 1882 Storms characterized him as "always having a smile on his lips." During 1886 Tippu Tip even stoically endured a Bible-reading in Swahili from visiting missionaries. A pleased Protestant noted the famous Arab and his companions "were very much pleased and astonished at the good Swahili, and listened quietly."[23] Many other Europeans, J. A. Moloney, for example, observed that the Arab leader "strikes you at once as a man of considerable intelligence"; all were surprised at his knowledge of Europe's affairs.[24]

Perhaps Tippu Tip's most outstanding trait was the personal vitality that propelled him to new conquests and attracted new followers. "His activity was astonishing," commented A. J. Swann; "he possessed a frank, manly character, enlivened by humour, and loved immensely to play practical jokes upon his intimate friends." "Touch on the subject of ivory with him," added another observer, "and he immediately becomes animated, his eyes full of fire." Although "he was benevolent in appearance and gentle in manner . . . ," concluded Herbert Ward, "he seemed to be full of restrained force."[25] Such characteristics elevated Tippu Tip over all other Arabs operating throughout the mainland, making him effectively the chief subordinate in the African interior of Zanzibar's sultan. Many Europeans, misunderstanding the Zanzibar political system, did not hesitate in considering Tippu Tip more important than the sultan. But Tippu Tip remained loyal to the sultan until the end of Zanzibar's independence. If there had been more men in Arab ranks with Tippu Tip's ability to understand the nature of the European threat that was building against the Arabs, the Zanzibar system and Arab way of life might better have weathered the assaults of the last two decades of the nineteenth century.

The expanding Arab commercial and political base in the center of the continent, although not much visited by Europeans before the 1880s, was one of the first Arab regions threatened. Leopold's schemes for the International African Association, utilizing Zanzibar as the initial penetration point for inland moves, changed quickly when Stanley in 1877 emerged at the mouth of the great Congo River. The Belgian king immediately sought to utilize the newly discovered internal waterway and from 1879 entrusted the task to Stanley. In slow but measured progress Stanley opened a road bypassing the rapids that blocked direct use of the Congo from the Atlantic; he thus cleared the way for an eventual incursion into the ivory regions hitherto dominated by Arabs.[26]

While Stanley advanced eastward, Barghash recalled Tippu Tip to Zanzibar to settle outstanding debts. The Arab still owed creditors for sums advanced for the caravan led inland over a decade earlier. Without hurrying, Tippu Tip accepted the summons, first carefully organizing the administration of his territories for his absence and preparing the several extensive caravans necessary to transport the fruits of his Congo labors.[27] During the long march there were many hardships for the thousands of individuals involved in the journey, as well as for Africans living in their path. In Ujiji's vicinity and in Uvinza excessive friction between the two groups caused serious fighting. Hore castigated Tippu Tip's "terrible progress from Manyuema to Zanzibar" for leaving "a whole track in his rear . . . stained and blackened."[28] While halted at Ujiji, Tippu Tip became acquainted with Muhammad bin Khalfan al Barwani, better known as Rumaliza, who joined the ranks of the Congo leader's adherents and in his subsequent career emerged as one of the most important interior Arabs.

Continuing along the caravan road, Tippu Tip attained Bagamoyo in November 1882, leading 2,000 porters bearing about 70,000 pounds of ivory. The long-absent Arab settled his debts. Stanley later affirmed he received £70,000 for the ivory, a sum that made Tippu Tip financially independent for the remainder of his life.[29] Barghash, naturally intensely interested in the affairs of the rich Congo, held long discussions with Tippu Tip and his associates. Afterwards, said Kirk, it was clear that Barghash fully understood "that the success of [Stanley's] Congo undertaking will directly affect the supply of ivory that now reaches the East Coast." The sultan decided Tippu Tip should return at once to the Congo to do all feasible in safeguarding the territory from European incursions. Leaving Zanzibar during 1883 Tippu Tip set forth both to uphold the orders of his sultan and to maintain his Congo domain.[30]

8 The Arab State in 1885

IF, IN THE mid-1880s, Barghash had paused to contemplate the changes occurring in East Central Africa since the beginning of his reign, the intelligent ruler of Zanzibar should have been well satisfied by the seeming strength of the Arab political and economic system. Zanzibar's commerce flourished, the customs house nearly doubling in size by the early 1880s, while royal revenues had climbed to about $1,250,000 annually.[1] The BuSaidi flag flew over a series of prosperous interior settlements whose Arab communities acknowledged Barghash as ruler.

In other inland centers where African leaders held firm sway Arabs held important positions in economic, political, or cultural affairs, while African rulers looked to Zanzibar as focal point of the East Central African world. And everywhere throughout this vast section of the continent individual Africans, drawn to the teachings of Islam, provided new recruits to the numbers of Muslims recognizing Barghash's influential office.

There are many indications, in addition to events at the principal locations of Arab activity discussed earlier, of the vigorous spread of Arab influence. In one typical happening, among the Sangu of central Tanzania, a people in contact with Arabs from the beginnings of their progress inland, an Arab individual, Amrani bin Massudi, arrived around 1867 to conduct a profitable trade. He returned to Usangu sometime later leading a raiding force against his erstwhile commercial partners. Barghash, advised of the resulting unrest, summoned the Arab to Zanzibar, then dispatched inland an expedition commanded by Sulimani bin Abedi after Amrani's refusal to comply. During the succeeding hostilities, in 1873, Amrani was killed, and Sulimani remained in Usangu as an influential advisor at the court of the Sangu ruler, recognized by Barghash and local Arabs as liwali. The Arabs maintained an important presence in Usangu until the colonial period.[2]

Another significant indication of Zanzibar's ties to the interior is the career of Mwinyi Mtwana. One of the most troublesome territories for caravans coming to and from the coast along the central route was Ugogo, aptly called by Burton "the rough nurse of rugged men." The semipastoral Gogo, politically divided into many independent units, jealously controlled the limited food and water available in their harsh country, thus ensuring adequate returns for sales to passing caravans. When Arabs reacted against their prices, the Africans disappeared, filling up water sources, often attacking weak and disorganized visitors. But, because of the even more difficult environment and peoples flanking the Gogo, Arabs endured the exactions, although, said Zanzibar physician Christie, "they have been vowing vengeance in silence."[3]

During the late 1870s, when forces under Nyungu ya Mawe worsened conditions along the Gogo road, Barghash reacted to improve Arab security. The sultan chose Mwinyi Mtwana, a coastman and long-time resident of the interior, to quiet the disorder. Mtwana, aided by his son, began combatting Nyungu and his local allies, particularly the ruler of Mdaburu, a fertile area astride the caravan road just before it passed to the inhospitable lands to the west. The sultan's agent was unable to gain victory until 1880, when he secured assistance from a passing group of Europeans[4] and then established himself as Barghash's regional representative, ruling over Mdaburu with the support of a subordinate African set in the defeated ruler's place.[5]

In succeeding years the Arab—pictured by Wissmann as "old, lean, one eyed"—consolidated authority over neighboring Africans. Although never defeating permanently all enemies, Mtwana, by the mid-1880s possessed a force with 500 guns, plus local allies, and was held by some observers to be the most powerful individual leader in Ugogo. Unfortunately for Barghash and passing Arabs, the sultan's delegate, once secure in his base, began imposing high charges on passing caravans. Since the complaints surfaced when Barghash struggled to preserve Zanzibar from the Germans, Mtwana and his family retained control until Germans stormed Mdaburu in 1893. The European victors executed Mtwana and his son after the battle.[6] Even if stationing Mtwana at Mdaburu hardly turned out to be a triumph for Barghash's administration, it must be regarded as an important step for the Arab state. If Barghash had been free to control the unruly agent, Mtwana, cognizant of the advantages coming from obeying the sultan, in time surely would have accepted terms. The fate of the Nasibu brothers served as a constant reminder to all Arabs of the dangers consequent to becoming an uncompromising foe of the unforgiving Barghash.

A very different type of interior extension of the sultan's authority occurred in 1880 with the founding near Mamboya by General Mathews of a fortified station occupied by men of Zanzibar's army. The reasons for the step are unclear, possibly coming from one of Mirambo's campaigns which caused the deaths of two Europeans; that event, according to Kirk, motivated Barghash to undertake construction of a line of posts into Unyanyembe to safeguard passage along the central route. The sultan stood prepared, claimed Kirk, "for the first time [to] assert a distinct claim . . . to the sovereignty over Central Africa." But French consul Ledoulx charged the 1880 venture was entirely Kirk's idea, Barghash unhappily complaining about the expedition's high cost. Whatever its origins, the progress of Mathews' command amply proved such distant station building barely within the capabilities of Barghash's Western-trained army. Mathews had prepared around two hundred soldiers, but the men, learning of the distant destination, refused to leave the coast, and over sixty deserted at Sadani. Placing some offenders in chains, Mathews finally moved inland, reached Mamboya, and built the post, leaving in occupation a garrison of about sixty. The sultan's soldiers then, however, acted without discipline, occupying a post—later depicted as "simply an inclosure with a few huts inside"—in a region generally free of trade route problems. In 1882 a passing missionary found only a few soldiers remaining on duty.[7] No other stations were built. The Mamboya post, even with its obvious weaknesses, stood as a mark of Zanzibar's influence. Later European arrivals often based claims on the presence of far less important holdings.

Most commentators on the Arab presence, from the nineteenth century to the present, have limited conclusions regarding the nature of the Zanzibar system in East Central Africa to strictures regarding its lack of political control over the peoples of the coast and interior. The capable G. K. Akinola stresses the inability of the sultans to create a functioning political unit joining Zanzibar, Pemba, and the coastal territories, thus creating by the mid-1880s only "an amorphous political unit without specific or clearly defined boundaries." Additionally, he blames the BuSaidi rulers for not following the examples of other nineteenth-century Muslim sovereigns by providing political and religious ideologies to win subjects' loyalties. Other scholars commonly assert that East Central Africa's Arabs, supposedly interested primarily in commercial matters, had no inclination before the mid-1880s to achieve outright political domination. Pioneer researcher Coupland decided: "As on the coast, so in the interior, their relations with the Africans were primarily commercial." Roland Oliver later added: "There was never any attempt at imperialism, never any attempt to assume the reigns of government."[8] More perceptive recent students of the Zanzibar state, while greatly increasing our knowledge of its development, have continued the interpretation. Sheriff characterizes the Zanzibar system as "a commercial empire . . . not built on a stable administrative or political structure, but on a system of influence and common economic interests." In roughly similar terms Philip Curtin sees the Zanzibar state as a "trading-post empire" utilizing European firearms not for conquest but for commercial exploitation of East Central Africa.[9] The nineteenth-century observers, of course, were partisan commentators, often playing down, even if they understood, the role of Arabs, the opponents of their efforts to seize control of African lands and peoples. The later scholarly commentators, whatever their feelings toward Arabs, usually have not considered the complete extent of the Arab representation throughout East Central Africa; instead they have based generalizations on judgments stemming from events that occurred in individual regions.

In reality, however, the Arabs never made sharp distinctions between political and economic matters. As they moved into new areas, arriving Arabs usually were not powerful enough to challenge existing regimes; initially they almost always reached agreement with Africans allowing the opening of some form of commerce. But if the Arabs had the opportunity to assume authority, as at Nkhotakota or in the Congo, they did so; if not, as at Tabora or Ujiji, they grabbed as much control as circumstances allowed. If Africans were strong enough to keep Arabs confined to trade, they perforce accepted this reality. Some nineteenth-century observers, followed by later writers, introduced another factor supposedly marking the impermanent nature of Arab presence. Harry Johnston, for one, claimed the Arabs of East Central Africa fell into two groups, indigenous Arabs and Arabs from Arabia. The latter, he stated, "came . . . to trade in Africa, and return . . . [home] when they have amassed a modest competence."[10] The proposition does not match reality. The Congo community possessed many important Arabs never planning a return to Arabia, men like Said bib Habib. And, demonstrating the confusion in classifying Arabs of various origins, Muhammad bin Khalfan, often cited by Johnston and others as a true Arab, had been born in East Africa, spent his entire life there, and apparently never evinced the slightest interest in returning to the land of some of his ancestors.

The European observers of Arab penetration were watching an ongoing process. Arabs, when opportunity offered, were ready to exercise political control, to accomplish elsewhere what had been achieved in the Congo. But even though their interior movement was continuous, it was not directly organized from any one central authority. Initiative always remained in the hands of individual Arabs entering new regions searching for profit and adventure. Kirk, recognizing that extending Zanzibar's authority meant an accompanying extension of British influence, often endeavored to make Barghash more involved in managing the details of Arab penetration. Yet whenever the sultan's British advisor became very active in supporting such policies he received admonitions from a Foreign Office reluctant to involve itself in the politics of the African interior. In 1881, for example, Kirk was firmly instructed to desist from committing Britain to any policy defining the inland extent of the sultan's dominions.[11]

Nevertheless Kirk persisted in efforts to make Barghash more interested in what he perceived as advancing Zanzibar's authority. When the sultan did not cooperate, the consul had harsh words for the Arab, in September 1884 castigating Barghash for "utter apathy to what takes place away from Zanzibar so long as he receives his revenue."[12] Kirk was mistaken. The sultan understood the realities of East Central Africa's Arab system. If he had to depend only upon the support of the Arabs of his realm to control interior events Barghash understood that undue interference in local Arab or African affairs was unfeasible. The abortive expedition sent against Mirambo had proved his lack of administrative apparatus for effective action away from the coast. And any unsuccessful intervention might lead aggrieved Arabs to seek arrangements with competing groups for the disposal of ivory and other products; the growing European presence made this alternative all too possible. Kemal Atatürk once aptly said: "Sovereignty is acquired by force and power and by violence."[13] Unable to remain sovereign over his Arabs through any of these tactics, Barghash remained committed to what F. J. Berg, when speaking of the coast, called the "Zanzibari preference for indirect rule,"[14] an indirect rule not in the European style of changing African institutions under the guise of preserving them, but a meaningful effort to incorporate local governing systems into a greater political entity. It was not an unusual stance; the much earlier African state of Carthage demonstrated also "that territorial sovereignty was not a precondition of port operations" for a flourishing empire benefiting, through commerce, most of its adherents.[15]

Zanzibar's sultans worked through traditions common for many centuries throughout the Muslim world. Claude Cahen's description of the millennium-earlier government of the Umayyads easily could stand for Zanzibar: "Very broadly speaking . . . [it] consisted of an organization of subjects, for the most part governed according to their own traditions and led by agents who came from among themselves . . . ," all under a ruler who was "no more than *primus inter pares*."[16]

We must equally stay free of European ideas of imperialism or colonialism. Arabs proceeded along a path where, even if becoming rulers of Africans, they operated in a pattern of cultural assimilation through the appeal of Islam. Whatever the exact degree of loyalty to the Arab state in Zanzibar, all Arabs and most Africans accorded its sultan a special position. Arab regional rulers, men such as Tippu Tip and Mwinyi Kisutu, gave adherence to the distant ruler who left them free to manage peoples under their control. African rulers, such as Semboja of the Shambaa, affirmed the sultan's overlordship without enduring Arab interference in state affairs. Others, such as Mutesa, treated the sultan as an equal whose friendship was of value to their polities. The ties in many instances may have been tenuous; nonetheless, they were real. If the beginning tide of Arab expansion, still a very recent phenomenon, had not been interrupted during the 1880s, the end result for much of East Central Africa probably would have been similar to the outcome of Islam's introduction in other world regions. Increasing numbers of Africans would have accepted the new religion, incorporating into their faith many local customs, finishing as an integral component of the Muslim community, its affairs directed by believers drawn from the ranks of the indigenous population.

Barghash, despite Kirk's opinions, was prepared to support a continuing inland extension of his state's authority. But he did so in a manner based upon his conception of the Zanzibar state, demonstrating his intentions during the unsuccessful negotiations concerning the award of a concession on the African mainland to a group of Britons.[17] What is important was Barghash's willingness to conclude an agreement. The Arab sultan, accustomed to conducting state business through intermediaries such as the Indians who staffed the customs service, apparently looked to the interested Britons to undertake a fundamental expansion of his administration, under their management, into the interior. Perhaps he saw that in the end the Europeans might usurp much authority. If so, Barghash was willing to accept the loss of freedom for some of his subjects, especially when the move was certain to increase his personal profits.[18] Barghash persisted in the search for a European-directed presence on the mainland, and in the early 1880s he concluded a concession with French merchant Rabaud. Kirk, claiming its terms were too loose for Zanzibar's interests, but really desiring to prevent non-British competitors from gaining influence, succeeded in making the sultan withdraw the concession.[19]

Thus, at the dangerous midpoint of the 1880s, apart from the limited mutuality of interests between British and BuSaidi, Zanzibar stood unsupported by powerful allies. Quarrels over minor matters often had occurred between Britons and Arabs, but there appeared little reason for suspecting any weakening of the long-standing arrangement. In mid-1884, for instance, a typical example of the usual frictions happened at Pangani. When a group of African Christians in the service of the Universities' Mission entered the town during the liwali's absence, they were seized and imprisoned by local Arabs. One African died while confined. Kirk pushed the reluctant Barghash to punish the perpetrators of this violation of Zanzibar's agreements with Britain; a British vessel accompanied the sultan's agent to Pangani to free the incarcerated Africans. In the end Barghash paid a $200 indemnity for the death and imprisoned the hapless liwali. Kirk blamed the affair on "an aggressive spirit" existing along the coast because of antislave trade measures, without being unduly troubled about the affair.[20] There had been many similar episodes in the past, and he doubtless foresaw more in the future.

The military weakness of the Arab system was not readily apparent so long as there were no determined enemies striking at the overall position of the Arabs of East Central Africa. Arab influence, even though recently characterized by the perceptive Frederick Cooper as "more than nominal and less than effective" for the coastal regions, still overmatched African military abilities. Zaramo raiding of 1878 and 1879, for example, led to successful punitive expeditions, with a principal Zaramo leader ending up in a Zanzibar prison.[21] The European influence in inland regions had grown, but Europeans remained a thinly spread minority, most of them seemingly immersed in the daily tasks of their several callings.

THE DOWNFALL OF
THE ZANZIBAR EMPIRE

9 Barghash, the British, and the Germans

> No amount of tinkering will keep the Zanzibar state to-
> gether after all that has happened, it is simply a question
> now of who picks up the pieces . . .
>
> —*John Kirk*

THE FIRST SIGNIFICANT steps leading to the end of the Arab political and economic complex in East Central Africa came from an unexpected source. The Society for German Colonization, an unimportant, underfunded organization founded in 1884 by a restless and unstable adventurer, Carl Peters, carried the German flag to lands claimed by Zanzibar. Peters and his associates, following difficulties concerning the choice of a suitable location for an overseas venture, looked to East Central Africa. One of the group, Graf von Pfeil, brought to his companions' attention a passage from Stanley's *How I Found Livingstone* referring to the potential wealth of the area behind the coast opposite Zanzibar. The German government, informed of the society's aims, took no official notice of their planned expedition. More importantly, the government did not forbid the venture, thereby clearly signaling possible later approval if Peters's schemes succeeded.[1]

The twenty-seven-year-old Peters, with three colleagues, Pfeil, Karl Jül-khe, and August Otto, embarked for Zanzibar. Arriving in November 1884, the four quickly and efficiently organized a caravan and crossed over to the nearby mainland. Their presence obviously had been noted by all; Kirk reported "there are mysterious Germans travelling inland" when questioned from London about German activity. The British consul did not appear overly concerned, even though remarking Peters's party probably was seeking concessions.[2] Moving quickly from settlement to settlement in the region behind the coast, Peters supposedly concluded

129

agreements, awarding sovereign rights to the German society, with ten Arab and African leaders. The most important individual signing a document was the old and established Mwinyi Usagara, generally held to be Barghash's representative for Usagara. Other signers included Salim bin Hamid, described by Peters as "since four years first Plenipotentiary of . . . the Sultan of Zanzibar in Nguru." Kirk investigated the accords, later claiming "the bulk of the treaties seem not to have been even obtained by fraud but deliberately concocted." Salim bin Hamid, visiting Zanzibar, explained he had welcomed Peters as a visitor from Zanzibar, protesting he had been asked to sign a piece of paper; "this he says is all he knows."[3] Such treaty-making ventures justly have been ridiculed, but we should remember that even the actual concluders of the accords did not take them overly seriously.[4] The practice was universal: at the same time that Peters was acting, Zanzibari agents, following similar procedures, were hoisting their flag in Ugogo.[5] The treaties were arranged, by whatever means, because in that era they were necessary as initial bargaining counters among European powers. With them the Society for German Colonization claimed possession of an estimated 140,000 square kilometers of East Central African territory.[6]

After securing enough treaties, Peters hurried to Berlin to win government approval, the German activity passing without notice in Zanzibar. The agents of the society, consequently, at an important moment had stolen a march on the hitherto dominant European arbiter of events in the Zanzibar sultanate, Kirk seemingly becoming too sure of, and satisfied with, his role as the sultan's most important advisor. His attitude was understandable; in the closing months of 1884, neither Kirk nor the Arabs expected an incursion from Germans whose activities heretofore had been limited almost entirely to transactions by the long-established Hamburg merchants. Nonetheless, the final scramble for territory was under way in East Central Africa, finding the British agent unprepared to provide either Barghash or the Foreign Office the advice necessary to safeguard their interests.[7]

One reason for the British government's several queries to Kirk concerning new European intrusions was the appointment of Gerhard Rholfs, a well-known explorer, as German representative to the sultan. Arriving in January 1885 the new consul impressed the local community, not for diplomatic skills, which apart from some knowledge of Arabic were little apparent, but by an immediately aggressive conduct toward Barghash.[8] In February, for example, Rholfs during a conversation with Barghash abruptly recalled the sultan's long-forgotten 1870 request for German protection, the result of a search for support in the looming succession to the declining Majid. When Barghash demurred, Rholfs produced a copy of the request; the disturbed Arab closed the interview by announcing he no longer was interested in this relic of the distant past. Nevertheless, the apparently tactless discussion obviously put the sultan on guard for any additional steps directed against his state. The conversation certainly worried Kirk. Additional uncertainty came also from the needlessly arrogant behavior of the German cruiser *Gneisenau*.[9]

Meantime, Barghash had been keeping an attentive eye upon the ongoing deliberations of the Berlin Conference (November 1884 to February 1885). When discussions concerning Zanzibar were held, the sultan was all too aware he was, as one Briton later said, only "an Oriental prince to whom are not accorded the usual rights prescribed by international law."[10] At that moment the British had decided upon a limited policy to protect their Zanzibar interests, inducing Barghash to make a "spontaneous" declaration against accepting any form of protectorate without first seeking British advice. Barghash, endeavoring to safeguard his conception of the extent of the Zanzibar dominions, altered the prepared document to read that he was ruler of both the coast and interior of East Central Africa. Both Britain and France assured Barghash of support against any conference measures, especially from Leopold's extensive Congo claims, threatening his dominions.[11]

Any statements concerning the eastern section of the Zanzibar dominions quickly became meaningless when the German government accepted Peters's treaties, in late February 1885, awarding an imperial charter to a new organization directed by Peters. The uncomplicated document allowed the German East African Company virtual unrestricted control of its yet vaguely defined territories. The arrival of the news in Zanzibar dumfounded Barghash and his advisors; the ignorance of the precise borders of the announced German protectorate—the charter merely stated it lay "west of the empire of the sultan of Zanzibar, and outside the suzerainty of other powers"[12]—immediately inaugurated a period of unsettling uncertainty. Barghash, aware of the power realities of East Central Africa, quickly sought support from Britain and France, the signatories of the 1862 declaration guaranteeing the integrity of his dominions.[13]

During April the protectorate's general location became public knowledge, the news causing great consternation among Zanzibar's Arabs since the claimed regions encompassed segments of the most important caravan routes to the African interior. Kirk hurried to Barghash's defense, stressing that Usagara was one of the few regions away from the coast where the sultan, with his Mamboya garrison, had an obvious right to recognized jurisdiction. Moreover, warned Kirk, the Germans assuredly appreciated the necessity for a coastal outlet for the inland protectorate, the company inevitably later seeking free transit rights and other concessions from the sultan, measures possibly leading to a total collapse of the Arab state.[14] Barghash, while awaiting hoped-for backing from Britain and France, speedily pushed to the offensive, formally protesting to the Germans, even before exact details about the protectorate were public, that the Arab and African signatories of agreements with Peters lacked rights to cede sovereignty over "places . . . under our authority from the time of our fathers." A little later Barghash informed Bismarck that the Zanzibar dominions stretched deeply into the interior "following the line of trade that has been in the hands of our subjects for many years," and providing a list of territories including Unyanyembe, Buganda, Ujiji, and the lands of the Chagga and Maasai.[15] The Germans summarily rejected Barghash's interpretations, maintaining that only Zanzibar, Pemba, and Mafia islands were under the sultan's "immediate control." On the coast, they alleged, the Arab held, in about thirty settlements, only customs houses, the lands between them remaining independent. As for the interior, the Germans ended, Barghash merely possessed commercial stations, private establishments stemming from his role as first merchant of Zanzibar.[16] Apart from a few minor elaborations of detail, this argument remained the basic German position throughout the succeeding stages of the quarrel resolving the fate of the Zanzibar sultanate.

While arguments raged over the Peters concession, another German threat emerged in the sultan's northern coastal territories. The restless Simba of Witu seized an opportunity to utilize German might against Barghash. Two adventurers, Clemens and Gustav Denhardt, already experienced in Witu affairs, concluded a treaty with Simba in April 1885. The Zanzibar reaction came too late to hinder the arrangement, the Witu treaty providing the German government with another welcome opportunity to intervene in Zanzibar's affairs.[17]

Barghash conducted the exchange of verbal thrusts with the Germans while anxiously awaiting the decision of the long-standing British allies of the BuSaidi dynasty, the only nation represented in Zanzibar possibly able to counter the proposed major diminution of his dominions. Kirk early in May succinctly spelled out the situation: "Sultan if left alone must yield or else seek other protection."[18] But, as leaders of secondary powers generally learn to their cost, great powers are not necessarily dependable allies. The British directors of foreign policy weighed the decision concerning Zanzibar's future against other significant considerations of general policy making German friendship appear more important at a time of potentially dangerous crises in Central Asia and elsewhere. But even if the British decided not to support Barghash against the Germans, important details of the exact extent of the seemingly inevitable loss of Zanzibar territory, perhaps even the loss of independence of the Arab state, remained for resolution. As early as the beginning of March 1885 Foreign Secretary Granville had dropped the possibility of opposing Germany's bid for a section of the sultan's dominions, although he stipulated that Zanzibar itself should be left alone. The Germans readily gave that promise. By the latter part of May a definite policy emerged: "Provided that British interests are not injured or the Sultan's established rights injured," the Foreign Office instructed Kirk, "H. M. G. are favourable to German entreprise in districts not occupied by any civilised powers." The sultan was denied the support of his traditional allies.[19]

In Germany, meantime, Peters, with his usual energy, was building an organization capable of meeting the new responsibilities in Africa.[20] The German East African Company's principal immediate problem was a serious lack of capital, the charter's announcement producing little impact on German public opinion. Peters perforce remained in Europe, conducting a spirited propaganda campaign extolling the supposed potentialities of the new "German East Indies."[21] One obvious source of possible assistance for the company was the German trading community in Zanzibar, the German government suggesting that the firms and company merge into one organization. But the Hamburg merchants, understandably wary of damaging established positions in the competitive Zanzibar marketplace through alliance with Peters's not very promising company, mostly expressed little interest. Only H. A. Meyer and Company, specialists in the ivory trade, demonstrated an active concern to bypass Arab and African dominance of the ivory-carrying trade by sending expeditions inland. The Meyer firm, despite the sultan's opposition, by 1885 already had breached the monopoly by sending agents to Tabora. One employee, Kurt Toeppen, combined firm business with a relief caravan to Pfeil, still holding on in Usagara.[22] Government pressure in the end partly overcame mercantile disinterest, with Bismarck personally playing an influential role. A compromise left business affairs on Zanzibar in the hands of the Hamburg merchants while the company concentrated upon its interior establishments.[23] The arrangement, possibly quieting the Hamburg firms' fears, did little to strengthen the finances of Peters's company.

While in Europe diplomats and businessmen engaged in their important activities, in Africa Arabs and their allies were in full competition with the Germany company, both groups attempting to secure as much territory as possible. Barghash dispatched Mathews in April on a secret mission to establish or reinvigorate garrisons at important locations along the coast between Pangani and Lindi. On April 9 in Bagamoyo the sultan's general called the citizens together, reading communications from Barghash and Kirk forbidding the sale of land to Germans and participation in the slave trade. A messenger sped inland from the town with the same message for the Arabs of Unyanyembe, Ujiji, and Buganda. Simultaneously, Zanzibari official Sayf bin Suliman was designated governor for Usagara, while letters and flags from Barghash went to indigenous local rulers. Mwinyi Usagara received one of the communications, showing it to Pfeil.[24] The sultan's determination, as small groups of Germans arrived to solidify and extend company claims, ensured a period of intense, dangerous rivalry. The Kilimanjaro region, well beyond the treaty-making of Peters, offers an example of the Arab-German competition. Barghash sent one of the most important coastal Arabs, Jumbe Kimameta, through the Pangani Valley to the Chagga of Kilimanjaro carrying flags for significant Arab and African leaders.[25] In early May, Mathews, commanding a large party of soldiers and porters, negotiated agreements with men previously in touch with Kimameta, including Shambaa chieftain Semboja and Rindi, Chagga ruler of Moshi. But the Zanzibari forces were followed closely by German rivals Jülkhe and Kurt Weiss, the two returning with ten accords duplicating much of Mathews' work. Semboja, however, refused an agreement with the Germans.[26]

Other Germans and Zanzibaris were active elsewhere in East Central Africa, especially in the disputed Usagara region. Missionary R. Price, for example, returning to Zanzibar from his Mpwapwa post, met followers of Bwana Heri, the coastmen reporting that their master planned to visit Mwinyi Usagara to determine what really had happened during Peters's stay. Later some Arabs did come to his settlement, protested the German flag, called a meeting to fine the old chief, and hoisted Zanzibar's flag. Pfeil, living nearby, was left undisturbed and asserted that the company flag was rehoisted without opposition after the Arab party's departure. A French visitor of January 1886, however, noted the presence of a thirty-man Zanzibari garrison, with the local population hindering the German gathering of provisions.[27]

Kirk persisted, meanwhile, in lecturing the Foreign Office that Barghash's rights "could never be set aside if the ordinary rules of law were regarded," while Barghash, doubtless heartened by the British consul's attitude, remained adamant before German pressure. His spirited reactions worried the Foreign Office; the officials feared Kirk's loyalty to the Arab state might lead to unwanted arguments with the Germans, Anderson remarking that Kirk, once "practically Sultan . . . [now] feels the German movement intolerable."[28] There was cause to worry; Bismarck advanced the simmering quarrel a few paces by protesting the entry of Zanzibari troops into asserted German territory, charging that "Germany would declare war, and might bombard Zanzibar" unless Barghash withdrew the men, and at the same moment aptly modifying the message by a pointed affirmation of Kirk's ability to resolve the issue. Soon after, Kirk was instructed to utilize his influence to meet German desires.[29] The British consul became worried himself on learning that Mombasa's liwali, Salim bin Khalfan al BuSaidi, described by missionary W. Taylor as "a truly honest servant of the Sultan," had, following orders, threatened any individuals selling goods to Germans. Since the open action clearly violated existing treaties, the ban quickly was canceled.[30]

Harsh reality ended Barghash's posturing. On August 7 five German vessels steamed into Zanzibar harbor, Commodore Paschen delivering to Barghash a final message rejecting his claims and calling for acceptance of the protectorates awarded the German East African and Witu companies. The alternative was war. Salisbury left British policy unchanged, advising Barghash to accept German terms. Thus abandoned, the sultan bowed to Paschen's threatening fleet, agreeing to the ultimatum on 13 August. The first step in the downfall and dismemberment of the Arab system focused upon Zanzibar had been accomplished.[31]

The Germans regarded the forced settlement as merely the initial move in attaining desired goals. The issue of transit rights across Barghash's coastal dominions had not been resolved, nor had the increasing list of German claims been discussed. Their resolution lay through determining precisely what constituted the territorial dominions of the Sultan of Zanzibar, a task given a commission with representatives of Britain, Germany, and France. Barghash, protesting Zanzibar's exclusion from the deliberations, was ignored.

As European diplomats conversed over Zanzibar's fate, in East Africa Germans, Arabs, and Africans persisted in increasingly hostile encounters. Many of the incidents occurred between the continuously aggressive members of Peters's company and the progressively more reluctant Africans they attempted to press into service as caravan porters. One affair, taking place near Mamboya, is representative. Two German officers, Rochus Schmidt (later a prolific writer on colonial matters) and Dr. Hentschel, commanded a caravan, according to African information, using the threat of force to recruit men. The African leader of the impressed porters' village, in company with a small party, followed the caravan. Becoming apprehensive, the Germans attempted to coerce a passing African into their service, the event leading to a quarrel and the shooting of one of the porters. The following Africans immediately opened fire, wounding both Germans. Schmidt suffered a somewhat serious injury while Hentschel, Kirk uncharitably noted, received "a flesh wound in the leg which did not prevent him from making his escape as soon as the fight began." Schmidt managed to reach nearby British missionaries, who helped him return to Zanzibar.[32] Lacking any organized military component, the German company was powerless before African resistance; fortunately for Zanzibar the German government, more and more dissatisfied with the company's doings, was not interested during this period in upholding its doubtful acts.

The three-power commission meanwhile commenced work, opening investigations along the southern coastal segment of Barghash's claimed dominions. The sultan did all that his limited resources allowed to buttress outward signs of Zanzibar authority, sending agents to prepare resident representatives for questioning, while a Zanzibari vessel preceded the Europeans to ensure that each local garrison was prepared—and reinforced if necessary—for the visit. Barghash's actions were not long kept secret; some of the commissioners noticed the same faces in more than one garrison, each European stressing or disregarding the conduct according to preconceived notions of the sultan's influence. The general findings of the commissioners showed a reasonably structured and working system of Arab government, perhaps a little more formally organized than was usual because of Barghash's priming, but nonetheless an administration suited to the needs of Arabs and Africans residing along the coast. There were liwalis present at major centers from Tunghi Bay northward, while minor places had akidas in residence, the officials often appointed from a corps of administrators serving during their careers in different coastal towns. Representatives of indigenous local peoples remained important in the administrative structure, their vital compliance stimulated by the fact they were "bound to visit Zanzibar once a year to pay their homage to the Sultan who then gives them certain presents . . ." Also present in most towns were qadis appointed by the sultan to preside over judicial affairs— the more important cases were settled in Zanzibar—and garrisons of irregular soldiers.[33]

Even during this supposedly deliberative process, German company members proved unwilling to contain the campaign to secure more of Barghash's territory. The company's resident director, Lucas, chartered a Hamburg merchant vessel and began to visit the coast in January 1886, presenting the craft as a German man-of-war. At Gazi the Germans found a weak link in Barghash's pretensions, meeting with the ever dissident Mbarak bin Rashid, only recently at peace again with Zanzibar's ruler. Sometime in late 1883 Mbarak and the liwali of Mombasa had quarreled, the result of unwise conduct by the official when Mbarak, strengthened by the gradual return of his former followers, began asserting predominance over the Digo as his hereditary right. Mbarak also endeavored, perhaps in alliance with fellow Mazrui Salim bin Rashid of Takaungu, to secure some type of authority over the Fulladoyo Watoro settlement. The liwali led his troops against Gazi in February 1884; Mbarak fled to an inland post in Shambaa territory, holding it for several months during what Kirk called an "irregular and ill-judged war" against forces drawn from Mombasa, Tanga, and Pangani. The desertion of his men, caused by the serious famine of 1885, finally forced Mbarak, in August, to flee accompanied by only a few companions. In a move related to the hostilities, Barghash summoned Salim bin Rashid to Zanzibar, placing the Mazrui under arrest for supposedly aiding Mbarak.

Mbarak, meantime, continued to be active, harassing African settlements around Mombasa and suddenly seizing an unexpected opportunity to profit from the confusion following the German intrusion into Barghash's dominions. Church Missionary Society bishop James Hannington, desiring to visit Fulladoyo, was warned by its elders of fears that his presence, perhaps implying a mission claim on the town, might lead Mbarak to attack. To allay suspicion Hannington arranged a meeting with Mbarak, the two arriving in Fulladoyo in early May. Hannington found Mbarak "a fine, handsome man, but . . . [looking] careworn and poor." During the conversations the Arab, disheartened at this low point in his long career, admitted to the bishop that "he was tired of his present mode of life, how could he get away from it?" Hannington had the answer: "I advised him to write to Sir John [Kirk], offer himself to the crown, and seek the Queen's protection." Mbarak accepted with alacrity. Hannington realized he had overstepped the boundaries of proper missionary conduct but considered the risk worth taking, peaceful resolution of Mbarak's position opening Fulladoyo to mission influence.

There was no chance of the British then offering Mbarak protection, the ongoing negotiations between Britain and Germany over the fate of Zanzibar precluding such aggressive action. But Kirk was interested, recognizing that Mbarak, even without a firm territorial base, possessed much influence around Mombasa. Moreover, he had heard rumors, later confirmed by Hannington, that Mbarak was prepared to intrigue against Zanzibar with the Germans and Simba of Witu. Mbarak in his letter clearly indicated he had other friends to turn to if the offer was refused. Thus Kirk approached Barghash, utilizing the danger of defection to convince the sultan to release Salim of Takaungu and come to terms with Mbarak. Barghash's offer included a guarantee of safety by the British agent in Mombasa, a yearly pension of $400, and a residence in Mombasa. Mbarak quickly rejected the proposal, Kirk concluding he anticipated better opportunities elsewhere. Hannington, after an inland venture, returned to Zanzibar to find the negotiations stalled and endeavored to keep them moving. But by July the bishop accepted defeat, hoping his intervention at least had established a basis for peaceful relations between Mbarak and his mission. Mbarak did leave the missionaries alone, although he resumed raiding around Fulladoyo. When in subsequent negotiations Barghash offered a choice of residence in Gazi or several other localities, Mbarak in November 1885 returned to his former stronghold, confirming allegiance to the sultan by sending his son to render homage in Zanzibar.[34]

When Lucas then landed in Gazi, Mbarak swiftly accepted his proposals, both German and Mazrui seeking to profit from their mutual opposition to Barghash's claims for mainland sovereignty. Recognizing Mbarak as an independent ruler, the German company received full cession of his rights over Gazi; the Arab in return gained protection and immediately hoisted the company flag. Barghash, following Kirk's advice, at once dispatched troops to remove the flag and punish Mbarak: "He ought to kill him and all his lot and have done with them," stormed Kirk. Unsupported by his company allies, Mbarak fled Gazi before arrival of the sultan's men. The aroused British and French representatives on the three-power commission simultaneously complained that German support for Mbarak meant the end of their work. The German diplomatic staff, appearing "quite taken aback" by the company's action, accepted British and French complaints, disavowing the treaty and prohibiting additional flag-hoisting for the commission's duration.[35]

Traces of the affair, even though Bismarck denied knowledge of Mbarak, lingered on in the diplomatic background. In March in London the German representative presented a memorandum advancing his interpretation of Mbarak's position in East Africa, describing the Arab as a "prince" of a legitimate dynasty with claims for territory predating those of the BuSaidi, thus making the latter "intruders and conquerors" in the disputed regions. In August Mbarak once more appeared as a discussion subject, the Germans alleging that the Mazrui, even though fleeing from Gazi, nonetheless maintained independence in the interior. Mbarak's pretentions obviously were being kept alive for possible use in the continuing effort to dismember Barghash's dominions.[36] Meanwhile Mbarak held on beyond the reach of Zanzibar's administration, doubtless hoping, but in vain, for active German support.[37] When Kirk proposed forceful intervention to end Mbarak's career permanently, Barghash, although extremely worried over the ties between the Mazrui chieftan and the Germans, demurred, fearing the latter might react similarly to his earlier planned step against Simba. Kirk reluctantly concurred, the recent capture on the coast of a company agent carrying gold, perhaps for Mbarak, justifying apprehension. Mbarak continued raiding into mid-1887. By then obviously abandoned by the Germans, he apparently concluded a new arrangement with the sultan, a missionary reporting the return of the Arab, a "tall, erect, vigorous looking man," to Gazi.[38]

With the Gazi affair resolved, the commissioners continued to work, visiting along the coast as far north as Lamu, with brief stops at the more distant Banadir settlements. The British and French delegates found as far north as Mombasa a continuation of the well-established administrative presence noted in the south. Information on Lamu was scarcer, the liwali being absent, but they nonetheless found a firm administration, describing the position of its liwali as second only to the governor of Mombasa in the sultan's coastal service. Banadir officials and garrisons similarly received favorable notice. Yet because of Schmidt's dissenting opinions the commissioners were unable to present any agreed-upon report concerning the coast—they decided against visiting the interior—until their governments intervened. The instructions to report what all agreed upon, which meant the minimal German view, accompanied a decision to make the final resolution of the Zanzibar dominions' extent in Europe.[39]

The East African atmosphere by this time was suffused with hatred for Germans because of their unrelenting excesses: they were "adui Allah," the enemies of God.[40] On shore in Zanzibar German sailors acted without restraint. Only the controls imposed by Barghash through Mathews' soldiers kept the peace.[41] Company caravan leaders and African porters persisted in disagreement, Kirk in March noting that "the shooting of porters is a common thing in German caravans," while the sultan entered the quarrels to demand justice from the German consul for two Arabs killed in Usagara. The consul had to admit German powerlessness in the recently recognized German territory. When Lucas endeavored to recruit an expedition to meet Barghash's embarrassing request, the effort foundered upon Zanzibari refusal to enroll. Similar impasses resulted when Germans sought redress for their grievances. A German caravan, for example, recruited 250 men in Pangani for a Kilimanjaro venture; once out of the town 247 deserted. The liwali denied all knowledge of the happening, doing nothing to assist the abandoned Germans. In face of such German complaints Barghash refused to allow registration of porter contracts, thus allowing Africans so inclined to desert after accepting advances in salary without fear of German apprehension.[42]

These disputes, all incidents potentially requiring redress by the German government, were dangerous enough. An even more fertile ground for disagreement opened when company agents began building stations in regions beyond German powers of protection. One party, led by Dr. Karl Schmidt, set off in 1886 to establish a post in Semboja's territory. The Shambaa leader rebuffed them, informing the Germans that a written letter of permission from Barghash was needed. Schmidt instead continued to Korogwe, building despite the protests of resident Africans. The station was not a success, the African subordinates of the Germans deserting whenever possible. Poor health finally compelled total evacuation. To guard against their return, Jumbe Kimameta immediately went to Korogwe, burning the German houses, although carefully preserving any remaining property from theft or destruction.[43] Another German endeavor at Dunda, not far from Bagamoyo, aroused more concern. Claiming the sanction of treaties made with local Africans, the Germans in March 1886 built close to the Bagamoyo caravan road. They erected shops for selling merchandise, began planting crops, and engaged in the military drilling of

African followers. Africans of the vicinity denied the existence of treaties, sending a delegation to the sultan protesting the German presence. Even though the German consul, when answering a query from the British and French commissioners, denied official backing for company pretensions, the affair was unsettling, particularly since the Dunda Germans soon caused difficulties in Bagamoyo.[44]

Despite their frenzied activity, many Germans active in East Africa became exceedingly discouraged at the lack of company accomplishment, the frustration increased by the dearth of financial resources available for the many remaining necessary tasks. By July most agents working in the interior, many in poor health, had returned to the coast and Zanzibar, making little effort to conceal their sense of failure. The company had spent over 690,000 marks without apparent result. The men of the Germany navy, many suffering from illnesses caused by service ashore, shared the disenchantment.[45] Still, the company stubbornly maintained its East African efforts, in September claiming about a dozen stations: a headquarters at Zanzibar, a general entrepot at Bagamoyo, and sundry agricultural or commercial establishments. About thirty Germans staffed them. In November a new group founded by Peters arrived, the German Plantation Society. Headed by agricultural expert Friederich Schroeder, the newcomers began work at Lewa in Usambara, subsequently founding several other stations, endeavoring to cultivate tobacco and other potentially profitable crops. The company also purchased a small steamer, hoping to move merchandise directly inland without paying dues at Zanzibar, an experiment which failed. As 1886 concluded, the Germans remained facing a troubled future, in serious need of new direction and capital.[46]

While company agents struggled in East Africa, in Europe Germans and Britons resolved the conflicting opinions concerning Zanzibar's future. By an 1886 agreement, the sultan's authority was restricted to Zanzibar, Pemba, and Mafia islands, a ten-mile coastal strip stretching from the Minigani River to Kipini, and limited enclaves around the Banadir ports. The mainland was divided into spheres of interest, the Germans receiving the territories as far north as the Umba River, with a dividing line extending inland to Lake Jipe and then westward to where the first parallel of south latitude touched Lake Victoria. To the north of the British sphere, the Germans gained recognition for a Witu protectorate located between Kipini and the northern extent of Manda Bay. The isolated Barghash could only accept the dismantling of his sultanate.[47]

The international pourparlers were matched by designs for strengthening the German East African Company, vital emphasis being given to measures for attracting still reluctant investors into company ranks. Peters, without success, even attempted to win support from British capitalists. In March 1886 a first significant reorganization occurred, Peters remaining president, but with several new members admitted into organization leadership. Yet, even with all the energetic striving of colonial enthusiasts, the company failed to secure sufficient capital until the German emperor, on behalf of the Prussian government, with an investment of 500,000 marks ensured its future. Considerable reorganization ensued: a new constitution adopted in 1887 left Peters, although still important, no longer enjoying an unfettered leadership role.[48]

Barghash realized he could not resist the German and British decision without losing even more of his dominions. But as he slowly moved to accept the 1886 treaty the Arab ruler encountered unrelenting German pressure. After the 1887 company reorganization, Peters left the fatherland with the mission of establishing a presence in Dar es Salaam and Pangani and, finally, launching the organization into profitable operations. The latter objective entailed reducing company holdings to four stations, the two planned for the coast, plus interior locations at Arusha and Mpwapwa. All others, excluding German Plantation Society posts, were scheduled for abandonment or sale. The arrival in Zanzibar of Peters and about thirty followers was not a welcome event for Barghash, but he was astute enough to accept Holmwood's advice not to dwell upon the German adventurer's past, instead offering full cooperation, including letters of introduction to Arab officials and use of a Zanzibari vessel. Holmwood in addition secured from Barghash a promise to transfer land and buildings at Dar es Salaam and Pangani to the Germans when needed, plus the major concession of leasing to the company, if asked by Peters, the entire coastal territory in the German sphere on terms similar to those recently granted the British for their section of the littoral.[49]

After unsuccessfully attempting the outright purchase of Dar es Salaam, Peters left Zanzibar in late May for that nearby port while Gustav Hörnecke led another company group to Pangani. At the northern town Hörnecke generally mistreated the residents, seizing and threatening individuals while trying to gain land and other property. At Dar es Salaam Peters behaved similarly, capping his misdoings by reportedly surrounding the liwali's residence with armed men and endeavoring to bribe a local leader to declare independence of the sultan and acceptance of German rule. When the coastman refused, a pistol held to his head by Peters led to the signed document wanted. Barghash at once protested the outrageous conduct, with the German vice-consul summoning all to Zanzibar for investigations. Even Peters recognized he had acted foolishly, endangering both the company future and his own position, apologizing to Barghash for the conduct of his men, insisting the charges were exaggerated, and promising to avoid future difficulties. Hörnecke was compelled to pay a fine for his misdeeds. Peters then drew closer to Holmwood, attempting to utilize the Briton's influence for German aims.[50] Nonetheless, even with the change in tactics, Peters had seriously damaged his colonial career. It was not to the interest of either the German company or the government to have affairs in East Africa continually in crisis. In Europe one German diplomat admitted that Peters had "seriously embarrassed" his country-men, reporting Peters had been reprimanded and instructed to concen-trate on developing what the company already possessed. Rumors of Peters's recall at government request were denied, but clearly the founder of the German presence in East Africa was under notice that his continued misdoings would not much longer be tolerated.[51]

Peters, working, said Piat, "with extraordinary activity," nevertheless did attempt to instill new vigor into the operations of the German East African Company and German Plantation Society. But Peters disregarded his instructions for reducing the numbers of stations: by September there were about thirteen in operation. The posts received varying evaluations, from the self-interested exaggerations of Peters to that of the generally disinterested explorer and scholar Hans Meyer, who in 1888 found several "in anything but a flourishing condition." Lewa appears to have prospered as much as its short existence permitted, while the others were subject to the usual fluctuations common to European pioneering stations in Af-rica.[52] Additional German reinforcements came during 1887, the Evangel-ical Missionary Society for German East Africa sending its first agent, J. J. Greiner, a capable man with experience in Ethiopia, to Dar es Salaam. By a December agreement with Barghash, Greiner secured for his mission a 100-year lease on land for an annual $50 payment. German Roman Catholic missionaries and a few private colonists arrived to settle inland from Dar es Salaam at Pugu later in 1887.[53]

Although frictions continued around stations, firm orders from Ger-many probably helped moderate excesses. In the interval of relative quiet Peters, after finally obtaining leases for Dar es Salaam and Pangani, began pressing Barghash for cession of the entire coastal administration. When Holmwood appeared hesitant, Peters reverted to his normal approach, darkly affirming that "means would be found to insist upon . . . com-pliance." There was no need for threats, since Barghash had promised Holmwood to award the Germans the same rights gained by the British East African Company. Peters had to draw back, explaining it was "no way my intention to press . . . the Sultan to cede anything to our company which he is not inclined to cede voluntarily." The whole matter, stressed Peters, was "a simple business affair." Barghash, hampered by increasing ill health, with little hope of saving much of his sultanate from the rapacious Europeans, grudgingly gave initial assent to German leasing of the coast. Negotiations regulating actual transfer followed during succeeding months, although Barghash died before signing a formal accord.[54] Peters, accompanied by several company members and a few important Arab officials, signaled his triumph by a ceremonial trip along the southern littoral in the sultan's vessel *Barawa,* explaining the proposed transfer to suspicious but outwardly polite Arab and African leaders. His associates studied development possibilities, while an accompanying physician treated the sick. Later a similar voyage along the coast north of Bagamoyo was made in the German vessel *Nautilus.*[55]

Many problems remained for the Germans, disease seriously hindering all work, with several mainland company agents dying.[56] Costs remained high, with inadequate revenues coming in to offset ongoing drainage of company resources. In commercial operations, the only feasible method of gaining revenues, the company failed in competition against Zanzibar's established merchants. The natural dissatisfaction in company headquarters in Berlin was increased by Peters's flagrantly aggressive and unbusinesslike conduct. At Mtanganyko, for example, an unlikely station on the British-protected coast, company agents, reinforced earlier in the year, during October were signing with Mbarak and other local notables agreements for gaining additional land.[57] Relations between Peters and the Arabs also had soured once more. The sudden death of the young Muhammad bin Salim, an influential advisor of the sultan often upholding German interests, commonly attributed to poison administered at Barghash's order, marked the ill feeling. In early November Peters, reacting to orders from Germany to abandon the negotiations concerning the coast concession if undue difficulties arose, formally reminded Barghash of existing bad relations, emphasizing the ability of a then present naval squadron to punish the Arabs for opposing German interests. The conversation, added to the general unease over the company's course, led in late November to Peters's recall. Returning to the fatherland and failing to satisfy critics, Peters, after a suitable delay to avoid harmful publicity, left the company's board.[58]

10 The Fall of the Arab State of Zanzibar

> But is it not contrary to all common sense and experience to suppose that a mere handful of foreigners can enter a vast territory, and treat the natives as a conquered people, without an army, without even a police to support them?
>
> —*Charles Smythies*

WHEN 1888 BEGAN, the German East African Company thought all obstacles blocking successful development finally had been overcome. But a turn-of-the-year incident at Mpwapwa better indicated the future. At the inland center a troubled sequence commenced when a few unruly Swahili soldiers of the Germans shot an ox. The soldiers, instructed to find the owner and pay compensation, during the search apparently insulted local African leader Kipangilo; an ensuing ruckus caused the death of a soldier. A few hundred Africans, prepared for fighting, quickly gathered; the Germans triumphed in a brief skirmish. The Church Missionary Society agents resident in Mpwapwa then helped mediate the two groups' differences. This petty quarrel, which could have had much more serious consequences, stands as a prime example of the misunderstandings between Germans and East Africa's inhabitants. Company men had arrived in Mpwapwa in August 1887, building a station without consulting the indigenous leadership. When Kipangilo sent the customary welcoming presents, the Germans repulsed the gesture, additionally refusing to visit the African until he personally came to salute them. Even though Kipangilo, reluctantly persuaded by the missionaries, complied, relations did not improve, and the Germans remained generally unsuccessful in gaining ivory. An underlying hostility thus was present for combustion whenever incidents occurred.[1] The same conditions existed in most coastal towns before the close of 1888.

In Zanzibar, Barghash died on 27 March 1888, his younger brother
Khalifa becoming sultan without incident. The new ruler, last of the independent BuSaidi sovereigns, described as "a tall, broad, well-built man
with a pleasant expression of countenance,"[2] had, because of stubborn and
futile opposition to Barghash, spent much of his life either in confinement
or in isolated locations, thus arriving on the throne with little knowledge
of the intricate matters, all calling for diminishing the powers of the sultan,
awaiting immediate decision. The prime issue was the signing of the concession for the administration by the Germans of the coast opposite Zanzibar.

Khalifa proved as determined in upholding the rights of his office as he
had been in resisting Barghash, demurring when German and British
agents endeavored to hurry him into signing a document fully composed
before his accession. British representative Charles Euan Smith, like most
Europeans contemptuous of Khalifa, probably because of the sultan's un-
familiarity, even disdain, for European ways, made it clear to the Arab that
he lacked strength to resist, confiding to the Foreign Office his opinion
that Khalifa had been "in a fog as to what he really did and did not want"
before finally recognizing obstinance endangered his position as sultan.
Khalifa did not forget Euan Smith's attitude, growing progressively more
hostile to the Briton during succeeding months. Still, the sultan realistically concluded the impossibility of checking the Europeans, instead
merely awarding a surface consent binding his future actions only when
sufficient pressure was imposed against noncompliance. By terms of the
arrangement, signed on 28 April 1888, the Germans received direction of
the coast administration from the middle of August, the beginning of the
Zanzibar fiscal year.[3]

Khalifa, however, let his Arab and African subjects know he had been
forced into signing, informing coastal visitors who came to Zanzibar to
greet their new sultan that "if they could in any way thwart German
enterprize on the mainland, such action on their part would afford him
satisfaction." Euan Smith, victim of his own mistaken certainty regarding
the sultan's character, denied this allegation, rather portraying Khalifa as
too timid for forceful action. But after signing the concession, reported the
French consul, Khalifa sent messages to coastal leaders informing them of
his mistreatment and the continuing threats to Zanzibar's remaining independence. The sultan did not need to add that a threat to the existing
system of administration in East Africa, with its focus on the Arab ruler of
Zanzibar, was equally a threat to their own jealously guarded local independence.[4]

During the first part of 1888 the Germans continued to hold operations
in existing stations. The earlier sense of failure persisted, but the April
concession brought new vigor. In mid-May a new director, accompanied

by a large staff, arrived to prepare to assume coastal authority. Ernst Vohsen, with previous commercial experience in West Africa, made a favorable initial impression on most Europeans, striving to remove the bitterness lingering from Peters's aggressive policies.[5] Vohsen's caution was well advised. According to a British missionary reporting in May, there were "talks all over the coast of making a clean sweep of all Europeans," while "Arabs are suggesting that all the native tribes should join and make a grand smash of all Europeans in East Africa."[6]

Vohsen arranged preliminary trips along the coast in June, traveling on a Zanzibari vessel accompanied by leading Arab officials representing the sultan. The visitors discussed with local authorities and prominent inhabitants the necessary details for beginning the new arrangement. Reportedly only minor differences of opinion occurred: Abd al Gawi bin Abdullah, liwali of Pangani, was the single Arab official grumbling openly about the future. The discussions were vital because Vohsen, despite the stated aim of winning local understanding, proceeded to issue a series of regulations presaging major modifications in the existing relationship between Zanzibar and the coast. A first proclamation dealt with commercial and administrative matters: most trade had to flow through seven designated ports—Tanga, Pangani, Bagamoyo, Dar es Salaam, Kilwa, Lindi, and Mkindani. Each henceforth became administrative center of a district where Arab and indigenous officials supervised local affairs under the surveillance of a resident German agent. A second proclamation concerned the fundamental issue of land ownership: all land had to be registered, with owners required to prove their rights within six months. A third proclamation announced a new judicial system: courts under the authority of the company agent were to be created in the seven designated major ports.[7] Clearly the German East African Company was inaugurating fundamental changes in East African life. And, just as clearly, the company, possessing limited military strength, had to proceed cautiously to achieve a peaceful transition from the Arab and African to the German style of administration.

As the critical transfer day approached, the Germans foolishly added unnecessary complications to the already tense atmosphere. Company officials wished their flag—the Southern Cross superimposed over German national colors—to fly alongside Zanzibar's standard before each town's company headquarters. Since the original agreement had not mentioned flag arrangements, the coastal peoples had time neither to discuss nor to understand the alteration. There were difficulties at Bagamoyo, the heart of the German concession. On 15 August a proclamation was read while Zanzibar and company flags were hoisted side by side before the company building. Liwali Amir Suliman al Lemki, without instructions from Zanzibar, at first refused to move the Zanzibar flag from its usual place before his residence. The armed German presence, however, allowed the exercises to pass without open friction. Vohsen then returned to Zanzibar, the formal takeover of administration, as elsewhere, scheduled for August 18th. But flag arguments continued, the resident company officials, assisted by a landing party from the *Möwe*, cutting down the liwali's flagstaff and transferring his flag to company quarters. Amir bin Suliman fled the town. With this foolish action, resentment at the unwanted company presence exploded: the jumbes, their followers, and the Arabs gathered in an unruly crowd. Even then the Germans evaded recognizing the seriousness of their acts; consul Gustav Michahelles, when Bagamoyo's Indian community protested about potential dangers, responded that the crowds were celebrating the Muslim New Year.[8]

The atmosphere was even more strained at other ports. At Pangani liwali Abd al Gawi, recipient of a humiliating order to report four times daily to receive instructions, joined other residents in protesting interference with the sultan's flag, setting off a series of events ending in warfare. The *Möwe* arrived on August 17, its threat outwardly resolving the flag argument, but when the vessel left Abd al Gawi once more refused cooperation with the company agents. During the recriminations between the aggressive, intolerant Germans and the suspicious, uncooperative Arabs and Africans, the former had been guilty of an incredible sequence of misdeeds. According to British missionary Farler, one very influential Arab, Said bin Hamadi, had been "knocked down and kicked because he refused to let his house" to the newcomers. The Germans also outrageously abused their Arab host's hospitality, "during his absence forcing his wives." When the friction continued, another German vessel, the *Carola*, anchored, sending ashore on the nineteenth a contingent which, while searching for the liwali, further added to the unrest by violating the sanctity of the local mosque. "With dogs at their heels," said one Pangani citizen, "the Germans strode into the sacred edifice, and . . . loudly demanded the whereabouts of the Wali." The landing party remained until the twenty-eighth; after its departure, German company resident Emil Zelewski immediately proved he had learned nothing during the previous fortnight. Ignoring the populace's excitable mood, he forbade landing of gunpowder from an Arab dhow; the order led to formation of an infuriated crowd which, without violence, confined the Germans to their headquarters.[9] There were similar stirrings at every company station.[10] By the end of August the entire coast was very tense, rumors indicating a general rising was likely.

The Germans in Berlin reacted with surprised concern to the actions of the company, one official describing company policy at Bagamoyo as "unjustifiable and reprehensible," withal maintaining that subsequent actions, including government expressions of regret to Khalifa made because

Germany did not want to "alienate [the] Sultan's confidence, nor weaken his authority," had alleviated the problem.[11] It was immediately apparent, however, that the Berlin functionaries had minimal influence over the fast-developing East African happenings.

The German company first turned to Khalifa for assistance in averting major hostilities; the sultan provided a few hundred irregular soldiers for distribution amongst the seven coastal stations. Vohsen left Zanzibar on August 29 for Tanga and Pangani, to his dismay discovering that all company authority had disappeared. On September 5 gunfire prevented his landing at Pangani, a boat from the *Möwe* receiving the same welcome at Tanga. The sailors withdrew, but on the sixth the Germans came ashore in force at Tanga, overcoming a determined resistance from liwali Zahora bin Swedi's garrison and the port's inhabitants. About ten townspeople were killed and two Germans wounded. The company men even then refused to leave their station without orders from Vohsen—some said they were too drunk to go—staying ashore until the *Möwe* came back on the seventh. While there, the Germans bombarded Tanga, the inhabitants fleeing and allowing the Germans to land unopposed. Meantime a British vessel had anchored off Pangani, moving away when its interpreter was fired on while attempting to go ashore. When members of the crew landed, they were met by a raucous crowd which "loudly and violently complained of recent German proceedings at Pangani declaring that they were going to put a stop to them." The visitors avowed British nationality, pushing forward their flag, but the coastmen proclaimed "they knew and cared nothing about flags, that all white men were the same and only came to seize the coast and rob the natives." The sultan's soldiers restrained the more unruly members of the crowd, the Britons quickly withdrawing when one leader, the Comorian Saleh, drew his sword.[12]

Vohsen regained Zanzibar on the sixth, seeking with Michahelles' concurrence additional support from Khalifa. The outraged sultan initially refused cooperation until Euan Smith's stressing of the dangers of German wrath reversed the attitude. Mathews and one hundred soldiers were dispatched to Pangani. Meanwhile Vohsen, observing company policies in ruins, began acting foolishly—and dangerously. Vohsen unsuccessfully sought German admiral Deinhard, hoping to convince him to bombard Pangani. Meanwhile at Pangani, Mathews found about eight-thousand Arabs and Africans gathered in opposition to the Germans, the townspeople strengthened by reinforcements from surrounding regions. They refrained from attacking the beleagured company men, allowing safe evacuation following talks with Mathews. The sultan's general, recognizing his inability to do more, returned to Zanzibar, bringing along five influential citizens desirous of presenting to Khalifa their version of events.[13]

The Pangani delegation unequivocally asserted determination in resisting reimposition of a company presence apart from non-German officials concerned only with customs. Any other course, warned the spokesmen, meant either war or a "general exodus" of inhabitants from the coast. The Germans refused—formally—to admit company blame for the coastal impasse, yet they had to recognize the seeming impossibility of returning company men to Pangani or Tanga. Deinhard still refused all offensive acts against the towns, in private conversations making little secret opinions blaming the company for the difficulties. Michahelles, accepting Euan Smith's assurances that Khalifa was uninvolved in the risings, agreed to let the Germans remain in the background while the sultan, utilizing Mathews and Arab administrators, attempted to regain control of the towns. Thus Vohsen was ignored, Bismarck accepting a one-month interval for the success of the sultan's endeavors, authorizing Michahelles to work along with Khalifa unless he decided that he was "playing false."[14]

As part of the scheme, Mathews and a small party of regular troops went to Pangani, where events at first appeared consistent with the script decided upon in Zanzibar. Mathews gathered the town's citizens for reading letters explaining Khalifa's future policies, also installing a new liwali, Suliman bin Nassir. But a different leadership had emerged in Pangani, demonstrating its influence by turning public opinion against Khalifa's British representative. Mathews, heretofore received everywhere with the deference due the commander of an effective army, now learned his life was in danger because he appeared to be a German supporter. The chastened Mathews discovered his men, in case of hostilities, could not be trusted to fight Pangani's people. The sultan's general, therefore, before any incident occurred that could possibly hinder Khalifa's reassertion of authority, returned to Zanzibar. He was not entirely discouraged since the new liwali, albeit against his will, remained in Pangani. Mathews and Michahelles decided to send additional soldiers to stabilize Pangani and Tanga.[15]

It was among the disaffected inhabitants of Pangani that the coastal opponents of the Germans found their best-known leader, Abushiri bin Salim. When Khalifa had been forced to sign the 1888 agreement, members of the Pangani community, among them Abushiri, Said bin Abeja, and Jehasi, began to discuss resistance. Abushiri, born possibly during the mid-1830s to an Arab father and African mother, by the 1880s a "stout, strongly built" man, had grown to manhood in Tanga, at an early age traveling into central Tanzania, reportedly seeing action in the wars against Mirambo. Returning to the coast Abushiri settled in Pangani, apparently coming into conflict with Barghash. Some sources blame the differences on Abushiri's previous adherence to Majid; others assert Barghash imprisoned the coastal Arab for participation in illegal activities.

German accounts later uniformly record Abushiri's defeat of a force sent
against him by the sultan in 1882. In reality the fight probably was a
minor affair; Abushiri bested a small group sent either to collect a debt
owed a Zanzibar Indian or to recapture him after an escape from the
sultan's prison. Abushiri was a typical representative of the influential
Afro-Arab coastal community, well aware of its historic rights and ready to
defend them when necessary. The emergence of a real leader, Euan Smith
had warned in mid-March, might unite the Germans' opponents into an
effective fighting force. Abushiri almost at once began to fill that role,
openly affirming during Mathews's stay that he planned to lead other areas
to resist the Germans. United behind Abushiri, the Pangani resistors
marked their local domination by forcing Mathews' departure. A so-called
moderate group remained in the port, its leading members including liwali
Suliman bin Nassir and Said bin Hamadi, but it possessed minimal influence.[16]

The coastal disaffection spread without requiring extra stimulation from
Abushiri. In Bagamoyo, although the jumbes continued to be resentful of
lost customs revenues, relations with the Germans, supported by offshore
vessels, remained peaceful until September 22. Then the town's inhabitants and the Germans began exchanging gunfire. The *Leipzig*, its officers
fearful for the safety of Deinhard, who was ashore hunting with the company station leader, were called upon by the beseiged Germans for assistance and landed about 200 men. In a hard-fought engagement the
Germans drove the resistors from the town, during the fighting killing
over 100 Arabs and Africans. Deinhard's party, warned of potential danger by friendly Arabs, returned unharmed. Much of Bagamoyo was destroyed during the hostilities, over 4,000 inhabitants seeking refuge with
the Holy Ghost priests. To prevent return of the defeated rebels, a contingent from the *Leipzig* continued in Bagamoyo, their presence allowing the
company Germans to go on the offensive.[17]

The Germans also were under seige in the sultan's southern ports. At
Mkindani two company officials, supported by about one-hundred Zanzibari irregulars, held a quiet flag-raising ceremony in mid-August, all
remaining outwardly calm until the early September reception of news of
the stirring occurrences to the north. By the middle of the month the
Germans were virtual, though unconfined, prisoners. Large groups of Yao
began gathering outside Mkindani, many of the settlement's citizens prudently evacuating their homes. When the liwali informed the Germans no
one would defend them from Yao attack, the two accepted the implied
threat, fleeing Mkindani by small boat on September 23.[18] In Lindi, where
company officials commanded a garrison of fifty irregulars, the two agents
had encountered increasing disobedience from the soldiers. When the Yao
began to collect on the town's outskirts, the Germans, assisted by Arabs

and Indians, fled Lindi by boat on September 25. The Mkindani and Lindi Germans were picked up soon after by German and British vessels.[19] The similarity of events at the two towns leads to suspicions of a conspiracy to remove, without bloodshed, the unwelcome Germans.

A similar outcome may have been envisaged for Kilwa, but German resistance instead brought disaster. Two agents, Heinrich Hessel and Gustav Krieger, facing a gathering of Yao, other Africans, and Arabs, on September 23 were given forty-eight hours to leave town. They refused, hoping to hold on until the expected arrival of a German vessel. Arriving before Kilwa on the twenty-third, the *Möwe*'s commander discovered the Germans under attack. Underestimating the seriousness of the fighting, the German officer, with orders to avoid a landing that could provoke the responses that occurred in the northern ports, did not intervene. Krieger and eleven Zanzibari soldiers were killed in the combat; Hessel, fearing capture, committed suicide. When representatives of the sultan later tried to land, the town's leaders asserted that Kilwa no longer recognized his authority, promising a return to allegiance only if the Germans did not return.[20] Most of Khalifa's soldiers, many belonging to the same ethnic groups as the resisters, also abandoned the southern ports, Mathews readily admitting the futility of expecting them to uphold the Germans.[21]

Dar es Salaam escaped the initial hostilities. There were rumors that Arabs planned to boycott ceremonies scheduled for August 16, and that a rising might occur, but when the day came, with the presence of the *Olga* in the harbor, events passed without incident. Liwali Suliman bin Saif, refusing German bribes, did not attend the festivities, returning, once the *Olga* departed, to make his opposition to the Germans public. Station chief A. Leue claimed support from members of the Arab community for keeping all peaceful. The liwali was recalled to Zanzibar, while in Dar es Salaam an undercurrent of suspicion and intrigue persisted. The Germans' enemies obviously awaited the outcome of the resistance elsewhere along the littoral.[22]

The disintegration of the company position left its interior stations in a very vulnerable status, particularly since relations between company and plantation society agents and their neighbors generally had been unfriendly. At Lewa on September 13 the appearance of an armed party caused all local workers to flee, the intruders destroying the tobacco crop and slightly wounding one of the Germans. After a general exchange of gunfire the Arabs and Africans withdrew, their mission accomplished: German work had eneded at Lewa. After an interval, negotiations for safe withdrawal of the company agents and visiting traveler Franz Stuhlmann took place in Pangani. Moderated by Suliman bin Nassir, an agreement was reached whereby Abushiri's men escorted the Germans to Pangani for payment of 4,000 rupees. Abushiri had offered to protect the abandoned

Lewa station from danger for an additional 1,000 rupees, but Koch refused. The Germans fired part of Lewa when leaving: the remainder was destroyed later by Arabs or Africans.[23]

The company's powerlessness was a fait accompli, its officials hanging on to coastal positions only when assisted by the German navy. The tactic of utilizing the sultan's administration to calm unrest proved fruitless, leaving the embarrassed German government the unwanted necessity of devising new policies. While admitting the mistake of flag-hoisting, the Germans interjected a new and significant explanation for hostilities, charging that the coastal peoples, fearing German interference with slave trading, had utilized company errors to begin an already prepared rising. The Germans stressed willingness for cooperation with Britain in any approach serving to restore peace. The British, fearing any action tending to threaten Zanzibar's independence, or stimulating Arab reactions along their section of the sultan's coast, found a worrisome ambivalence in German conduct, questioning why, despite German affirmations, their navy participated in offensive actions. The Germans responded, unconvincingly, that government orders must have been delayed, insisting no new ventures were planned, but admitting the necessity of not publicly announcing such prestige-damaging orders.[24]

German response to the East African dilemma included a 30 September 1888 dispatch to Khalifa describing the disorders as directed as much against his authority as against the company's. The Arab ruler, by this time thoroughly disillusioned with Europeans, withdrew to Zanzibar's remote eastern shore, leaving government business to two trusted subordinates, Pira Dewji and Muhammad Bakusumar. Answering Bismarck's letter in most undiplomatic style, Kahlifa, listing company misdeeds, awarded full responsibility to it for the war. Arabs had wanted peace, insisted the sultan: the Germans instead "spat upon our flag everywhere and said we were no longer the Sultan but that they were the Sultan." The Zanzibar government, he concluded, bore no blame for the coastal inhabitants' continuing attitude. Khalifa's perfectly justified attitude was reinforced by letters from different parts of the littoral, his subjects affirming willingness to return to traditional concepts of allegiance, but only if German administration was not restored.[25]

The Germans, then not desiring problems with the British-backed sultan, ignored Khalifa's strictures, instead seeking a course that would satisfy domestic critics. Utilizing the slave-trade theme, the Germans proposed, with British collaboration, blockading the sultan's coast, thus preventing both trade in slaves and shipment of munitions. The Foreign Office, even though Salisbury judged the slave trade a "potent cause" of the coast hostilities, found the proposal unappealing, regarding it justly as aiming to quiet internal German criticism by giving the impression of effective action against the Arabs. Yet it was impossible openly to resist joining the Germans in view of the long British campaign against the slave trade. Moreover, Salisbury and his advisors feared to allow German operations in East African waters "unless . . . shaped and controlled by at least an equal English force." The British leader, however, declined to permit German vessels to blockade the British sphere, while specifically warning that any offensive action against Zanzibar was unacceptable. The Germans willingly gave assurances, stressing that they planned only a blockade, not attacks on coastal settlements. Euan Smith thus was ordered to gain Khalifa's consent, the sultan, after desultory resistance, complying. The blockade opened on 2 December 1889, with each nation responsible for patrolling its section of the coast. The French, concerned over potentially troublesome incidents arising from treatment of vessels flying their colors, dispatched two vessels to Zanzibar. Their commanders were instructed to limit activities to ensuring that French vessels did not carry slaves. The Italians, then commencing their East African imperial venture, sent one vessel, while the Portuguese agreed to watch over their Mozambique coast.[26]

During the negotiating interval, relations between Germans and Arabs turned even more bitter, some of the former reacting badly to the obvious inability of regaining any initiative against their opponents. Unsuccessful deliberations were attempted with groups living near Dar es Salaam and Bagamoyo, while trade remained stagnant because of indigenous control of their environs. The German navy shared the low morale, suffering serious health problems. As a result of shore duty 110 of 150 sailors from the *Leipzig* came down with fever, the vessel eventually sailing to Zanzibar for service as the fleet's floating hospital. Deinhard nevertheless retained a thirty-man garrison ashore at Bagamoyo, probably, thought Euan Smith, as a restraint upon company actions. The admiral steadfastly refused Vohsen's continuous striving for additional offensive support. Meantime Khalifa, continuing in seclusion, increasingly drew German ire, Vohsen's repeated demands including a publicly expressed desire for an indemnity covering all company financial losses.[27] Perhaps the frustration helps explain the actions of the German fleet at the end of October. The *Sophie* steamed to the minor northern port of Whindi, responding to company allegations that the town served as a receiving center for arms and ammunition. Whindi's inhabitants refused to communicate with the Germans, suffering in return the bombardment and burning of their settlement.[28]

Among Europeans most involved in the breakdown of Zanzibar's authority were resident British, French, and German missionaries. Members of the Universities' Mission to Central Africa especially regretted past failures to arrange British treaties of protection with Africans around Magila. Now, when the Germans advanced territorial claims, the missionaries, regardless of past fulminations against influences coming from Muslim Zanzibar, uniformly sprang to the sultan's defense. The missionaries admittedly were in a difficult situation, balancing between upholding the interests of their African neighbors and Zanzibar, while reluctantly necessarily accepting the new German rulers. Smythies illustrated the dilemma in February 1886 when a German caravan visited Magila. Since its leader kept his men in chains to prevent desertion, the missionaries endeavored to satisfy both Africans and Germans, refusing the group permission to camp on mission property while simultaneously not demonstrating personal hostility to the caravan leader.[29] The Church Missionary Society had similar worries, its leaders' questions to the Foreign Office regarding their future in the German sphere causing British officials to seek and receive assurances of the German government's intention to "protect and assist them to the best of their ability and to the same extent as German missions."[30] The French nationals of the Holy Ghost Mission, with little chance of meaningful intervention by their government, took a more cautious stance, stressing that they were members of an international church. Fortunately, the Arabs, despite bitterness at French failure in defending Zanzibar's interests, continued to recognize the missionaries as neutrals.[31] The German missionaries, both Protestants and Catholics, inevitably suffered the consequences of their nationality.

The British and French missionaries, perforce accepting partition, found it troublesome to live with the Germans. The British churchmen, because of their government's involvement and because of their reaction to German misdeeds, became an especial embarrassment to the Foreign Office, hindering, so its officials felt, efforts to safeguard the position of the sultan—and Britain. One Universities' Mission agent, for example, wrote in the society's periodical about the supposedly striking decline of British influence in Zanzibar, the disgruntled Euan Smith hotly countering: "British influence has . . . never been stronger than at the present moment." When asked if the reply should be shown to the mission's directors, Salisbury, perhaps reacting to the near truth of the charge, demonstrated the underlying hostility to missionaries, caustically directed withholding any answer, adding, "but show it to them the first time they come to ask for anything." All doubtless agreed with Anderson's comment on another matter: "Even the most educated missionaries in East Africa seem hopelessly muddleheaded."[32]

The events of August 1888 and succeeding months drew strong missionary reaction; Farler, with his usual bluntness, published recollections of problems caused since 1885 by Germans, concluding with a recital of the excesses that preceded the hostilities. This, plus other missionary criticism, was close enough to the truth to require public German response usually stressing Arab hostility to envisaged measures against the slave trade.[33] More important, for both British officials and missionaries, was the continued safety of the Christian settlements now in the midst of coastal resistance. The missionaries had no intention of leaving their stations: Farler, for instance, in early 1888 reported nearly 1,000 Africans under Christian instruction in scattered villages in his district, a success in danger of foundering if Europeans withdrew.[34] But the government feared public blame for losses endured by missionaries living in dangerous localities; Euan Smith quickly wrote to the mainland stations, placing thereby in the public record a formal statement calling for evacuation of individuals beyond official protection. The request was renewed once the potentially unsettling blockade came under discussion. Smythies, a determined and vigorous man, replied as expected, agreeing, if circumstances permitted, to the departure of female missionaries, the males leaving only if "their staying would constitute a greater danger" to their African followers.[35]

Then occurred events apparently justifying Euan Smith's apprehensions. Hamid bin Suliman, visiting Pangani for discussions concerning evacuation of the Magila missionaries, learned they were forbidden to leave, the Pangani Arabs asserting hostilities were directed only at Germans. On Hamid's recommendation Abushiri guaranteed missionary safety, promising an escort to safety whenever the consul ordered. Euan Smith accepted Abushiri's participation, securing also Khalifa's agreement for a small party of Arabs to accompany Smythies to Magila to arrange the departure of the European women. The decision, however, raised some of the problems that made missionaries unpopular with the secular leadership, forcing Euan Smith to arrange with Deinhard postponement of the blockade in order not to endanger completion of the withdrawal. Accompanied by Nassir bin Suliman, Smythies arrived at Pangani on 12 November 1888, after minor hindrances meeting Abushiri and other Arabs. They assented to the march inland, although first advising Smythies that consent of the jumbes, "who have always been allowed a share in managing the affairs of Pangani," also was required. The jumbes specifically wanted a portion of the anticipated payment for arranging missionary removal, expressing particular concern since they had not yet been paid for returning German travelers Hans Meyer and Oscar Baumann. Smythies, refusing entanglement in ransom details, considering the matter the responsibility of secular authorities, allowed Nassir bin Suliman to make payments totaling 1,500 rupees. While the discussions went forward, Smythies provided a striking example of Abushiri's character. When a large, threatening crowd of local inhabitants pushed to the doorway of the building where the Arabs and bishop conversed, Abushiri strode forward, blocking all entry and informing the mob their "quarrel was only with those foreigners who had oppressed the people, that he guaranteed the safety of the missionaries, and he would see me safe up to Magila, even if he had to fight his way up," resolving that "no one should enter unless they killed him first." The crowd dispersed. With details arranged, Smythies left Pangani on November 13, attaining Magila without difficulty. The bishop lingered for some time at the station, the departing group of five women and three men journeying to Pangani and Zanzibar without incident. Smythies in late December returned safely to Zanzibar via the northern port of Wanga.[36]

The Church Missionary Society agents, also warned to evacuate interior stations, responded in much the same tone as the Universities' Mission. "Apparently they do not wish to discourage martyrdom," morosely commented one Foreign Office member. A sensible reason for remaining at mission bases was the undoubted danger facing individuals who left usually secure havens among Africans they knew and trusted for the uncertainties of the road: to Price of Mombasa, withdrawal was "only a change of risks."[37] The society quickly became involved in intricate negotiations concerning the safety of its personnel when missionaries from Buganda and Mpwapwa, partly in answer to the government request, decided to make for the coast. R. P. Ashe and Mr. and Mrs. Steven Pruen marched eastward through rumors that all Europeans were to be killed. They received a Euan Smith letter advising return to Mpwapwa. But when the missionaries attempted to comply, their porters refused; the provident arrival of an escort commanded by Abdullah bin Bwana Heri resolved the impasse, the rescue resulting from intervention by Euan Smith and Khalifa. Ashe later claimed a meeting had been held in Sadani following reception of letters from Zanzibar, most important men speaking in favor of killing the missionaries. Bwana Heri, however, citing past favorable treatment by the British, decided to provide safe passage. The story is possible, but unlikely, since the coast Muslims up to that time generally had not turned against the British. Abdullah did his duty, escorting the missionaries to Sadani, complaining while marching of Khalifa's treaty with the Germans. Henceforth Sadani would stand as an independent entity, declared the young Arab. In late November the party reached the coast where, said Ashe, Bwana Heri greeted the missionaries with "cold but studied politeness." After minor hindrances an Arab official sent by the sultan returned the group to Zanzibar.[38]

By the end of November 1888, Abushiri, sharing decision making with other Arabs but dominating military questions, made a significant resolution, resolving to leave Pangani for offensive actions against the Germans. With an estimated 800 supporters following a red and white flag bearing a Qur'anic sura, Abushiri marched first to Sadani, holding fruitless discussions for gaining Heri's adherence in his campaign. But the Sadani chieftian shared the convictions of many coastal leaders, his real interests not extending beyond defending his own region. Moreover Heri regarded Abushiri with almost as much suspicion as he did Germans, this lack of unity among Arabs and Africans enduring all during the succeeding warfare.

Abushiri's army entered Bagamoyo's environs in early December, hoping to capture the coast's major ivory terminal. Hostilities around the settlement had never entirely ceased, the naval garrison and offshore fleet continually safeguarding company headquarters. The Germans made frequent sallies into surrounding settlements, striving in late November, for example, to apprehend local resistance leader Salim bin Abdallah. The foray failed, its leaders, Gravenreuth and Bülow, suffering minor wounds; in a typical reaction they ordered the summary execution of their African guide for supposed complicity in the defeat. As elsewhere, Arab and African resentment remained directed only against Germans. French missionaries lived in relative security, while the British were equally tolerated; the local attitude showed when a Universities' Mission man, blown coastward when sailing off Zanzibar, went aground near Bagamoyo. The villagers first fired at the newcomer, desisting when they learned his nationality, later aiding his return to Zanzibar.[39]

Abushiri encountered willing allies at Bagamoyo, among them jumbes Bomboma, Makanda, Sima Mbili, Marere, and Fimba Mbili. The combined Arab and African forces attacked German positions on December 5. Most of Bagamoyo's buildings were destroyed during the fighting, about 2,000 of the remaining population joining other refugees at the Holy Ghost Mission. During the combat the Germans failed to protect Nyamwezi traders, the Arabs securing a large booty in ivory and slaves from the defenseless Africans, their arms impounded by the company. On December 24 Abushiri once again attacked Bagamoyo, the Germans a second time repulsing the Arabs, the attackers losing 100 while twenty-five of the German followers were killed or wounded. The Arabs and Africans retreated to a fortified location between the town and the Kingani River, henceforth raiding neighboring territories. The Germans accepted a defensive stance; Deinhard, angry over losses suffered by his men during the land fighting, refused support for offensive movements.[40]

The Bagamoyo strife immediately engulfed nearby Dar es Salaam where, despite overbearing conduct toward Arabs, company resident Leue had maintained local peace. Outside the town the countryside continued loyal to Arab and African leadership, among them Shindu, Salim bin Sayf, and Akida Sulamini. On 23 and 24 December they struck, the combined company and naval defenders driving the attackers from the town, both sides then settling into essentially defensive stances.[41]

The war affected more than relationships between the sultan, Germans, and coastal Muslims, the African peoples of the immediate hinterland inevitably becoming involved. The powerful Shambaa ruler Semboja offers the major example of the reaction to events sparked by failure of the company administration. Semboja, before German arrival, had acted in close political and commercial concert with Zanzibar's Arabs. Semboja experienced little interference from Germans before August 1888, but when fighting began at Pangani, Semboja nonetheless dispatched assistance—Baumann said 800 men—for Abushiri. In the succeeding months, however, Semboja avoided a major role, satisfied with German evacuation of Shambaa lands. But Semboja did become embroiled in controversy due to treatment of two German travelers, Hans Meyer and Oscar Baumann, an involvement ending with a very complicated settlement that influenced other happenings during the coastal war. After leaving Pangani on August 27, Meyer and Baumann suffered desertion by most of their porters, and reached Semboja's capital as virtual prisoners. Eventually receiving permission from Pangani to return to the coast, the two were seized during the journey and conducted in chains to the town, probably in retaliation for the chaining of a captured Arab to the funnel of a German vessel. In Pangani, Meyer and Baumann learned they were prisoners of Abushiri, the Arab supposedly intending their death unless he received a 10,000-rupee ransom. Envisaging escape as impossible, Meyer paid the sum by check, adding 2,000 rupees to the original amount "as interest." Shortly thereafter the two Germans were permitted to return to Zanzibar.[42]

Regaining Zanzibar, Meyer attempted to honor his pledge, leaving 12,000 rupees with Euan Smith for eventual transfer to Abushiri; the consul accepted the sum ostensibly to avoid placing Khalifa in an affair possibly leading to complications with Germans. But after discussions with the sultan, doubtlessly browbeating the Arab ruler into compliance, Euan Smith announced the unlikely circumstance of Khalifa taking responsibility for settling the affair, not intending to allow such extortion in his dominions. Meyer's money was returned. Since Abushiri did not immediately demand the funds, it appeared a successful resolution of the problem. Yet, not long after, fifty loads of supplies that had been sent to Pangani by the Universities' Mission were seized, the town's jumbes apparently reacting to the delay in receiving their share of the Meyer ransom. The astutely applied pressure swiftly brought Smythies into the matter; the bishop judged the sum should have been paid and thus chided Euan Smith for interference. The bishop, then acting in his usual forceful manner, resolved the impasse, proceeding directly to Pangani, the liwali immediately releasing the mission goods for transport by Smythies to Magila. The tangled Meyer affair continued troublesome, Abushiri warning Euan Smith of his refusal to accept responsibility for the safety of the Mpwapwa and other inland missionaries without payment of the ransom. The Briton threatened Khalifa with blame for any disaster befalling missionaries; the sultan, as customary, demonstrated complete indifference to consular intimidation.[43]

Once Abushiri passed to the offensive, the general intensification of hostilities inevitably caused a worsening of European security. The first war-related death of a non-German missionary immediately ensued. Arthur Brooks of the London Missionary Society, heading coastward from Urambo, reached Mamboya, there learning of the uncertainties ahead. John Roscoe and the other resident missionaries previously had written Euan Smith concerning their isolated position, the consul replying that the war made it impossible for arranging supply caravans, promising instead the dispatch of an escort to conduct them to the coast. Brooks temporarily joined the Mamboya party, waiting for the escort until local shortage of provisions raised fears that his men might desert. Deciding to continue, Brooks wrote Bwana Heri seeking reassurance about the route; the letter carrier disturbingly returned, said Amani wad Mabruki, minus either his gun or a reply. Three other Africans of the caravan claimed the carrier bore the news that all Europeans going to Zanzibar were to be killed in retaliation for general European support of Germans. Brooks, Amani explained, while preparing a return to Mamboya, was interrupted by arrival of men from Sadani and Uzigula. The missionary was killed as he greeted the newcomers, his followers scattering as men were seized and caravan loads plundered. Whatever the minor differences in the several African versions of the killing, all witnesses clearly placed responsibility upon men subordinate to Bwana Heri.[44]

Securely in control of Sadani and its environs, Heri, hitherto universally regarded as a friend of Europeans and a loyal adherent of the sultan, was at once presumed guilty by Euan Smith. To prevent future aggressions against British missionaries—he particularly worried about the expected journey of the Mpwapwa-Mamboya group—Euan Smith attempted to force Khalifa into accepting responsibility, with the German consul pushing the sultan into making "widely known his own anger at and his intention of punishing the murderers of Mr. Brooks." The Briton proposed that Khalifa, with German permission, and perhaps even assistance, send an expedition against Heri, envisaging a Sadani victory as a possible first step in regaining Zanzibar's lost coastal authority. As usual bowing to Britain's imperious representative, Khalifa promised, if the Germans joined in, to dispatch the men. The Germans, however, decided against involvement, the aroused Deinhard complaining that he had warned the missionaries, charging that their perpetual disregard of advice was a hindrance to military planning. Khalifa then countered that it was impossible for Zanzibar to act alone, the conclusion supported by a chastened Mathews admitting his soldiers' undependability. Salisbury meantime cautioned Euan Smith against retaliatory action by the sultan, fearing that intervention in favor of a Briton obligated a similar response for all Germans killed on the mainland. The consul changed tack, receiving German permission to arrange reception of the Mpwapwa-Mamboya missionaries and to arrest Heri. The latter task, in view of the realities of the day, probably was merely a tactic for encouraging the Sadani ruler to make known the names of Brooks's murderers. Then in the midst of an intrigue aiming to unthrone the uncooperative Khalifa,[45] Euan Smith drew upon the sultan's supposed attitude to discredit his standing with the Foreign Office, informing Salisbury of receiving reliable information from a member of Khalifa's Mamboya garrison implicating the sultan in complicity in Arab hostility to missionaries. In Foreign Office discussions of the Brooks affair, officials judged the evidence concerning Khalifa's participation too weak for formal reaction, even though Kirk concluded the sultan "undoubtedly" had given orders leading to the killing.[46]

Bwana Heri, despite the circulating allegations, had not changed his policy of succoring non-Germans; in December 1888 he offered the Mpwapwa-Mamboya missionaries assistance in reaching the coast. Later, when Holy Ghost priests wrote concerning help for an inland trip, Heri promised aid, although suggesting that the Frenchmen not leave from Sadani since the path westward had passed from his control.[47] The Germans meanwhile, vowing all possible cooperation in finding Brooks's killers, evolved an interpretation of Heri's position in East Africa that endured through the continuance of hostilities, informing the British that the Sadani ruler was "not an official of the Sultan of the ordinary type, but a local chief, whose allegiance was little more than nominal, who had been entrusted by His Highness with temporary authority." The matter rested for the moment.[48]

Abushiri, then conversing with Baur of the Holy Ghost Mission concerning release of the Pugu missionaries,[49] informed Euan Smith of his interpretation of the reasons behind Brooks's death. The Arabs, explained Abushiri, had serious grievances against the British, with bitterness coming especially from participation in the blockade and missionary reception of Mombasa slaves. These feelings, the Arab warned, endangered the lives of the Mpwapwa-Mamboya Europeans; broadening the threat by adding that Brooks's death "was but the precursor of the murder of the missionaries at Magila." Both mission societies stood firm, Smythies emphasizing the persistent good relations between his followers and Arabs. Yet even in that usually stable relationship there were disturbances: in March 1889 when African Christians landed materials for Magila near Pangani, three women were detained. Euan Smith went to Khalifa, the sultan ordering his Pangani liwali into action. The governor first presented the captors a letter from the sultan, holding back the desired ransom of fifty rupees, but the coastmen, exclaiming "we want our money all the same," taunted that "an Englishman was murdered at Sadani and who was punished for it?" Receiving the money, they released the women. When, despite the continued official warnings, the churchmen went on with their work, an aroused Foreign Office member sputtered helplessly about the "further evidence that the missionaries will never learn."[50]

Much of Admiral Deinhard's resentment toward missionaries stemmed from the time-consuming negotiations necessary to secure their release from Arabs. Once the hapless German Catholics, chained and in a "most pitiable condition," arrived in Abushiri's camp, Baur began to mediate deliberations between Germans and Arabs. The proceedings were difficult, Abushiri seeking a substantial ransom, necessary for meeting the heavy expenses required for continued warfare. Although striking the chains from the Germans, Abushiri refused their surrender, even after receiving a 6,000 rupee ransom, unless sixteen Arabs seized by the *Leipzig* were liberated. During the negotiations Baur and Abushiri were together when the Germans shelled the Arab camp, the Frenchman providing a revealing picture of the resistance leader. "While shells from the German men of war were bursting around him," reported the admiring priest, "he entirely refused to listen to the prayers of his attendants to seek a place of safety until his negotiations were terminated."[51]

The approach of the Mpwapwa-Mamboya missionaries, including the pregnant Mrs. Roscoe, caused a new round of ransom deliberations. When messages from Zanzibar finally reached Sadani, Abdullah bin Bwana Heri, acting for his father, refused assistance, leaving Euan Smith helpless to assist their journey.[52] Then, in mid-March, Abushiri, learning an armed Arab party had left the coast to intercept the missionaries, announced to Baur the dispatch of men to guarantee the Europeans reaching the coast safely, the Frenchman, certain of Abushiri's good faith, being ready once more for service as intermediary if the Germans concurred. Deinhard consented. Abushiri did not miss the opportunity for profit, seeking payment of the long-delayed Meyer ransom, plus all additional expenses incurred for helping the group to safety, in return for the Europeans' release. British consul Albert Hawes, temporarily replacing Euan Smith, hurriedly reminded Khalifa of his alleged responsibility for the Meyer payment, threatening to hold him accountable if noncompliance led to harming the captives. Khalifa angrily denied ever promising payment, strongly protesting what he considered unjustifiable British harassment.

Meantime Abushiri released the Roscoes, holding C. S. Edwards and W. E. Taylor until he gained the Meyer ransom. When the Germans, delaying a scheduled shelling of Pangani, became restive, Hawes advanced the necessary sum from consulate funds. But then another missionary, Douglas Hooper from Uyuwi, fell into Abushiri's grasp, the Arab claiming additional compensation for his liberation—the freeing of Masud bin Slayman, an Arab imprisoned in Zanzibar for involvement in the death of a British naval officer. The talks concerning Hooper dragged on until April 21, British admiral E. R. Freemantle blaming Deinhard for delaying permission for Masud's deliverance.

An important reason for settlement came with the East African arrival of Hermann Wissmann; the impatient new commander of German forces regarded missionary-imposed delays as "a great obstacle" to his plans. When Masud rejoined his companions, Hooper was freed. At some stage during the drawn-out process Courmont of the Holy Ghost Mission noted some Arabs pressing for the death of the missionaries, although liwali Ismail of Whindi convinced them otherwise. In all, the ransomed missionaries brought Abushiri about 12,000 rupees, the sum drawn from Meyer, the British consulate, and the Church Missionary Society. The Arab immediately offered to bring down the remaining Mwpapwa residents; the British consul quickly declined before Abushiri, questing augmentation of his limited financial resources, intervened once again.[53]

There was no solution possible within existing German policies for ending hostilities in East Africa. After talking to Vohsen as the discouraged director prepared to return to his homeland—he had been recalled in mid-January 1889—W. S. Price "gathered . . . that the Company is defunct—nothing for it but either to abandon the enterprise or for the Imperial Government to take it in hand." With the rabid European imperialistic climate of the 1880s, withdrawal was impossible, the German government inevitably moving to intervention to quiet opponents berating nonpunishment of Arab and African resisters portrayed as participants in the slave trade and as miscreants blocking the fruits of Western civilization. Vohsen stressed these themes after reaching Germany, publicly blaming Khalifa for lack of cooperation. Consul Michahelles similarly increasingly placed responsibility for the rising on slave-trade supporters.[54]

During December French representative in Berlin Herbette reported that Bismarck was beginning to assume direct charge of formulating policy toward East Africa, the step marking a change to active intervention to end hostilities through military defeat of Arab and African resisters. Later the well-known German explorer Hermann Wissmann, after talks with Bismarck, was selected for an investigatory mission to East Africa. The change in Bismarck's reasoning occurred contemporaneously with agitation led by Cardinal Lavigerie for a European crusade against the slave trade, thus allowing the chancellor opportunity to utilize the Roman Catholic block within the legislature for more forceful policies.[55] Wissmann's appointment effectively prejudged the outcome of the policy review. The thirty-five-year-old officer was an avowed advocate of breaking the power of East Central Africa's Arabs, during 1887 succinctly explaining "the deliverance of Equatorial Africa from the thraldom of the Arabs has become my life's object." A missionary who met Wissmann after his 1888 crossing of the Congo portrayed "a man who came with a heart boiling over what he actually saw . . . The man was mad with the truth of it."[56]

Events quickly went forward, decision for a campaign against Abushiri and other resistance leaders coming even before Wissmann left for East Africa. The new policy, supported by an initial Reichstag authorization of £100,000, aimed first at ending all armed opposition, following with renewed striving for commercial development. The German leadership, for a semblance of continuity with earlier promises to the British, blamed the change on the force of national public opinion, accepting without demur the reaction that any move against Zanzibar "would be very strongly opposed." Thus, by early February, Wissmann, appointed Imperial Commissioner, held authority over the German company, with promise of four small steamers granting some independence from the Imperial Navy. His orders, in brief, were to defeat the Arabs.[57] Immediately deciding that only a force made up of African troops could succeed, Wissmann, with Salisbury's "benevolent support," began to recruit among the unemployed, experienced soldiers—mostly Dinka and Shilluk—available since the Egyptian defeat in the Sudan.[58]

The accounts of Wissmann's forthcoming intervention were received with dismay by most European residents of East Africa. Euan Smith, responsible for the safety of British subjects, reacted sharply, fearing the missionaries would become an immediate "sacrifice" to German urge for battle. And, prognosticated the consul, the Germans were backing a mistaken policy. Arabs informed Euan Smith that they planned to avoid major battles, concentrating instead upon commerce-destroying raiding, allying with the East African factors of disease and climate to wear down German will to fight. Euan Smith concluded the Germans required many thousands of troops for victory over "fanatical and bitter enemies," recommending instead utilization of the sums voted for war to buy off the coastal leadership. Even this might not work, he warned, since many areas permanently had rejected Zanzibar's domination. In short, the consul judged, "nothing of a permanently beneficial character can be expected" from Wissmann's expected campaign. The opinion was shared by others, the Hamburg merchants, for example, similarly awarding Wissmann little chance of victory, recommending policies in line with Euan Smith's.[59] The advice, if heard by Wissmann, was ignored.

While Wissmann prepared his campaign, coast hostilities continued, Arabs and Africans attacking Dar es Salaam and Pugu in early January 1889. Unwisely providing the local population specific stimulation, the Germans in October 1888 awarded Africans liberated from a captured dhow to the care of the German Protestants in Dar es Salaam, their presence serving as a constant bitter irritation to former owners. The attack, under joint leadership of Suliman bin Sayf and Shindu, was well planned. The former, an influential Arab once serving Barghash, supposedly sold all his Zanzibar property before battle to avoid possible retaliation. It was a common happening, many Arabs passing back and forth from Zanzibar during the war. The Germans knew an attack was intended, learning of it from Brother Oskar, a German member of the Holy Ghost Mission, and from local Arab and African sources. But they did not know the exact timing, the Arabs, about 1,000 strong, striking unexpectedly on January 11. During the hard fight the mission station and most of the town were destroyed, only the presence of the German navy allowing the company to continue holding on. In the confusion of combat many liberated slaves held by the mission were retaken by Arabs. The German Roman Catholics also had been warned of danger; confident of sharing the immunity enjoyed by the Holy Ghost Mission, they refused evacuation. Pugu was surprised on January 13, four missionaries becoming prisoners, three perishing, and two escaping. The Arabs struck Dar es Salaam again on January 17, once more without victory. In the several engagements the attackers lost over 100 men. The imprisoned Pugu Catholics added a new complication for the Germans, the Arabs at first refusing liberation unless Dar es Salaam and Bagamoyo were evacuated. Eventually Abushiri secured control of the captives, beginning negotiations for release through the mediation of the Holy Ghost fathers.[60]

Sultan Khalifa during this troubled period became even more resentful of European-imposed pressures. The Arab ruler no longer received adequate revenues, because of the disruption of commerce, collecting from the coastal dominions from August through the end of November 1888 only 80,809.25 rupees. Before hostilities, the customs paid over 71,000 rupees monthly. Thus, by the beginning of 1889 Khalifa, not sending the salaries of officials, helplessly watched the outward signs of Zanzibar authority fading. The remaining members of the Lindi garrison, for example, unpaid for months, deserted in March. The coastal peoples, reacting to the change, often asserted more independence. In Sadani during January, when Khalifa sent men to assist in the return of some British missionaries, the inhabitants dispersed them, clamoring that communications between Zanzibar and the interior were prohibited. Khalifa's British ties also eroded. "The Sultan believes in us no more, and how could he?" a Briton concluded. "His present policy seems to be to promise everybody everything, and do nothing." The attitude left Khalifa dangerously exposed, the German company threatened forced payment of the full war costs while the British consul plotted with rivals for the throne. In early February, Euan Smith, not mentioning his own role, began to stress Khalifa's anti-

European stance, asking and receiving permission to deport the sultan's principal advisors Pira Dewji and Muhammad Bakusumar, also warning of a possible Arab coup against the supposedly inept Arab sovereign. French consul Lacau, however, observed the true flow of events, noting Euan Smith's active stimulation of plotters under the leadership of Khalifa's brother Ali. Salisbury, unaware of his agent's duplicity, reacted against removing Khalifa. Anticipating unwanted complications with the Germans over selecting a successor, Salisbury warned the conspirators that Britain would not recognize any government resulting from a coup. Ali, carefully avoiding antagonizing the British, postponed his hopes for the sultanate.[61]

After the January 1889 fighting in and around Dar es Salaam, the Arabs and Germans abstained from major hostilities, both awaiting Wissmann's arrival. Abushiri in early March participated in one skirmish near Bagamoyo, a disturbance during the combat leading the Arab into an interesting sequence of pourparlers with the British and Germans. On March 5 an emissary from Abushiri informed Euan Smith that his master had been fired at by one of his own men, an act attributed to German bribery. "Under these circumstances," explained Euan Smith, "he had sent to tell me confidentially that he would come over and give himself up to me at the British Consulate if I would send a verbal message to him to the effect I would guarantee his life." Since the messenger carried only a verbal declaration, the consul temporized, doubtlessly requesting more information from Abushiri.[62] Whether or not the shooting incident occurred, Abushiri obviously wanted a dialogue with his enemies, in succeeding days advancing terms for peace, including receipt of 10,000 rupees for distribution among his followers and a safe conduct on the promise of withdrawal to Arabia. Euan Smith thought the proposals reasonable, judging that Abushiri so far had not driven the Germans to extreme hostility—Deinhard, in fact, during the missionary negotiations had characterized the Arab as a "thorough gentleman." The German government, after mulling the offer, informed Salisbury it would "be glad if Bushiri were to disappear," although refusing formal guarantee of his life. While requesting "absolute secrecy," the Germans sought British assistance in continuing the talks, suggesting an inquiry as to whether Abushiri might go to India rather than Arabia. In East Africa Deinhard accepted this opportunity for peacefully resolving the war, concluding a truce with Abushiri, both Arabs and Germans then waiting to allow Wissmann the chance to participate in the deliberations.[63]

Wissmann reached Zanzibar on 31 March 1889, simultaneously beginning preparations for war and taking notice of the existing truce. Abushiri, meantime, believing the Germans willing to negotiate, carried on with assistance from missionaries Taylor and Baur. His more comprehensive proposals included his designation as liawali of the coast opposite Zanzibar at a salary of 4,000 rupees per month, appointment of all qadis by the liwali, retention of customary rights by the jumbes of Bagamoyo, upholding of traditional property rights, and continuance of slave sales not violating existing treaties. In return the Germans were offered free exercise of the coastal concession, but without the right of erecting fortified stations.[64]

Although Wissmann later castigated the Arab's terms as "outrageous" and "comic," purporting that he accepted and even extended the truce only because of unreadiness for immediate hostilities, it does appear that the commissioner, at least initially, sought to seize advantage of a chance for ending Abushiri's resistance. According to Smythies, passing on "most private" information gained from the Holy Ghost fathers, Wissmann sent counterproposals to Abushiri, accepting the Arab as liwali, under German authority, of the northern coast at a monthly salary of 3,000 rupees. An alternative proposal offered Abushiri 100,000 rupees for withdrawing, with his followers, from German territory. Abushiri, dealing through British consul Hawes, considered the suggestions reasonable, but admitted lack of confidence in the Germans, fearing the discovery, after his submission, of some excuse for retaliation. Realistically recognizing German and Arab mistrust, Hawes advised Abushiri, if he had qualms about the future, to accept the second set of terms. As the discussions spiritlessly dragged on, both sides growing weary of delays, it became apparent that agreement was unlikely. The judgment of Lacau and others that Wissmann never intended coming to terms, unless Abushiri abjectly surrendered, is sensible. The Berlin government, less sure of victory than its self-confident young officer, might have welcomed provisions removing Abushiri from the scene, but the absence of strong interest in successful negotiation by Germans in East Africa ensured failure.[65]

Seizing upon a supposed truce violation Wissmann, on 8 May 1889, led his troops, about 730 Africans—including 200 Nyamwezi present in Bagamoyo—and 60 Europeans, against the Arabs. The Germans estimated their opponents at about 600 Arabs and Africans occupying a camp strongly fortified under Jehazi's direction. Contrarily, Douglas Hooper, a recent visitor to the enclosure, reported half that number of poorly armed and fed men. The different accounts, apart from probable German exaggeration, perhaps are explained by arrival of over 200 men from Mombasa. The Germans successfully stormed the unprepared stronghold, killing about 100 defenders, among them liwali Ismail of Whindi. They lost forty African followers. Abushiri, apparently not realizing the truce's termination, was elsewhere during the attack.[66] The defeat left Abushiri without significant military support, one group of disgruntled men, blaming him for the loss, refusing further service. He also

lost the ransom paid for the Pugu missionaries. The Arab commander
eventually fled the Bagamoyo region, joining the Arabs of Kondoa. Meanwhile, the Germans maintained pressure on their enemies, mounting follow-up expeditions around Bagamoyo and Dar es Salaam. Suliman bin
Sayf was defeated, while the Germans regained Pugu, destroying the village of the leader responsible for raiding the Catholic mission. Shindu and
Suliman bin Sayf fled north, joining the remnants of the defeated
Bagamoyo Arabs.[67]

Pangani was Wissmann's next objective. Anticipating the danger, some
town leaders sought a peaceful settlement, sending an agent to Zanzibar to
communicate through Gerald Portal with the Germans. The Germans of
the 1880s portrayed the proponents of a negotiated accord as representing
the wealthier Arabs, but there is little evidence for the assertion.[68] When
the talks ended in impasse, the Germans, on June 5, approached Pangani
in force, sending a boat toward shore to test the inhabitants. When met
with gunfire, the Germans countered on the seventh with a bombardment
followed by a landing by over 800 men. The outnumbered defenders fled,
the Germans burning the town. There had been little actual fighting, both
sides suffering minor losses. The victors then withdrew, Wissmann apparently not wishing to weaken German strength by dividing forces among
the many coastal centers. Soon thereafter liwali Suliman bin Nassir arrived
in Zanzibar, reporting much difficulty in gaining permission to leave Pangani. After attempting explanations for the failure of previous negotiations, the liwali, returning to Pangani on a German vessel, ventured to
reopen talks. The citizens refused permission to land, calling the Arab the
sultan's friend, not theirs. When they opened fire, Suliman abandoned the
task. The final attack on Pangani occurred on July 9, the Germans clearing
away the defenders with a Maxim gun. Sixty to seventy Arabs and Africans
were killed, among them Said bin Abeja. The Germans continued on to
Tanga, its leaders on July 12 agreeing to discussions, but when Arab
hotheads fired guns into the air the Germans, fearing attack, drove the
inhabitants from the town.[69]

Wissmann next directed his methodical campaign against Sadani. About
400 men landed, following a bombardment, meeting fierce resistance, the
defenders later asserting thirty German casualties. Destroying the town,
the Germans withdrew. Anticipating continuing stiff opposition from the
doughty Bwana Heri, Wissmann opted for negotiations, justifying the
decision by describing the Sadani leader as an independent ruler fighting
exclusively for his own territory, not guilty of actions requiring German
punishment. The arrival in Pangani shortly after its capture of Tippu Tip's
son Sefu gave Wissmann the idea of sending the young Arab to Sadani for
talks with Bwana Heri. Sefu, after consulting Khalifa, agreed to the mission. Landing in Sadani in July, Sefu found himself in a very dangerous

position, the inhabitants preventing a meeting with their chieftain, castigating Sefu as a friend of the Germans, and rejecting presents of food brought for Heri on the grounds of fear of poison. Informed his life was in jeopardy, Sefu left in haste for Zanzibar. Later two influential Zanzibar Arabs made a final unsuccessful effort to arrange terms. Despite additional hostilities in November and December, however, 1889 ended with Bwana Heri still unconquered by Germans.[70]

While the Germans regained possession of most of the northern coast, Abushiri gathered new contingents at Kondoa. During July 1889 he sought Kami support, but the Africans, suspicious because of his close ties with their Hehe and Mbunga enemies,[71] rejected proposals for attacking the Holy Ghost Tununguo mission. Abushiri had altered his attitude toward the French priests, reacting to their conduct during the Bagamoyo fighting. He considered that the missionaries should have warned him of the forthcoming German offensive, even more importantly suspecting the presence in his camp of Christian Africans passing information to the enemy. Bishop Courmont admitted the reasonableness of the last charge, since a former African member of the mission, visiting the Arab camp disguised as a mission resident, did spy for the Germans. Because of the threat the missionaries evacuated Tununguo, Longo, and Morogoro, gathering at Mhonda prepared to resist the Arabs. The missionaries escaped hostilities, the Kami declining to participate unless the influential Kingo Mkubwa, son of Kisabengo, joined in. But Kingo refused to get involved against Europeans. Left to his own resources, Abushiri instead struck the German company post at Mpwapwa.[72]

Both Germans and Britons at Mpwapwa had declined evacuation, each rejecting the possibility of inclusion in the seemingly distant war. Missionary Price justified his decision by Gogo promises to defend the station. But in June 1889 the British learned Abushiri planned to capture Mpwapwa, thus gaining more prisoners for ransom. The missionaries informed German commander Giese; all the Europeans, continually hearing rumors, remained unconcerned. On June 23 Abushiri and 150 men surprised the German post, killing one officer. Giese precipitously fled, his African subordinates successfully resisting Arab attack. Reaching Mpwapwa chieftain Kipangilo's residence, Giese sought assistance, but when the African sounded the war drum only a few of the settlement's warriors answered. The missionaries, uninvolved in the fighting, hid in the bush until the Arabs left. Most of the Germans' African troops, obviously disillusioned with Giese's conduct, abandoned the post, leaving the officer with no alternative but flight to the coast. Kipangilo, assuring the missionaries of his people's support, explained the lack of response to the Arab incursion as a legacy of earlier German conduct.[73] Learning that Abushiri intended to return to Mpwapwa, Kipangilo queried Arab intentions, gaining assurances that both Africans and missionaries were not in danger, the Arabs merely seeking to seize the German property. When Abushiri's men entered, one, a former resident of the Mpwapwa mission, confided to Price suspicions of his leader's attitude concerning the Europeans. Abushiri, arriving on July 5, commanded 200 followers, offering the Britons safe conduct to the coast. As long as he lived, the Arab vowed to Price, he intended to fight Germans, spreading disorganization throughout their territories. Price's African friend soon warned that Abushiri had decided to seize both Kipangilo and the missionaries; the latter immediately under shelter of darkness abandoned Mpwapwa for the Kisokwe mission. Abushiri's men, looting and destroying the deserted station, despite initial rumors left the region without further harassing the Britons.[74]

Giese, with assistance from Holy Ghost fathers, regained the coast on July 26, spreading unfounded reports that Abushiri personally had killed his Mpwapwa associate. Reacting to the first defeat since his arrival, Wissmann vowed henceforth war without mercy against Arabs, offering a 10,000-rupee reward for Abushiri—dead or alive. He organized a major expedition, designed both for restoring German interior authority and for reopening the principal trade route to German controlled ports, marching inland in early September with about 600 soldiers, plus 1,500 homeward-bound Nyamwezi bearing presents to stimulate future commerce. To humiliate his opponents, Wissmann brought along three Arabs captured while supposedly spying for Abushiri; they were chained by the neck, "à la manière antique" said the French consul, carrying heavy loads. The missionaries meantime remained untroubled by Arabs, all danger ending when Wissmann's expedition entered Mpwapwa on October 12. The German commander quickly and brutally quieted all potential opposition, publicly executing the three Arab prisoners, leaving their bodies on display. Stationing a garrison of over 100 men, the Germans hurried back to the coast war. The campaign had been a clear triumph, many along the route, including the Kondoa Arabs and Kingo Mkubwa, accepting terms from the powerful invaders, while several smaller German side expeditions defeated minor groups of resistors.[75]

With the bulk of the German military committed to the Mpwapwa venture, Abushiri, strengthened by Africans from the lower Kilombero Valley, the Mbunga,[76] proved his skill as a strategist, avoiding Wissmann and assailing the depleted coastal garrisons. The Arab and African command, 6,000 strong, divided into several segments, burst into the territory behind Bagamoyo and Dar es Salaam, plundering the indigenous Zaramo while moving eastward. The Germans collected all available men, the main column under Gravenreuth, on October 20 meeting Abushiri and 2,000 Mbunga at Jombo, firing salvo after salvo into the charging African ranks. Just as German ammunition ran short, the Mbunga withdrew from the battlefield. In other, less dramatic combat, smaller parties of Mbunga also were defeated. Although ammunition shortage prevented German pursuit, the Mbunga, hurrying homeward, suffered severe harassment from revenge-seeking Zaramo. Abushiri had to flee punishment from his erstwhile allies, the Africans reacting against earlier assurances of easy victory.[77]

The coast blockade continued while Arabs and Germans fought on the continent, even though participating Europeans quickly discovered it was not an effective war measure. The northern coast was lightly patrolled, the British taking to heart warnings of Nassir bin Suliman and other Arabs that appearance of Germans would precipitate an immediate rising. There was, in any case, little reason to irritate Arabs in regions not directly involved in the war. Before the end of 1888 even some Germans considered the blockade counterproductive, keeping traders away from the coast while unnecessarily arousing the littoral's inhabitants. The fleet was "heartily tired and disgusted with it," the German consul told Euan Smith, most dissatisfaction arising from the nature of activities required at sea. Small boats left the men-of-war to seek out indigenous small craft, many little more than canoes, sailing in coastal waters, much energy being expended without significant return. According to one account, Germans searched 1,500 Arab and African boats; only three were seized. The British fared about the same: one vessel by the end of 1888 had searched 104 dhows, not uncovering a single violation. Later, Admiral Freemantle, in reporting 1,300 searches, lamented: "The net result has been the taking away of one gun from a passenger, which I have ordered to be restored to him." German officer Hirshberg typically emphasized the boredom of the task, finding solace only in frequent participation in operations ashore. By 1889's close, six German vessels, carrying about 1,500 men, seven British vessels with a similar complement, and the few ships of the French, Italians, and Portuguese had shared in patrolling. But during the year the numbers involved grew smaller, by September the German contingent dropping to two small craft operating around Zanzibar.[78]

Meantime the Germans diligently hunted the defeated Abushiri, hoping to prevent a new Arab offensive. After failing to gain allies in Usagara, Abushiri, by the end of November, endeavored to reach either Bwana Heri or Semboja, the worried Germans fearing that they would cooperate in an attack upon Pangani. The Arab did reach Sadani, where Heri, in combination with other local leaders, planned offensive action against the French missionaries at Madera. When German moves prevented the scheme, Abushiri headed for Semboja's capital.[79] The Arab chieftain, however, after his several defeats, had lost the initiative, the reward for his capture tempting many formerly passive Africans. An old enemy, Zigula chief Muhammad Sowa, informed the Germans of Abushiri's whereabouts. A small expedition, guided by Sowa's men, hurried from Pangani to his place of refuge, during the quest capturing some of Bagamoyo's fleeing jumbes. Abushiri finally was seized by Africans and handed to the Germans.

Wissmann rushed to Pangani to confront his enemy, the commissioner and Abushiri, Euan Smith learned, engaging "in earnest and animated conversation" until two hours before the Arab's execution. In a mockery of the principles they claimed to be advancing in Africa, Wissmann and his subordinates garbed Abushiri in his best clothes for photographing, then reposing the Arab, to mark German victory, "with a bare head, chains on his legs and arms and a halter around his neck." Abushiri, not unnaturally, since his captors had been behaving like civilized men, reportedly did not realize the Germans planned an immediate execution. Acting in the East Central African manner, the Arab, expecting a pardon, offered henceforth to serve the Germans. Then, so his captors alleged, when he realized the German intentions, Abushiri began blaming others for the main responsibility of opposing the Germans. Such statements, not in line with Abushiri's previous conduct as a war leader, must be doubted. It is certainly possible the Germans were constructing an unfavorable image for propaganda use in the continuing campaign. To conclude the sorry affair, "the ropes were so badly adjusted as visibly to prolong . . . suffering . . . for more than twenty minutes."[80]

Much information concerning the barbarous treatment of Abushiri and his colleagues probably came from Pangani's liwali, Suliman bin Nassir; he additionally told Khalifa that Abushiri had made statements to Wissmann "of a character highly injurious to H. H. and, indeed, directly implicating him in the recent disturbances on the German coast line." Khalifa, worried over the charges, had even more cause for unease when Wissmann, while dining with Euan Smith on December 16, the day after Abushiri's death, spoke of recovering a box of the Arab's documents, many containing "treasonable matter." Despite hints of the documents' contents, the only incriminating evidence the Germans apparently possessed against the sultan were Abushiri's last words, revelations including the assertion that he, if victorious, expected to become the sultan's liwali for the coast, explaining away lack of direct proof with claims of Khalifa's cleverness. The German government, however, realizing the unfinished conquest of the coast, recognized Khalifa's usefulness for restoring their territory's prosperity, joining the British in agreeing not to make Abushiri's reported last remarks public, treating as "most secret any statements . . . which may be damaging to the good faith of the Sultan of Zanzibar." Both governments reaffirmed commitment to maintaining "the supremacy of the Sultan of Zanzibar." Interestingly enough, during these deliberations the British learned from the Germans that Abushiri's documents included letters from William Mackinnon of the Imperial British East African Company which,

Salisbury confided to Euan Smith, "were full of most imprudent expressions against Germany and concerning his future plans." They too remained secret.[81]

Abushiri's death was a major blow to continued coastal resistance. He had been the only important leader prepared to leave his home territory, striking wherever the Germans appeared vulnerable. Abushiri did not have a successor, the inhabitants of each settlement usually waiting behind their defenses for the inevitable German attack. Wissmann's continuing triumphs convinced Semboja of the necessity of reaching accord. After Pangani's fall Semboja sent an agent, bearing gifts, to the Germans. Wissmann welcomed the opportunity for a peaceful arrangement with the formidable inland chieftain, in January 1890 dispatching K. W. Schmidt, along with agents of the German Plantation Society, to commence rebuilding the Lewa station. In ensuing negotiations the Shambaa leader formally pledged loyalty, accepting until his death in 1895 a monthly salary from the Germans, additionally agreeing to a 4,000 rupee compensation for the losses to the Meyer and Baumann caravan. When the two complained that the settlement slighted their interests, Wissmann forthrightly stressed that Semboja, a valuable addition to German ranks because of his strong local authority, had played a minimal role in opposing Germans.[82]

Wissmann resumed active campaigning on 4 January 1890, leading a large expedition against Sadani. Its inhabitants, sheltered behind earthworks, poured forth a heavy answering fire, the surrounding dense bush preventing significant hand-to-hand combat. In the end superior German firepower drove Sadani's defenders from the town. The engagement, the impressed Wissmann informed Smythies, "had been more real fighting than any that he had had." Returning again to Sadani at the end of January, the Germans attempted to storm Bwana Heri's nearby inland Palamakaa fortification, once more failing to capture the coastal chieftain. By March rumors of possible peace negotiations circulated, but another German attack near the end of March met the usual determined resistance; this time, however, the invaders remained to occupy the town's ruins. The situation hardly was satisfactory for either side, the fugitive Bwana Heri, with a 10,000 rupee reward offered for his capture, continuing active in Sadani's environs. Both sides now were ready for serious deliberations, the Germans requesting that Khalifa arrange a peace, consenting in advance to the reestablishment of Heri and his family in Sadani. The sultan at once began talks, with Wissmann hurrying back from his southern campaign to participate.[83] Heri offered to accept terms if restored to the position he possessed before the rising, if Zanzibar's foreign consuls guaranteed his safety, the request probably motivated by Abushiri's fate. The Germans, although refusing a role for foreign consuls, gave general acceptance. Heri refused to come to Zanzibar during the negotiations, doubtedless fearing both the Germans and Euan Smith, the latter still seeking the murderer of Brooks. On April 6 Bwana Heri, Jehazi—his chief of staff—and Abdullah, with about 400 followers, entered Sadani; the old warrior, as a sign of submission, awarded Wissmann his sword. The German reciprocated by supplying the ragged defenders with needed provisions, plus 2,000 rupees for reconstructing the town mosque.[84]

From the negotiations' onset Euan Smith had reminded Wissmann of the Sadani leader's alleged responsibility for the Brooks affair, accepting the German request to await the outcome of negotiations, then immediately renewing demands for satisfaction. Wissmann, less concerned with retribution for the death of a British missionary than for a stable peace with a formidable rival, first countered that the long, damaging hostilities had been enough punishment. When the aroused Briton firmly stressed the general opinion holding Heri culpable, Wissmann consented to taking some unspecified action within two or three months, adding that he personally regarded the "scoundrel" Abdullah as guilty. The British accepted the delay. During the interval Euan Smith gained new information, the most important coming from Charles Stokes, the recipient during long confabulations with Heri of the names of five supposed murderers, part of a group sent by the Sadani chieftain to capture Brooks, thus allowing Heri to emulate Abushiri by holding the Briton for "reward or ransom." The caravan men, however, judging as minimal their chances of sharing the ransom, killed Brooks for his property. The disorganized conditions of the war, explained Heri, had prevented punishment of the guilty individuals. It was a plausible story, usefully shifting blame from Sadani's important ruler. The Germans took no further action, despite British reminders during 1890 and 1891.[85]

Once the coastal centers north of Dar es Salaam fell, Wissmann turned attention to the southern coast where resistance groups had experienced few contacts with Europeans since the events of 1888. Indian traders remaining in most towns had not been harmed, although during 1889 they had encountered increasing pressures because of the blockade and general degeneration of commerce. The few inland Europeans similarly were untroubled, the Universities' Mission men in Newala traveling to Lindi without incident.[86] There were possibilities for peace, Wissmann standing prepared to negotiate with all but the Kilwa leadership, excluding the latter because of the deaths of the company agents. In early 1890 the Germans prepared to utilize Khalifa as intermediary, the sultan sending Hamid bin Suliman south with powers to disarm resisters. Salisbury stopped the involvement, warning a failure might later allow German claims of the sultan acting as an "embarassement to their action." The desire to end hostilities was obvious in some towns, Mkindani's leaders, for example, dispatching to the sultan a list of specifications for a settlement, basically asking for a return of the old coastal system. The Germans delegated Nassir bin Suliman for deliberations with receptive leaders, with tentative arrangements probably being concluded at Mkindani and Sudi. With arrival of new Sundanese recruits, Wissmann was ready for a final offensive; in early May 1890 a large expedition arrived before the strongly defended Kilwa. Following heavy shelling the Germans occupied a virtually empty town, the defenders fleeing before the invaders' superior might. Later the Germans apprehended three individuals determined guilty of the deaths of the company agents; they were executed publicly. Along the remainder of the coast the Germans encountered little opposition. At Lindi there was minor fighting, some fearful Arabs forcing over twenty Indians with them into the bush. When Wissmann refused all negotiations without their return, the Arabs complied, local leader Said bin Salim arranging terms. In most settlements the existing leaders, subsequent to surrender, entered German service.[87] The entire coast, at last, was under final German control.

During the last two decades scholars have undertaken the analysis of African opposition to European invaders, attempting to determine patterns of resistance. The Arab-German war has been awarded a place in this literature, Abushiri and other participants gaining honored niches in the gallery of resisters of Europe's imperialism. There is little argument concerning the causes of the Arab-German war. Salisbury and other contemporaries stressed the slave trade as a prime underlying reason for the troubles, with a few modern interpreters concurring. But most individuals of the late 1880s realized the German company did not plan significant steps against slavery or the slave trade. The principal reason for conflict was the treaty forced upon Arabs and Africans and the subsequent inept company actions.[88] In the most extreme recent interpretation of the war, Walter Rodney asserted that all revolutions, including Abushiri's, "contributed to greater unity and ultimate freedom," a generalization unfortunately too encompassing to possess any meaning. The hostilities along the coast certainly added little to the growth of unity in the future Tanzania. Abushiri fought without broad support from the peoples of the coast, at the height of his career leading about 2000 followers, the usual core of Arabs and Africans numbering only 300.[89] When the Arab leader did secure African backing from the Mbunga, they proved as interested in attacking other Africans as in fighting Germans. By the time the war terminated, the legacy was as much of divisiveness as of unity.

Another exponent of the resistance school, Robert D. Jackson, singled out three individuals—Abushiri, Bwana Heri, Semboja—as vital leaders of the rising. "These men," he postulated, "had developed an entirely new vision of the political future of the Tanganyikan coast and had rejected both the Germans and the Sultan." Jackson's interpretation appears the exact opposite of reality, moreover demonstrating the scholarly dangers of linking resistance ideology with insufficient knowledge of events.[90] Perhaps Abushiri might be regarded as a new type of leader, but the evidence is not overly strong, the Arab rather appearing to be a very typical member of the Arab coastal leadership springing to defend his threatened home-land's existing political, economic, and social organization. Abushiri did not attempt the destruction of the sultan's existing role: if victorious the Arab, recognizing the need for the island's commercial facilities, most likely would have come to terms with Zanzibar's ruler. But, responding as any dynamic coastal chieftain would, Abushiri demonstrated through negotiations with Germans his readiness, if necessary, to substitute Germans for the sultan, as long as the former granted terms allowing return to prewar conditions. The other principal resistance commander, Bwana Heri, clearly fought only to preserve patterns of life existing in his small state. Semboja does not belong in the company of Abushiri and Heri. Enjoying a different, less intimate, relationship with Zanzibar, Semboja, once fighting erupted, limited participation to sending minimal assistance to Pangani. Closely observing Arab defeats, he made the best possible terms for his state.

Khalifa has not received much consideration as a resistance figure in the Arab-German war, treatment that parallels the usual neglect awarded the career of the last independent BuSaidi ruler. John Iliffe, for example, dismisses Khalifa as "an ignorant and unstable British puppet," blaming the sultan for setting the stage for hostilities through a supposed desire to secure monopoly profits from the German concession arrangements. Thus, concludes Iliffe, the war was a "popular uprising" against both Germans and Umani, with Khalifa working with the Germans to preserve even a limited hold upon his former subordinates. But Khalifa signed the concession only because of overwhelming German and British pressure. Afterward Khalifa consistently did all possible within his limited means to hinder the Germans. He delayed making necessary decisions, simultaneously stimulating resistance among coastal inhabitants by letting all know, in very clear terms, his opposition to the German presence. The Germans and others noted the sultan's efforts, although sufficient evidence never emerged to allow formal connection of Khalifa and the resisters.[91] Khalifa accomplished what was most important, maintenance of an attitude of resistance to the hated Germans, providing thereby a useful focus for the opposition to the intruders into the Zanzibar dominions, even attempting occasionally a more active role through endeavoring without success, to draw other powers into supporting the Arabs.[92] Khalifa deserves rehabilitation. Despite the constraints of his office, Khalifa strove courageously against the enemies of the Arab system. In the fair judgment of one local chronicler: Khalifa "dwelled well with the people as he cared for the common people and the populace loved him . . ."[93]

While the Germans regained possession of the coast, they simultaneously maintained steady pressure upon Khalifa. A principal cause of friction was the determination of the final sum to be paid when, according to the concession, reckoning was drawn from the first three years' receipts. The decision, binding the future, was important, affecting a principal source of Khalifa's revenues. Unfortunately for Khalifa, at the end of the first year, revenues had fallen to a sum 80 percent below average: the three years' receipts were estimated at 13,500,000 rupees, or 450,000 yearly. Khalifa held the average should be at least 600,000. The Germans made the ongoing talks even more unpleasant, stressing the old threat of making the sultan responsible for total government and company war expenses. The tension exacerbated in January 1890, the unpopular Vohsen returning to carry forward negotiations.[94]

Khalifa was spared resolving the problem, the harassed ruler, hardly free from pressure for an instant since becoming sultan, dying suddenly on February 19, 1890. His departure, unregretted by most Europeans, caused no transition problems. Ali attained his reward for ceasing to plot, by general European agreement succeeding to Zanzibar's throne.[95] The new sultan, with close ties to Euan Smith and facing immediate German pressures, naturally fell into the British camp, so much so that by mid-1890 French representative Ottavi reported Arabs scornfully describing Ali as "mamluk" of the British. But Ali had limited options, any ruler of Zanzibar, even more than in the past, holding office only if backed by a strong foreign power. As Euan Smith warned, "the comfort of his position" depended upon maintaining satisfactory relations with Germany, a course possible only through British support. Ali accepted the inevitable, in June concluding a provisional accord for eventual acceptance of British protection, in return gaining a guarantee of his throne.[96]

The German pressure persisted, Ali receiving an offer of 2,000,000 marks for cessation of his coastal strip, plus a waiver of all German claims (then estimated at 1,000,000 marks). "Is it fit for me to hear such words and could a Sultan tell such things to his people?" countered Ali. "Is my kingdom a camel that is to be bargained for and sold in a few minutes?" The Germans raised the bid to 3,000,000 marks. In Europe the negotiations were more sedate, by early July Salisbury indicating he judged not a "bad bargain" an arrangement awarding Ali a capital sum paying, at 8 percent interest, about £2,000 or £2,500 yearly. On September 25 the Germans, for about £200,000, invested by the British in the sultan's name, received outright possession of the coast opposite Zanzibar. Ali, much regretting the loss of the heart of Zanzibar's dominions, complained vigorously that the amount was too small, but the time had passed for anyone to heed the protests of Zanzibar's sultan.[97]

The German coast deliberations accompanied other discussions between Germany and Britain leading to general resolution of their remaining East African differences. A treaty of June 1890 gave Britain a protectorate over the sultan's island and coastal dominions. Ali agreed to this disposition of his state, but any supposedly free decision by the hapless Arab sovereign was aptly ridiculed by French Foreign Minister Ribot's cynical reminder to the British ambassador: "Your Lordship had recently described him as an Indian rubber manikin who could be pinched into any shape."[98] In Zanzibar most Arabs, understanding the impossibility of preserving independence, quietly accepted the protectorate, apparently considering the British a lesser evil than the Germans. The resident European merchants, Germans included, also generally favored the outcome. But the Germans of Wissmann's victorious army, as well as imperial enthusiasts in general, were shocked at the decision, regarding Zanzibar as the ultimate seal for their East African triumphs. It had not been an unreasonable hope: by this time Germans in Zanzibar outnumbered other Europeans by ten to one. Wissmann particularly reacted to the island's fate, finding the verdict, made without his participation, an injurious slight to the prestige of a man openly advertising himself as very close to the German emperor. "German discontent here . . . is very marked," chortled Euan Smith, the "Acting Commissioner"—Wissmann was in Europe—"and whole body [of] Wissmann's officers are meditating immediate resignation."[99] European diplomatic considerations had prevailed, the British protectorate sealing the end of Zanzibar's independence.

In preceding years the northern coast of the Zanzibar dominions had been the subject of discussions between Barghash and British interests grouped around William Mackinnon. In a preliminary agreement of May 24, 1887, a new organization, the British East African Company, received for fifty years full political and judicial rights along the coastline between the Umba and Kipini, in return annually paying the sultan a sum at least equal to existing customs collections. A long period elapsed before completion of final concession arrangements, but on September 3, 1888, the British concern, henceforth known as the Imperial British East African Company, received its charter. During the interval, company representatives were active in Zanzibar and along the coast, endeavoring to resolve problems potentially leading to crises once administration of Arab territory began.[100]

The most obvious impediment to satisfactory Arab-British relations remained the long irritating presence of runaway slaves in the Christian missions surrounding Mombasa. The missionaries naturally had viewed

German aggressions against Zanzibar with apprehension, fearing the effect upon their Muslim neighbors' attitudes. Since the British provided Barghash and Khalifa the only hope for European assistance, the missionaries escaped harm, even though unrest caused by quarrels over slaves persisted. In mid-1885, for instance, the British vice-consul in Mombasa had flogged Swahili individuals caught dealing in slaves, the punishment resulting in a public meeting of Mombasans dispatching a protest to the sultan. Barghash, immersed in efforts to save Zanzibar, ignored it.[101] Nevertheless, the runaway issue continued fundamental to local Arab opinion. The Rabai station had grown to considerable size, the missionaries admitting the presence of about 2,000 Christian inhabitants, while an official British visitor reported a community of around 3,000. William Jones and other African Christians managed the settlement; the residents clustered in quarters comprised of houses built in the styles of their respective homelands. The Bombay Christians persisted in acting independently. When, in early 1886, the mission Europeans appointed an indigenous African Christian as an evangelist, the Bombay group, resenting the step, burned his house during the night, the unfortunate African barely escaping alive. The size and ethnic complexity of Rabai made effective working of European authority impossible: even if missionaries had attempted controls, their supposed charges probably would not have obeyed. Instead the Britons continually complained to the consular staff in Zanzibar about Arab conduct. But visiting official E. Berkeley in June 1887 blamed the missionaries for local frictions, upholding Arab complaints and working out an agreement with the liwali and missionaries allowing aggrieved owners of missing slaves the right of search at Rabai. The free African community, however, did not modify its conduct; when one owner ventured to utilize the accord, the Africans advised a speedy exit. Subsequently, even though Jones personally offered to conduct inquiring Arabs around the settlement, no owners dared visit Rabai. Despite other consular interventions, the missionaries continued to avoid serious consideration of the slave issue, acting either from indifference or from ignorance, perhaps self-imposed, of the magnitude of the number of slaves living on mission land. The missionaries instead worried more about the possibly unsettling effects of British administration, especially after war commenced in the German sphere, W. S. Price emphasizing his determination to uphold the mission separate from all company doings.[102]

Meanwhile company officials designed positive measures for winning Arab support, thus providing Mbarak bin Rashid, still the most influential individual around Mombasa, and still raiding his neighbors, an opportunity for profit. Berkeley, arriving in the concession to conclude treaties with groups residing beyond the sultan's dominions, stressed that Mbarak's proferred "friendship was a matter of real importance to the success of the proceedings," thus promising the Arab full utilization of company influence in persuading Barghash to allow a return to Gazi and the release of captured followers. In a June 9, 1887, accord Mbarak, declaring that he "placed all his country and peoples under the British East African Association," hoisted the Zanzibar flag.[103] The stubborn Barghash adamantly refused any change in Mbarak's status, but Khalifa, sympathetic to all his brother's enemies, complied. Mbarak quickly sent his son and most important subordinates to Zanzibar to mark the new ruler's accession, the Mazrui party returning with rich presents, $1,000 in cash, and a promise that Mbarak would regain Gazi. In July Khalifa sent Mathews to Mombasa to accompany Mbarak to Zanzibar, the former rebel utilizing the visit for private conversations with company leaders, apparently agreeing, in return for a subsidy, to recognize company authority and cooperate in measures against the slave trade.[104]

The initial company staff, headed by George Mackenzie, a man with extensive experience in Muslim lands, landed in Zanzibar on October 6, 1888. Mackenzie promised to work quietly within the concession boundaries, steadily building a favorable reputation by successful development measures in coastal towns. To assist, and perhaps help moderate, the company, Khalifa seconded Mathews to their service, all arriving in Mombasa on October 15, reassuring the Arabs about the future, confirming existing officials' positions, and commencing repair of a mosque. Mbarak conferred with Mackenzie and Mathews, Mackenzie afterwards recommending that the Mazrui help to administer the coast between Wanga and Kipini, along with ten principal followers receiving company salaries. In addition to a monthly payment of 1,000 rupees, Mbarak also collected 2,000 rupees for keeping armed men ready for company service. Mackenzie, obviously determined to retain Mbarak's support, explained: "He is well placed there [Gazi] to stem any tide that may set from the South. He is a man we *must* keep in favour." By March the sultan did seem disposed to appoint Mbarak liwali of the coast, demonstrating a receptive attitude by returning all remaining seized properties and individuals.[105]

The missionaries threatened company endeavors, the runaway slave problem at once presenting the wary officials with a first significant confrontation with Arabs. "The missionaries are just as great slave holders as we are," the slave owners of Mombasa said to Mackenzie, "the only difference is they take or get slaves for nothing while we have to pay for ours." To signal their distress the Muslims asked abolition of the mission. Price firmly contested the charges, asserting that the Arabs "have absolutely no cause for complaint," uncharitably alleging any missing slaves probably were at Fulladoyo or Ribe, and blaming much of the Arab attitude on Mathews' conduct, characterizing the general as a friend to Arabs and an enemy of the missions. An exasperated Euan Smith rejected the effort to avoid responsibility for runaways, upholding Arab protests while warning Price that the constant Arab irritation in seeing their slaves protected by the British flag endangered both company and missions. Promising measures "of an exceedingly drastic and stringent character" as the likely outcome of failing to resolve the issue, the consul in the meantime announced dispatch of Hamid bin Sulayman and over 100 soldiers to strengthen Mombasa's liwali. Mackenzie, working skillfully, managed to shelve the Arab resolution, stilling protests by creating a commission—himself, Mathews, liwali Salim bin Khalfan bin Amir al BuSaidi, and two members of the Rabai community—with the task of ascertaining the size of Rabai's fugitive population. Price agreed to surrender any slaves discovered.[106]

Before investigations commenced, Price, suddenly recognizing the seriousness of matters once denied, directed Jones "to make a clean sweep of the settlement." Worriedly confiding to mission headquarters reports of about 400 refugees prepared to defend their freedom, with aid anticipated from other Rabai Christians, Price discovered matters passing even beyond control of Jones. When Price's count proved faulty—there were about 900 fugitives—the missionaries persisted in denying responsibility; Binns, then in Britain, elaborated the many difficulties of regulating mission Africans' "free masonry," their "false practices," such as name changing, making slave discovery impossible. Finally, and unfairly, Binns blamed all on Jones: "He will not give up a slave under any conditions whatever, if he can possibly help it."[107]

To avoid the unwanted crises, Mackenzie quickly changed the original scheme. Apparently judging that only about 100 to 150 slaves were involved, Mackenzie offered an arrangement enabling slaves, for $25, to purchase freedom. The Arabs, doubtless grateful at the prospect of gaining some return for lost property, knowing all too well the Rabai Africans' demeanor, agreed without demur. Calling the numbers found "nothing less than a revelation," Price, bowing to government pressure, accepted Mackenzie's solution. But more and more slaves left hiding, the final total for Rabai and other stations reaching over 1,400. After once more altering his scheme—the British government finding the slaves' working for the company to earn the freedom money little to their liking—Mackenzie gained financial resources from private and official sources, paying £3,100 to liberate the fugitives.[108]

Despite the arrival of smaller numbers of runaways at mission stations during the next few years, the long-standing problem at last had been resolved. With a firm British administration seeking coastal stability, Arabs for a time were guaranteed safe possession of slaves, a rather ironic outcome of the much-heralded European drive in East Central Africa against slavery and the slave trade. But, as elsewhere in the African colonial world, humanitarian sentiments regarding slavery considerably declined once a specific European power gained responsibility for governing peoples who possessed slaves. The British company demonstrated its position when the question of the continuing legality of slave-holding within the Zanzibar sultanate surfaced. Euan Smith, in December 1888 suggesting the time was ripe for abolishing slavery in Zanzibar and Pemba, thought the step might fittingly accompany ending the naval blockade of the sultan's coast. Broaching the inclusion of the company sphere to Mackenzie, the consul encountered stiff opposition. "Slavery under existing circumstances here is an absolute necessity," reacted Mackenzie. "If suddenly abolished the country would be utterly ruined."[109] Discounting serious resistance in Zanzibar and Pemba to determined British action, Euan Smith, despite contrary German reports of Arab opposition for ending slavery, persisted in pressing for abolition, by the close of December alleging consent from Khalifa and the principal Arabs. As was his wont, the consul attributed decisions to the sultan which, if actually made, were the result only of Khalifa's desire to be rid of the overbearing British agent. When inaction followed, Euan Smith noted Ali bin Said's willingness to strike against slavery, the Foreign Office, however, ignoring the already rejected plans for removing Khalifa from the throne.[110]

While temporarily in Europe, with the slavery issue remaining under consideration, Euan Smith traveled to Germany for conversations with Bismarck. The consul discovered the chancellor at first hesitant, fearing consequences in German territory. Finally, Bismarck gave approval for action to mark the end of the blockade.[111] Bowing to British and German desires, Khalifa publicly proclaimed on 20 September 1889 the abolition of slavery for new arrivals into Zanzibar and Pemba after November 1, 1889, also conceding to Britain and Germany rights to search vessels for slaves in Zanzibar waters. Portal additionally secured from the sultan a promise to free all slaves born after 1 January 1890, a concession not included in the public proclamation since it went beyond the German consul's instructions.[112]

The triumph turned out stillborn, the September proclamation gaining minimal notice in Zanzibar or along the coast. When in January 1890 Wissmann, pleading ignorance, asked the returned Euan Smith for clarification, the consul admitted removal of all notices from Zanzibar's public places and the nondispatch of copies to the coast. Khalifa side-stepped his promises, warning Euan Smith that actual enforcement might end with abandonment and death for all affected children, another Arab adding that liberation would lead owners to "send their slaves in thousands 'en masse' simultaneously to Zanzibar to demand work and maintainance from foreign consuls." Nonplussed, Euan Smith recommended abandoning compliance until Britain possessed sufficient authority to enforce obedience.[113]

With the declaration of Britain's Zanzibar protectorate a new decree forbidding buying or selling slaves was promulgated on August 1, 1890. Ignoring the extreme opposition, Euan Smith predicted acceptance since the Arabs feared even more stringent measures. "This decree," he exulted, "really settles the whole question of slavery in the Zanzibar dominions." But the first publicly posted copy of the regulation was torn down, an armed guard being required to keep others in view. Apprehensive European residents at night posted guards, fearing a general rising. Resistance similarly came from the Germans, their representative first protesting a step "injuriously affecting the Arabs on the German Coast line," even though the decree concerned only the islands. German Governor J. von Soden took a calmer view, however. Not intending to enforce the potentially disturbing regulation in his recently conquered colony, he promised cooperation at an unspecified future date. Further opposition came from the British-occupied coast, where Mbarak was reported to be antagonistic to the changes. Both French and American consuls predicted the decree's early demise, the former's opinion buttressed by Khalifa explaining he had issued the proclamation merely as a sop "to satisfy public opinion in England," expecting affairs in Zanzibar and Pemba to continue unchanged.[114] The consuls were correct; Zanzibar's population ignored the slavery regulations. Euan Smith soon admitted as much, countering British company opposition by explaining drastic enforcement never had been intended. By 1891 Mathews reported the open selling of slaves, business simply moving to less obvious locations.[115] Slavery remained a legal institution in Zanzibar and Pemba until 1897 and in British East Africa until 1907. In German East Africa, slavery continued to be legal throughout the German period, finally losing recognition after the British World War I conquest.[116] Clearly, the crusade against slavery assumed a different aspect once lands dominated by Arabs fell to Europeans, abolition then signifying potential economic and political disruption. Freedom for individual Africans had to await the administrative convenience of the new rulers.

The British attitude toward slavery, matched by careful company treatment of Arabs, kept the British-administered coast tranquil for some years. "Altho[ugh] the people were familiar with the disturbances going on in the south," commented a British visitor to Lamu in November 1888, "they were unaffected and going on in the even tenor of their way." Others, not responsible for keeping the peace in the sultan's dominions, poured scorn upon the undramatic stance of company administrators, H. F. Behr, for one, discovering a British variant of the old divide and rule technique, "pay and rule."[117] The company directors, comparing the peace in their sphere with the fighting along the German coast, justly paid the critics little heed. About the only practical change occurring in the northern coastal administration was the company paying of the sultan's troops, a welcome step for the soldiers because of Khalifa's financial problems. Mackenzie adroitly gained additional goodwill, while working to strengthen the company position, by advancing one quarter of the capital for a venture by local traders seeking a route to Tabora, hoping thereby to secure ivory blocked inland by the Arab-German war.[118]

Although Mbarak bin Rashid never received the sought-after appointment as liwali of the British coast, his relations with the company continued satisfactory. When Wissmann accused the Gazi Arab of aiding Bwana Heri, Mackenzie sprang to Mbarak's defense, proving the charges false. Mbarak, in fact, stayed free from all involvement in the German war, refusing action when one northern firebrand in 1889 unsuccessfully "strongly urged all the other coast chiefs to join hands with one another and with Bushire and to drive all the Europeans, Germans and English, into the sea." Relations between Euan Smith and Mbarak did cool somewhat by the second half of 1890, the consul charging failure in living up to the company agreement because of charges of taking slaves. The usual complaints against Mbarak's raiding also continued. Company director Francis de Winton, stressing the need for quiet in the concession, ignored the strictures, even defending Mbarak when a letter of encouragement sent to the unfriendly ruler of Witu was discovered.[119]

Left virtually unsupervised by the British until 1894, Mbarak profited by utilizing his company position for personal ends.[120] Then, in 1895, a Mazrui succession dispute caused a final crisis.[121] Salim bin Khamis of Takaungu died in February, a company official designating his son Rashid, considered "well-disposed to English Rule," as liwali. Salim's nephew, Mbarak bin Rashid—hereafter called the younger Mbarak—disputed the choice, forcing an unanticipated confrontation between Briton and Arab. The British administration in East Africa, led by Arthur H. Hardinge, just then assuming control over company territories, had not been consulted concerning Rashid's selection. Although doubting the wisdom of the choice, Hardinge felt obliged to accept Rashid. The younger Mbarak persisted in opposition, finally attacking the new liwali. It was impossible for Mbarak, receiving over 1,900 rupees monthly for upholding British authority, to remain uninvolved. "His interest," said Hardinge, "was on our side, but his honour and prestige with his own people on the other." In discussions with Mathews and other Britons, Mbarak initially proceeded cautiously, requesting a free hand in resolving the succession quarrel, and suggesting that the younger Mbarak be placed in his custody. Suspicious that Mbarak was somehow advancing his own interests, the British refused. Hardinge finally offered Mbarak only one choice: unconditional surrender of his younger namesake. The Briton knowingly accepted the risks of refusal. "A conflict with him was inevitable, sooner or later," he postulated, "if our authority on the mainland was to be more than a name: and we may as well get it over at the outset."

Mbarak characteristically did not bow, joining the combat against the British. Many coastal Arabs and Africans sided with the resisters. In Zanzibar many Arabs, including the sultan, showed sympathy for Mbarak, but apart from a tense atmosphere and probable arms smuggling, there was no open opposition. Mbarak again proved militarily skillful, requiring Hardinge to call Indian reinforcements to end the war. After a difficult campaign the old Arab accepted defeat, crossing into German East Africa in April 1896 with about 3,000 followers. The British later allowed most of the rank and file to return home, but Mbarak ended his days in morose exile in the German colony.[122]

Mbarak's defeat marked the beginning of permanent eclipse for the British coast's Arab community. Although the Arabs for some time continued trading into the interior, they gradually sank into a position of economic and political insignificance. Hardinge, regarded by some as a pro-Arab official, did have plans to utilize Arabs in government service, yet neither he nor his successors ever implemented them. When the legal status of slavery ended in 1907, the Arabs, losing their work force, faced economic ruin, subsequent unsympathetic British policies sealing decline. The later move of British East Africa's capital inland to Nairobi confirmed Arab relegation to a largely ignored niche among the colony's peoples.[123]

The transformation in the island and coastal world was a deathblow to the East Central African Arab political and economic system. The Arabs still maintained bastions in inland regions, especially the Congo, but the loss of Zanzibar and the coast presaged final European triumph.

11 War in the Interior

> We must be prepared for a combination of the Arabs of
> the interior against European progress generally and
> whatever the result of the conflict which will ensue, the
> existing trade . . . will be ruined.
>
> —*Frederick Holmwood*

THERE HAD BEEN signs of confrontation between Arabs and Europeans in
inland East Central Africa even before the direct stimulation toward hostilities provided by Germany's offensive against Zanzibar. Some Europeans in the 1880s, observing the increasing difficulties with Arabs,
advanced the theory of a widespread movement requiring central direction
and inspiration. Their thinking regarding Islam, conditioned by the
Mahdi's triumph in the Sudan, awarded a unity simply not existing in the
African Muslim world.[1] Henry O'Neill, British consul in Mozambique,
reasoned of the fighting at Karonga: "It is at Zanzibar that the chief actors
reside: thence the sinews of war have been furnished: and only at that
place therefore can the evil be really nipped." In Zanzibar Euan Smith,
although denying Khalifa's participation, concurred, speculating: "It may
be that . . . it is their ambition to establish in Central Equatorial Africa
another Mahommedan Kingdom." Later he became more positive: "There
is reason to believe that this is the result of a plan of organized action
among all the Arabs of the interior."[2]

The supposed fears of the Arabs concerning the future of the slave trade
strengthened European conclusions regarding a general stirring among
Muslims. The Germans, through the slave theme, quickly connected the
Karonga war with their coast problems. A prime exponent of this general
view was the well-known missionary Robert Laws, who insisted the Arab-
European fighting at Karonga was "no mere isolated spurt . . . but part of
a concerted scheme for resuscitating the slave trade to more than its previous vigour. The slave trade and this alone is the mainspring of the whole."[3]

The Arab conspiracy theory was revived during the 1950s by Roland Oliver and other scholars asserting opinions familiar during the latter part of the nineteenth century. Oliver, for the years between 1884 and 1888, spoke of a concerted movement encompassing all Arab centers from Buganda to Lake Malawi. "Missionaries . . . noticed two things of profound significance," Oliver claimed, "that the Arabs were now aiming at political power, and that they were seeking to drive out the European."[4] The argument, both in the nineteenth and twentieth centuries, is based upon a fundamental misinterpretation of the nature of the East Central African Arab presence.[5] The firm direction some Europeans postulated for the various interior conflicts contradicted their usual remarks concerning Zanzibar's lack of authority in regions away from the coast. As the following sections will demonstrate, the Arabs reacted in specific localities to specific European pressures. By the 1880s the Europeans of several nationalities represented in East Central Africa were interfering with economic, political, and social patterns established by Arabs. When local pressure became too intense, war resulted. In a few instances the Sultan of Zanzibar became involved in the often reluctant decision to fight. In most cases, with troubles enough of his own in Zanzibar, the Arab ruler left his subjects and allies to make their own decisions, subsequently providing, whenever possible, what little help he could for their cause.

12 Lake Malawi

> I have now come to this conclusion, after five years' expe-
> rience in this part of Africa, that the presence of Arabs is
> incompatible with the introduction of European civilisa-
> tion, and, sooner or later, the Arabs must go from Cen-
> tral Africa.
>
> —*Harry Johnston*

THE GERMAN INTRUSION into the sultan's dominions had no immediate
impact among Arabs of the Lake Malawi region. The trade from the lake
to the coast, both in ivory and slaves, continued with full vigor, Arabs and
Europeans sharing in apparent harmony the market at the busy commercial center of Karonga. The Arabs, grouped behind Mlozi, Msalama, Kopa
Kopa, and Salim bin Najim, faced African Lakes Company agent L. Monteith Fotheringham. The company during 1885 had considerably
strengthened its local influence by signing agreements placing some
Ngonde under British protection. The accords did not receive official
recognition, but their conclusion left the company men with a special
relationship to the Ngonde.[1] Later, European participants described hostilities as inevitable, the result of a long-planned Arab scheme,[2] but this
characterization was largely a retroactive effort to place blame upon Arabs.

During July 1887 a large caravan commanded by Ramadan, the Baluchi
subordinate of southern Lake Tanganyika Arab leader Kabunda, arrived in
Karonga bearing an estimated 15,000 pounds of ivory. As often happened, Fotheringham lacked adequate merchandise for completing transactions with Arab visitors; Ramadan and his followers, while awaiting
return of the company steamer *Ilala,* settled down to enjoy the amenities
of Karonga life.[3] Then occurred an apparently unpremeditated act of violence, not an unusual happening in any of the interior's bustling trading
centers. According to the Europeans, accepting the Ngonde explanation,
some of Ramadan's men entered Kasote's village, there arguing with an

African who, under the influence of alcohol, struck an Arab with an ax. In retaliation the caravan men seized some livestock. It was a dangerous moment, Kasote informing Fotheringham he planned to attack an Arab settlement. Much of the threatening talk, however, was part of the normal negotiating process for redressing an alleged affront. But affairs began moving out of control when, during discussions between the contending parties, an Arab from another group wounded the African leader, thus stimulating a general outburst that resulted in the killing of Kasote and his son by Ramadan's men. Fotheringham refused Ngonde demands for honoring the company treaties by leading them against the Arabs. Carefully guarding his ivory stores Fotheringham, not fearing involvement, seemingly regarded the unrest as one of the usual problems caused by Arab caravans waiting for completion of business, seeking to utilize his local prominence by mediating the dispute. The Arabs, gathered behind the influential Salim bin Najim, rebuffed the Briton's first proposal involving surrendering the concerned Arabs, reasonably offering instead payment of compensation to the aggrieved Africans. The latter, used to the interplay of such negotiations, rejected the first sum suggested, threatening to resume the fighting, but soon after closing the quarrel by accepting a larger amount. The affair had been a normal occurrence, settled without inordinate bloodshed. What might have been a dangerous incident passed, all in Karonga returning to their usual daily patterns. Salim bin Najim, without fears for the future, journeyed to the coast, leaving much valuable property with his remaining associates. The Europeans were equally unconcerned about the future, company agent Nicoll leaving Karonga, accompanied by many African employees.

There seemed little reason to expect a different outcome when new disorders occurred at the beginning of October. In another fracas the chief of Mpata, Mwinyi Mtete, was killed by Arabs, the Ngonde claiming that an argument over the price of sugar cane caused the Arabs to open fire, the latter countering that Mtete acted first. Followers of Mtete, Mlozi later asserted, seized an Arab slave, accepting a cloth for ransom, but then not returning the captive, the treachery leading friends of the slave to kill Mtete. Mlozi professed unawareness of his people's involvement, a believable statement in view of subsequent happenings. The Ngonde, in this case not close to the company and not seeking its mediation, reacted to their leader's loss by striking suddenly at the Arabs, killing about thirty women—some of them Mlozi's wives—and five men. Peacefully purchasing foodstuffs, and not expecting difficulties, they were unprotected. Naturally enraged, the Arabs counterattacked. Once more Fotheringham had to decide his role, the Ngonde, as the Arabs began winning the fighting, bringing considerable pressure upon their only available source for outside support. To the watching Europeans, even those who discounted a preconceived Arab plan, the disorders provided Mlozi and his colleagues a long-awaited opportunity for seizing the lakeside settlement and endangering the company position. Still, proof is absent for justifying a preconceived Arab attack. Certainly the Europeans must have recognized that, even if the Arabs did plan to impose domination on the Ngonde, striking the company station, home of their yet useful and valued trading partners, was not a necessary next step.

Fotheringham opted to attempt to end hostilities, making contact with the still-waiting Ramadan. But, reported the Briton, Ramadan rudely announced fighting would continue until "the country was now the Arabs and Mlozi was the Sultan of Konde." The Arabs, added Ramadan, intended to expel the defeated Ngonde, settling in their place the Henga, a lakeside people who had fled the Ngoni earlier and been allowed by the Ngonde to settle in the region. The Henga joined the Arabs, according to some even stimulating them to greater activity.[4] Ramadan clearly demonstrated minimal animosity toward Fotheringham, cautioning the European to remain in the company station if shooting began, the thought probably prompted mostly by fears for his ivory. Not surprisingly Fotheringham, in constant communication with Ngonde leaders, openly refused recognition of Mlozi's claimed dominance, asserting that he planned to write the British consul about the ongoing troubles. Mlozi "defies the Consul to do anything," said Fotheringham, calling the quarrel, because of Arab losses, a matter for Arabs and Africans alone.

Until mid-October Fotheringham avoided actions that might possibly motivate Arab inclusion of Europeans in the Ngonde disagreement. Despite stiff African resistance, the Arabs and their allies seized many Ngonde villages. Three settlements near the company station, however, were left alone, numerous refugees seeking shelter in the security provided by European proximity. Fotheringham attempted to intervene on the refugees' behalf, asking for assurances of the three villages' continued safety. The Arabs refused. The refugees then began to leave, the Arabs, taking the villages, informing the protesting Fotheringham they could return only upon payment of tribute. During this dangerous period the company agent acted as a careful diplomat, receiving the Kyungu at the station, but requesting departure when combats occurred nearby. Mlozi responded with equal reserve, assuring Fotheringham that he did not intend to attack Europeans, in return asking similar assurances. Fotheringham avoided commitment, beginning in his station what he described as defensive preparations. The rearrival of the *Ilala* helped lessen tension between Arabs and Europeans, Ramadan and the agents discussing delayed business affairs even as Fotheringham continued fruitless mediation efforts. Ramadan remained disappointed, sufficient merchandise not coming in the steamer, without complaining excessively about the new delay, a fair indication that the Arabs lacked plans for offensive action against the African Lakes Company.

The fighting intensified in mid-October; on one occasion men of the Arabs and Europeans—each claiming the other fired first—exchanged shots near the station. To prevent escalation, Fotheringham hurriedly sent Mlozi his view of the incident, the message leading to an important conference attended by Fotheringham, Mlozi, Msalama, and Salim bin Nassir, the latter recently arrived from the Nsenga Arab community. Mlozi advanced his explanation for the war, Fotheringham concluding that the Arab had abandoned the goal of ruling all Ngonde, promising to leave free the company station and three adjacent villages. Mlozi, nevertheless, did intend to continue the war against the Kyungu. After the meeting the Arabs evacuated the three villages, although, for whatever reason, soon returning. All stayed quiet, the *Ilala* sailing for the south on October 19. While inconclusive talks went on between Arabs and Europeans, some displaced Ngonde began to return to swampy lands near their lost villages, beginning minor hostilities that culminated on October 27 in a major Arab and Henga attack, the fighting closing with the defeat of the Kyungu. Blaming the extensive Ngonde losses on Arab treachery, the Europeans pictured the combats as unprovoked massacres, reacting by stepping up the hitherto desultory process of fortifying their station.

The *Ilala* reappeared on November 4 with a load of trade goods and a small group of European reinforcements, among them Consul Henry O'Neill from Mozambique. A. G. Hawes, consul for the lake area, had been absent when the steamer reached Blantyre; the visiting O'Neill, after reading the letters requesting consular assistance, decided to attempt arranging peace.[5] While Ramadan and other Arabs settled accounts, O'Neill assumed command of the Europeans, stressing the need for remaining on the defensive. After the *Ilala*'s departure the settlement was peaceful, both Britons and Arabs passing to and from the company headquarters on commercial matters. O'Neill, meantime, with little to offer the victorious Arabs, vainly endeavored to negotiate accord between Ngonde and Arabs. The Europeans made one vital decision during this period, offering refuge to many defeated Ngonde; by mid-November 1,500 gathered around the station. The Arabs, in turn, may have suspected Fotheringham and his compatriots, persistently upholding Ngonde interests, of intending action on the Africans' behalf. Nonetheless, at that moment, the Arabs appeared as little organized for war as the British.

Then, war came quickly, minor hostilities beginning on November 23, the next day the Europeans opening fire on advancing Arab forces. Driven back without difficulty, the Arabs besieged the station. How do we, a century later, assess responsibility for the war? The British of the 1880s, plus their modern spokesman A. J. Hanna, considered the Europeans forced to choose between maintaining their version of order at Karonga or recognizing the consequences of Arab domination. "If the white men remain," said a missionary, "it will be only by the permission of the Arabs and on payment of powder, cloth and caps." The unstated but assumed implication was that the Arab alternative was unthinkable for representatives of European civilization.[6] Modern scholars have offered more balanced opinions concerning the conflict, stressing changes in the local balance of power leading to friction and the possible planned political ambitions of Mlozi,[7] or the stubborn European refusal to accept Arab efforts to resolve their African quarrel without mutual hostilities.[8] The evidence supports the latter view, Mlozi and the Arabs, whether or not actively plotting eventual war with the Ngonde, moved offensively only when problems with Africans extended beyond the normal, ever present, minor quarrels. But the general European resolve of the late 1880s for subduing Arabs inevitably drew representatives of other European interest groups into a war originally between Arabs, Africans, and British traders. The Arabs appear no more at fault for the war than the British, perhaps even less so, since the latter, not originally involved in the fighting, made decisions placing themselves on the Ngonde side. Even if the Arabs did make the final overt attack, their motivation for action by then was understandable.

The war quickly turned against the Arabs. Doubtlessly aware the company's Nyakyusa allies were marching to relieve Karonga, Mlozi lifted the siege on November 28, the liberated defenders destroying the abandoned Arab camp. The British then commented upon the superior construction of Arab fortifications, a fact which should have been remembered during the continuing warfare. The British and their African allies passed to the offensive, although the large numbers participating and the differing aims of Africans and Europeans hampered successful campaigning. Salim bin Nassir's settlement was destroyed, delays in the attack allowing previous Arab evacuation.

In early December company forces defeated the Henga. When the *Ilala* reappeared, bringing Hawes, John Moir, John Buchanan, and other Europeans, the British, now possessing sufficient ammunition, with the remaining African allies on December 23 successfully attacked Mlozi, the victory marred by immediate breakup of the advancing army, the Africans forgetting the enemy while looting the Arab camp. The onset of the rainy season and ammunition shortage then closed the initial phase of the war. In deliberations concerning the immediate future, O'Neill, judging the Arabs "weak and dispirited," proposed talks, but Hawes, mistrustful and voicing official caution, recommended evacuating Karonga until more effective action became possible. Fotheringham and the company men strongly objected, adding to a natural reluctance to abandon the station an opposition to forsaking African allies. In the end Fotheringham and a few companions remained in the area while Moir went south with Hawes to secure additional European support. When the steamer left in early January the Britons, accepting an African request, evacuated Karonga for a nearby location.[9]

The clash at Karonga was of major significance, causing reevaluation by each Arab and European group of its general position. To many the war signaled an inevitable happening, confirming Arab and European extremist opinion about the impossibility of coexisting peacefully. On the European side, belief immediately emerged of an overall Arab conspiracy. British officials involved in the fighting quickly explained to skeptical superiors, but to a more receptive general public, that they took action only in response to Arab aggression. O'Neill asserted his arrival had saved Karonga, the Arabs deferring attack when British defenses were weak, advancing for Foreign Office consideration Robert Laws' opinion that Arabs planned "the establishment of a powerful Mohammedan Empire in Central Africa."[10] While not prepared for participation in the war, Laws and the Free Church brethren readily assisted the African Lakes Company against the Arabs. "Most earnestly do I long for the restoration of peace," intoned Laws, "but peace based on wickedness would be a hollow affair." Most British missionaries made similar decisions. Universities' Mission agent W. P. Johnson, although disassociating himself from Laws' contention that company men were "our defenders," nonetheless admitted Arab influence was "most deadly." When his London office, recalling Steere's strictures,[11] queried Johnson about involvement in the war—the mission steamer was used by the company—he answered forthrightly, "I am very sorry not to be able to stand apart neither looking for European protection nor fearing coast prejudice, but I do not think we can take this position. Consul Hawes writes in a way that makes it a matter of duty to succor his party as far as men of peace may do so." Kerr Cross of the Free Church mission, and Tomory of the London Missionary Society, both medical men, also aided company forces.[12] A local European consensus had emerged, if not in direct supporting actions, certainly in spirit. The missionaries, coming to Africa with stereotyped views of Islam, naturally closed ranks when trouble occurred, blaming all on the Muslims.

Similar unity did not emerge for conducting the war. During the lull in the Karonga fighting, differences of opinion concerning future conduct surfaced between the aggressive company leaders and consular officials. The company agents, for example, learning of a large Arab caravan waiting at the Deep Bay Lake crossing, wanted to attack, even though the Arabs were not implicated in the war. Hawes reacted against the proposal, fearing company recklessness might unnecessarily broaden Arab-European hostilities, endangering all Europeans residing in the lake region. Later, in

February, when Moir proposed reoccupation of Karonga, charging further delays allowed augmentation of Arab strength while African friends lost confidence, his plans did not receive official sanction.[13]

Laws meantime helped organize opinion for negotiations, the Europeans during a February meeting at Bandawe agreeing on terms for the Arabs. The Muslims, in return for the company not seeking compensation for losses, were to raze their stockades, evacuating Karonga within two months. Securing company guarantees of remaining on the defensive, consular agent Buchanan—Hawes had left on leave—steamed to Karonga on the mission vessel *Charles Jansen;* Johnson provided Buchanan with the appearance of acting independently from the company.[14] The deliberations opened at Karonga on 20 March 1888, Mlozi, Kopa Kopa, and Msalama representing the Arabs. Mlozi persisted in blaming Fotheringham for the war, declining Buchanan's countering suggestion of hearing Fotheringham's version of events. When these necessary recriminations had ended, Buchanan got down to business, reporting African Lakes Company claims of losing property worth £700, the Arabs immediately replying, regardless of the merits of the demand, that payment was impossible, claiming equal damages during the fighting. Buchanan then advanced the Bandawe proposals, but from the Arab viewpoint the terms were ludicrous. They held Karonga, with little likelihood appearing that the company would find the strength to drive them away. The negotiations closed without result.[15]

Both before and after the abortive negotiations, British officials, pushed by fears of a general Arab movement, sought alternative means for resolving the dispute. Ignoring the charges concerning the Zanzibar government's role, they naturally thought of utilizing the sultan's influence. The distant Foreign Office found the idea sensible, instructing Euan Smith to bring the sultan's "moral influence" against the Lake Malawi Arabs, "and also to subject them to the material pressure of the stoppage of the supplies upon which they depend." Khalifa obligingly promised, doubtlessly realizing his inland subjects would respond as they wished. Finally, frustrated since Mlozi's Arabs seemed to "have but little connection with this port or with the coast," Euan Smith settled for a dual policy: Khalifa both summoned them to Zanzibar and dispatched a representative to the lake to implement orders. Ali bin Surur, depicted by Johnson as "a weak vessel," but characterized by Euan Smith as "a very apt, intelligent man," was chosen for the onerous task, receiving instructions to order Mwinyi Kisutu to "isolate and weaken" the Karonga Arabs. He left for the lake in August 1888.[16]

The lakeside Europeans had not waited for policy evolution in London and Zanzibar, returning to Karonga during the Buchanan-Mlozi negotiations. Unopposed by Arabs, they began to rebuild the destroyed company establishment, simultaneously considering schemes for renewing fighting.

There was a minor peace tentative, the British utilizing a visiting Nsenga Arab, Majid, who earlier had reported much opposition to the war among his community, as intermediary. "All the Senga Arabs," said Fothering-ham, "are wild at Mlozi for spoiling the trade," even promising to assist the Europeans if war continued. Mlozi did not answer the message: since Moir included in the terms a demand for an indemnity, the attitude hardly was unexpected. The company forces, about 8 Europeans and 500 Afri-cans, attacked Mlozi's stockaded settlement on April 10, 1888, the de-fenders greeting the assailants with heavy gunfire supported by a sally from Kopa Kopa's nearby stockade. The British, with their leader Moir wounded, retired. During the combat Msalama's fields, and thus his food supply, had been ruined; otherwise victory belonged to the Arabs. Another British effort, against Kopa Kopa's village, followed during the next week, with similar lack of success. Both sides then settled into defen-sive stances, concentrating upon strengthening fortifications.[17]

The British, awaiting reinforcements, remained resolved to carry on the war. Among the several arriving recruits was one individual destined for a major role in the European conquest and administration of Africa. Freder-ick D. Lugard, an officer in the Indian army, landed in May, because of his military background immediately taking command of the company men. But Lugard, whatever his military talents, was then probably mentally unsuited for command, because of an unfortunate affair of the heart suffer-ing which, according to an army medical board, was the cause of a "mental depression" so serious that his examiners judged "the state of this officer's health . . . so unsatisfactory as to unfit him for the command of an expedi-tion." Lugard's sympathetic biographer, Perham, was not permitted to publish the diary covering this part of her subject's life. "This diary was, indeed, a most terrible document," she commented.[18] Lugard's state of mind is relevant, perhaps influencing his faulty strategy against the Arabs. Additionally it expresses one of the lasting themes running through Euro-pean involvement in Arab and African affairs—the desire to submerge personal sufferings, even to the point of death, in a supposedly cleansing combat against the perceived forces of darkness. There was fanaticism in nineteenth-century Africa, but not all on the side of the Muslims.[19]

Lugard turned out just the man the aggressive agents desired, im-mediately announcing that if the British did not take the offensive, they might as well evacuate Karonga. He started active preparations in early June, leading a scouting party to investigate the nature and strength of Arab positions, discovering the fortifications impressively built and strongly manned, the defenders' gunfire compelling withdrawal before adequate surveillance was accomplished. Fotheringham later admitted they had been "unable to get a proper view of Kopa Kopa's," but planning for the attack went ahead unabated. There was no other choice but to attack, Lugard subsequently explained, the Arabs being too cowardly to fight in the open, a sufficient indication of the military naïveté of the supposedly trained officer.

The British collected an impressive army, about 350 Africans and 25 Europeans, the latter including some of East Central Africa's first European mercenaries—paid £1 weekly—among them, said Lugard, "a number of desperados from the gold fields" of South Africa.[20] The combat commenced on June 16, some of Lugard's command, to divert Arab fire, rushing at one side of Kopa Kopa's stockade, the major body advancing against the opposite flank of the fifty-square-yard fortification. The lines of the attackers immediately became disorganized, the men stumbling into ravines not discovered by the scouting party. Struggling forward through a very damaging fire from the loopholed stockade, the dismayed troops encountered a mud wall over six feet high, surmounted by long poles topped with thorns. Blasting powder, for use against the walls, did not arrive because of the confusion within ranks. While bravely endeavoring to scale the wall Lugard was wounded, his men later finding him "lying at [the] side of [the] path covered with blood and in a very helpless condition." The disheartened Britons and Africans, their progress hopelessly checked, retreated. Content with the outcome, the Arabs left the withdrawal unopposed. Now regading the Arab fortifications as beyond the capacity of their military resources—Buchanan called them "almost impregnable"—Lugard and the company leaders decided to send for artillery, in the interval, with many Europeans hampered by illness, contenting themselves with minor skirmishing against their Arab enemies.[21]

No significant military action occurred during the rest of 1888. The British, seizing Deep Bay, interrupted at least one Arab coastal route, thereby partially damaging the flow of supplies to Karonga. With their fields ravaged, the Arabs endured food shortages; in August reports indicated they were "already feeding on leaves and roots and mice." Their opponents were little better off, many Ngonde dying of starvation.[22] When Lugard, recovered from his wounds, returned in late October, the Europeans, their numbers dropping as recruits left because of the nonarrival of promised arms, regained heart. The officer wrote Mlozi expressing willingness for talks, Mlozi of the Lake Tanganyika Arabs appearing to hear his proposals. It was not a fruitful encounter; Lugard, acting as if he possessed military supremacy, informed Mlozi that the Sultan of Zanzibar had ordered the war stopped and restitution made for British losses, warning that his envoy soon was expected at Karonga. But, commented Lugard, if Mlozi and his allies peacefully evacuated their stockades, he guaranteed safe exit, a necessary promise in face of Ngonde hostility. The Arab delegate brought the terms to Mlozi; nothing more was heard of them.[23]

Even before learning of the several British defeats, Salisbury had expressed displeasure at consular officials becoming involved in the ongoing hostilities.[24] The Foreign Office, of course, feared an Arab rising. Yet the lack of Arab unity was obvious. During the Lugard conversations Mlozi of Tanganyika had cheered the Europeans with information that his community, men loyal to Tippu Tip, were uninterested in the quarrel. Later, in 1889, Kabunda attempted mediation, hoping to reopen trade with the African Lakes Company. Even in the distant Congo, Arab spokesmen in April 1888 informed James Jameson of the war, blaming their fellow Muslims and indicating that Tippu Tip was so angry he threatened to send men to bring Mlozi and the other Arabs to Zanzibar. This doubtless was empty rhetoric, but the feeling of noninvolvement seems apparent.[25]

Near the end of November Khalifa's agent reached the British camp. Described by Fotheringham as "a plain, unostentatious coast Arab . . . [a] born diplomat, skilled in all the ruses of his office," Ali bin Surur faced formidable obstacles. The British did not trust him, and worse, expressed racist scorn. True to his perceptions, Lugard considered Ali "a mere Swahili . . . despised" by lighter-skinned Arabs. And the Europeans' commitment to seeking peace via negotiations continued tenuous, the company openly standing against any terms that left the Arabs resident in the northern lake region. Even if the sultan's envoy truly did want his coreligionists bowing to Europeans, which is doubtful, there were few reasons for Mlozi and the others to pay attention to an Arab from Zanzibar. They were men of the interior, still independent, minimally impressed by the representative of a sultan who was then losing authority to demanding Europeans. Nonetheless Ali relayed Khalifa's instructions to Karonga's Arabs: "Go to the . . . [British] speedily and beg their pardon and request their forgiveness." If they disobeyed, warned the sultan, "I will stop every one sending you goods and other necessities." Receiving the envoy with customary tokens of respect, Mlozi allegedly promised obedience, blaming other Arabs, particularly Salim bin Nassir, for beginning the war. Ali summoned Salim to Karonga, leaving for the Nsenga community when the Arab declined to come. Once Khalifa's agent departed, Mlozi, probably never taking Ali seriously, forgot about Zanzibar's distant ruler.[26] An interesting side result of Ali's conversations with Mlozi came from the presence with the envoy of a "trusted native," Chimbomo, sent by the British to observe the talks. Mlozi astutely treated Chimbomo with friendship, carefully impressing upon the African the strength of Arab fortifications. When Chimbomo told his tale, many Africans supposedly lost courage, deciding that the Arabs never could be driven away.[27]

Ali bin Surur regained Karonga in January 1889 without comforting news for the British. The Nsenga Arabs had listened politely, otherwise paying the envoy scant heed. Continuing to talk with Mlozi proved fruitless, Lugard regarding his conduct as a delaying tactic allowing Arabs to receive additional supplies, and perhaps it was. The British, however, profited equally from the slow-down, their field pieces arriving in mid-January. This news did not alter Mlozi's attitude, the Arab earlier informing Fotheringham: "Nor can you make us afraid, for we are men of war from our childhood . . . As for cannon and mortars, we knew them long ago. If God bids us to live, we live. If we die, we die."[28] By this moment, the Karonga British had become increasingly insecure, news of the Arab-German war signaling to them the long-feared general Arab outburst. On February 21, 1889, the lull in hostilities ended, Lugard turning the field pieces against the Arabs, the shells merely passing through the supple pole stockades without exploding. The British judged the Arabs suffered heavy casualties during the firing, but, even if losses occurred, the termination of shelling left battle lines unaltered. Negotiations, by letter, ensued with the Nsenga Arabs, Salim bin Nassir, to Lugard's disgust, refusing to intervene while concluding that Mlozi would fight on to the end. Renewed shelling took place on March 13, again without important result. Lugard had had enough. He announced Ali bin Surur had been acting in bad faith—although in February firm Arab opponent John Moir praised his efforts—and on April 8 left for Zanzibar and Europe for consultations concerning Karonga's future. Laws optimistically maintained the British stand had blocked Arab domination of the lake region, yet, in reality, Lugard's campaigns had not changed the stalemate existing at his arrival.[29] The Arabs, avoiding offensive activity, persisted in their Karonga establishments.

The war continued in desultory fashion although some discouraged Europeans abandoned Karonga. Buchanan concluded the time was near when the Arab question "must be taken up by a strong power or left alone altogether." The company agents, nevertheless, hung on, as determined as ever to combat Arabs, with Moir even requesting official permission to strike at Arabs living in territory now presumed to be in the German sphere. Hawes, then acting consul in Zanzibar, merely answered that prior Foreign Office approval was necessary. Meanwhile, in the apt phrase of Cross, affairs remained "gloomy enough," the combatants on both sides suffering the effects of food shortages and smallpox.[30]

In Zanzibar, Lugard encountered general official disfavor regarding the unsuccessful fighting around Karonga, reacting with his version of responsibility for failure. He castigated Ali bin Surur, charging the Arab never worked toward the stated aims of his mission, in the end really joining Mlozi. Khalifa countered angrily, blaming Lugard from the beginning of mistreating the envoy, not listening to advice, and instead insisting on war. Ali, explained the sultan, finally had been driven by Lugard from the British camp.[31] The recriminations soon involved other Britons. Lugard criticized Buchanan for hampering the war effort: if he had "not told the

Arabs that the quarrel was not one of the British govt., they would have given in to the demands made at the time for them to quit the country . . . the govt. should be responsible for all that has happened on that account." Lugard blamed Moir, a man he held "void of the sense of truth," for military failure, alleging that the company agent's harsh demands for compensation had ensured collapse of negotiations with the Arabs, not mentioning that he had dealt in the same unrealistic manner. Buchanan simply replied that he followed orders, Hawes upholding his subordinate and labeling the British venture at Karonga "a chapter of failure, quarrelling and discontent." The obvious inability either to gain victory or secure acceptable peace, said Hawes, merely exacerbated bitterness among the group, the consul agreeing that Moir, "by his crushing demand for ivory and bales of goods, upset the whole of the negotiations."[32]

The contesting Britons' fulminations further strengthened unfavorable Foreign Office opinion regarding the lake war. Lugard's reports, the officials judged with apparent satisfaction, "leave no doubt of his opinion of the hopelessness of this campaign. He will hardly return." "The Co. and Capt. Lugard are at their wit's end how to get out of this scrape they have gotten into," noted Anderson.[33] The general public proved equally unreceptive to assisting actions against Arabs. A campaign, backed by such luminaries as the explorer Cameron, to raise £10,000 to continue the struggle after nine months' work collected only £3,000.[34] But at this late date in the accelerating imperial age the government, under pressure from influential missionary and other interested parties, could not remain uninvolved in the unresolved Karonga episode. Influential mission propagandist Horace Waller, for example, spoke for most enthusiasts when insisting the government bore responsibility for defending the company. "Lord Salisbury," he trumpeted in face of all evidence, "has given the greatest license for the Moirs to fight it out with the Arabs."[35]

A new consul, Harry Johnston, was appointed for the region, a more influential and talented man than his predecessors.[36] With the existing military stalemate Johnston had good opportunity to end the costly war, the company awarding the consul full authority over its agents and promising to accept any accords concluded with the Arabs. Johnston proceeded in careful, logical fashion, first stopping in Zanzibar to secure from Khalifa letters and gifts for the Arabs of Lakes Malawi and Tanganyika "directing them to act in all things upon the advice of the English and to further English interests by every means in their power." To buttress chances of success, the consul recruited Swahili aides for the planned operations.

After attaining the lake, Johnston first negotiated with Mwinyi Kisutu. During the fighting the jumbe had continued in cordial relations with Europeans, a sensible decision since they had never interfered significantly in his sphere. Johnston, of course, knew of Kisutu's conduct, his estimate of the Arab chieftain's usefulness to the British increasing after initial discussions. Recognizing that the company agents' anti-Arab stance almost had brought Kisutu into the war, Johnston quickly won the Arab to the British side. Kisutu, then described by missionary A. C. Murray as "a tall thin old man of perhaps sixty, with a chronic cough," was realist enough to seize the opportunity, accepting an arrangement that guaranteed his existing position. In a treaty of September 22, 1889, the jumbe gained British protection within recognized boundaries, consenting to follow "in all matters" the advice of the local British agent, in recompense receiving yearly payment of 3,000 rupees. The sum, paid by the African Lakes Company, came as compensation for ending charges levied on ivory purchased by Britons. In addition Kisutu promised cooperation in the forthcoming negotiations with Mlozi, providing the consul with letters for the northern Arab leader and sending an agent to speak with Mlozi, pledging military support if peace did not ensue. Later Johnson stressed the agreement's importance, reasoning that the jumbe's actions "turned the whole tide of Arab feeling on Nyassa and Tanganyika in our favour." Although exaggerating the Arab's influence, Johnston had proceeded intelligently, recognizing, as other Britons had not, the necessity of gaining the backing of Arab leaders who held positions of power and influence if they wished to win British predominance without warfare.

Johnston next sailed to Karonga where a truce had been arranged in his name. The consul judged the outcome of additional fighting as uncertain: even though "Arabs were eating rats, leather, and roots, besides being scourged by a terrible outburst of small pox," the British forces lacked ammunition. Johnston accepted the company contention of Mlozi's responsibility for the war, concluding that Ali bin Surur had joined his cause through "threats or bribery, and had disappeared." Ali, however, claimed being held a prisoner by the Nsenga Arabs.[37] But Johnston did not allow such judgments to cloud the perception of a primary British need for peace. The deliberations began with the jumbe's representative visiting Mlozi with assurances of the consul's good faith. Satisfied, Mlozi met Johnston for talks on October 19. The British agent presented Khalifa's letter, later noting that the missive had "an excellent effect," and that "he was amazed at the prestige still attaching in these far off regions to the name of the Sultan of Zanzibar." During the meetings, attended also by Kopa Kopa, Msalama, and other Arabs, a reasonable settlement, acceptable to both sides, emerged. Ceasing the hostilities, each belligerent forswore seeking revenge for past deeds, allowing all refugees freedom to return home. The Arabs promised henceforth to leave undisturbed Africans under British protection, with all disputes between the company and

Arabs being settled by the British consul. The Arabs also consented to restrict their stockades to a designated, less strategic area, removing all existing settlements within a year.

The treaty obviously was a one-sided document, favoring the British. But it was a practical arrangement. By this time many of the more astute Arabs, aware of developments elsewhere in East Central Africa, realized survival depended upon gaining workable relationships with the more powerful Europeans now controlling coastal outlets for their commerce. Johnston offered, without major affront to the proud defenders of Karonga, opportunity for closing the profit-destroying quarrel on conditions well short of total surrender. They had to agree to move from existing locations, but if the future brought peace and the return of satisfactory trade, this was acceptable. Not all Britons thought the terms satisfactory. "British prestige," lamented Lugard, "was sacrificed by the conclusion of the treaty." He reasoned Mlozi could not be trusted, a judgment echoed many years later by Oliver, who characterized the treaty as "a cynical compact which would last just as long as Mlozi conceived the rival forces to be evenly balanced."[38] The Arabs, with even more justification because of future British conduct, could have said the same of Johnston.

A few years of relative quiet between Arabs and Europeans followed in the lake region. Passing under British rule, and known as British Central Africa, its first governor was Harry Johnston, his duties including, instructed Salisbury, "by every legitimate means in your power to check the slave-trade." Because of an initial tolerance of the existing Arab presence, and especially the satisfactory working relationship with Mwinyi Kisutu, Johnston gained a lasting reputation as a pursuer of pro-Arab policies,[39] a very mistaken interpretation. Johnston merely accepted the fact of insufficient military resources for an alternative policy, generally attempting to isolate the northern lake Arabs from the Yao, leaving to the future any resolution of the Arab issue. Even before taking office Johnston had decided that it was preferable to utilize Arabs in subjugating Africans rather than striking head-on as recommended by the various European crusaders against continuation of the slave trade. Thus Johnston first concentrated on overcoming the spirited Yao resistance to imposition of alien rule.[40]

Meanwhile the Arabs continued to trade ivory, some participating in the slave trade when opportunity allowed. A visiting Belgian officer in 1893 described relations between Arabs and the African Lakes Company as "the best," the profitable ivory business serving as a strong "bond" between them.[41] In the north conditions had not changed much since conclusion of the 1889 treaty. Mlozi, recently married to a daughter of the jumbe, remained the dominant local leader. There were reports of occasional arguments with company agents, all passing without interrupting the satisfactory ivory trade. Buchanan visited the Arab in 1891, checking one of the periodic charges of implication in slaving activities. Still Mlozi's opponent, Buchanan nevertheless admitted he had not yet violated the British treaty. During their talks Mlozi emphasized loyalty to the Johnston administration, even offering help in apprehending slavers, firmly reminding Buchanan he was not receiving the subsidies given the jumbe and other local rulers.[42]

From early 1892 Johnston openly avowed that an acceptable lasting arrangement with Arabs was impossible. "I am anxious to clear all the Arabs out of British Central Africa one by one," he said, "except men like Jumbe who are really good leaders of the people and loyal allies to the Queen."[43] Still, until other resisters were conquered, Johnston did not move. Mwinyi Kisutu until his death kept Johnston's trust. If the jumbe did participate in the slave trade, as several observers reported, he discreetly avoided confrontation with his European superiors. Kisutu's valued assistance against the administration's enemies doubtlessly offset any charges brought, particularly since Johnston steadfastly maintained that the Arab consistently moved toward a fully legitimate commercial position. Kisutu died in July 1894. His son and successor, Mwinyi Heri, involved in local rivalries and suspected of plotting against the British, was deposed in December 1894 and dispatched to Zanzibar. No new jumbe was appointed.[44]

Before the end of 1894 Johnston was ready to break the remaining power of the Arabs. Receiving reports of Mlozi not acting as a proper British subordinate, Johnston in July 1895 visited the north to bring the Arab into compliance. Mlozi refused to meet the governor, sending what Johnston regarded as a hostile letter. He decided to proceed against Mlozi and his supporters before they organized resistance or fled, although it is most doubtful the Arabs had either course in mind. Returning, with the assistance of a German steamer, in early December, Johnston attacked the estimated two or three thousand defenders of the strong Arab stockades.[45] The British, with artillery, possessed clear military superiority. The Arabs and their followers suffered heavy losses while putting up a fierce resistance. After one shell exploded the Arab powder supply, a lull occurred in the fighting, a white flag appearing on Mlozi's stockade. The Arabs were willing to talk with the Europeans, but Johnston refused discussions with anyone but Mlozi and his fellow leaders, a challenge eventually accepted by Mlozi. "He came a short way out of the main gate," said a British observer, "and desired that the Commissioner might come up and speak to him face to face." Fearing treachery, Johnston demurred briefly, in the end both Mlozi and the Briton advancing closer, allowing talk "from a short distance." Mlozi asked the terms offered for Arab surrender, Johnston replying they must put down their arms and deliver the stockade at once, in return receiving their lives, nothing else. After some thought Mlozi concluded "that the Arabs meant to fight it out to the end, and that if the British wanted them they must come in and take them." The shelling resumed. Later a Henga leader arrived from the Arab camp, informing the British of the location of Mlozi's headquarters. After several direct hits resulting in the wounding of Mlozi "a tremendous sortie" came from the stockade, the remaining women and children utilizing the diversion to reach safety. In the following action the British forces breached the Arab defenses, pouring into the settlement and defeating the Arabs in bloody hand-to-hand combat. Mlozi, still in the ruins of his house, rejected surrender, his enemies storming it and capturing the Arab, who was "stupid with his wound." About 2,000 defenders died in the stockade, plus many others killed by the pursuing Ngonde.

Emulating Wissmann's treatment of Abushiri, Johnston tried Mlozi before a Ngonde court sitting under his presidency. The captured Arab, retaining dignity until the end, merely informed his enemies of his readiness to meet his fate. "What is the good? These people are resolved that I shall die. My hour is come." Quickly found guilty and condemned to death, Mlozi was executed on December 4.[46] His death marked the end of Arab power in the Lake Malawi region.

13 Buganda and Lake Victoria

In 1884 Mutesa's successor, his unstable son Mwanga, was chosen by the powerful officials who customarily bore responsibility for selecting a kabaka.[1] The officials hoped for success in dominating the young, inexperienced ruler. Such striving occurred after every kabaka's accession, but now the challengers included factions, grouped around adherents of Islam and Protestant or Roman Catholic Christianity, that were strong enough to reverse the growth of monarchial might accomplished by Mutesa. Each African faction sought the active support or advice of Arabs and Europeans resident in Buganda. In the forthcoming dramatic happenings, however, the Arabs, in contrast to their role in most of East Central Africa, took a secondary place, assisting, not controlling, the Ganda Muslims in struggles against the Christian Ganda and their European allies.

Mwanga, possessing neither his father's talent nor his ruthless, determined efficiency, became kabaka at a most dangerous time. Divisions within Buganda endangered stability just when Europeans commenced their frontal attack upon East Central Africa's independent polities. The Arab community during the first months of the new reign increasingly became at odds with Mwanga, angered at the failure, as promised, to pay Mutesa's debts. Missionary O'Flaherty by July 1885 painted Arab standing at low ebb. Outside events soon reversed the Ganda ruler's feelings. German aggressions against Zanzibar, plus Britain's progressive abandonment of Barghash, were related in full detail to the Ganda leadership, the Arabs stressing the united European front compelling their sultan's surrender of his mainland holdings. The Baluchi Ismail and Ali bin Sultan, the important Tabora Arab, were leading proponents of this interpretation.[2] In November the Christian community learned the shattering news of Bishop Hannington's death, killed by Mwanga's orders when attempting to enter Buganda. Masudi bin Suliman, the long-resident Arab, carried out the initial arrest.[3] The Arabs remained on the offensive into 1886, Ali bin Sultan "bribing," said Mackay, both Mwanga and the *katikiro* (chief minister) to refuse entry of all Europeans. "Perhaps the main cause of Arab hostility," he added, "is their fear of competition in trade," noting that they were "exultant" over a reported Barghash letter forbidding Tabora's Arabs to supply a residence to a German ivory trader.[4] The British missionaries made their plight known in Zanzibar, although the best the distant British consul could manage in their behalf was a letter for Mwanga, the missionaries unhappily learning that the message was carried by old opponent Sulayman bin Zahayr, then en route as Barghash's representative in Buganda.[5]

While struggling against the many hindrances that blocked exercise of full authority, Mwanga during 1886 found the Christian Ganda's independent attitude an increasing irritant. The hostility broke forth in May when Mwanga began the famous persecution of Ganda Christians. Although over one hundred perished, some refusing the opportunity for recanting, persecution was less serious than Mutesa's 1876 action against Ganda Muslims. By these trials the Christian Ganda had their group loyalties even more refined, standing thereafter as a coherent body against all opponents. But the haphazard nature of the killing must not be ignored. Losing his temper the kabaka ordered the killings. Once calmed, Mwanga discontinued the persecution, soon turning to a policy of utilizing the Christian and Muslim factions, mostly young men, in his ongoing campaign against the older chiefs.[6]

The Arab community was strengthened in April 1887 by the arrival of Sulayman bin Zahayr at the head of a large caravan. The letters he bore from Zanzibar supposedly counseled Mwanga to send away resident Europeans, unscathed, before they harmed Buganda. Other Arabs, including Ali bin Sultan and Hamis Belul, joined the newcomer in speaking against the missionaries, particularly Mackay, still the Arabs' most vocal adversary. "I cannot go to court without encountering these wretched Arabs," lamented Mackay, "and the King takes apparent delight in seeing them storm at me." Unwilling to side completely with the Arabs, Mwanga, however, ignored the expulsion advice.[7] The Britons complained of Arab activity in Zanzibar, Euan Smith pressuring Khalifa into recalling Suliman and Ali bin Sultan. Soon after, an agent of the sultan was on the road to Buganda carrying letters to Mwanga and the resident Arabs, counseling good treatment of the British, making particular reference to the newly created Imperial British East African Company.[8]

Before the dispatches arrived, Buganda's political structure had been changed radically by armed rebellion against Mwanga. By the latter part of

1888 the older leaders had lost much influence, causing Mwanga's reevaluation of the Christian and Muslim role. But when the kabaka began plotting to breask them, his intrigues inevitably leaked to Christian and Muslim leaders. They struck against the kabaka in September 1888. Unsupported by any substantial group of his people, Mwanga fled the country, the rebels allowing the escape. It had not been a rebellion of aggrieved Muslims and Christians against a persecuting ruler; it was instead a rising of privileged factions acting determinedly to maintain threatened positions. The rebels intended to appoint Mwanga's brother Kalema as kabaka, the disorder attending the coup leading instead to the designation of the more available Mutebe, a not very energetic upholder of traditional Ganda life and religion.

Neither Arabs nor Europeans played much, if any, role in these stirring happenings, the young Ganda not requiring outside assistance. Both Arabs and Europeans did not lament Mwanga's ouster. The Europeans, rejoicing in the departure of the man responsible for the deaths of Hannington and the African Christians, hoped the Christian Ganda rise to positions of authority signaled the onset of more propitious times for adherents of their faith. The Arabs had equally few regrets, the deposed kabaka having roused their ire by continued nonpayment of debts and by closing the recently opened trade to neighboring Bunyoro. The exultant victors reorganized the government, Mutebe immediately proclaiming freedom of religion, the opening of trade to Bunyoro, and a lowering of import taxes, all measures welcomed by Arabs and Europeans. The principal state offices were filled following decisions by the Muslim and Christian victors, the Christians securing the largest share. Catholic commander Honorat Nyonyintono became katikiro.[9]

In the resulting unstable political situation rivalries among the factions obviously ran deep, Catholics, Muslims, and Protestants all watching their compatriots suspiciously. Mutebe, a weak and unwise sovereign, failed to master his unruly subjects' strivings. According to the missionaries, Arabs and Ganda Muslims quickly became disenchanted with Mutebe's rule, the former displeased at failure to honor promises for repaying Mwanga's debts, while both justly feared a future in a state dominated by Christian officials. Mutebe increased the unhappiness by not fulfilling an earlier promise to accept Islam: emulating Mutesa, the kabaka refused circumcision. Instead Mutebe strove to build an alliance of supporters from among the older chiefs, his actions thus increasing already dangerous tensions. In early October 1888 the Muslims, in the kabaka's presence, accused the Christians of plotting his deposition, following the confrontation with a surprise attack driving them from Buganda. Withdrawing in good order, the Christians found refuge in nearby regions beyond the reach of Buganda's new government. Although the supposed plot had led Mutebe once again into promising conversion, his hesitations quickly returned after the Christian removal. Deciding to resolve the problem through assassinating the principal Muslim leaders, the kabaka mismanaged the attempted coup, the Muslims then easily deposing Mutebe. Kalema became ruler, the circumcision issue being resolved by the Muslims carrying through the operation before the new kabaka secured the throne. A believer in the tenets of Islam, Kalema became Buganda's first Muslim ruler. The Arabs had an unimportant role in the foregoing events, although they participated in the effort to establish a Muslim state by responding with all resources at their disposal to assist their Ganda brethren after Mutebe's abortive plot. The new ruler, in one of his first official diplomatic acts, marked the change in the character of the Ganda state by writing the Sultan of Zanzibar, requesting from the titular leader of East Central Africa's Muslims firearms and gunpowder, teachers and books, the Zanzibar flag, and the stoppage of additional Christian missionaries from coming to Buganda. European traders, however, were welcome. Unfortunately for the Muslim Ganda, the harassed Khalifa, his sultanate beset by Europeans, could do nothing useful to aid the distant Muslim polity.[10]

The missionaries, expelled unharmed after the Muslim victory, retreated to the south shore of Lake Victoria, Mackay awarding first place in the agitation causing the departure to Suliman bin Zuhayr. That Arab, along with Said bin Sayf of Magu, Mackay later claimed, attempted without success to persuade local Africans to expel the missionaries from their new location. Mackay sent to Zanzibar the names of Suliman and other Arabs who had participated in the Buganda events, accompanying his hopes for punishment with a request for a £2,000 indemnity as compensation for destroyed mission property. Khalifa, however, declined action without more proof of actual involvement by the named Arabs.[11]

The fugitive Mwanga, not abandoning hope of regaining Buganda's throne, found refuge at the Magu Arab center. Watching his limited resources disappear into Arab hands, Mwanga soon desired to move elsewhere, opening communication with nearby British and French missionaries. To the British, Mwanga spoke of attempting, with mission assistance, to reach the East African coast, the missionaries in November agreeing to arrange for him to meet Irish trader and caravan leader Charles Stokes. The Magu Arabs meantime, having drained nearly all of Mwanga's wealth and not wishing intermixture in Ganda intrigues, allowed the former kabaka's departure, a shortsighted decision opening the way for total destruction of the Arab position in Buganda. Arriving at the Catholic Bukumbi mission in December, Mwanga announced preparations for regaining his throne. In April 1889 Nyonyintono came to Bukumbi, reporting Kalema's loss of non-Muslim Ganda allegiance through unwise policies. Despite the perceived strength of the Muslims, including possession of about two thousand firearms and abundant ammunition, refugee Ganda opinion turned in favor of war, Mwanga pressuring the Catholics by announcing departure for the coast if a contrary resolution was taken. Mwanga's firmness sealed the decision to fight: the former kabaka was essential, providing legitimacy to the Christian cause.

The Protestant Ganda also entered the discussions, seeking the advice of their missionaries concerning the proposed campaign. The Britons, both mistrusting Mwanga and fearing Muslim strength, counseled against participation, but the Protestants, determined to regain their lost homeland, disregarded the opinion. Stokes entered the deliberations, offering valuable logistic support. His adhesion gave the vital use of a lake vessel and needed supplies of firearms and ammunition. During the delay before the campaign's opening, Stokes endeavored to utilize his many Muslim trading contacts to detach the Magu Arabs from the Ganda Muslims, offering protection from the Christians in return for neutrality. The Arabs ignored him, answering instead Kalema's appeal for assistance by dispatching the boats of Said bin Sayf and others with war materials for the Ganda Muslims. Near the end of April the Christians, acting quickly, surprised the Arabs, in a fierce battle destroying both vessels and cargoes. No quarter was given during the fighting, about 150 Muslims losing their lives. This most important Christian triumph, boosting the morale of the recently united Catholic and Protestant factions, caused some Muslim supporters to abandon the war, and, by establishing Christian supremacy on Lake Victoria, prevented the Muslim Ganda from receiving war supplies. At about the same time a Protestant group, commanded by Ham Mukasa, captured a caravan led by Khalfan bin Farid. Restraining his men from killing the Arab, Mukasa delivered the Arab to Stokes, the trader wisely beginning ransom negotiations, asking the Magu Arabs for war materials in return for Khalfan's release.[12]

The Christians continued on toward Kalema's capital, Stokes once more attempting to divide Arabs and Africans, delaying the attack while awaiting an Arab reply. No answer came, some Arabs later denying that they had ever received Stokes's offer. In any case the Arabs probably had decided upon fighting alongside the African Muslims. The Christians attacked on October 5, after extremely harsh combat defeating the Muslims, the survivors fleeing toward the Bunyoro frontier. The Arab quarter of the capital was destroyed, along with considerable property, including over 1,000 ivory tusks, while about thirty coastal traders were killed. Other Arabs and their supporters perished in the disorganized retreat, the Ganda peasantry, reacting to the extreme measures adopted by Kalema for spreading Islam, assisting the Christians in harrying Muslims. All circumcised captives were killed. A few Arabs survived the rout, Said bin Sayf losing a son and all property, later returning to Magu in Stokes's company.

The war was not over, however; the Muslims, reorganizing ranks in the Bunyoro border region, remained a potent enemy, still possessing an estimated 500 to 1,000 firearms and a small supply of ammunition. The Muslims hoped for succor from Kabarega, *mukama* (ruler) of Bunyoro, the Ganda's staunch foe, but he at first hesitated. Then, apparently deciding continuation of internecine Ganda strife to Nyoro advantage, Kabarega provided the Muslims with war materials and fighting men. The reinvigorated army entered the Ganda capital in triumph in November. The Muslim success was shortlived, the still united and determined Christians, utilizing the ransom provided by the Magu Arabs—forty tons of powder and sixty firearms—reoccupying the capital in February 1890. Kalema, leading the battered Muslims back into Bunyoro, nonetheless continued to be a dangerous opponent, prepared, with the ever present possibility of Kabarega's assistance, to exploit any frictions between the yet mutually suspicious Christian Ganda factions. When Kalema died from smallpox in April, the Muslims chose Mbogo, a brother of Mutesa, as new leader.[13]

The 1890 partition of East African territories occurred while Ganda hostilities remained unresolved, Buganda falling within the British sphere. Its initial administration fell to the Imperial British East African Company, agent Frederick Jackson marching inland at the beginning of 1889 with instructions prohibiting involvement in the Buganda war. Although receiving appeals from Mwanga and the missionaries, Jackson obeyed orders, merely informing the embattled Christians that acceptance of company rule implied support for their cause. Mwanga also fruitlessly sought assistance from Stanley's returning Emin Pasha expedition. The Ganda Christians thus defeated the Muslims without outside aid, apart from Stokes's contribution, awaiting the eventual arrival of British company representatives with apprehensive curiosity.[14]

Mwanga, although restored as kabaka, no longer possessed effective authority over his Christian subjects. The victorious Protestants and Catholics, warily watching each other, divided state offices, remaining united only because of the very real threat from the Muslims encamped on the Bunyoro border. The Muslims frequently raided deeply into Christian territory, in April and November 1890 even threatening the capital. With firearms gained from the British company the Christians in August temporarily drove the Muslims back into Bunyoro, although Kabarega compelled their reoccupation of the border camp once the Christians withdrew. By this time some Muslim Ganda, weary of the long war, vainly sought from Kabarega permission to move elsewhere. Others wrote their Christian brethren requesting approval to reenter Buganda, not receiving a reply since no mention was made of submission to Mwanga's regime.[15]

At the end of 1890 British company resident Frederick Lugard boldly led a small detachment of Zanzibari troops into the Ganda capital. Unchanged in attitude toward Muslims, Lugard regarded resolution of the persisting hostilities as necessary for establishing British supremacy. Rumor now awarded the Muslims an army of 4,000 men, 2,000 with firearms, plus 200 coastal Arabs and their subordinates. After negotiations Lugard, in May 1891, marched against the Muslims and their Nyoro allies, leading an accompanying Ganda army of over 20,000. A brief combat quickly established Christian supremacy, the fugitive Muslims, leaving behind about 200 dead, unpursued by Lugard's unwieldy command. The Muslim Ganda still remained unsubdued, but with all offensive capabilities destroyed. The Christians, at last free from invasion, began to intensify the long-simmering Catholic-Protestant rivalry, the quarrel in January 1892 erupting into open warfare. The Protestants, cleverly managing Lugard's supportive involvement, triumphed. Buganda henceforth was dominated, under the British, by the victorious Protestants. The Catholics, yet a significant grouping, were allowed possession of one province, the British at the same time attempting to remove the last hindrance to secure control of Ganda affairs by resolving the Muslim problem, a change that also allowed use of Muslims as a possible check against any Catholic stirrings.[16]

Lugard's assistant, Williams, demonstrated the new attitude, reportedly constructing a mosque and informing the reluctant Protestants that the Muslims, equally the kabaka's subjects, deserved treatment similar to the Catholics. The dispirited Muslims responded favorably, in May agreeing to terms. Mbogo led the survivors into Ganda territory, thus finally terminating the long, debilitating war. Accompanying the Muslim Ganda were the remnants of their Arab allies. Most were, said Lugard, in "an utterly destitute state," describing one individual as "in a miserable plight. Sick, covered with ulcers, all his ill-gotten ivory lost, his sole desire to get out of the country." Deciding the wisest policy was to forget the past, Lugard did not punish the hapless Muslims, allowing the survivors, about 140 in number, including slaves freed by the British, passage to the southern shore of Lake Victoria.[17] Meantime, Suliman bin Zahayr, erstwhile leader of the Buganda Arabs, suffered for his role, arriving in Zanzibar in April 1890 to face British charges. Lacking proof of the Arab's role, Euan Smith influenced the new sultan to seize Suliman's ivory, variously estimated in value between $20,000 and $40,000; Stokes's opportune return to Zanzibar provided the necessary evidence for a decision. Suliman, fined £3,000 (£2000 for satisfying the missionaries) received additional sentence of five years' banishment from Zanzibar, shortly afterward a modification permitting residence on the island, under surveillance, for the same period.[18]

The important Arab involvement in Buganda's affairs had ended. Their presence had resulted in one of the most far-reaching conversions to Islam occurring in any of the territories reached by the influence of Zanzibar, culminating in the effort by African converts, assisted by their Arab mentors, to establish a Muslim state. The failure before the Christian Ganda, acting with minimal European backing, left the Christians in control of Buganda when the British representatives of the new European imperialism arrived to seal defeat of the Muslim cause.[19]

14 German East Africa

THE TRAUMATIC COASTAL events after 1884 inevitably affected relations between Arab and European in the region of the major inland trading routes. In the central caravan carrefour of Tabora, the Arab community had not recovered the unity lost after the death of the Nasibu brothers. For obscure reasons Barghash never appointed a new liwali, the community falling under the supervision of the most important resident Arabs, including Said bin Juma al Harthi, Ali bin Sultan, and Sayf bin Said bin Hamid al Bessar. Said bin Juma, a prosperous agriculturalist and trader dealing with the Congo and Lake Victoria regions, emerged as unofficial liwali. In 1886 visitor Edvard Gleerup described the Arab, then about fifty-eight years old, as "noble looking . . . a very pleasant person . . . [who] knew more of European conditions than any Arab I have met." To Mackay, despite his role in the Arab-European quarrels of Buganda, Said was "perhaps the most respectable Arab here, at any rate the quietest and least malicious." Said bin Juma maintained his position in Tabora until his death in about 1890. The other leading Arabs left official business to him. Sayf bin Said, a flourishing agricultural entrepreneur, and Ali bin Sultan, one of the longest-resident Arabs and an active trader to Buganda, appeared content in exercising influence under the mantle of Said's authority.[1]

The first Europeans to suffer from the new political circumstances facing East Africa were members of an unfortunately timed Tabora venture by H. A. Meyer and Company of Hamburg. Seeking an inland base for breaking the Arab and African ivory monopoly, the firm dispatched two caravans from Zanzibar in mid-1885, Kurt Toeppen's arriving in Tabora in September and Eduard Harders's in November. Despite reports that Barghash had ordered his subjects to refuse the Germans housing, the Meyer agents negotiated permission for settling from Said bin Juma and ntemi Isike. In return the Arab received a percentage of all ivory sales; the

African gained gifts—and the hope of more. Toeppen and Harders, both experienced East African residents, immediately began purchasing ivory, in six weeks securing about 27,000 marks worth. The traders lived isolated from neighboring Europeans, the White Fathers in Tabora, the Church Missionary Society men in Uyuwi, and the agents of the London Missionary Society at Urambo. When Toeppen wrote concerning visiting Uyuwi, the missionaries, remembering the previous European resident trader's fate, and fearing the German might be a member of "a German Annexation Society," requested him, if so involved, not to come since "we should become mixed up with him in the minds of the natives." Respecting their apprehensions, Toeppen explained his connections, adding that he, like most German traders, opposed seizing the sultan's territory. Harders maintained a similar careful attitude toward the White Fathers. After the first burst of commercial activity the Meyer agents, met by rising Arab competition, conducted little additional business, Toeppen returning to the coast in March 1886 to report the Arab attitude to Barghash. Harders, apparently reacting to Arab pressures, began to act aggressively, according to local sources threatening his government's intervention. The important Arab Muhammad bin Kassum later effectively summed up the Muslim response: "If he had come with soldiers and cannon there would have been some meaning in his behaviour, but alone!" Harders died from yellow fever in April 1886, the firm's property falling prey to some Arabs and Isike.[2]

Another member of the Hamburg company then on the road to Tabora, Hermann Giesecke, with previous North African experience, at first encountered little opposition from Arabs, even regaining some pillaged ivory. His efforts to secure the rest, partly reportedly held by Muhammad bin Kassum, failed. As Arab-European tensions heightened the German's unprotected position in the Nyamwezi capital became increasingly insecure: there were two attempts on Giesecke's life, both perhaps merely warning him to leave. Barghash's imposition on the Tabora community of a $4,000 penalty for Harders's losses naturally further aroused the Arabs. The firm finally decided to close the agency, Giesecke packing his remaining ivory—some had been stolen by Arabs—and abandoning Tabora in September 1886. Giesecke was shot and grievously wounded a few days later, dying on October 3, his traveling companion, Tippu Tip, then en route for the coast, safely bringing the German's remaining ivory to Zanzibar. Because of Tippu Tip's powerful influence some Europeans, notably Stokes and Wissmann, implicated him in the killing. Missionary Arthur Brooks said the same about Said bin Juma. There is no evidence of any role by Tippu Tip, the murder of an individual European not fitting the known attitudes of the Arab leader. He, in fact, blamed Muhammad bin Kassum and Said bin Juma for the deed. Although the European charges are understandable, from the Arab viewpoint there was little reason, if anyone knew of the plot, to restrain hotheaded members of their community, German actions along the coast removing all Arab sympathies. The trader attempted to outcompete Arabs at a moment when their normal channels to the coast suffered the effects of the German incursion into East Africa. It was a foolhardy effort, Giesecke paying with his life.[3]

Determined to punish someone for the murder and ivory losses, German consul Michahelles pressured Barghash to take measures against Said bin Juma, the Arab then having considerable ivory in the hands of a Bagamoyo Indian merchant. British representative Claude Macdonald adroitly served both British and German interests, allowing the Indian to subtract Said's debts, the sultan impounding the residue. According to information received by Mackay from an Arab source, the affair caused an irritated Barghash to dispatch "an angry letter to Saidi [bin Juma?] (the Arab who evidenced the theft) blaming him for not concealing the Arab theft." As more information became available, the general European consensus about guilt fell upon Muhammad bin Kassum, Mackay reporting that he had hired the actual killers, while Wissmann learned during his second Congo journey that the Arabs considered Muhammad "a great man" for disposing of the German. Muhammad, at least at first, only admitted responsibility for ivory thefts. Since he joined the Congo Arab community after the incident, the single remedy for the Germans was persuading the sultan to recall him and confiscate his Pemba estate, using the proceeds, perhaps with the addition of Said bin Juma's lost ivory, as partial compensation for the Meyer losses. Muhammad bin Kassum continued beyond German reach until, during the Arab-German war, he returned to East Africa, marching from Tabora with 600 Manyema to assist Bwana Heri at Sadani. Learning en route of the Heri-Wissmann peace settlement Muhammad halted, his men returning to their homeland. Continuing coastward under an assumed name, but betrayed by Arab rivals, he was seized by Germans in May 1890. Despite British advice and Arab protests that he stand trial in the sultan's courts, the Germans tried Muhammad at Bagamoyo. The Arab was hanged on June 27, 1890.[4]

Charles Stokes, the only other significant European trader operating in the interior, remained active during these troubled years, moving with large caravans between Lake Victoria and Zanzibar. He profited from an efficient management of affairs based upon close alliance with African leaders, especially the Nyamwezi Mitinginya of Usongo. At the beginning of 1887 Stokes reported that Arabs were openly threatening his life, along with the missionaries at Uyuwi, blaming them for the death of an important Arab among the Sukuma. But the Britons were not involved, the scare passing without incident. Stokes returned the dead Arab's property to Zanzibar, there exulting in the fact that he had so far conducted six cara-

vans, each numbering from 700 to 1,000 porters, in safety to the coast.
Despite his role in the Buganda war between Muslims and Christians,
Stokes never experienced major difficulties from Arabs, doubtlessly because of his powerful African friends along the caravan route and his
record of fair commercial dealings with all.[5]

In 1889 Stanley conducted the reluctant Emin Pasha, evacuated from
his embattled Sudanese post, into German territory.[6] Wissmann naturally
sought to utilize the great African experience of the unemployed German
for the benefit of his administration. Emin received command of a large
expedition destined to establish German authority in the far interior. Wissmann ordered Emin to the shores of Lake Victoria, acting there and in the
lands extending toward Lake Albert both to end Arab influence and to win
over Africans. After Emin left the coast Wissmann hired Charles Stokes to
work in union with the Pasha, in the Irishman's words "to induce Arabs in
[the] interior to accept peacefully the German rule." The influential trader,
regarded by Euan Smith as "a distinct power in East Central Africa,"
accepted the assignment on the condition that warfare was not contemplated. Wissmann readily concurred, the serious German lack of military
resources precluding extensive campaigning away from the recently conquered coast. The German leader, for the same reason, ordered Emin's
avoidance of Tabora and its large Arab community.[7]

Emin's expedition, numbering about 700 soldiers and porters, marched
inland in April 1890. The German conducted the first significant negotiations with Kondoa's Arabs, the small, apprehensive community quickly
accepting German rule. Sahir bin Sulayman, "the most respected among
the Arabs here," according to Emin, received appointment as liwali. The
Arabs of the related Irangi settlement similarly later followed suit.[8] Emin,
meantime, despite orders, apparently rethought the course of his expedition, requesting from Wissmann additional men for the occupation of
Tabora and Karagwe. When the force attained Mpwapwa in June, encountering Carl Peters, returning from a fruitless mission to seek Emin,
and some White Fathers, all urged gaining control of Tabora, the Pasha
readily agreeing that the important center, vital to European communication with the coast, should not be left under Arab domination.[9]

The Tabora Arabs, aware of Emin's progress, began to discuss future
conduct, one faction, led by fierce old Ali bin Sultan, talking of war, while
another, behind Sayf bin Said, more realistically contemplated negotiations. The Arabs decided upon submission, making the choice in discussions carried on with a Bagamoyo trader, the Baluchi Ismail, sent by
Wissmann for talks with the Tabora community. Wissmann simply asked
acceptance of German rule, allowing the Baluchi, a man known to all, to
emphasize Muhammad bin Kassum's fate as a warning to individuals contemplating hostile actions against Germans. With troops wanting for an

effective garrison, Wissmann did not desire a more formal agreement, considering the Arabs likely to violate its terms. Greeted by Ismail with news of the Arabs' decision, Emin, after cordial discussions, concluded an agreement on 4 August 1890. The Arabs recognized German rule, with Sayf bin Said receiving appointment as liwali. The more reluctant Isike also came to terms. Wissmann's renewed orders for Emin to avoid Tabora did not arrive until after the negotiations.[10]

Wissmann's hesitations concerning premature treaty-making proved justified only for Isike, the Arabs henceforth not offering much cause for worry. By the 1890s the economic importance of Tabora declined, the European conquests on the East African coast and in the Congo forcing a shift to more locally focused commerce. The Muslim community, burdened as always by debts to Zanzibar's Indians, nonetheless remained prosperous, but it no longer included many of the most important Arabs of the East Central African interior.[11] Accepting the fact of Emin's treaties, Lieutenant Sigl, originally ordered to found a post at Usongo, established at Tabora. Arriving in early 1891 Sigl, commanding only seventy men, followed orders, refraining from playing an active role in the region. The Arab community, estimated at eighty coastal Arabs, plus another 5,000 Muslims, cooperated, avoiding open displays of slave-trading activity. Isike did not prove so tractable, his resolute resistance against encroachments upon his authority ending during 1892 with intermittent warfare. Most Arabs followed Sayf bin Said in siding with the Germans. Isike was defeated and killed in January 1893, the Germans not severely punishing the few Arabs who supported the ntemi, merely imposing a fine and a new loyalty oath.[12] There were no additional significant difficulties between Arabs and Tabora's European rulers.

Before leaving Tabora, Emin had considered marching westward for Ujiji, placing its major Muslim community under German authority, then continuing to his northern goal via Rwanda. Conversations with missionaries and others emphasized the dangers facing Europeans around Lake Victoria, Emin thus holding to the originally scheduled route, merely dispatching a letter offering the Ujiji Arabs an agreement similar to the Tabora community's. Rumaliza, heading the Ujiji Muslims, deftly returned willingness for an arrangement when the Germans arrived at his settlement.[13]

"As regards the Arabs in Magu, they will simply have to submit to whatever I think proper, and if they object they will be expelled from the country," warned Emin in September 1890 while setting forth for Lake Victoria. The Magu Arabs, shaken and disorganized after the recent defeats by the Ganda Christians, had not overcome losses in manpower and merchandise. Said bin Sayf, with other Arabs, had departed for Tabora and the coast. The remaining Muslims, uncertain of the future, either withdrew from the exposed lakeshore, many settling at Masanza, or sent gifts to Mwanga, hoping to ward off retaliation. During 1890 the Arabs did conduct some commerce with a British agent in Buganda, but they later withdrew inland when Peters passed through the region on his return journey to the coast.[14] After arriving at the lakeshore Emin, gathering complaints from Africans and White Fathers concerning supposed Muslim aggressions, quickly summoned the Arabs to German headquarters. Receiving no reply, Emin sent Franz Stuhlmann, with about 100 men, neither Arabs nor Europeans apparently making serious efforts to negotiate. In the ensuing battle the German troops, with superior weaponry, easily routed the Arabs, Stuhlmann's men summarily executing about six Arab prisoners. In a simultaneous incident a few Arabs came to Bukumbi for talks with the White Fathers about arranging terms with Emin, the priests conducting the Arabs to the German station. Apparently desiring Stokes to return the Arabs to the coast, Emin entrusted them to Catholic Ganda for delivery to Bukumbi and Tabora. The Africans, soon after leaving the Germans, mistreated and then drowned the Arabs. Emin most certainly had not intended this outcome, his past career not indicating the slightest inclination for the summary punishments often given by other contemporary Europeans. There is some uncertainty concerning the two unfortunate affairs, but, whatever the details, Emin received blame for his African and European subordinates' excesses. Wild stories explaining the Arab deaths spread widely through East Central Africa—in one popular version Emin, coveting the Arabs' property, simply ordered their deaths—the resulting resentment playing an important role in the German officer's subsequent death.[15]

The German conquests did not halt the growth of Islam, the numbers of Muslims steadily augmenting in German East Africa and British Tanganyika. In 1957, 31 percent of Tanganyika's population claimed adherence to Islam. The Christian European conquest, however, as elsewhere in East Central Africa, eventually relegated Muslims to a secondary rank among the territory's Africans.[16]

15 The Congo

> I came to this country and by my own wealth and power
> and at risk of my own life conquered these people years
> before you knew they existed and now you question my
> right to do with them what I please.
>
> —*Tippu Tip*

IN NOVEMBER 1883 Stanley, aiming for the ivory-rich lands of the Upper Congo, landed at Arab-dominated Stanley Falls, for the first time bringing into direct relations the Europeans and Arabs of the Congo. Both groups wanted control of the region's abundant ivory, opening a competition about whether it would continue flowing to the established Indian Ocean market of Zanzibar or to new lower Congo River factories of the Congo Independent State. The first encounter was peaceful enough, the Zanzibari followers of Stanley easing potential tensions between the two groups. Nyangwe Arab Abed bin Salim al Khethiri, described by Tippu Tip as one of the richer men of the region, collecting over 200 frasila of ivory monthly, was present, reporting a near brush with the Europeans, but recognizing Stanley, "the English American," the Arabs instead waited to learn the reason for the visit. Many Muslims quickly proved willing to trade ivory to the agents of Leopold's state, Abed bin Salim significantly noting: "They say Europe is easy of approach from where we are." About 7,000 pounds of ivory changed hands, the transfer depriving Barghash of an estimated £7,000 in customs revenues. Other information reaching Zanzibar included rumors that the Arabs were given State flags to hoist between Stanley Falls and Nyangwe, additionally agreeing to gather all remaining ivory for sale to Europeans, with payment made in Muscat to escape the sultan's retaliation. In all, later explained Tippu Tip, Abed bin Salim became so friendly to Europeans that "the people stopped him and were to fight him," forcing negation of the flag offer and canceling of some ivory transactions. Well satisfied with the general results obtained, Stanley

THE DOWNFALL OF THE ZANZIBAR EMPIRE

departed on December 10, leaving behind an agent, Andrew Binnie, with about thirty African soldiers, to begin constructing a station on one of the islands below the falls. Accompanying Stanley downriver were about ten Arabs and their property, hopefully advertising the river route advantages to the Muslim community.[1]

The news of Stanley's anticipated arrival at the falls stirred the directors of Arab policy in Zanzibar. Kirk, worried about the individualistic character of the Arabs, fretted: "If they can sell their ivory at a profit to the agents of the Association on the Congo they will do it."[2] Barghash was furious, demonstrating his anger during a meeting with French representative Lacau, ignoring the usual introductory formalities so much a part of Zanzibar political etiquette, protesting that Leopold, after accepting his help in Congo-related affairs for seven years, now endeavored to seize the most productive Arab territory. Barghash announced his intention of preventing the recently arrived Association expedition commanded by Jerome Becker from leaving the island, threatening with death any subjects who accepted service with the Belgians. Becker, instructed to march for Nyangwe, cultivating good relations with Arabs along the route, never left Zanzibar.[3] More importantly, Barghash ordered his subjects to hurry to Nyangwe and nearby regions prepared for potential hostilities. The directive was heeded. Said bin Habib, then en route to Zanzibar after many years of inland trade and travel, heard the news on Lake Tanganyika's shores, at once returning to Nyangwe, while the son of Mwinyi Kheri, visiting Zanzibar, immediately went back to Ujiji. Scores of lesser Arabs followed suit. In August 1884, partly because of the westward movement, Arthur Brooks judged Ujiji "deserted and decayed." It even was rumored that Barghash had commanded Tippu Tip and Juma bin Salim to bring in chains to Zanzibar any Arabs discovered selling ivory to Europeans.[4]

Kirk was not at all certain of the efficacy of Barghash's instructions. "From what I know of Tippoo Tib I do not think it possible he would take part in any attack upon Europeans," said the consul; "on the contrary I think he personally would be pleased to trade with the merchants from the West Coast and remittances by bills would be accepted by . . . his creditors."[5] In more recent times, Belgian historian Ceulemans contended Barghash had little real control over Tippu Tip's actions.[6] Yet the Belgian priest might have recognized that men often loyally follow leaders lacking effective secular sanctions for enforcing strict obedience. Tippu Tip, however powerful in his Congo domain, accepted Barghash's authority as reality, striving as long as the Arab sultanate remained viable to carry through his sultan's wishes. Regaining the Congo Arab settlements in late 1884, Tippu Tip immediately began undoing some of Stanley's breach of the Zanzibari system. Commanding a caravan with over 1,000 armed men Tippu Tip met no resistance when calling for explanations from Abed bin

Salim. "When he knew he had disobeyed," laconically remarked Tippu Tip, "he was sorry." Tippu Tip then arranged affairs to prevent, as much as possible, future ivory deliveries to Stanley's men.[7]

Before Tippu Tip's arrival Binnie, heeding Stanley's instructions for not meddling in Arab concerns, had lived peacefully with his Muslim neighbors, keeping occupied with building projects and cultivating the station gardens. In July 1884 Arvid Wester replaced Binnie, continuing the same careful policy. But the increased number of arriving Arabs, the result of Barghash's urgings, inaugurated a period of more difficult relationships. The Arabs wished to go down river past the State station, stepping up pressure in October when a leading Arab, Mwinyi Amani, entered Stanley Falls. After heated arguments, during which the young Arab threatened to use force, Wester reported signing a treaty prohibiting Arabs from passing the seventh cataract of the falls and from raiding in State territory. The State, in turn, limited its concerns to the lands below the named cataract. There appears little reason for Amani's conclusion of such an agreement, particularly if he knew its meaning, but Wester made the claim.

Arabs continued to arrive, Tippu Tip joining with a large armed party raising the total around the falls to about 1,200. In discussions with Wester, Tippu Tip denied Amani's right to negotiate, refusing to recognize the recent treaty, and announcing, as Barghash's representative, that all territory in the Congo region belonged to Zanzibar. Probably the Arab repeated the statement made to Hore in 1886. "He tells me himself," said the missionary, "that he *claims* right to the West coast and could take it if he likes but he has enough and does not wish to raise his hand against Europeans." To prove his assertion Tippu Tip announced to Wester his intention of leading a large expedition downriver past the State post, warning that any attempt at interference meant war. Tippu Tip, however, did not force hostilities, explaining with his usual diplomacy that his mission was to ensure that all ivory went to Zanzibar, with Wester's best possible reaction being the evacuation of the station. He even offered assistance in moving its property. But realizing Wester had orders to uphold, Tippu Tip promised to leave the post in peace if the Europeans did not interfere with Arabs. With only thirty men under his command, Wester wisely remained quiet when the Arabs moved downriver. With Arab supremacy established—American visitor E. H. Taunt saw slaves sold, the Arabs "not attempt[ing] the slightest concealment"—Wester lived cordially until departing in 1886. The State weakness and Tippu Tip's determined stance had preserved the working of the Zanzibar system.[8]

The dissatisfied directors of the Congo Independent State, hampered by limited finances, were powerless before the presence of Arab expeditions in their claimed territories. In January 1885 State officer Alphonse Vangele steamed upriver, hoping to convince Tippu Tip to cease raiding, additionally carrying an invitation for the Arab to visit Europe. Tippu Tip checked the nonplussed Belgian's arguments by reiterating Barghash's rights over all territory down to the Atlantic coast. Endeavoring to regain his thrust, Vangele countered that the extent of the sultan's possessions was a matter for discussion between representatives of their sovereigns, attempting to return to the question of raiding. Tippu Tip remained obdurate, denying the validity of the October 1884 treaty. Then, doubtless to prevent the talks from ending in an impasse possibly causing further problems, Tippu Tip, as a sign of goodwill, suddenly offered recall of his bands from the disputed regions of the Lomami and Aruwimi rivers if the State in return guaranteed that the African inhabitants would trade with Arabs. The Muslims, he disingenuously explained, raided only because Africans refused to trade. Such an arrangement, Vangele answered, required an interval of time after the cessation of raiding. Thus both sides had maintained face, the discussions terminating on an openly cordial note. During the talks Vangele demonstrated lack of awareness of Tippu Tip's character by asking why the Arab did not reject Barghash's authority, and act instead as an independent ruler of Manyema, thereby profiting by shipping ivory downriver to the Atlantic. Tippu Tip simply remained silent at this callous suggestion that he betray his sultan. The raiding did not cease after Vangele's departure, Tippu Tip's men continuing active in their existing localities, while Mwinyi Moharra kept busy along the Lomami. When British missionary George Grenfell visited Tippu Tip later in 1885 he found the Arab fully confident of his strength and not disposed to alter his commercial and administrative methods. "He is making large plantations, talks of building a stone house, and says he is expecting 2,000 more men," said Grenfell.[9]

Leopold, obviously unhappy, considered schemes by Congo governor Francis de Winton for a military expedition against the Arabs. But harsh economic reality precluded offensive action, the State during 1885 suffering serious lack of financial resources which, continuing until 1890, almost caused failure of Leopold's African enterprise. An additional weakening factor was the composition of State forces, the large numbers of Zanzibari making officials doubt the outcome of any conflict.[10] Wester, his service time expired, merely was replaced in February 1886 by another officer, Walter Deane, bearing the usual orders against provoking the Arabs into open hostilities. In contrast to Wester, who always recognized the weakness of his position and acted accordingly, Deane took a more aggressive stance, protesting to Tippu Tip about alleged mistreatment of Africans. European visitors noticed visibly cool relationships between the Arab and State commanders, yet contacts on an official level appeared satisfactory enough when in April Tippu Tip, recalled by Barghash, once again set off for Zanzibar, leaving the reliable Muhammad bin Said in charge of Arab affairs.[11]

The Arab and European tolerance for each other's presence ended in August 1886, a smoldering quarrel igniting into hostilities. Two opposing explanations were offered for responsibility for breaching the peace: nonetheless, the main facts are clear. According to information from Muhammad bin Said and his followers, a woman, variously described as a slave, wife, or concubine, fled to the State post, Deane refusing Arab requests to surrender her to her husband or owner. The Arabs, claiming that Deane previously had given shelter to other fleeing slaves, feared the effect of his attitude upon their remaining slaves, moreover asserting that Deane resisted their demands because of involvement with the woman. "But he had seen the woman sweet," charged Muhammad bin Said. Deane began to prepare for war after his refusal, the Arabs maintained, while they, countered Tippu Tip's agent, "held ourselves and all this for fear of our master Sayid Burgash." Momentary calm came when a State vessel docked, and the Arabs reported that the Europeans advanced unacceptable terms in the ensuing talks. When the vessel left, the Arabs accused Deane of beginning the fighting that ended with the loss of the State post. A later study by Belgian officer Francis Dhanis confirmed Deane had been guilty of raiding before the final conflict.

The European view of the episode, presented by Deane, State official Camille Coquilhat, and Grenfell—the latter conducting interviews at the falls after the fighting—agreed that a woman, fleeing from mistreatment, sought refuge at the station. Since she could not prove her case, Deane, after unsuccessfully endeavoring to purchase her freedom, returned the woman to her husband or owner on promise of no punishment being awarded. Once again mistreated, she returned to the post, Deane again offering to buy her freedom, then refusing to compel her to leave. There is conflicting information among Europeans concerning Deane's involvement in other slave affairs. When the State vessel anchored on August 22, Deane received neither sufficient reinforcements nor ammunition supplies. The situation clearly was dangerous, Grenfell reporting that in an interview between Deane and Muhammad bin Said the Arab had commented in direct fashion on the officer's behavior, pausing "to inquire whether Mr. Deane had well considered what he said, and whether he could take care of his head?" When Deane responded affirmatively, Muhammad departed in anger. After the vessel left, about 800 Arabs attacked the post.[12]

Whichever explanation is accepted, Deane, at a time when Arabs were still answering Barghash's orders to uphold his Congo claims,[13] bore responsibility for forcing a quarrel which he and a garrison of under fifty men had no chance of winning. The result was a transparent indication of the strength of the Congo Arabs and of State weakness, a fact further demonstrated by State inability to take action to regain the lost post.[14] The news of the fighting aroused Arabs everywhere in East Central Africa, both in jubilation over victory and in anticipation of possible European reaction. German traveler Wissmann, then in Arab territory, learned that many Muslims were gathering for the expected European return. Moreover, Wissmann decided that Tippu Tip's son Sefu, to him "a passionate, suspicious, and cunning fellow," more or less held him hostage until acertaining his father in Zanzibar was not considered responsible for the falls embroglio.[15]

While the dramatic events transpired, Tippu Tip had been prosaically proceeding on the march to Zanzibar, unknowingly entering into a critical stage in his career. The forthcoming decisions the Arab magnate had to make were of the utmost importance due to the fact, now obvious to even his most devoted subordinates, that Barghash was losing the struggle to preserve his state. Tippu Tip had to answer this question: what should his reaction be to the pending transformation in the affairs of East Central Africa's Arabs? With his growing wealth, plus the rigors of the long trips to Zanzibar, it was not surprising that Tippu Tip meditated over the future even before learning the results of Deane's misplaced zeal, admitting in July 1886 to Hore desires for a "more settled life and occupation under some European government or other extensive enterprise."[16] There had not yet occurred any important difficulties between Tippu Tip and Europeans to hinder such an arrangement; all during his long career the Arab generally maintained the best personal terms with explorers, missionaries, and government officials. In November 1885, for example, missionary soldier Léopold Joubert noticed a caravan en route to Zanzibar with "curiositiés" of Manyema sent by Tippu Tip to Europeans in Zanzibar.[17] The expressed desires for a quiet life, however, probably were just vocal musings, the still active Tippu Tip then germinating in his mind another major undertaking, an expedition to relieve Emin Pasha, the German reportedly holding huge stocks of ivory. Wondering if the British might award him the task, Tippu Tip admitted his readiness to proceed to Europe for discussions concerning the project.[18]

Tippu Tip landed on Zanzibar in November 1886. His arrival, remarked French consul Raffray, accompanied the "curious coincidence" of Barghash requesting from him a copy of the Berlin Act. The conversation occurred at a moment when the city was swept by rumors that the sultan intended to create an independent state in Manyema, if the Germans made continuing in Zanzibar impossible. The thought perhaps had entered Barghash's thinking, but probably never seriously. Except for brief journeys away from Zanzibar, and his short Indian exile, Barghash had lived his life along Africa's east coast, possessing limited knowledge of the continent's interior, while the increasing serious illnesses of his last years effectively precluded residence away from the Arab court's easy conditions.[19] While contemplating the future, Barghash endeavored to keep his powerful Congo subordinate under wraps, asking Tippu Tip to refrain from visiting European consulates. Although complying, Tippu Tip nonetheless remained his usual alert self, at once making known to the Belgian consul his good intentions toward Leopold. When in December news of the Stanley Falls fighting reached Zanzibar, Tippu Tip immediately secured permission to visit Belgian consul Cazenave, in their meeting denying forcefully any Arab fault, stressing that Deane, from his arrival, had blunted the previously satisfactory relations existing between Arab and European. And, the Arab asserted, Deane on several occasions before the period of troubles had attempted to purchase the female slave whose flight ended in conflict. Muhammad bin Said, continued Tippu Tip, was a man of peace, as was he: if they intended to fight the State, would he have left for Zanzibar? Tippu Tip concluded by alleging willingness to live in peace with Leopold, withal reminding the Belgian that he possessed the power to defend himself when necessary, offering, if Leopold so desired, to travel to Belgium to discuss the future.[20]

Other significant conversations occurred with Barghash and Holmwood. The harassed sultan, Tippu Tip said years later, had lost hope in the struggle for his dominions. "I really do not want the hinterland at all," Barghash admitted. "When I heard Sayyid's words," concluded Tippu Tip, "I knew that it was all up." The news of the Deane affair confirmed the impression that when seeking advice from the sultan, Tippu Tip disappointingly discovered "his power all gone." Thus Tippu Tip requested and received permission from Barghash to inaugurate talks with the British. In dealing with Holmwood Tippu Tip demonstrated himself a strong, yet flexible, leader, explaining Arab preparedness for uniting against European attempts to regain the lost State post, even claiming Muslim readiness, if pressed, to call a jihad. Then, sharply turning emphasis, the Arab announced willingness to place himself at British disposal to solve the problems arising from the Deane crisis, proclaiming eagerness to cancel the planned search for Emin and to return to the Congo once Salisbury requested his services. But there were conditions; behind his smooth approach lay the undoubted strength of the Arab position. "He is . . . averse to taking such a step," explained Holmwood, "unless he is assured that he will meet some officer of the Association who is acquainted with the country and who knows something of the language, as in the event of his being met by unjust and impracticable demands on the part of the Association he considers . . . he would be unable to restrain the Congo Arabs from combining against the Association." In short, no officer of Deane's type was wanted. The Foreign Office, then uninterested in involvement in that part of Africa, rejected any connection with the Arab, one official noting he might be "a very awkward protegé." Tippu Tip simply was informed to work for peace.[21] Yet, even without a positive response from London, Tippu Tip had opened a valuable communication channel with Holmwood would soon bring important benefits.

Thus by the close of 1886 the Arabs held practical domination of the

Upper Congo, facing little obvious threat from the inept and weak Congo Independent State forces. Several travelers visited the area in that year, providing some indication of the growth and development of the prosperous Arab territories. Nyangwe, rich in provisions because of healthy agricultural prospects, and well stocked with merchandise from the continent's east coast, had a population of about 10,000. Oskar Lenz did not notice a mosque, but there were many Muslims, both Arab and African, in residence. One of the town's first settlers, Abed bin Salim—"partially compelled," said Wissmann, by the sultan to return to Zanzibar for paying debts, and perhaps to answer for the earlier dealings with Stanley—headed for the coast during 1886, his first visit since arriving in the Congo twenty-eight years previously. The pioneer Arab died while traveling to Muscat. Another early settler, Juma bin Salim, still resided near Nyangwe, where Wissmann found 500 tusks of ivory piled before his house. Old and ill, Juma died before the year's end. Lenz considered Said bin Habib the greatest merchant residing in Nyangwe, although Mwinyi Moharra probably remained the town's most powerful Arab. Kasongo, growing steadily, still appeared of lesser standing than Nyangwe, its population reaching 8,000. The trade brought by Tippu Tip's constantly entering and leaving caravans, plus the town's rich agricultural holdings, guaranteed healthy prosperity. Other smaller Arab settlements shared in the good times, as did lesser African villages aligned with Arabs. There was, regretfully, another side to life in the Congo. The Arabs persisted in raiding, becoming especially active in lands north of the Aruwimi and west of the Lomami and Sankuru.[22]

The power realities of the Congo, making Tippu Tip, in Stanley's description, "an uncrowned king of the region between Stanley Falls and Tanganika Lake," had to be faced by State authorities when in 1886 Stanley set forth to relieve the beleagured Emin Pasha. The expedition was scheduled to proceed to its goal through State territories, Leopold seizing advantage of his contract with Stanley to turn the venture to benefit his schemes for northeast expansion. Since the expedition was to be organized in Zanzibar, Stanley and Leopold recognized Tippu Tip's assistance as essential, particularly since the Arab, uncertain about Stanley's exact goal, was strengthening his position around the falls, the vital starting place for a northeast journey. It was rumored there already were 3,000 followers of the Arab chieftain in its vicinity. Consequently Stanley thought of offering Tippu Tip a State position, the Arab receiving an annual salary in return for acceptance of State authority. Stanley claimed he advised Leopold's adoption of this tactic, "it being a far cheaper, and more humane method to disarm his hostility than the costly method of force," especially, as he exaggeratedly informed de Winton, since the Arab was preparing at Zanzibar "for the most important raid of all—that is, down the Upper

Congo." Stanley neglected to add that the State then lacked the ability to do otherwise.

Meantime in Zanzibar, Tippu Tip continued discussions with Holmwood concerning some form of agreement with Leopold, openly unimpressed by the Briton's warnings of an eventual Belgian return in armed steamers up the Congo River. When Stanley reached Zanzibar in February 1887, the three, Tippu Tip, Holmwood, and Stanley, extended the pourparlers. During the meetings Tippu Tip once again demonstrated skill as a negotiator by deftly emphasizing his ability to block the progress of Stanley's expedition. At one moment in the conversations, becoming "exceedingly wroth," the Arab dramatically exhibited three shells, sent by Muhammad bin Said, used by Deane against his men. Accustomed to Arab methods, Stanley calmly announced readiness for combat. Alternatively Stanley offered Tippu Tip the post of governor of the Stanley Falls district, his duties to include defense of State territory, suppression of the slave trade, and abstention from State lands below the falls, all for the nominal annual salary of £30. Substantial profits, of course, naturally would flow to the holder of the office. Leopold recognized the value of the agreement, and Barghash advised acceptance, allowing formal conclusion on 24 February 1887.[23] The Arab had made an important decision, granting significant concessions to Europeans because of the realization Zanzibar no longer was much of a factor in African politics. Commercial considerations were uppermost in his mind when the agreement was signed, Tippu Tip confirmed in a Reuters interview; the changing situation in East Central Africa due to the German arrival caused a sharp decline in Arab profits from the Congo trade.[24]

The revelation of an alliance between one of the most famous of Africa's Arabs, known chiefly to Europeans as a major slave-trade participant, and the self-proclaimed humanitarian Congo Independent State, shocked many Europeans. Missionaries cried out against agreement "with perhaps the vilest wretch Africa ever saw," "the robber and murderer of hundreds and thousands of our fellow-creatures in the heart of Africa." Henceforth, declaimed Horace Waller in disgust, he would call the State "Tippootibia."[25] Much of the Belgian press opposed the appointment, as did many anti-Arab individuals within State ranks.[26] Jerome Becker and a few others, regarded by contemporaries as pro-Arab, defended the arrangement as a practical step in the peaceful development of the immense domains claimed by the State, Becker noting he earlier had suggested to Leopold a similar alliance.[27] Doubtless, many Arabs, though leaving little record of their feelings, similarly discussed Tippu Tip's adhesion to the Europeans. Some indication of opinion surfaced when the Arab leader assumed the new appointment at Stanley Falls.[28] Realistically, despite the general satisfaction in ruling circles, many problems remained for both

Arabs and Europeans, neither Tippu Tip nor Leopold yet contemplating any definitive surrender of rights each felt he possessed in the Congo. As Tippu Tip later said: "I was given Belgian flags to plant in every one of the places which were mine by right."[29]

Nonetheless, for the moment, the latent hostilities between the State and Tippu Tip ceased, the new agent accompanying Stanley's expedition in the steamer journey to the Congo River mouth. As Stanley prepared for Emin's quest, Tippu Tip had occasion for studying the ongoing progress of State work along the river's lower course, remaining enough of an acute observer to comment to an official stressing State power: "Yes, it is a large country *on paper*." Encountering missionary reproaches for the supposed excesses of his past career, the coolheaded Arab simply countered: "Ah, yes! I was a young man then; now you see my hair is turning gray; I am an old man and shall have more consideration." The Arab governor reached the falls in June 1887, the watchful men on shore inadvertently firing on his boat, flying the State flag, before realizing their leader's presence.[30]

Although immediately welcomed by his own followers, Tippu Tip discovered other Arabs regarding with grave suspicion his alliance with Leopold, rightly fearing their overpowerful rival intended furthering his personal dominance of the Upper Congo. Said bin Habib was a particularly outspoken opponent, refusing to recall his raiding parties when Tippu Tip so requested. "He is in the act of spoiling my work," complained the new State official. Tippu Tip reported his first efforts to Holmwood, emphasizing the bringing of stability to some areas by checking Arab raiding. "I made the people go back to their own villages in an orderly manner," he announced, adding, "in some other villages people have not yet returned, because they are still afraid—Inshallah! I shall make them hasten." Yet because of such forceful actions, he lamented, "all the Arabs have become antagonistic to me." Thus, although not doubting his ability to control the local situation—"I alone am quite enough for them but I need some one to stand by me"—Tippu Tip suggested Holmwood "should write to the great Sultan of Belgium to send to me Europeans and about 40 or 50 soldiers." But Stanley, although sanguine over affairs at the falls—"Tippu Tip will make the very best Governor that could be found for that distant station"—at that early moment ensured the Arab's distrust of the State's real intentions. Tippu Tip became most upset when Stanley failed to deliver supplies of gunpowder agreed upon during their first deliberations, threatening to go to Leopoldville himself for the goods, then bill Stanley and return to Zanzibar if the charges were rejected. All Tippu Tip received in return for his fulminations were vague promises, their nonsatisfaction persisting as a continuous irritant in the evolving relationship between the Arab and the State.[31]

Ignored by State authorities after Stanley's departure, Tippu Tip became increasingly restive. The officers of Stanley's rear guard, frequently communicating with the Arab, sympathized with his expressed unhappiness, Edward Barttelot deciding Tippu Tip was "justly aggrieved" by violation of promises made when he agreed to return to the Congo. To Jameson, after a year of waiting, Tippu Tip fumed: "If I find all the power gone from the Belgians as it is from the Sultan, then I will take it all myself."[32] The State finally reacted to its governor's complaints, Guillaume Van Kerchkhoven arriving in May 1888 for discussions; he was the first State officer ashore since Deane's enforced departure. During their conversations Tippu Tip and Van Kerckhoven, reported Barttelot, had a "tremendous row," the probable result of arguments over the Arab's planned activities in the Aruwimi region. Van Kerckhoven promised resistance to any Arab incursion into State-claimed territory. There also may have been discussions concerning the securing of Tippu Tip's support for Leopold's schemes of northeast expansion. No resolution of any issues discussed was attained, with Jameson noting in June that relations between the two were "decidedly strained at present." But no open crisis occurred, the Arab and Belgian curbing their emotions and leaving the problems unsettled. Tippu Tip did gain one aim with the landing, shortly after Van Kerckhoven, of a State party bringing the long-awaited European resident.[33] A chief reason for the delays in fulfilling the terms of the February 1887 accord was admitted by Baron van Eetvelde: even if the State lacked excuses for distrusting Tippu Tip's good faith, "still he did not think that an Arab was to be trusted." Henceforth, he vowed, there would be a permanent agent at the falls, the State regarding it dangerous for Tippu Tip to "remain without an European to control him."[34]

Already well aware of Belgian ambivalence and facing continuous opposition from rival Arabs, Tippu Tip did not wait supinely for the State establishment of his future perimeters. Knowing of the European rivalries for African territory—E. Glave in an 1887 encounter was much impressed by the Arab's knowledge of European affairs—he ventured in mid-1888 into exploratory diplomacy. Writing his brother Muhammad bin Masud, then in Zanzibar, Tippu Tip stated awareness of European claims for the African interior, lamenting the coastal concession planned between Germans and Arabs: "We were astonished on hearing this extraordinary news." As a de facto independent interior ruler, Tippu Tip informed Muhammad of the necessity of safeguarding his own interests, advising friendliness to Germans. "You need not be ashamed to join with Europeans," he explained, "inasmuch as our Sultan has already done so." Tippu Tip suggested that his brother, bearing a list of lands supposedly under his influence, go to the Germans to discuss some form of arrangement. The Belgians, he added for good measure, held only the region around Stanley Falls, and even that really was his. But, after this important advice, Tippu

Tip changed course, requesting Muhammad first to see the British consul—it, of course was no accident that all this information ended in British
hands—and inform him that Tippu Tip, following British counsel, had
entered into agreement with Belgians who then began to claim his territories. Tippu Tip stressed the Congo Arabs' ability for repelling anyone
seeking possession of their holdings. But, said the Arab, he regarded the
British as friends, significantly adding: "I do not think they are willing to
see me in the hands of any other people or in trouble."

If the British had been interested in the section of Africa under Tippu
Tip's influence, they had the opportunity to profit from consultations with
the Congo chieftain. The British, however, not intending to interfere in
the Congo, did not respond; Euan Smith merely observed "that Tippoo is
not wholly free from a tendency to double dealing and from a not un-
natural desire to make the best terms for himself in the conflict for territory
which he evidently considers is about to take place in Central Africa between the European powers." It was not "double dealing," of course, the
Arab acting with statesmanlike ability in trying to secure outside assistance
for maintaining his Congo domains.[35] During 1889 Tippu Tip continued
to keep a line of communication open to the British, in March, for example, writing to the Zanzibar consul requesting assistance in informing
Leopold of his loyalty to the State, at the same time asking the king for the
delayed firearms. They were needed, explained Tippu Tip, because "now
all the Arabs are my enemies. They say I am the man who gave up all the
places of the mainland to the Belgian King." The favor was asked, Tippu
Tip informed Gerald Portal, since it was the British "who put me in the
friendship of the Belgian King." Tippu Tip concluded by announcing he
intended to return to Zanzibar to pay homage to Khalifa, although a more
likely reason was the chance for discussion of the issues raised in the several
letters to the British. The beginning of the Arab-German war, however,
caused postponment of the journey.[36]

While Tippu Tip endeavored to sort out his future, the State took an
important step toward circumscribing Arab power. As early as October
1886 it had been suggested to Leopold that building stations near the
mouth of the Aruwimi and on the upper reaches of the Lomami and
Sankuru was necessary to check Arab expansion.[37] In 1888 the idea was
joined to Leopold's desire to extend State boundaries to the northeast, the
king selecting Becker to head an expedition to the Nile. Before Becker set
off, Van Kerckhoven led an advance party to the Aruwimi region, establishing a State post at Basoko without informing Tippu Tip. In February
1889 Becker arrived at Stanley Falls, hoping for Tippu Tip's support for
the northeast venture, the king offering 50,000 francs for each State post
established. Tippu Tip, not liking State conditions, was not interested,

Becker's mission ending without result except for the stationing of an agent at the falls to purchase ivory. The Basoko post also remained.[38]

The obvious challenge was matched by another disturbing State initiative, a decree prohibiting sales of firearms and ammunition, a serious hindrance to Arabs then feeling the effects of the disruptive Arab-German war. In February 1889 an angry Tippu Tip burst into the State post at the falls, protesting the decree, emphasizing loyalty to the State, and asserting continuation of the regulation would be regarded as violating the contract binding him to Leopold. If satisfaction did not come within six months, stormed the Arab, he considered the agreement void. At the same time Tippu Tip complained to Van Kerckhoven about the Basoko post, although he did not demand its removal.[39] Nevertheless, despite strained relations, during 1889, Arab and Belgian remained at peace. One sign of the persisting intimacy was the sending in April of the first State representative to Kasongo. When State agent Nicolas Tobback of Stanley Falls declared that "nothing would please the Arabs more than living in good relations with us," many Arabs and Europeans shared the sentiment.[40]

The year 1890, without anyone realizing it, marked an important turning: Tippu Tip for the last time left the territories he had so much influenced. The Arab leader, in his early fifties, stood at the peak of his career, doubtless planning for his expected return new methods of development. Realizing the precariousness of relations between Belgians and Arabs, Tippu Tip was open to new alternatives for buttressing his local standing. Zanzibar no longer figured as a useful source of support. "The new Sultan of Zanzibar has abandoned me completely," lamented the Arab to Van Kerckhoven; "I am a wingless bird perched on a tree branch which my enemies wish to fell . . ." The only substitute, he emphasized, was more assistance from the State.[41] But Tippu Tip could leave the Congo without undue worry, his power still placing him at the forefront of the Arab community. "He is indeed a remarkable man . . . ," remarked Herbert Ward in 1889, "still as active and supple as a youth, and brim full of vitality and energy." Tippu Tip's wealth was enormous; during the same visit Ward exclaimed in wonder: "I think there must have been thirty tons of ivory lying in front of his house."[42] By this period the profits from his many trading ventures had been invested in ownership of land and buildings in Zanzibar, Tippu Tip additionally lending extensively to Arab newcomers into his lands, both for profit and to ensure recognition of authority.[43] Yet if much had changed for the Arab first entering the region over twenty years previously, he persisted in the plain pattern of dress and adornment common to his Arabian and Zanzibari ancestors. "There was nothing particular in his appearance to indicate in any way his being a remarkable man," observed Jephson in 1887. Once Ward asked Tippu Tip to explain this unostentatious manner of living. "'Ah' he replied, 'it is better that I should live in a house like this, because it makes me remember that I am only an ordinary man, like others. If I lived in a fine house with comforts I should perhaps end by thinking too much of myself.' "[44]

When leaving for Zanzibar, Tippu Tip, as usual, left his Congo domains under the direction of a small, interconnected group of chieftains. His son and expected heir Sefu bin Hamid, a popular individual, assumed overall control. Normally a resident of Kasongo, although often visiting Stanley Falls, Sefu was absent in Zanzibar when Tippu Tip headed for the east coast, returning to the Congo in late 1890. At his side, with direct responsibility for territories from Kasongo to Kabambare, was the trusted Muhammad bin Said; he managed affairs when Sefu was absent. By this time Kasongo clearly was the principal urban center of the upper Congo; it was, in Trivier's astonished eyes, "truly a city." A walk of two hours' duration was required for passing from one side of the town to the other, its residences interspersed among fields of rice and other crops.[45] Nyangwe continued under Mwinyi Moharra's firm leadership; he commanded an estimated 4,000 armed followers. The other influential Nyangwe Arab, Said bin Habib, the opposer of Tippu Tip's State-inspired orders, left during 1889 for a long-postponed return to Zanzibar. Said died on the march, closing one of the most eventful careers of any East Central African Arab. At Stanley Falls, a bustling center of trade, Tippu Tip's nephew, Rashid bin Muhammad bin Said al Murjebi, in 1890 depicted by a Belgian visitor as "a long and lean *gaillard*, with dark eyes and a hooked nose," was in charge. Other leading Arabs were Hamid bin Ali at Kirundu, Muhammad bin Hamis bin Galaf, known as Nserera, at Riba Riba, where Said bin Abedi also resided, and Muhammad bin Khalfan, the latter's reach extending from Kabambare to the eastern shores of Lake Tanganyika. Ngongo Lutete retained his important command as leader of Tippu Tip's forces along the Lomami and Sankuru.[46]

When Tippu Tip began the long journey to Zanzibar, leading some 3,000 men in several caravans bearing his ivory,[47] there was no expectation of immediate difficulties between European and Arab. Some later commentators have thought otherwise. G. A. von Götzen concluded after conversing with the Arab in 1894 that he left foreseeing future difficulties. British historian Slade's characterization of Tippu Tip as an "uncertain ally . . . it was not surprising that he had decided to leave for Zanzibar when he saw fighting was imminent," also does not fit the reality of the era.[48] To postulate inevitable conflict, with hindsight's wisdom, is to accept the myopic view that Congo Muslims were only "Swahili slave-traders . . . and their followers," people with whom long-term peace was not possible.[49] Since State officers then purchased Africans from the Arabs, any distinction based on slave dealing is rather difficult to maintain.[50] Tippu Tip left merely to sell ivory in Zanzibar, a move under contemplation for over a year, to revisit his island homeland, and to undertake the pilgrimage to Mecca.[51]

An additional unpleasant reason for the exact timing of the journey was the need to answer charges brought by Stanley against Tippu Tip's conduct during the Emin Pasha expedition. In the general aftermath of bitterness over the heavy loss of life that marred the return of the reluctant Emin, Stanley blamed Tippu Tip's alleged failure to supply porters for his rear guard as a principal cause of difficulties. Upon discovering that the Arab's agent held £10,000 paid for ivory bought from Tippu Tip by Becker, Stanley succeeded in placing it under injunction. Missionary Swann reported Tippu Tip "bursting with indignation" at Stanley's action. Sultan Khalifa acceded to the British wish to try the case in their consular court, although the British did strive to avoid appearance of siding with Stanley in the dispute, fearing that the Arabs might react by moving closer to the Germans. Wissmann, for instance, cautioned Sefu that the British, wishing to ruin his father, really supported Stanley. He advised the young Arab to look to the Germans for assistance. The competition between British and Germans largely stemmed from rivalry over drawing the interior trade to the ports of their coastlines. Sefu, arriving at Sadani in July 1889, had an early taste of the contest when Wissmann relaxed all German regulations, allowing his caravan, caught in the disorder of the Arab-German war, to pass freely to Zanzibar. British officials, by their dual role in the forthcoming court deliberations, thought they had won a major advantage in the rivalry. Others were not so sanguine, Henry Johnston urging a halt to the judicial process, fearful of the result a decision favorable to Stanley might have on Arabs in contact with his administration.[52]

Tippu Tip may have been aware of some of these machinations, but as always he proceeded in deliberate fashion upon his appointed task. When departing Stanley Falls, around April 1890, he advised the indigenous Genya to avoid all difficulties with Europeans and left behind there and at other settlements a prosperous and generally quiet region. Along the route the Arab chieftain renewed contacts with various European residents, at a September meeting with the Ujiji White Fathers insisting he no longer had anything to do with the slave trade: "Since I have promised my sovereign not to raid for slaves, I have kept my word." Also meeting with his associate Rumaliza, then at odds with the Europeans around the lake, Tippu Tip counseled that explosive Arab to remain at peace. And Tippu Tip gave his ongoing British policy a fresh turn, an agent of Johnston on southern Lake Tanganyika soon receiving a message that Tippu Tip and his associates desired "to have a consultation and understanding on all matters . . . they want no troubles or misunderstandings with the English, and would take the English flag if we would give it to them . . ." Since the Germans threatened the Arab lakeside position, the reason for the communication was obvious.[53]

Meantime Leopold, acting to ensure continued stable relations with his Arab subordinate, sought British aid in Zanzibar. "I am very anxious that nothing should be neglected," said the king to Euan Smith, "in order to strengthen Tippu Tib's allegiance to the state."[54] The consul complied, talking with Sefu while awaiting Tippu Tip, particularly about the Congo Arab's long-discussed visit to Belgium, advising against the trip because of the notoriety arising from the Emin controversy. Sefu stimulated British and Belgian interest during the conversations, claiming his father had important news relating to the nature of his State position. In a related move, Leopold sent Louis Haneuse to Zanzibar to discuss with Tippu Tip the issues outstanding between Arab and European, including in the agenda a renewal of the Becker proposals for a northeast move, this time with more independent initiative left to Tippu Tip, and for Arab recruitment of large numbers of Africans for State service. Delays in Tippu Tip's progress, the result of illness, plus the Belgian's similar ill health, caused the latter's withdrawal from Zanzibar before the Arab's arrival.[55]

While the Congo Arab community lacked its wisest leader—the only individual possessing both the prestige and the power required for holding its more intemperate members under control, plus the vital experience necessary for dealing with Europeans in a manner allowing the Arab viewpoint to be listened to instead of being summarily dismissed as the plaint of slavers—it faced a new barrage of European initiatives. One challenge rose from the State's continuing financial weakness; with its resources by 1890 almost at an end, there emerged a policy of government commercial monopolies. To assist State officers, purchasing ivory for government account since 1885, an 1891 decree forbade selling ivory to foreigners. By 1892 ivory provided significant profits for Leopold, the Congo exports elevating Anvers's ivory market to third place among European cities. This was also the period when Leopold, preserving their resources for the State, issued the September 1891 secret decrees closing the Aruwimi, Uele, and Ubangi districts.[56] When news of the first ivory measures reached Zanzibar and Europe, van Eetvelde repeated previous disclaimers that instructions had been issued that violated the agreements setting up the Congo Independent State. Instead he blamed the rumors on an Arab effort "to stir up commercial rivalry and suspicion between European Powers in Africa." Any measures taken, he added, were designed only to block the contraband trade from the east coast.[57] Still, the State actions, though irritating, were not immediately troubling to Arabs: they remained the principal collectors of ivory, selling to whoever made the best offer. Leopold continued to be unconcerned with forceful steps against Arabs, his interests centering on expanding frontiers and increasing revenue. The attitude was sound—and necessary: in January, State military strength was listed at only 3,127 soldiers.[58]

As elsewhere in Africa policies expressed in Europe did not control local events. Moreover, Leopold's musings concerning peace were endangered by contradictory policies supporting extension of State influence. The sending of expeditions from Basoko to the territories around the Aruwimi, Uele, and on toward the Nile led to conflict with Arabs. A Van Kerckhoven venture aiming for the region's effective occupation presaged cessation of existing Arab penetration. Beginning in late 1890 the expedition's advance sections encountered Arab groups around the confluence of the Aruwimi and Bomokandi rivers. The Arabs were attacked and defeated, the Belgians' African followers inflicting major losses on the fleeing enemy. Other combats continued into 1891. During the engagements the State seized great amounts of booty, including over ten tons of ivory. The disastrous Arab losses, in men and property, included caravans sent by Sefu, Rashid bin Muhammad, and Mwinyi Moharra to a territory considered for years their own. In reality the State, by allowing its officers to clear the region of Arabs, had declared war on the Congo's Arab community, setting off a sequence of happenings that culminated in its destruction. The responsibility for the initial action was clear, British representative Roger Bannister, for instance, learning from African State soldiers that their officers had rejected all Arab efforts to avert conflict. The Belgians, however, justified the fighting, explaining that the expedition's officers before heading northeast had held talks with Rashid, reminding the Arab of regulations prohibiting passage of Arabs beyond the Aruwimi. Rashid supposedly responded that he had sent none of his men there, agreeing that the Belgians might deal as they chose with Arabs they encountered. It was not a very convincing explanation. When news of the victories reached Leopold, he welcomed the triumphs, ordering his men to seize every opportunity for ending the role of the raiding—and competing—Arabs.[59]

Arab bitterness at their losses caused some leaders to plan revenge. Sefu, holding true to instructions, merely wrote to Zanzibar about State aggressions, any answer naturally requiring many months.[60] During the interval the Arabs were further aroused by the execution at Basoko of three Arabs charged with raiding and by news of the Jacques' expedition, ostensibly sent against the slave trade, arriving on Lake Tanganyika.[61] The general unease among Arabs resulting from these several European offensive movements coincided with the entry of private European traders seeking ivory, an event not necessarily causing problems since the traders did not plan to bypass Arabs, but rather to purchase their ivory. The group, the Société Commercial de Katanga, led by Arthur Hodister, was the result of careful planning inaugurated a few years previously. Hodister, a much-traveled and experienced man, who had visited Zanzibar, had been active in the Congo since 1883. As an agent of another company, he had undertaken during 1890 an exploratory venture into Arab territory, visiting Kasongo, Nyangwe, and other centers, establishing cordial relationships with the Arab leadership. Both Tippu Tip and Moharra held friendly meetings with the Belgian trader. After returning to Europe, Hodister advocated a scheme for commercial development of the region between the Lualaba and Lomami, envisaging Arabs selling ivory to agents of a new company. Hodister considered Arabs, at that particular stage of the Congo's history, "a natural intermediary" between Africans and Europeans, trade serving as a means both of keeping the peace and influencing Arabs. When ivory resources were depleted, Hodister foresaw Arabs turning quietly to agriculture. His proposals accepted, Hodister was named director of the new organization. Returning with about twenty followers to the Congo in February 1892, Hodister immediately began preparations to make his scheme reality.[62]

Landing at Stanley Falls in March, Hodister's group discovered the hostilities along the Aruwimi and Bomokandi had had a profound effect upon Arab opinion. In one of his last letters Hodister reported a conversation with Rashid, the obviously unhappy Arab—Hodister found him "dejected and sorrowful"—protesting the difficulties of following Tippu Tip's instructions. If the State desired the Arabs to leave, Rashid avowed, then its officers should say so and the Arabs would comply. Other Arabs, not interested in the indirect diplomacy of Rashid's conversations—an Arab departure causing a catastrophic drop in the ivory trade—openly talked of war. The Société agents additionally encountered problems in business dealings, the Arabs having lost much property in the combat with the Belgians. Nonetheless, Hodister experienced little open animosity, Arab leadership at the falls sending letters of recommendation to Arabs the trader intended to visit. Before leaving, Hodister learned that the region's State agents were buying ivory in the Arab zone, complaining over this clear attempt at undercutting his venture. As part of the effort, State officer Isidore Michiels went to Nyangwe in March, discussing with Moharra the building of a station at Riba Riba. The veteran Arab leader, furious at the losses suffered by Arabs in the north, replied he wanted neither government nor private Europeans at Muslim centers. The dangers of the Arabs not distinguishing between the two soon became all too manifest. But Hodister, confident in the strength of his personal relationships with Arab chieftains, persisted in his original schedule, the expedition dividing into two sections, one aiming for territories along the Lomami, the other for the Nyangwe-Kasongo region.[63]

Then, with sudden fierceness, the Arabs struck at some of the Europeans. The Nyangwe-Kasongo group, led by Gaston Jouret, went upriver from the falls in late March, encountering along the way Michiels returning from Nyangwe. The Belgain officer reported his stormy interview with Moharra, attempting to convince Jouret to desist from the goal of creating commercial establishments. The private traders, considering Michiels' information vague, moreover regarding him as a competitor for ivory, did not pay much heed. The Société men continued on to a satisfactory welcome at Kirundu, after some trading advancing to Riba Riba on April 24. At first resisting the landing, the inhabitants changed attitude when they learned that the traders were Hodister's men. Nsesera appeared friendly enough, explaining he lacked authority to allow a trading post at Riba Riba, and charging Michiels had threatened to return in force to build. In early May, Tobback, State commander at the falls, joined the other Belgians. Despite repeated warnings of the dangers of residing among Arabs, the unworried traders again ignored the official advice. Shortly thereafter Jouret's party left for Nyangwe, while Tobback returned to the falls for talks with Sefu. One Société agent, Alfred Noblesse, stayed at Riba Riba, commencing work on a station; Michiels, on Tobback's orders, remained as an observer.

Reaching Nyangwe on May 17 Jouret strove without success to change Mwinyi Moharra's opinions, the Arab responding that the aggressive doings of the State had altered earlier circumstances. Jouret attempted to prolong the deliberations until Hodister's expected arrival, hoping his influence might prevail, but without success. Moharra ominously then informed the Belgians that two Europeans already were dead, protesting that he did not want to see them harmed. A planned continuation of the voyage to Kasongo had to be scrapped because of local hostility. Providing the troubled party with letters of safe conduct and an escort, Moharra sent the Belgians on their return downriver. But the Nyangwe men soon deserted, Jouret's group continuing to Riba Riba, where they were prevented from landing. After a difficult trip, during which Jouret perished, the survivors gained Stanley Falls. While Jouret traveled to Nyangwe, the two Belgians at Riba Riba had faced increasing trouble. There later were arguments concerning the role of each man, official E. Hinck alleging Noblesse had forced the issue by building despite contrary Arab orders, while Société agent C. Doré countered by questioning why the State had allowed its own man to remain at Riba Riba if the situation was as dangerous as claimed. Wherever fault resided, on May 10 Noblesse was killed at work; Michiels, trying to escape, shared his fate. Hodister meantime, hearing rumors of his colleagues' difficulties, headed for Nyangwe to discus matters with Moharra. Arriving at Riba Riba on May 15, probably unaware of the Belgian deaths, Hodister and three companions were killed while landing. Other agents of the Hodister expedition lost their lives, either by Arab action or by the hardships of flight to Stanley Falls.

It appears very likely that the outbreak against the Belgian traders was a spontaneous reaction to the Van Kerckhoven expedition. Mwinyi Moharra, despite his anger, had not been hostile to the Société men in his power while at Nyangwe. They reported his words against establishing as not spoken in anger, but rather as those of an individual determined to avoid future dealings with Europeans. It later appeared the Nyangwe chieftain had left orders to prevent, by force if necessary, government officials from building at Riba Riba, not envisaging the arrival of Hodister's party. Both Moharra and Nsesera were reported to be angry when they learned that Hodister had been killed. The Belgian trader had arrived in the Arab zone at the worst possible time. Blinded by self-confidence, plus distrust of government competition for Arab ivory, he unknowingly led his men into disaster.[64]

Whatever the exact cause, ten Europeans had died, seven directly from Arab attack, the largest number of Europeans killed by Arabs in East Central Africa at any one time. Both Rashid and Sefu denied knowing any more concerning the tragedy than the State officers knew. They protested their loyalty to the State and the orders of Tippu Tip. A subsequent study made by Francis Dhanis awarded blame to Moharra, Ceulemans agreeing. Tippu Tip, later in life after important quarrels, blamed Muhammad bin Khalfan. More likely, the blame for the deaths lay with Arabs and Africans reacting to the human and material losses caused by Van Kerckhoven's men. There clearly was no general plan, some Belgians being attacked while others were left alone. The frustrated and bitter Muslims simply struck at some intruding Europeans. There is no evidence at all involving Tippu Tip. As succeeding events demonstrated, his faction entered into final conflict with the State only with the utmost reluctance. It appears a reasonable surmise to this historian that, had Tippu Tip then been in the Congo, he might have checked the quarrels, preventing outbreak of a full-scale war. In any case, no general Arab move followed the Hodister tragedy, although the anxious Belgians at Stanley Falls learned that Moharra had ordered that all Europeans henceforth entering Arab territory should be killed. State officer Louis Chaltin nonetheless went up the Lomami into the Arab zone in late June without encountering resistance.[65]

The Congo Independent State leaders, fearing the consequences of widespread warfare, reacted to the news by vigorously counterattacking the Société Commercial de Katanga. Additional difficulties were unlikely, Leopold assured British representative Edward Monson, the entire embroglio probably arising because of "some offense against the domestic honour of the Arabs." The diplomatic explanations were matched by a vigorous press campaign featuring interviews by leading Congo officials. Opponents of the government case concluded that "the inauspicious [State] ivory policy is the sole cause of the revolt."[66]

With Leopold's fears concerning the results of general conflict, the Hodister episode might have passed without immediate reaction. But before the echoes quieted, with the Arabs still apprehensive over the European reaction to the deaths and aroused over their losses in the northeast, a major intervention by State officers against the vital interests of Tippu Tip precipitated the final clash. Ngongo Lutete, the forty-year-old trusted lieutenant of Tippu Tip, with other subordinates, had remained active during 1890 in the Lomami and Sankuru territories. The State Lusambo post, on the right bank of the Sankuru, founded the previous year to check Arab advances, inexorably had its officers drawn into the tumultuous politics of this frontier region. In August 1890 Ngongo Lutete invaded lands above Lusambo, chastising a local chieftain, Mpania Mutombo, for joining in alliance with the Belgian garrison. The officer in command, G. Descamps, held palavers with Ngongo, warning the African military commander to cease raiding. He refused and soon after in sharp combat the State forces defeated Ngongo's 7,000-man army.[67] The fighting gave the African his first experience of the strength of well-armed, disciplined State troops, coming at a time, Ceulemans claims, when Ngongo was unhappy over the precedence given Sefu by Tippu Tip in the border region's command.[68] It appears doubtful that Ngongo expected to be favored over his Arab master's son; even if some resentment was present, it did not surface until a subsequent State victory. Meanwhile, the Arab lieutenant became more familiar with European ways, in February 1891, for example, receiving at his camp the Belgian explorer Alexandre Delcommune. Rashid bin Muhammad, probably curious about Delcommune's presence, visited Ngongo at the same time, Delcommune reporting the extreme deference shown the Arab by the African. The Belgian seized the opportunity, explaining to Ngongo the advantages of leaving the Arabs and joining State forces.[69]

The urgings had little apparent result. Ngongo Lutete in 1892 once again led his followers into the Lusambo sphere, remaining determined to defeat Mpania Mutombo. From April 1892 Lusambo was commanded by Francis Dhanis, a headstrong young officer ready to disregard orders when he decided they hindered State progress. In two combats in May, Ngongo Lutete suffered two defeats, Dhanis winning immediate control of all territory between the Sankuru and Lomami. Tippu Tip's lieutenant had enough, the losses pushing the African into arranging peace negotiations. Dhanis, ignoring instructions for remaining on the defensive against Arabs, jumped at the chance to separate Ngongo from his superiors. During talks in August and September the African made his desires for independence from the Arabs clear, complaining of their treatment, and asserting that they "for some time past had paid him neither for his work nor for the ivory he sent them." Agreement came on September 19, Ngongo accepting Congo Independent State rule. Lupungu, another important Arab ally, followed Ngongo's example. From the Arab viewpoint the Belgian action in detaching the Africans was an aggressive measure striking at the heart of their Congo system, while Ngongo and Lupungu, by accepting the State offer, were guilty of treasonous conduct.[70]

Some indication of Arab reactions to the several State pressures is available. Two State agents, J.-F. Lippens and Henri De Bruyne, both present in Kasongo in 1892, observed excitement grow in the Arab community as news arrived of the Europeans' doings in the northeast and along Lake Tanganyika, the death of Hodister and his companions, and the Ngongo Lutete treaty. Mwinyi Moharra, although seemingly not contemplating offensive action, prepared to oppose any State move from Stanley Falls into the Arab zone, summoning assistance from all Arabs. Tippu Tip's faction continued to be committed to their absent leader's orders, even though most individuals naturally sympathized with Moharra's martial preparations. Before news of Ngongo's treaty arrived, the two Belgians were not at all sure of the resolution of the debate raging over the merits of peace or war. When the September events on the Lomami became known, opinion in Kasongo veered toward the more aggressive Arab leadership. Even the two Belgians, agreeing the original State pact with Tippu Tip guaranteed control of the territory surrendered by Ngongo, considered Sefu justified in upholding Arab interests. Sefu, reluctantly, with full awareness of the dangers involved, began preparations for joining Moharra, but only if Ngongo's defection remained unresolved. On October 1, with De Bruyne in tow for use in hopefully successful negotiations reversing Dhanis' policies, Sefu, commanding an estimated 10,000 men, marched southward. During the subsequent correspondence and discussions between Arabs and Belgians, De Bruyne, recognizing the reluctance of Tippu Tip's son for hostilities against the State and believing Arab forces capable of defeating his colleagues, strongly urged peaceful resolution of the Ngongo Lutete affair.[71]

Dhanis stood ready to oppose an Arab crossing of the Lomami. Ngongo rejected all advances, answering Sefu's embassy with "a magnificent velvet cloth destined, he said, to serve as the shroud of Tippo-Tip's son." The Belgians, reacting similarly to Wissmann on the East African coast and the Europeans on Lake Malawi, were not interested in a settlement. "Those ridiculous pretentions naturally were rejected," exclaimed Chaltin with customary nineteenth-century European arrogance. Sefu, probably realizing that the captive De Bruyne passed on information about Arab plans for crossing the Lomami, let him do so, hoping the data might cause a rethinking of policy by the outnumbered State troops. No changes occurred. In late November the united State forces under Dhanis, with African allies numbering several thousand men, joined combat when Sefu started across the river. The Arabs, during a brief battle, were defeated, losing many men in the panic of a disorganized retreat following the first fighting. Sefu was wounded, while his son was killed. As a consequence of the decisive victory, all Arab territory east of the Lomami lay open to the confident Dhanis's poised army.[72]

Until the Lomami battle there had been little sign of any concerted action against the Congo Independent State nor of any desire on the part of the latter for war with Arabs. Dhanis had pushed beyond orders, while Sefu, reacting against his father's directives with considerable misgiving, had struck to arrest serious State aggression. Sefu, realizing Ngongo's unpunished desertion meant virtual disintegration of Arab influence, had to go to war. Rashid bin Muhammad, remaining at Stanley Falls, in early December before learning of the Arab defeat, informed Tippu Tip that the Arabs in his faction did not wish war. "The Christians will not leave Gongo because he is very strong," he reasoned, emphasizing that his group still intended to obey orders, but warning that Mwinyi Moharra and Rumaliza argued for fighting. "God knows what will be the consequence of this," concluded the harassed Arab. When hearing of Sefu's defeat Rashid upheld Arab conduct. When Sefu asked the Belgians why they were assisting the rebellious Ngongo, they replied, according to Rashid, "No slave has power like this, he is the Sultan of his town." The answer, to the Arab, made war inescapable.[73] Tippu Tip, isolated from Congo events in distant Zanzibar, waited in anguish for news, writing his friend Becker affirming Sefu's orders forbidding fighting. After all, commented the worried Arab, if the Congo Muslims had planned war they would have struck immediately after Van Kerckhoven's aggression. Tippu Tip also confided to Becker and French consul L. Labosse that Ngongo, at the time of the treason, held much of his master's property, along with a major share of the 10,000 firearms he claimed to have sent inland since Livingstone's day. "All my riches, my men and my guns are in his hands," he lamented. How then could Sefu do anything but fight?[74]

The State government, unsure of the future, restrained its natural jubilation. There were no orders for additional hostilities. But the belligerent Dhanis planned to continue the offensive, by December talking of pushing on toward Nyangwe, Kasongo, and Lake Tanganyika. Whatever the opinions of his superiors, Dhanis had declared war on the Congo Arabs, adding his actions to the equally provoking conduct of Van Kerckhoven and Jacques. Ceulemans postulates that Dhanis, unaware of the effects of his operations on the larger Congo Arab community, only thought of defending the Lomami border when battling Sefu. The explanation is not convincing. If an Arab had interfered to gain the loyalty of a principal African State subordinate, Dhanis, and most fellow officers, immediately would have intervened. Dhanis acted when the opportunity came for detaching Ngongo from his masters, subsequently rejecting all Arab endeavors to heal the breach.[75]

After the Lomami fighting, the Arabs began to gather in Kasongo. With Dhanis advancing, there no longer remained any alternative to full-scale war. Lippens and De Bruyne were killed in retaliation for Sefu's defeat, although the young Arab bore no responsibility for the deaths.[76] Emin Pasha also suffered from the rising tide of hostility. Entering Arab territory in October Emin, unprepared for trouble, was killed while greeting the men of Hamid bin Ali. The Pasha had come to fight the Arabs, Rashid told Tippu Tip, but the unfortunate German, leading a very small expedition, was simply a victim of the general unrest—and his past conduct to Lake Victoria's Arabs.[77] In the Arab-State hostilities the opposing forces probably were roughly equal in numbers, Dhanis initially commanding three or four hundred State troops and 20,000 African allies. The State forces naturally possesed better arms, the Arab supporters almost all owning only antiquated weapons.[78] With each succeeding triumph, the numbers of the State's African allies increased. The first combat between the advancing State army and the Arabs occurred on December 30, the Arabs losing the contest. A little over a week later, Mwinyi Moharra, charging at the forefront of his men, was wounded during another State victory, the doughty Arab warrior dying shortly thereafter. Uniformly defeated in subsequent encounters, the Arabs sustained substantial losses due to ruthless African follow-up activity against fleeing troops.[79]

Dhanis marched directly toward Nyangwe, the principal Arab commanders regrouping their battered contingents to defend the important settlement. A search for a suitable crossing over the Lualaba delayed the advance, but by late February Genya fishermen assisted the passage of State forces. In early March Dhanis held Nyangwe, the Arabs evacuating before the State onslaught. It was an important triumph, giving Dhanis control of a principal Arab stronghold, the town's unexpected size and wealth drawing delighted murmers of amazement. The occupation vindicated Dhanis's conduct, the resolute Belgian staking his future on success at Nyangwe, one officer later recounting Dhanis's reception of two letters from superior officers, one advising attack if victory appeared possible, the other, from the governor general, recommending a defensive stance. "We did not know whether we should be praised or blamed for what we had done," another officer remarked; "we knew Tippoo Tib was probably in Europe, and might have arranged the whole affair with the King." Losing heart, Sefu and Mwinyi Pembe, Moharra's son, sought negotiations, but the victors rejected anything except complete Arab capitulation.[80]

The Arabs withdrew to Kasongo, beginning preparations for resolutely defending their principal Congo base. The Belgians arrived on April 22, pausing to survey the impressive defenses facing them. Muhammad bin Said apparently contacted Dhanis, suggesting talks, but the offer was spurned. ,Striking against Kasongo, the State forces found Arab fortifications unfinished, the surprised defenders abandoning their positions, the retreat degenerating into total rout. The Belgians again were impressed with the luxurious Arab way of life, the booty taken including twenty-five tons of ivory and ten tons of gunpowder. After fighting ceased, Dhanis halted his rapid advance, the Belgian supply lines becoming far too extended for efficient operations. The respite allowed the fleeing Arabs one more opportunity to regroup their disorganized followers, still a considerable force, for a new test of strength.[81]

While the main concentrations of Arab and State forces awaited the next battle, several State columns moved against smaller Arab settlements. Chaltin proceeded upriver from Basoko, occupying Riba Riba before heading for Stanley Falls, while Pierre Ponthier seized Kirundu, both Belgians eventually rejoining the main camp at Kasongo.[82] At the falls, hearing of one Arab loss after another, Rashid, although becoming increasingly restless, steadfastly upheld Tippu Tip's orders. But as 1893 went on Tobback reported that Rashid was growing more hostile, in one instance in April throwing at the agent his contract with the administration, complaining about not receiving enough compensation for all the trouble caused him by the State. Tobback, lacking a strong garrison, simply remained calm. By May trouble was at hand for the State, Rashid abandoning his stance before the pressure of new Arab arrivals. Fighting began on May 15, the Arabs striking before the anticipated entry of Chaltin. Tobback managed to hold out until Chaltin broke the siege, Rashid and others fleeing to the principal Arab camp.[83]

Now fully supported by the State, Dhanis in July made ready an advance across Arab territory toward Lake Tanganyika. Rumaliza's decision to support the Congo Muslims brought new spirit to the disheartened Arab army. During an October meeting, when most Arab leaders spoke hopefully of arranging a peace whereby Arabs accepted State rule, Rumaliza scornfully repudiated compromise. Dhanis, the Arab correctly realized, intended to accept only abject surrender, preferring above all to resolve the Arab question by their total defeat. When Muhammad bin Said, for example, once again tried to open a discussion, the message went unanswered. The Belgians resumed the offensive in October, meeting the Arabs in fierce fighting around their newly established fortifications near Kasongo. Strengthened by Rumaliza's resolve and leadership the Arabs beat back the attackers; during the fighting Rumaliza's men crossed the Ulindi River and erected four forts endangering Dhanis' Kasongo camp. Checked for the first time during the campaign, while reporting heavy losses to his army, Dhanis considered the situation dangerous, calling for reinforcements in men and supplies for use against the strong Arab forts defended by men with modern weapons. Skirmishes continued for the rest of the year. In November, fighting reluctantly but with consistent bravery, Sefu died from battle wounds.

In early December Muhammad bin Said, based in Kabambare, endeavored to conduct reinforcements into the main Arab camp, a move which if successful might seriously have compromised Dhanis's position. When State forces pushed the Arabs back to Kabambare, Muhammad bin Said, his martial resolve ended, abandoned the war, heading for Zanzibar. In mid-January 1894 Dhanis finally succeeded in storming the Arab fortifications, driving their defenders eastward, many drowning in the rush to cross the Ulindi. Rumaliza fled to Kabambare, the Belgians attacking and seizing the town before he reordered the disorganized Arabs. Although Rumaliza escaped, Rashid bin Muhammad, Muhammad bin Hamis, and other Arabs, plus most Arab war materials, fell into enemy hands. One Arab participant in the fighting, his charges matched by other Arabs for previous battles, complained that the Belgians attacked Kabambare during a truce of their making. The Belgians do not mention a truce, so it remains the Arab word against theirs. With Arabs fleeing in disarray before the conquering State army, Dhanis marched on, on February 10 linking with the advancing column of the Belgian forces from Lake Tanganyika, the union signaling final defeat for the Congo Arabs.[84]

Before the Arab defeats, Tippu Tip, progressing slowly, with his large ivory caravan, had reached Bagamoyo in July 1891. During the trip he maintained contact with the British, still his most useful allies. "On my arrival at Tabora and Ujiji," he informed Euan Smith, "many people told me that the English will do harm and make you sorry, and I was thinking that what they told me may be true . . . But," said the Arab, "I came anyhow." After visiting by invitation the Germans in Dar es Salaam, Tippu Tip sailed to Zanzibar, discovering that he was even more a celebrity than previously, the various Europeans strenuously competing for his favor. The French staged a reception in his honor; the Germans loosened coastal regulations, allowing 400 of his slaves passage to Zanzibar, where, the French consul charged, they were sold or given away. The British, playing down their role in the pending Stanley-Tippu Tip case, offered help in its resolution. The Germans also allowed Sefu's return inland with supplies of gunpowder and other merchandise. Tippu Tip accepted attention, rebuffing only the Belgian consul's advances, alleging nonpayment for five months of his salary as governor. He did, however, enter into dealings to supply the State with large contingents of men for work on a planned railway. Announcing to all the intention of visiting Europe, then planning a long-deferred visit to Mecca, Tippu Tip delayed his departure until after the expected arrival of Rumaliza. During the interval the British, accepting the judgment of Kirk and others that Tippu Tip's victory in court was likely, and reacting to intervention by Johnston, Leopold, and Mackinnon, succeeded in quashing the charges against the Arab.[85]

Then came news of the war. Caught in Zanzibar, Tippu Tip was powerless to organize relief expeditions. In early 1893, reacting to one of Sefu's defeats, Tippu Tip angrily refuted Belgian renditions of Congo happenings, approaching the British with a scheme for proceeding to his inland domain, promising, if his expenses were covered, to carry out an evacuation of Arabs—and doubtless their ivory—while making all Muslims submit to the State. The proposal was not accepted. When news of Sefu's death came, Tippu Tip, enraged at his son's loss, blamed all on Belgian treachery, charging that they had "asked the Arabs to make a peace and during the negotiations treacherously attacked them in the early dawn." There were rumors that Tippu Tip intended to march for the Congo through German territory, but British representative Hardinge remained unapprehensive, cynically concluding: "He has too many interests in Zanzibar to afford a break with us." Naturally, once the first shock of the magnitude of his disaster, both personal and monetary, had passed, Tippu Tip realized the only rational course was acceptance of Allah's will, closing the period of his life relating to inner Africa.[86]

Tippu Tip's property losses, particularly in ivory, were estimated at 500,000 rupees.[87] More important were the casualties among the Arabs during and after the fighting. Hinde reported "an almost incredibly large loss of life," placing the total at 70,000, the figure including the numerous Africans actively supporting the Arabs or merely caught in the war zone. Among the dead were many Arabs, one reporter noting that in the heat of battle "the white Arabs were hung or shot."[88] Many refugees did succeed in regaining Zanzibar or the east coast, Tippu Tip and other wealthy Arabs assisting them, and the children of families never returning.[89] Other Arabs fell into Belgian hands. Among those executed after "trials" were Hamid bin Ali, Nsesera, and Hamisi bin Hamid. Rashid bin Muhammad and Said bin Abedi won acquittal, the former remaining in the Congo as a State official.[90] Many of the less important Arabs also stayed on, accepting relatively easy terms offered by the State. Africans once serving the Arabs in many cases simply changed masters, entering the State army.[91] Stanley Falls continued as a principal Muslim settlement, although the focus of development under the Belgian rulers shifted to other regions and peoples of the Congo.[92]

With most of his fortune intact—just before leaving the Congo he sold 30,000 kilograms of ivory—Tippu Tip became one of British Zanzibar's most influential citizens. Estimates of his wealth varied widely. "He is now said to be the richest native in Africa, having property to the value of about

$800,000," said Frank Vincent; others mentioned possession of a well-invested £50,000, plus several plantations and great numbers of slaves. His "spare, sinuous figure, alert and upright, with no sign of age about it, save the greyness of the beard," remained well known, Tippu Tip busied himself with the normal affairs of an island aristocrat, at the slightest opportunity "giving interesting reminiscences of his African experiences with Livingstone and Cameron, not forgetting Mr. Stanley." He visited the mainland at least one more time, accompanying the sultan in 1898 on a trip inland by railway from Mombasa past Kibwezi. Tippu Tip, the greatest of all Zanzibar Arabs active in nineteenth-century East Central Africa, died on June 13, 1905.[93]

16 Lake Tanganyika

> You obtained India by force and we never disputed your
> right, why do you dispute ours?
>
> —*Rumaliza*

BY THE MIDDLE of the 1880s Muslims representing several of East Central
Africa's important Arabs were active in the lands bordering Lake Tanganyika, the Ujiji community concentrating along the northern shores, with
the southern regions shared by several groups. Tippu Tip, following the
1867 defeat of Nsama III, claimed authority among the Tabwa, Lungu,
and their neighbors, his brother Muhammad bin Masud developing the
territory as a trade dependency of Tabora. When Muhammad left for
Zanzibar in 1876, leadership passed to the Baluchi Hassan Bondare, better known as Kabunda, a man of imposing mien depicted by F. Moir as a
"polished gentleman," "a dignified and cultured Arab." Based in the Lofu
River valley Kabunda contracted alliances with local African leaders, living
in relative harmony until 1883. Preparing to return to Zanzibar the fruits
of his years of trading and raiding, Kabunda quarreled with his African
associates, through successful pillaging accumulating even more booty for
the journey. Leading over 3,000 men the Baluchi traveled via Tabora,
there suffering the misfortune of encountering Tippu Tip. The powerful
Congo Arab, perhaps upset, explained Hore, because Kabunda had left
the region without appointing a successor, or according to others, because
of Kabunda's raiding without permission, imposed a fine to offset the
supposed misdeeds. The amount, about ten frasila of ivory was not important, Tippu Tip rather acting to formalize his asserted rights over the
southern lake region. Kabunda returned to his former haunts by 1887,
thereafter remaining among the ranks of Arabs who acknowledged Tippu
Tip's authority. Free from any important European presence, Kabunda
and other southern Lake Tanganyika Arabs avoided significant difficulties,
dealing without rancor with the London Missionary Society and the Lake

Malawi Europeans. Kabunda accepted agreement with Harry Johnston in 1889, living peacefully with Europeans until his death in late 1894.[1]

Meanwhile, in Ujiji, a young Muslim destined to become one of East Central Africa's principal Arabs, was gaining authority. Muhammad bin Khalfan al Barwani, called because of military prowess Rumaliza ("the one who utterly finishes"), born in the 1850s near Lindi, won local renown by the late 1870s, in succeeding years becoming especially active in the northern lake regions. In 1881 Tippu Tip encountered Rumaliza in Ujiji. Apparently much impressed with the young Arab's abilities—a missionary called Rumaliza "the most enterprizing Arab in Ujiji"—Tippu Tip brought him to Zanzibar. Concluding some form of arrangement, the two Arabs henceforth worked closely together, Rumaliza emerging as one of Tippu Tip's foremost subordinates, a vital link in the chain connecting the Congo to Zanzibar.[2] During his years of influence Rumaliza had frequent contacts with Europeans, in 1883 Jane Moir describing him as "a tall, very thin, middle-aged man, extremely quiet and gentle in his manner, but with a certain dignity about him." London Missionary Society agents Hore and Swann, knowing Rumaliza well, characterized the Arab as "an educated and liberal minded man free from many of the prejudices of the half-castes and others who have not 'seen the world.'" "His manners," said Jameson, "are those of an English gentleman."[3]

Rumaliza earned these plaudits despite following policies that stimulated European fears and opposition. Returning to Ujij. from Zanzibar at the end of 1884, "with," said missionary F. Coulbois, "a band of brigands and the airs of a sovereign," plus abundant supplies of arms and ammunition, Rumaliza began to make an impact in the lake region. Among European residents it became established opinion that Barghash, as part of the reaction to the growing European threat in the interior, had awarded Rumaliza official appointment as "ruler over the countries in the north." To Hore, Rumaliza was one of the "powerful and direct agents of the Sultan of Zanzibar." There is no direct evidence Rumaliza actually received Barghash's commission, although it is exceedingly likely that the sultan, then sending Tippu Tip to block the Congo Independent State's advance, encouraged his associate in strengthening Arab holdings around the northern shores of the strategic lake. The leader of the Ujiji Muslims, Mwinyi Kheri, did not oppose Rumaliza, the two not interfering in each other's spheres. At Kheri's death in 1885 Rumaliza, natural successor to the old liwali, never received formal appointment from Zanzibar, the ceaseless pressure on the sultan probably making it impossible to award such an important office to a man in frequent controversies with Europeans.[4] And not all Ujiji Arabs favored Rumaliza, members of the long-existing anti-Kheri and Rumaliza faction in 1886 asking Barghash to name a liwali from their ranks. Msabah bin Njem al Shahini, present in

Ujiji since the 1870s, claimed the title from 1886 but, whatever his justification, remained powerless before Rumaliza's might.[5]

The Arabs, of course, had competitors for influence in the lake region. The Germans asserted sovereignty over the eastern shore; the western, after astute diplomacy by Leopold, fell to the Congo Independent State.[6] Both were incapable, until the 1890s, of making their claims reality, thus leaving Arabs to deal with Europeans already settled around the lake. The longest residents, agents of the London Missionary Society, accepted failure in Muslim-dominated Ujiji, in 1883 moving their main base to the lake's southern end. Relations with Arabs remained cordial. When Tippu Tip stopped in Ujiji in 1886 they received formal assurances of friendship, plus a promise, later honored, of halting disturbances in their southern neighborhood.[7]

The lakeside representatives of the International African Association and the White Fathers, two more aggressive groupings, did not share Arab benevolence. The former, with Emile Storms commanding stations at Karema and Mpala, gained increasing unpopularity with Arabs and Africans, Hore precisely stating local feeling: Storms "has fought with the natives, has taken possession of African soil and planted flagstaves, which prompted by the Arabs, is to the natives the worst crime of all . . . The Arabs are very angry about the A. I. A. and would have made trouble long since, but . . . they know themselves unable to face their 200 to 300 guns." But the Arabs did not have to deal with Storms, Leopold, heavily involved in the difficult progress up the Congo River, deciding against maintaining the Lake Tanganyika posts. Fearing that rival Europeans, especially Germans, might occupy the abandoned holdings, Leopold early sought an alternative. When Cardinal Lavigerie requested Leopold's permission to expand the White Fathers' work in State-claimed lands, the king agreed, asking in return the Catholics to be established as near Karema as possible, allowing the missionaries, if the need arose, temporary control over his posts. The White Fathers eventually honored the agreement. In 1884, wanting locations in regions freer from Muslim influence, they founded a station in Marungu, near Mpala. Storms provided full assistance, the officer and the priest in charge, Isaac Moinet, becoming very close associates. When in 1885 the Association evacuated Karema and Mpala, the White Fathers took over the stations.[8]

The White Fathers and the Arabs, even before the transfer, were reacting like two competitive, expansive rivals, all too often working in the same localities. Relationships for a time remained stable, however, even after Rumaliza's 1884 return from Zanzibar. The creation of an orphanage at Kibanga was achieved without problem through Mwinyi Kheri's assistance, but such help did not come automatically. In 1883 P. Guillemé gained permission from Africans for an Uzige settlement, other mission activity delaying a move until June 1884. Then arguments developed concerning Kheri's attitude, the Frenchmen finally learning they might stay only if they accepted Arab sovereignty and paid tribute. When all appeals failed, the priests evacuated the station in January 1885. Rumaliza's increased activities also brought Arabs into the environs of Kibanga, located on the route to the Congo Muslim centers. Yet the Frenchmen at first encountered few hindrances. Throughout 1886 the missionaries repeatedly exchanged gifts with Rumaliza's men, in August receiving a friendly visit from the Arab chieftain.[9]

With Storms's departure for Europe the White Fathers passed to a new stage in their occupation of the lake region. The strength of Mpala led surrounding Africans, reacting to the increasing Arab activity in Marungu, into recognizing missionary authority, signaling their status by paying a small tribute for whatever protection the Frenchmen might provide. Moinet, recognizing the obvious limitations of missionary martial ability, uneasily accepted such arrangements, but they were made, by August, with an estimated 6,000 Africans covered by agreements, with numerous others tied to the priests through less formal relationships. Thus the White Fathers had a new role, directing a political entity by 1887 growing to 20,000 inhabitants, henceforth requiring decisions relating to internal order and defense. The fathers flew their own flag, a red cross on a white background, beginning to administer their version of justice, executing Africans found guilty of theft and murder. Since some Africans independently fought Arabs in the mission's name, the priests awarded military leadership to Léopold Joubert, a former papal zouave and French soldier, then a lay member of the mission.[10] In truth, the organization of the Mpala settlement was already familiar enough to the region's Africans: newcomers had arrived, establishing a base, buying slaves, enforcing new regulations, and expanding authority. The Arabs had been doing it for years.

Relationships between Arabs and White Fathers steadily deteriorated, the roving bands of Rumaliza and other Muslims actively raiding and traversing the environs of Kibanga and Mpala. When the missionaries remonstrated with Rumaliza he answered merely: "In the country I am not master of my men, they are savages who don't understand anything especially when hunger drives them." The Kibanga neighborhood, with an Arab post nearby, especially suffered, large numbers of Africans fleeing for safety to the mission. Still, the station was left alone, one Arab avowing the sultan had ordered all against molesting Europeans. Kibanga remained indefensible, its continued existence depending upon Rumaliza's goodwill.[11] But the Arab, after visiting Tippu Tip at Nyangwe during 1888, began to rethink his attitude toward East Central Africa's Europeans. Obviously worried over the policies of the Germans and the Congo Independent State, Rumaliza realistically decided to try to preserve good terms with the representatives of the major powers based on Zanzibar. Rumaliza had a special reason for moderating his Arab companions' hostility to Europeans: desire for appointment by Barghash as liwali of the Lake Tanganyika region. The Arab chief actively began to court British and French missionary support, hoping to motivate their nation's agents in Zanzibar to intervene in his favor.[12]

Events in Europe undermined Rumaliza's hopes. Cardinal Lavigerie during the 1880s had been rethinking mission policies toward East Central Africa's Arabs. In 1880–1881 the prelate instructed his priests to shun conflicts with Arabs, avoiding wherever possible regions under Muslim influence, an impossible goal since both normally sought the most favorable African areas. In 1881 Lavigerie, through the pope, failed to convince the European nations to act against Arabs. A more serious venture followed in 1886: the cardinal, striving for concerted European action, proposed to hold Barghash responsible for hostile Arab deeds in the interior, reasoning that the sultan alone held practical inland influence. The scheme foundered in great-power discord, France, Britain, and Germany all opposing intervention.[13]

Left to his own resources, Lavigerie advanced a time-honored European remedy, a crusade against the representatives of Islam. In an August 1888 Bruxelles speech an impressed British diplomat reported a church "thronged" with listeners responding favorably to the Frenchman's advocacy of a cause "as holy as that which led Godfrey de Bouillon and his 20,000 men to the Holy Land." A favorable public response followed, 2,700 Belgians and Frenchmen volunteering for service as crusaders.[14] Lavigerie also visited Britain, publicly and privately attempting to move the nation possessing the longest record of actions against the slave trade. Neither government nor private organizations responded favorably. "There is no use crusading in a country you cannot keep after you have conquered it," cynically reasoned Kirk, "and no use driving the slaver out unless you put something better in."[15]

The ready popular response in Belgium and France did not deceive the eminently practical Lavigerie into adopting policies intolerable to governments with African interests. Leopold especially did not favor an international movement, fearing its effects in his loosely held domain. Nonetheless, Leopold recognized an opportunity for strengthening his position against the Arabs by turning antislavery enthusiasm into assistance for the financially troubled Congo Independent State. After negotiations with crusade leaders Leopold deftly incorporated the movement, subordinating crusader schemes to State control. Expeditions, their leaders receiving appointment as State officers, soon were under way.[16]

While the crusaders worked in Europe, relations between Arabs and White Fathers worsened. Arab incursions in the south continued as more and more caravans headed westward, Rumaliza's men over the next two years establishing in sundry Marungu locations. In August 1887 Joubert defeated one group of Muslims; all expected additional combats. The Frenchman fully realized that his opposition might cause general warfare, but he judged that the Arabs must be checked if the mission was to maintain authority over its African followers, a decision matching Sefu's response to Ngongo Lutete's defection.[17]

Not yet abandoning hope of working with Europeans, Rumaliza avoided direct pressure on the missionaries, in 1890 once again trying for British approval by aiding a mission sent by Johnston to negotiate treaties in northern lake territory, in the process vainly requesting inclusion under the British flag. Grateful for Rumaliza's assistance, Johnston counseled Euan Smith "to please make much of him," without causing any change in policy.[18] Tensions continued, some Africans in White Fathers' territory calling in Arab allies in a local quarrel. Joubert quickly defeated them. But possessing meager military resources—150 guns and limited ammunition—the embattled Frenchman petitioned succor from the antislave trade crusaders. The request was accepted, Joubert supplying the European organizations with the plight of a supposed hero to fuel their propaganda drives for financial support. Joubert meantime continued limited defensive operations, beginning in April a post which they hoped would block Arab passage southward. All major Arab advances were checked, a fortunate lake storm aborting one serious move against Mpala in June 1890. But the Frenchman's overall position remained inherently insecure, Rumaliza threatening war if hindered again, while the defenseless Kibanga mission prevented any thoughts of mission offensives. The doughty French soldier puzzled Rumaliza; in February 1891 the Arab queried Joubert for a definition of his exact status: was he a White Father, a State officer, or an independent agent? Wryly observing the question was "a little indiscreet," Joubert kept silent.[19]

With a British option still closed, Rumaliza in 1890 had to contemplate the arrival of Germans at Ujiji, Emin Pasha from Tabora commanding cessation of hostilities against Europeans and acceptance of German rule. The bombastic talk previously circulating in Ujiji suddenly ceased; White Father Bridoux described Rumaliza as "nearly at my feet" while seeking mission intervention with Emin. Rumaliza answered Emin cordially, promising settlement when the German arrived, the opportunity passing when the Pasha turned instead toward Lake Victoria.[20] If the Germans had entered Ujiji their limited power in the lake region might have allowed agreement, Rumaliza, once in German service, perhaps avoiding collision with the oncoming Belgians. Free from effective German sovereignty, the Arabs debated their future, Rumaliza emerging as leader of the more moderate Muslims. Hoping to ensure the future, Rumaliza during 1891

and 1892 flew the German flag over Ujiji, concurrently claiming suzerainty over the lake region as Tippu Tip's lieutenant, deputized for bringing the territories under Congo Independent State rule. Joubert,
previously almost speechless with rage when he learned that Tippu Tip
had arrived at the lake as a State Agent, simply ignored Rumaliza's assertion. In communications with Europeans the latter kept to his policy of
openness, expressing willingness to accept terms from the Germans once
they reached Ujiji.[21]

The first antislave-trade expedition's October 1891 arrival at Karema
effectively precluded success for Rumaliza's diplomatic tergiversations.
Bearing Leopold's commission as State representative, Jules Jacques, its
commander, was an officer of the same mold as Dhanis, his attitude immediately making war between Belgian and Arab inescapable. Jacques,
with instructions including the standard pious advice about peaceful measures, authorization to tax ivory leaving State-claimed lands, and the building of a station, from the start affronted Rumaliza and the Arabs, ignoring
local diplomatic usage by neglecting to visit Rumaliza on arriving in his
sphere. Then Jacques set off on a reconaissance trip, thinking of building
at Mtowa until the resident Arabs' determination to resist if he acted
without Rumaliza's permission compelled withdrawal. Selecting a site for
interdicting Arab passage south of the Lukuga, Jacques began the future
Albertville, meanwhile seizing four Arab followers who visited the camp.
After a one-sided court martial, three—one escaped—were executed on
charges of spying and of attacking nearby Africans. In January 1892 the
first hostilities came, Jacques destroying a neighboring Arab post. Other
skirmishes ensued.[22]

From Rumaliza's perspective the rumored Belgian wishes for peace
were a sham. "We obeyed your words strictly and hoisted the Belgian
flag," complained Rumaliza to Tippu Tip, "and now in return they come
to fight us." The Arab chieftain continued his British ties, utilizing Swann
as a negotiator. "The Arabs appear to be sincere in their desire to arrive at
a modus vivendi with the two powers to the East and West of them, and
declare their willingness to pay fair duties and abide by just laws," concluded the missionary, still much impressed by the Ujiji chieftain. An
agent sent by Tippu Tip, influential Lake Tanganyika Arab Nassir bin
Suliman bin Juma, in mid-1893 said the same. Yet all negotiations proved
abortive, the inevitable result of Jacques's approach: the Arabs were offered only the opportunity to surrender. The Arab reaction was clear when
Jacques visited Ujiji in March 1892, the consequence of a communication
from Kasongo resident Lippens reproaching his aggressive conduct.
Greeting Jacques as an enemy, the Arabs scornfully laughed at explanations justifying the Albertville executions. Rumaliza and Jacques blamed
each other for existing tensions, the meeting ending without beneficial

result. Any other alternative scarcely was likely if Jacques believed in his June 1892 description of Tippu Tip and Rumaliza as "two scoundrels, the two greatest assassins in all Africa." As for peace, Jacques had advised his superiors, "it is impossible here!"[23]

Meantime Jacques levied the ivory tax, bringing on serious hostilities. The Arabs naturally sought to avoid the imposition, estimates of the amount ranging between 20 percent and 50 percent of the ivory's value. The charge on one small caravan ended in fighting near Jacques's headquarters in April 1892, the Arabs killing one officer while defeating State forces.[24] Then the Arabs ranged around the Belgian post, erecting their own strong fort. Jacques, forced to the defensive, attempted to negotiate through Swann, the missionary offering to reduce the ivory tax, but all deliberations foundered in the continuing combats. Threatened by steady Arab pressure, causing some African allies to abandon the Belgians, Jacques summoned Joubert's assistance, the Frenchman arriving with additional levies drawn from the recently entering caravan of Alexandre Delcommune. With 450 men, two-thirds bearing firearms, Jacques on August 27 struck at the Arab fort, the attack failing before the sturdy Arab defense, the State troops breaking because of losses and lack of ammunition.[25]

Secure within his fortifications, Jacques settled down to an inconclusive siege, both Arab and Belgian forces suffering from smallpox and famine. Arab success, however, was transitory, Jacques receiving reinforcements and supplies from his European backers in early 1893. The State authorities, fearing the upset of efforts to win Tipper Tip's support in recruiting laborers to build a Congo railway, sent Albert Long with orders for Jacques to resolve the problems with the Arabs. Made even less receptive to instructions by news of Dhanis's campaign, Jacques, without offering a single concession, merely requested that Rumaliza demonstrate good faith by lifting the siege. Rumaliza probably would have ignored the message, but whatever his reaction, the siege suddenly ended when Arab forces, breaking before famine conditions, without informing their commander evacuated Albertville's environs.[26]

Rumaliza stood before a critical crossroads, facing a decision compelled by inexorable State pressure, news of the Congo war, and fear of the Germans reaching Ujiji. He continued the various approaches to Europeans, sending both Muslim agents and Swann to the Belgians, but by this time Jacques' attitude must have convinced the Arab there was little future under State rule. Service under the Germans, busily involved elsewhere in their new colony, remained a feasible alternative. German agent in Tabora Sigl, receiving a friendly communication from Rumaliza, planned to appoint the Arab as governor, in June 1893 marching for Ujiji. At about the same time Wissmann, commanding a German antislave trade society expedition on Lake Malawi, informed Swann he intended to appoint Rumaliza Ujiji's liwali. Perhaps, if the Congo situation had been different, Rumaliza might have waited to discuss the future with Sigl or Wissmann, but the reports of Dhanis's advance, plus Jacques's doings, motivated the Arab—who little trusted European promises—into joining the Manyema Muslims. In July 1893 leading up to 6,000 men, around four thousand with firearms, Rumaliza marched toward Kasongo.[27]

Following Rumaliza's departure the Belgians quickly and easily ended Arab domination of Lake Tanganyika.[28] Fleeing the Congo defeats, Rumaliza discovered he no longer was welcome in his former capital. Shortly after his exit for the Congo war Sigl entered Ujiji, appointing the old, nearly blind Msabah bin Njem liwali. Still hoping to utilize Rumaliza's influence, the Germans allowed a temporary return to Ujiji for securing any remaining property, plus promise of safe conduct to the coast. But Rumaliza's old rivals chased him away. After apparently failing in negotiations with the Belgians, conducted through Sef bin Rashid, the Arab, after various unclear adventures, including participation in the Hehe war against the Germans, reached a safe exile on the East African coast. Defeat brought bitterness, Rumaliza, Muhammad bin Said, and Tippu Tip quarreling over the disposition of property held in German territory. Although Rumaliza won the resulting court case, the success was temporary, the once powerful Tanganyika Arab ending his career as an obscure coastal Muslim.[29] In Ujiji the Arab community, broken in power and vitality by losses in war and the closing of the Congo territories, lacked heart for resisting the Germans. Sef bin Rashid, once in the service of the International African Association, succeeded Msabah as liwali, living cordially with the German rulers until he retired just before World War I.[30]

Epilogue

WITH ZANZIBAR'S LOSS of independence and the eventual defeat in battle of East Central Africa's principal Arabs, a chapter in the region's history ended. Even though Islam remained a vigorously present religion, increasing the number of its adherents throughout much of East Central Africa, the loss to the Christian European invaders generally relegated Muslims to secondary roles in the newly created colonial political entities. Islamic centers created during the years of Zanzibari activity persisted, but they usually declined to subordinate rank behind cities established or reinvigorated during the European period. Conquered Africans and their descendents naturally gravitated to the influences brought by the technically superior, conquering West, accepting its religion, or at least attending its schools. Thus the leaders of the African groupings who led the resistance against the Europeans after World War II commonly represented the Westernized classes of Africans. While Muslims often participated in the drives to independence, they generally remained—except in Zanzibar, Pemba, and the East African coast—distant from leadership levels. The process begun before 1800 by many now nameless Muslims, intensified by the BuSaidi and their Arab and African adherents during the nineteenth century, could not withstand the powerful European invaders. The Zanzibar system, even though binding many East Central Africans and Arabs together in political, economic, and social concerns, by the 1880s still remained a loosely integrated structure inspired by past Umani and African precepts. With more time and greater intermixture between Arab and African, a firmer union might have evolved. But that is idle speculation. The Zanzibar system crumbled during the 1880s and 1890s, leaving the future to the very different world created by Europeans and, eventually, by their African inheritors.

Abbreviations

AA	*African Affairs*
AD	Allemagne, Dépêches Politiques des Consuls, MAE
Adm	Admiralty, PRO
AEC	*L'Afrique Explorée et Civilisée*
AH	Allemagne, Dépêches Politiques des Consuls, Hambourg, MAE
AIA	Association Internationale Africaine
AngD	Angleterre, Dépêches, MAE
AOM	Archives de l'Ancien Ministère d'Outre-Mer, Paris
APF	*Annales de la Propagation de la Foi*
A-T	*Africa-Tervuren*
B.	*Bulletin*
BEM	*Blackwood's Edinburg Magazine*
BG	Bombay Government
BKK	*Beiträge zur Kolonialpolitik und Kolonialwirtschaft*
BL	British Library
BMA	*Bulletin des Missions d'Afrique (d'Alger)*
BS	*Bantu Studies*
BSAF	*Bulletin de la Société Antiesclavagiste de France*
BSARSC	*Bulletin des Séances, Académie Royale des Sciences Coloniale*
BSARSDM	*Bulletin des Séances, Académie Royale des Sciences d'Outre-Mer*
BSBG	*Bulletin de la Société Belge de Géographie*
BSE	*Bulletin Général de la Congrégation du St. Esprit et de l'Imé. Coeur de Marie*
BSG	*Bulletin de la Société de Géographie*
BSGM	*Bulletin de la Société de Géographie de Marseille*
BSIRCB	*Bulletin des Séances de l'Institut Royal Colonial Belge*

BUM	Boston University, Mugar Library
BUP	*Boston University Papers on Africa*
CA	Central Africa
CA	*Central Africa*
CAMOP	*Central African Mission, Occasional Papers*
CCZ	Correspondance Commerciale, Zanzibar, MAE
CDZ	Consular Despatches, Zanzibar, NA
CI	*Le Congo Illustré*
CLMS	*The Chronicle of the London Missionary Society*
CM	*Calwer Missionsblatt*
CMI	*Church Missionary Intelligencer*
CMIR	*The Church Missionary Intelligencer and Record*
CMS	Church Missionary Society Archives
CPC	Correspondance Politique—Consulats, MAEB
CR	*The Contemporary Review*
CSHFMR	*The Church of Scotland Home and Foreign Missionary Record*
CTSM	*Chronique Trimestrielle de la Société des Missionaires de Notre-Dame des Missions d'Afrique*
CWTW	*Christian Work Throughout the World*
DBZ	Despatch Book, American Consulate, Zanzibar, NA
DGB	*Deutsche Geographische Blätter*
DKB	*Deutsches Kolionalblatt*
DKZ	*Deutsch Kolionalzeitung*
DP	Dhanis Papers, Tervuren
DRGS	*Deutsche Rundschau für Geographie und Statistik*
EB	*L'Etoile Belge*
EMM	*Evangelisches Missions-Magazin*
enc.	enclosing, enclosure(s)
FO	Foreign Office
GJ	*The Geographical Journal*
GM	*The Geographical Magazine*
GWE	*Gott will es!*
HFMRFCS	*The Home and Foreign Missionary Record of the Free Church of Scotland*
IB	*L'Indépendance Belge*
IJAHS	*International Journal of African Historical Studies*
IOE	Enclosures to Secret Letters Received from Bombay, India Office Archives
J.	*Journal*
JAH	*Journal of African History*
JAI	*Journal of the Anthropological Institute of Great Britain and Ireland*
JAS	*Journal of the African Society*

JB	*Le Journal de Bruxelles*
JMGS	*The Journal of the Manchester Geographical Society*
JRAS	*Journal of the Royal African Society*
JRGS	*The Journal of the Royal Geographical Society*
JSA	*Journal of the Society of Arts*
KJ	*Koloniales Jahrbuch*
LMS	London Missionary Society Archives
MA	*Le Mouvement Antiesclavagiste*
MAC	Ministère d'Alger et des Colonies
MAE	Archives du Ministère des Affaires Etrangères, Paris
MAEB	Archives du Ministère des Affaires Etrangères, Bruxelles
MAGD	*Mittheilungen der Afrikanischen Gesellschaft in Deutschland*
MBB	*Missions-Blatt aus der Brüdergemeine*
MC	*Les Missions Catholiques*
MCB	Archives Africaines du Ministère des Affaires Etrangères, Bruxelles
MFGDS	*Mitteilungen von Forschungsreisenden und Gelehrten aus den Deutschen Schutzgebieten*
MG	*Le Mouvement Géographique*
MGGH	*Mittheilungen der Geographischen Gesellschaft in Hamburg*
MGGW	*Mittheilungen der kais. und kön. Geographischen Gesellschaft in Wien*
MH	*Der Missions- und Heidenbote*
ML	*Mission Life*
MMC	Ministère de la Marine et des Colonies
MP	Mackinnon Papers, School of Oriental and African Studies
MR	*The Missionary Register*
ms.	manuscript
NA	National Archives, Washington, D.C.
NJ	*The Nyasaland Journal*
NOM	*Nachrichten aus der ostafrikanischen Mission*
NRC	Naval Records Collection, NA
NRJ	*The Northern Rhodesian Journal*
P.	Proceedings
PM	Peabody Museum, Salem, Mass.
PM	*Dr. A. Petermann's Mittheilungen aus Justus Perthes' Geographischer Anstalt*
PP	*Parliamentary Papers*
PRGS	*Proceedings of the Royal Geographical Society*
PRO	Public Record Office, London
PZ	Politique, Zanzibar, MAE
R.	*Review*
SGI	Secretary, Government of India

SGM	*The Scottish Geographical Magazine*
SL	Smythies Letters, UMCA
SLRB	Secret Letters Received from Bombay, India Office Archives
SLRV	Secret Letters Received (Various), India Office Archives
Soc.	*Société; Society*
SSI	Secretary of State, India
TBGS	*Transactions of the Bombay Geographical Society*
TNR	*Tanzania Notes and Records*
tr., trans.	translator
trim.	trimestre
UJ	*Uganda Journal*
UMCA	Universities' Mission to Central Africa, Archives
UMFCM	*The United Methodist Free Churches' Magazine*
u.v.	unindexed volume
VGEB	*Verhandlungen der Gesellschaft für Erdkunde zu Berlin*
WP	Waters Papers, PM
Z.	*Zeitschrift*
ZA	Zanzibar Archives
ZAE	*Zeitschrift für Allgemeine Erdkunde*
Z and M	Zanzibar and Muscat, NA
ZG	*Zanzibar Gazette*
ZGEB	*Zeitschrift der Gesellschaft für Erdkunde zu Berlin*
ZM	Zanzibar Museum
ZP	Zanzibar Protectorate

Notes

INTRODUCTION

1. ZP, *Administrative Reports for the Year 1929* (Zanzibar, 1930), 34, and *Debates of the Legislative Council. Twenty-First Session 1946–1947* (Zanzibar, 1947), 27–28.

2. A good description of this mixture is Hasani bin Ismail, ed. and trans. Peter Lienhart, *The Medicine Man: Sifwa ya Nguvumali* (Oxford, 1968).

3. W. G. Palgrave, "Observations made in Central, Eastern, and Southern Arabia during a Journey through that Country in 1862–1863," *JRGS* 34(1864), 153; Horner, 1 July 1869, *BSE* 7(1869–1870), 275; Harold Ingrams, *Arabia and the Isles* (London, 1942), 22.

4. New, 2 February 1864, *UMFCM*, 21(1878), 214; Arthur N. West, "A Visit to the Universities' Mission in Central Africa," *ML* 5(1875), 246.

5. See Norman R. Bennett, *A History of the Arab State of Zanzibar* (London, 1978), 113. For *ridda*, see W. Montgomery Watt, *Islamic Thought: The Basic Concepts* (Edinburgh, 1968), 62.

6. Steere in *ML*, 7(1876), 490.

7. For a useful discussion of these issues, Bernard Lewis, *Race and Color in Islam* (New York, 1971). Lewis, however, confines his thought largely to the central Islamic lands, thus not meeting some of the problems existing in the frontier regions of East Central Africa. See also Watt, *Islamic Thought*, 97. For discussions of specific relevance to East Africa, Frederick Cooper, *Plantation Slavery on the East Coast of Africa* (New Haven, 1977), 23–28, 35, 37, 195–199; August H. Nimtz, Jr., "The Role of the Muslim Sūfī Order in Political Change: An Overview and Micro-Analysis from Tanzania," (Ph.D. diss., Indiana University, 1973), 245–247, 307–315.

8. Palgrave, "Observations," 151.

9. Allen to Penney, 19 May 1881, A.1.IV, UMCA.

10. Hamerton to Aberdeen, 31 July 1844, in Hamerton to Willoughby, 2 September 1844, IOE 71; Emily Ruete (trans. Lionel Strachey), *Memoirs of an Arabian Princess* (New York, 1907), 182.

11. J. Ross Browne, *Etchings of a Whaling Cruise, with Notes of a Sojourn on the Island of Zanzibar* (London, 1846), 244.

12. Otto Kersten, ed., *Baron Carl Claus von der Decken's Reisen in Ost-Afrika in den Jahren 1859 bis 1861* (Leipzig and Heidelberg, 1869), 9.

13. Livingstone to Clarendon, 18 May 1866, FO 84/1265. Muhammad bin Salah later confirmed the statement; Horace Waller, ed., *The Last Journals of David Livingstone* (London, 1874), I, 279–280.

14. Fred L. M. Moir, *After Livingstone* (London, n.d.), 162.

15. Livingstone to Clarendon, 1 November 1871, *PP* 1872 (c.598), 5.

16. J. Spencer Trimingham, *Islam in East Africa* (London, 1962), 24–25, and *The Influence of Islam upon Africa* (New York and Washington, 1968), 30–32, 80.

17. Hutley, ms. "Mohammedanism in Central Africa," in Hutley to Thompson, 12 September 1881, W. Griffith to Thompson, 13 March 1882, CA 4, LMS.

18. John Hanning Speke, *Journal of the Discovery of the Source of the Nile* (London, 1863), 110; W. P. Johnson, "Steamer for Lake Nyassa," *ML* 15(1884), 171.

19. *BSAF* (1891–1892), 22. See also Goodrich to Granville, 19 February 1885, 19 March 1885, FO 84/1702; Smythies in *CA* 5(1887), 176.

20. Henderson in *CSHFMR,* 14(1884), 314; Janson, journal, 19 January [sic], unindexed papers, UMCA; Waller, *Livingstone's Journals,* I, 73.

21. Johnson elsewhere contradicted himself, explaining that he had met in a Yao town a teacher who "quotes and reads the Koran fluently." W. P. Johnson, "Seven Years Travel in the Region East of Lake Nyassa," *PRGS,* 6(1884), 513. R. S. Hynde, "A Trip to Lake Shirwa," *CSHFMR,* 18(1891–1892), 314; Johnson extract, 29 August 1881, A.1.VI, UMCA.

22. Steere to UMCA, 27 July 1876, in Kirk to Derby, 19 February 1877, *PP* 1878 (c. 2139), LXVII, 281. The attitude persists in modern works: see P. Ceulemans, *La Question Arabe et le Congo (1883–1892)* (Bruxelles, 1959), 39; H. Alan C. Cairns, *Prelude to Imperialism: British Reactions to Central African Society 1840–1890* (London, 1965), 132–133.

23. Edward A. Alpers, "Towards a History of the Expansion of Islam in East Africa: The Matrilineal Peoples of the Southern Interior," in T. O. Ranger and I. N. Kimambo, eds., *The Historical Study of African Religion* (Berkeley and Los Angeles, 1972), 181–186. For the Ganda, see below, p. 93.

24. Trimingham, *East Africa,* 11, 27; Franz Stuhlmann, *Handwerk und Industrie in Ostafrika* (Hamburg, 1910), 88.

25. Aidan Southall, "The Problem of Malagasy Origins," in H. Neville Chittick and Robert I. Rotberg, eds., *East Africa and the Orient* (New York, 1975), 213.

26. Quoted in Abbot to Webster, 12 March 1851, Z and M, 3, NA.

27. Samuel Baker, *Exploration of the Nile Tributaries of Abyssinia* (Hartford, 1868), x.

28. Richard F. Burton, "The Lake Regions of Central Equatorial Africa . . . ," *JRGS* 29(1859), 53; Rigby quoted in R. Coupland, *The Exploitation of East Africa, 1856–1890: The Slave Trade and the Scramble* (London, 1939), 42; Rigby to Pelly, 8 October 1861, FO 800/234.

29. David Livingstone, *Missionary Travels and Researches in South Africa* (New York, 1868), 36, 399; Livingstone to Clarendon, 20 August 1866, *PP* 1868–1869 (4131–1), LVI, 16; F. D. Lugard, "Uganda: Its Value to British Trade," *JMGS,* 8(1892), 110.

30. A. M. Mackay, "Muscat, Zanzibar, and Central Africa," *CMIR,* 14(1889), 21; Alfred J. Swann, *Fighting the Slave-Hunters in Central Africa*

(Philadelphia, 1910), 87; J. Rose Troup, *With Stanley's Rear Column* (London, 1890), 228, 236.

31. See Alison Smith, "The Southern Interior," in Roland Oliver and Gervase Mathew, eds., *History of East Africa* (Oxford, 1963), I, 271.

32. Allen to Heanley, 18 July 1877, A.1.IV, UMCA.

33. Waller, *Livingstone's Journals*, II, 143.

34. Verney Lovett Cameron, *Across Africa* (London, 1877), II, 12.

35. F. D. Lugard, "Lake Nyassa and Central Africa," *JMGS* 5(1889), 349; Goodrich to Granville, 19 March 1885, FO 84/1702; Cameron, *Across Africa*, I, 113; Adolphe Burdo, *Les Belges dans l'Afrique Centrale: De Zanzibar au Lac Tanganika* (Bruxelles, 1886), 286, 305; Paul Reichard, *Deutsch-Ostafrika* (Leipzig, 1892), 93–95.

36. For the changing development of the concept "Arab," see Albert Hourani, *Arabic Thought in the Liberal Age, 1798–1939* (London, 1970), 260ff.; Watt, *Islamic Thought*, 117–119.

37. See A. C. Unomah and J. B. Webster, "East Africa: The Expansion of Commerce," in John E. Flint, ed., *The Cambridge History of Africa* (London and Cambridge, 1976), V, 270ff., and my review of this book in the *American Historical Review*, 83(1978), 244–245.

38. For an example of the changing manner in which the inhabitants of Zanzibar viewed themselves, ZP, *Report of the Census Enumeration of the Whole Population on the Night of the 28th–29th March, 1931* (Zanzibar, 1931), 1–2.

39. Michael F. Lofchie, *Zanzibar: Background to Revolution* (Princeton, 1965), 76; John Felt Osgood, *Notes of Travel or Recollections of Majunga, Zanzibar, Muscat, Aden, Mocha, and Other Eastern Ports* (Salem, 1854), 35; Edward Steere to M. Steere, 28 October 1865, A.1.III, UMCA.

40. G. N. Sanderson, *England, Europe & the Upper Nile, 1882–1899* (Edinburgh, 1965), 7; Victor Giraud, *Les Lacs de l'Afrique Equatoriale* (Paris, 1890), 473; "Exploration du Koango par le lieutenant Dhanis," *MG* 9(1892), 39.

41. F. T. Haig, "Arabia as a Mission Field," *CMIR* 12(1887), 411; Marcel Luwel, "Verney Lovett Cameron ou l'échec d'un concurrent de Stanley," in *La Conférence de Géographie de 1876: Recueil d'études* (Académie Royale des Sciences d'Outre-Mer, Bruxelles, 1976), 99; Gordon, 7 November 1888, *CMIR* 14(1889), 159; Nourse to Farquhar, 8 December 1822, Adm 7/47, PRO; Kerr Cross to Smith, 27 January 1888, *The Times* (17 May 1888), 6; Kirk to BG, 22 April 1869, *PP* 1870 (c.141), LXI, 47; E. Trivier, *Mon Voyage au Continent Noir* (Paris and Bordeaux, 1891), 179.

42. Mgr. Bridoux, "Un Première Tournée Pastorale au Tanganika," *MC* 22(1890), 537; West to Elwes, 18 November 1874, A.1.V, UMCA; Euan Smith to Salisbury, 29 September 1890, FO 84/2064.

43. "Les Arabes du Haut Congo," *CI* 1(1892), 130.

44. Cairns, *Prelude*, 211–212; Hore to Thompson, 11 February 1888, CA 7, Hore to LMS, 28 November 1885, CA 6, LMS.

45. Elst to Caraman, 14 April 1885, CPC 18; Becker interview, *IB* (27 May 1893).

46. George Schweitzer, ed., *Emin Pasha: His Life and Work* (Westminster, 1898), II, 45.

47. Norman Daniel, *Islam and the West: The Making of an Image* (Edinburgh, 1960), 45; Bernard Lewis, *The Middle East and the West* (Bloomington, 1967), 30.

48. See, for example, Lucy Mair, *African Kingdoms* (Oxford, 1977), 12, or

Ronald Robinson and John Gallagher, with Alice Denny, *Africa and the Victorians* (New York, 1961), 224.

49. Kirk to Granville, 27 August 1873, *PP* 1874 (c. 1064), LXII, 72; Kirk to BG, 27 August 1872, E–62, ZA.

50. Livingstone, *Missionary Travels*, 724.

51. See Cooper, *Plantation Slavery*, for the East African system.

52. Leslie B. Rout, Jr., *The African Experience in Spanish America: 1502 to the Present Day* (Cambridge, 1976), 174–179, 237–239; David Brion Davis, *The Problem of Slavery in the Age of Revolution, 1770–1823* (Ithaca, 1975), 164ff.

53. E. P. Thompson, *The Making of the English Working Class* (New York, 1963), 592.

54. P. Charmêtant, *D'Alger à Zanzibar* (Paris, 1882), 162; Salisbury quoted in Roland Oliver, *The Missionary Factor in East Africa* (London, 1952), 122.

55. Coupland, *Exploitation of East Africa, 392;* Jean Stengers, "The Congo Free State and the Belgian Congo before 1914," in L. H. Gann and Peter Duignan, eds., *Colonialism in Africa* (Cambridge, 1969), I, 267; Oliver, *Missionary Factor,* 109.

56. B. H. Warmington, *Carthage* (Baltimore, 1964), 9; Daniel, *Islam and the West,* 240.

57. Daniel, *Islam and the West,* 113.

58. See Steven Runciman, *A History of the Crusades* (Cambridge, 1951), I, 128ff.

59. Margery Perham, ed., *The Diaries of Lord Lugard* (London, 1959), I, 19; F. D. Lugard, "Nyassa-Land and Its Commercial Possibilities," *PRGS* 11(1899), 689; Roland Oliver, "Some Factors in the British Occupation of East Africa," *UJ* 15(1951), 55.

60. Harry H. Johnston, *British Central Africa* (New York, 1897), 72; L. Monteith Fotheringham, *Adventures in Nyasaland* (London, 1891), 32; F. D. Lugard, "The Fight against Slave-Traders on Nyasa," *CR* 56(1889), 336.

61. Ruth Slade, *King Leopold's Congo* (London, 1962), 107–108.

62. Ceulemans, *La Question Arabe,* 294, 298.

63. L. H. Gann and Peter Duignan, *The Rulers of German Africa, 1884–1914* (Stanford, 1977), 13.

64. Jacques, 10 August 1892, *MA* 5(1892–1893), 43.

65. Horace Waller, "The Two Ends of the Slave-Stick," *CR* 55(1889), 528.

66. Anthony Low, "British Public Opinion and the Uganda Question: October–December 1892," *UJ* 18(1954), 96.

67. Euan Smith to Salisbury, 1 November 1888, u.v., ZA.

68. Compare Charles van Onselen, *Chibaro: African Mine Labour in Southern Rhodesia, 1900–1933* (London, 1976), 112–113.

69. Ceulemans, *La Question Arabe,* 325.

70. Robert Schmitz, *Les Baholoholo* (Bruxelles, 1912), 572; Colin Turnbull, *The Lonely African* (Garden City, 1963), 52.

CHAPTER 1

1. This section summarizes material presented more fully in Norman R. Bennett, *Zanzibar,* 14ff.

2. François Coulbois, *Dix Années au Tanganyka* (Limoges, 1901), 14; Edward Steere, *The Universities' Mission to Central Africa* (London, 1875), 12.

3. See Massieu to MMC, 9 October 1822, O.I. 17/89, AOM.

4. Hamerton to Wyville, 8 May 1850, E–11, ZA; Hamerton to Malet, 5 September 1850, IOE 104.

5. Norman R. Bennett and George E. Brooks, Jr., eds., *New England Merchants in Africa: A History through Documents, 1802 to 1865* (Boston, 1965), 414–415.

6. R. E. Robinson, "The Partition of Africa," in F. H. Hinsley, ed., *The New Cambridge Modern History* (Cambridge, 1962), XI, 611; G. K. Akinola, "The Sultanate of Zanzibar, 1870–1890," (Ph.D. diss., University of Ibadan, 1971), 109, 178.

7. W. E. Taylor, *African Aphorisms; or Saws from Swahili-Land* (London, 1891), 25.

8. Bennett and Brooks, *New England Merchants,* 380. See W. Montgomery Watt, *Islamic Thought,* 40–41, and *Islam and the Integration of Society* (Evanston, 1961), 36, 65; H. Lammens (trans. E. Dennison Ross), *Islam: Beliefs and Institutions* (London, 1968), 11–12.

9. A. C. Unomah and J. B. Webster, "East Africa," 273. J. L. Krapf, among other contemporaries, pointed out Said's real title: *Outlines of the Kisuáheli Language with Special Reference to the Kiníka Dialect* (Tübingen, 1850), 9.

10. See J. B. Kelly, *Sultanate and Imamate in Oman* (Chatham House Memoranda, December 1959), 5.

11. Steere to A. Steere, 1 September 1864, A.1.III, UMCA.

12. Abdul Mohamed Hussein Sheriff, "The Rise of a Commercial Empire: An Aspect of the Economic History of Zanzibar, 1770–1873," (Ph.D. diss., University of London, 1971), 112ff.

13. C. Guillain, *Documents sur l'Histoire, la Géographie et le Commerce de l'Afrique Orientale* (Paris, 1856), II, 251.

14. Bennett, *Zanzibar,* 49.

15. Abdullah bin Salim received an annual subsidy of $1,200 and additionally did not pay duty on merchandise imported into Zanzibar. Rigby to Anderson, 14 April 1859, IOE 140.

16. Lamu notables, for instance, received a subsidy of $450. Holmwood to Prideaux, 17 November 1874, in Prideaux to Derby, 24 November 1874, FO 84/1400.

17. Hamerton to Secret Council, 14 May 1841, in Hamerton to Willoughby, 14 May 1841, IOE 35.

18. Notes sur la cote orientale d'Afrique tirées du travail de M. Loarer, O.I. 2/10, AOM; Richard F. Burton, *Zanzibar: City, Island, and Coast* (London, 1872), I, 265; Christopher, journal extracts, 8 May 1843, in Haines to Willoughby, 22 May 1843, IOE 60; J. L. Krapf, *Reisen in Ost-Afrika ausgeführt in dem Jahren 1837–55* (Kornthal, 1858), I, 194; John Felt Osgood, *Notes,* 67; Otto Kersten, *Decken's Reisen 1859–61,* 102.

19. Elton to Kirk, 14 Dec. 1873, in Kirk to FO, 17 Dec. 1873, FO 84/1376.

20. Watt, *Islamic Thought,* 35.

21. Rigby to Anderson, 4 April 1859, IOE 140.

22. Kersten, *Decken's Reisen, 1859–61,* 127; Bennett, *Zanzibar,* 81.

23. Adrian Germain, "Note sur Zanzibar et la Côte orientale d 'Afrique," *BSG,* 16 (1868), 535, Mrs. Charles E. B. Russell, ed., *General Rigby, Zanzibar and the Slave Trade* (London, 1935), 340; Ernst Hieke, "Aus der Fruhzeit des Deutschen Afrikahandels. Das hamburgische Handelshaus Wm. O'Swald & Co 1831–1870," (typescript, Staats- und Universitäts-Bibliothek, Hamburg), 145; letter, 22 March 1858, *PM,* 4(1858), 254; Kersten, *Decken's Reisen, 1859–61,* 128.

24. Frederick Cooper, *Plantation Slavery*, 115.

25. See Jablonski to Thouvenel, 26 January 1862, PZ 3.

26. Pelly to Stewart, undated [1862], FO 800/234; Rigby in *PP* 1871 (420), XII, 43.

27. Krapf in Playfair to Russell, 1 June 1864, FO 84/1224; Dupré to MMC, 5 October 1861, in Chasseloup-Laubat to MAE, 29 November 1861, PZ 2.

28. Webb to Seward, 17 March 1869, DBZ.

29. Mehemet Ali to Rombaix, 24 August 1864, and succeeding letters, E–38; Rombaix to Majid, 23 May 1867, E–55; Kirk to Rombaix, 20 June 1870, E–60; Kirk to BG, 31 December 1872, E–62: ZA.

30. Kirk to FO, 13 January 1872, E–62, ZA.

31. Steere to Penney, 8 January 1881, A.1.III, UMCA; Lagougine, Traite des esclaves à Madagascar et à la Cote orientale d'Afrique, in Note pour le Cabinet du Ministre, 31 August 1872, O.I. 14/56, AOM.

32. Pelly to Forbes, 30 October 1861, Pelly to Senior Naval Officer, 22 November 1861, E–27; Playfair to Anderson, 23 May 1863, E–32: ZA; Krapf letter, *PM* 9(1863), 159.

33. Churchill to Stanley, 27 September 1868, E–41, Kirk to Gonne, 10 April 1869, Kirk to Majid, 14 August 1869, Kirk to FO, 23 April 1869, Adm. to Kirk, 12 March 1869, E–57, ZA; Kirk to FO, 25 February 1870, FO 84/1325; Norman R. Bennett, *Studies in East African History* (Boston, 1963), 34.

34. For harassment, Rebmann, 29 October 1861, in Pelly to Forbes, 10 January 1862, E–31, ZA; for violence, see below, Ch. 5, and Marguerite Ylvisaker, *Lamu in the Nineteenth Century: Land, Trade, and Politics* (Boston, 1979), 94.

35. Kirk to BG, 1 May 1871, E–61, ZA; Tozer to Steere, 21 March 1871, addendum of 29 March, A.1.I, UMCA; Webb to Ropes, 26 February 1871, J. Tharia to Ropes, 22 April 1871, Ropes Papers, PM; Kirk to Vivian, 10 June 1871, *PP* 1871 (420), XII, 94.

36. Steere to "My Dear Lord," 5 May 1875, A.1.III, UMCA; Kirk to Wedderburn, 9 March 1871, in Kirk to SSI, 9 March 1871, SLRV; Kirk to BG, 30 August 1871, E–61, ZA; Bennett, *Zanzibar*, 104–107.

CHAPTER 2

1. The Somali region will not be included in this volume. For a recent analysis, Lee V. Cassanelli, "The Benadir Past: Essays in Southern Somali History," (Ph.D. diss., University of Wisconsin, 1973).

2. The basic source for the region in the nineteenth century is Marguerite Ylvisaker, *Lamu*. Shahabudin, 14 February 1870, FO 84/1392; Kirk to Derby, 8 December 1875, FO 84/1417; Holmwood to Prideaux, 1 December 1874, in Prideaux to FO, 8 February 1875, E–71, Kirk to FO, 6 November 1873, E–63c, ZA; W. F. W. Owen, *Narrative of Voyages to Explore the Shores of Africa, Arabia and Madagascar* (London, 1833), I, 364.

3. Smee to Hamilton, 6 April 1811, Add. Mss. 8958, BL; Ylvisaker, *Lamu*, 69ff.; C. S. Nicholls, *The Swahili Coast: Politics, Diplomacy and Trade on the East African Littoral, 1798–1856* (New York, 1971), 301–302.

4. Rodger F. Morton, "Slaves, Fugitives, and Freedmen on the Kenya Coast, 1873–1907," (Ph.D. diss., Syracuse University, 1976), 149–155; Ylvisaker, *Lamu*, 81–93; Cochet to MAE, 3 October 1856, CCZ 2.

5. Cooper, *Plantation Slavery*, 81ff.; Charles New, *Life, Wanderings, &*

Labours in Eastern Africa (London, 1873), 166; Holmwood to Prideaux, 1 December 1874, in Prideaux to FO, 8 February 1875, E–71, ZA; Kirk to FO, 6 November 1873, FO 84/1376; Gissing to Kirk, 14 September 1884, in Kirk to Granville, 8 October 1884, FO 84/1679.

6. Peter Langer Koffsky, "History of Takaungu, East Africa, 1830–1896," (Ph.D. diss., University of Wisconsin, 1977), 12ff.

7. Thomas T. Spear, *The Kaya Complex: A History of the Mijikenda Peoples of the Kenya Coast to 1900* (Nairobi, 1978), 124–125, 146; John Lamphear, "The Kamba and the Northern Mrima Coast," in Richard Gray and David Birmingham, eds., *Pre-Colonial Trade: Essays on Trade in Central and Eastern Africa before 1900* (London, 1970), 75ff.

8. Hans Meyer, "Die Mombassa-Kilimandscharo-Route in Britisch-Ostafrika," *PM,* 37(1891), 257–263; Lamphear, "The Kamba," 92.

9. See below, p. 40.

10. Krapf, Journal of a voyage made in February and March 1850 . . . , C.A5/M1, CMS, Journal, 20–25 February 1852, *CMI* 4(1853), 93–109, and *Travels, Researches, & Missionary Labours during an Eighteen Years' Residence in Eastern Africa* (London, 1860), 339; Steven Feierman, *The Shambaa Kingdom: A History* (Madison, 1974), 93ff.; Oscar Baumann, *Usambara und seine Nachbargebiete* (Berlin, 1891), 124, 162ff.; Erhardt to Venn, 9 April 1853, FO 54/15; Burton, "Zanzibar," 278–288.

11. Feierman, *Shambaa,* 110ff.

12. Playfair to Havelock, 9 April 1864, in Playfair to Wedderburn, 11 April 1864, SLRV 1; Hamerton to Willoughby, 9 February 1842, SLRB–1; Handford to Lang, [November–December] 1884, G3.A5/02, CMS; Burton, "Zanzibar," 217; Kersten, *Decken's Reisen 1859–61,* 19ff.; L. A. Ricklin, *La Mission Catholique du Zanguebar: Travaux et Voyages du R. P. Horner* (Paris, 1880), 15; New, *Life,* 54; Holmwood to Prideaux, 8 February 1875, E–71, Kirk to FO, 31 May 1873, 6 November 1873, E–63B, Smith to FO, 26 July 1875, E–72, ZA; Guillain, *Afrique Orientale,* II, 254; Krapf, *Reisen,* I, 180; Spear, *Kaya Complex,* 138; Pelly, Memo. on the trade of Mombasa, 28 March 1873, in Frere to Granville, 5 April 1873, FO 84/1390; Fred J. Berg, "Mombasa under the Busaidi Sultanate: The City and Its Hinterland in the Nineteenth Century," (Ph.D. diss., University of Wisconsin, 1971), 103, 94–95.

13. Burton, *Zanzibar,* II, 71; New, *Life,* 224; Decken, 5 March 1861, *ZAE,* 10(1861), 305; Rebmann to Hamerton, 1 May 1855, ZM.

14. Spear, *Kaya Complex,* 189–190; Deimler, 8 May 1857, *CM* 30(1857), 52; Rebmann, 22 April 1858, *CM* 31(1858), 66; Jacobs, "Pastoral Masai," 89–95; Jacob Hildebrandt, "Von Mombasa," 255–256.

15. Burton, *Zanzibar,* II, 145–147; Ricklin, *Horner,* 10; Kurt Toeppen, "Handel und Handelsverbindungen Ost-Afrikas," *MGGH* 7(1885–1886), 227; G. A. Fischer, "Bericht über die im Auftrage der Geographischen Gesellschaft in Hamburg unternommene Reise in das Massai-Land," *MGGH* 5(1882–1883), 37–38, and *Mehr Licht im dunkeln Welttheil* (Hamburg, 1885), 11; Ludwig von Höhnel, *Discovery of Lakes Rudolf and Stephanie* (London, 1894), I, 24; Oscar Baumann, *Durch Massailand zur Nilquelle* (Berlin, 1894), 124–125, and *Usambara,* 72ff.; Hardy report, April 1811, Add. Mss. 8958, BL; W. Westendarp, "Der Elfenbeinreichtum Afrikas," *DKZ,* 2(1885), 446; Loarer, No. D, Ports au Nord de Zanguebar, O. I. 2/10, AOM; Kitchener to Rosebery, 15 March 1886, FO 84/1798.

16. G. Meinecke, "Pangani," *DKZ* 7(1894), 154; J. Kirk, "Visit to the Coast

of Somali-land," *PRGS* 17(1872–1873), 340; Charles New, "Journey from Pangani, viâ Wadigo, to Mombasa," ibid., 19(1874–1875), 318.

17. Krapf, *Reisen*, I, 224; Burdo, *Zanzibar au Tanganika*, 485; Fischer, *Mehr Licht*, 9.

18. Franz Stuhlmann, *Mit Emin Pascha ins Herz von Afrika* (Berlin, 1894), 40; S. Tristram Pruen, *The Arab and the African: Experiences in Eastern Equatorial Africa during a Residence of Three Years* (London, 1891), 224; Reichard, *Deutsch-Ostafrika*, 327–328; Rochus Schmidt, *Deutschlands Kolonien: I. Ost-Afrika* (Berlin, 1894), 175.

19. Walter T. Brown, "The Politics of Business: Relations between Zanzibar and Bagamoyo in the Late Nineteenth Century," *IJAHS* 4(1971), 635, 639; Nimtz, "Sūfī Order," 141–149, 171–172; Mgr. Gaume, *Voyage à la Côte Orientale d'Afrique pendant l'année 1866 par le R. P. Horner* (Paris, 1872), 126; Burton, "Lake Regions," 45, 87; *BSE* 13(1883), 45; A. Leue, "Bagamoyo," *BKK* 2(1900–1901), 11ff.; Otto Ehlers, "Ein Besuch in dem Küstengebiete von Deutsch-Ostafrika," *DKZ* 1(1888), 321; H. F. von Behr, *Kriegsbilder aus dem Araberaufstand in Deutsch-Ostafrika* (Leipzig, 1891), 138; Eugen Krenzler, *Ein Jahr in Ostafrika* (Ulm, 1888), 71; New, *Life*, 46.

20. Paul Reichard, "Das afrikanische Elfenbein und sein Handel," *DGB* 12(1899), 151–157; J. F. Elton, "On the Coast Country of East Africa, South of Zanzibar," *JRGS* 44(1874), 236; "Dr. A. Roscher's Tagebuch über seine Reise nach dem Lufidji, 6. Februar bis 24. März 1859," *PM* 8(1862), 1–2; J. H. Speke, "On the Commerce of Central Africa," *TBGS* 15(1858–1860), 141; Lyndon Harries, *Swahili Prose Texts* (London, 1965), 181–183; Guillain, *Afrique Orientale*, III, 375–380; Richard F. Burton, *The Lake Regions of Central Africa* (New York, 1860), I, 31.

21. Nourse to Adm, 5 January 1823, Adm 7/48; Thomas Boteler, *Narrative of a Voyage of Discovery to Africa and Arabia* (London, 1835), II, 48; Loarer, Ports au Sud de Zanguebar, No. A, O.I. 2/10, AOM; Bisson excerpt, 23 July 1848, in Belligny to MAE, 9 January 1850, CCZ 1; Kitchener to FO, 10 February 1886, FO 84/1797.

22. Report on the Proceeding of the French . . . , in Hamerton to Willoughby, 9 February 1842, FO 54/4; Loarer, Ports au Sud de Zanguebar, No. A, I.O. 2/10, AOM; Krapf, *Travels*, 344; Burton, *Zanzibar*, II, 342–343; Kirk to FO, 27 August 1873, E–63c, ZA; Neville Chittick, "The Early History of Kilwa Kivinje," *Azania* 4(1969), 156; Kersten, *Decken's Reisen 1859–61*, 146–147; Edward Alpers, "A Revised Chronology of the Sultans of Kilwa in the Eighteenth and Nineteenth Centuries," *Azania* 2(1967), 150, 152, 163; Sheriff, "Zanzibar," 65ff.

23. Chittick, "Kilwa Kivinje," 157; Decken, 26 October 1860, *ZAE* 10(1861), 135; Kirk to FO, 27 August 1873, FO 84/1375; Kirk to FO, 25 January 1872, E–66, ZA.

24. Seward to Gonne, 27 November 1866, Seward to FO, 23 December 1866, E–36, Kirk to Churchill, 6 March 1868, E–42, Kirk to FO, 27 August 1873, E–63c, ZA; Waller, *Livingstone's Journals*, I, 25; Churchill to Gonne, 4 March 1868, in Churchill to SSI, 14 April 1868, SLRV 48; John Gray, "The British Vice-Consulate at Kilwa Kivinje, 1884–1885," *TNR* 51(1958), 181; Webb to Ropes, 12 November 1867, Ropes Papers, PM; Steere to Penney, 19 October 1881, A.1.III, UMCA; Edward Steere, *Central African Mission: Its Present State and Prospects* (London, 1873), 11–12 and in *PP* 1871 (420), XII, 71; Chittick, "Kilwa Kivinje," 157; Patrick M. Redmond, "A Political History of the

Songea Ngoni from the Mid-Nineteenth Century to the Rise of the Tanganyika African National Union," (Ph.D. diss., University of London, 1972), 33ff.
25. For the following paragraphs: Andrew Roberts, "Nyamwezi Trade," in Gray and Birmingham, *Pre-Colonial African Trade*, 39–51; Aylward Shorter, *Chiefship in Western Tanzania: A Political History of the Kimbu* (Oxford, 1972), 116, 216ff.; Sheriff, "Zanzibar," 136ff.; *Maisha ya Hamed bin Muhammed el Murjebi yaani Tippu Tip* (Supplement to the East African Swahili Committee Journals, No. 28/2(1958) and 29/1(1959), 39, 65; Baumann, *Massailand*, 234, 242–243; Paul Reichard, "Die Bedeutung von Tabora für Deutsch-Ostafrika," *DKZ* 3(1890), 67; Burton, "Lake Regions," 180ff.; Burton, *Zanzibar*, II, 292.
26. Loarer, "Exploration de la Cote orientale d'Afrique . . . ," January 1846, O.I. 2/10, AOM.
27. Ebenezer Burgess, 11 September 1839, *The Missionary Herald* 36(1840), 119.
28. Roberts, "Nyamwezi Trade," 51; Coulbois, *Tanganyka*, 41.
29. See John Roscoe, *The Baganda* (London, 1911), 269, 412–413.
30. Baumann, *Massailand*, 243; Reichard, "Afrikanische Elfenbein," 139, 149. For the Kamba hunters, Gerhard Lindblom, *The Akamba* (Uppsala, 1920), 572.
31. Speke to Rigby, 12 May 1861, in Russell, *Rigby*, 239; Heinrich Brode (trans. H. Havelock), *Tippoo Tib* (London, 1907), 19–20; Jablonski to Lhuys, 28 May 1866, CCZ 3; Kirk to Clarendon, 30 May 1869, in Reginald Coupland, *Livingstone's Last Journey* (London, 1945), 93; Ch. de Vienne, "De Zanzibar à l'Oukami," *BSG* 14 (1872), 356; Reichard, "Tabora," 67.
32. Burton, *Lake Regions*, II, 424; James Augustus Grant, *A Walk across Africa* (London and Edinburgh, 1864), 48–51. For the various villages of Tabora, Sleman bin Mwenyi Tshande, "Meine Reise ins Innere Ostafrikas bis zum Tanganyika," in C. Velten, *Schilderungen der Suaheli* (Göttingen, 1901), 9.
33. Speke, *Journal*, 91; Cameron, *Across Africa*, I, 81.
34. Henry M. Stanley, *How I Found Livingstone* (London, 1872), 193–194; Waller, *Livingstone's Journals*, II, 182.
35. Burton, "Lake Regions," 58; Reichard, "Afrikanische Elfenbein," 159–161; Harries, *Swahili Prose Texts*, 179; Fischer, *Mehr Licht*, 13–14; D. Jeram to Kirk, 5 June 1886, E–90, ZA.
36. Burton, *Lake Regions*, II, 229.
37. For details, Norman R. Bennett, *Mirambo of Tanzania, ca. 1840–1884* (New York, 1971), and "Isike, *Ntemi* of Unyanyembe," in Mark Karp, ed., *African Dimensions: Essays in Honor of William O. Brown* (Boston, 1975), 53–55.
38. Pelly to Forbes, 27 November 1861, E–27, 1 January 1862, E–31, ZA; Jablonski to MAE, 2 February 1862, CCZ 2.
39. Pelly to Stewart, 18 April 1862, 15 July 1862, E–31, ZA; Jablonski to MAE, 7 January 1865, CCZ 2; Seward, Report on the Commerce of Zanzibar . . . 1864–1865, E–36, ZA.
40. Burton, *Zanzibar*, I, 378, 479; Edward Steere, *Collections for a Handbook of the Nyamwezi Language* (London, n.d.), 5; Sleman bin Mwenyi Tshande, "Meine Reise," 10; Livingstone to Maclear, 17 November 1871, *PRGS* 17(1872–1873), 71.
41. Vienne to MAE, 20 October 1871, CCZ 3.
42. "Leben des Herrn Amur bin Nasur," in C. G. Büttner, *Anthologie aus der Suaheli-Litteratur. Zweiter Theil. Uebersetzung* (Berlin, 1894), 162; Prideaux to FO, 21 May 1874, E–64, Prideaux to FO, 21 September 1874, Unyanyembe

Arabs to Hashim bin Sualim, 23 Ramathan 1291, in Elton to FO, 22 December 1874, Elton to FO, 24 December 1874, E–65, Note, E–67, ZA; Stanley, *Livingstone*, 190, 219–220; Dutrieux letter in *La Flandre Libérale*, 30 May 1879, Extraits de Presse, A.I.A., 1, MAEB; Waller, *Livingstone's Journals*, II, 183.

CHAPTER 3

1. Hamerton to Aberdeen, 2 January 1844, *PP* 1845 (632), XLIX, 143; John Robb, *Medico-Topigraphical Report on Zanzibar* (Calcutta, 1879), 7.
2. Krapf to Coates, 10 January 1844, Willoughby to Hamerton, 21 November 1844, E–6, ZA: R. C. Bridges, "The British Exploration of East Africa, 1788–1885, with Special Reference to the Activities of the Royal Geographical Society," (Ph.D. diss., University of London, 1963), 99ff.
3. Krapf to Coates, 25 February 1846, C.A5/M1, CMS.
4. Krapf to Venn, 10 April 1852, 12 May 1854, Erhardt to Venn, 27 December 1853, C.A5/M1, CMS; Krapf, 12 April 1852, *CMI*, 3(1852), 192; Krapf to Jomard, 30 August 1853, *BSG*, 7(1854), 261; Krapf to Kuhlman, 3 October 1854, in Belligny to MAE, 28 January 1854, PZ 1; R. C. Bridges, "Introduction," in J. L. Krapf, *Travels, Researches, and Missionary Labours during an Eighteen Years' Residence in Eastern Africa* (London, 2nd ed., 1968), 29–32; Hamerton to Malet, 3 June 1853, E–3, ZA; Norman R. Bennett, "France and Zanzibar, 1844 to the 1860s," *IJAHS* 6(1973), 628–630.
5. See R. C. Bridges, "Krapf and the Strategy of the Mission to East Africa, 1844–1855," *Makerere J.*, 5(1961), 41–45.
6. Ibid., 39; Rebmann to Hamerton, 27 November 1854, 23 January 1855, ZM; "Die ostafrikanische Mission," *EMM* 2(1858), 96–101; Venn to Playfair, 24 May 1865, E–46, ZA.
7. Erhardt to Young, 9 August 1854, C.A5/M1, CMS; Hamerton to Clarendon, 16 February 1854, FO 54/15; Rigby to Anderson, 10 May 1859, E–26, ZA; Rebmann, 19 September 1858, 28 April 1860, *CM*, 32(1859), 4, and 33(1860), 67–68; "Voyages of the Candace to the East Coast of Africa," *CWTW* 1(1863), 609–612; Georg Haccius, *Hannoversche Missionsgeschichte* (Hermannsburg, 1910), II, 238ff.; "Das Suahelii Sultanat," *MH* 11(1889), 138–142, 162–165.
8. John Anthony Patrick Kieran, "The Holy Ghost Fathers in East Africa, 1863–1914," (Ph.D. diss., University of London, 1966), 17ff. See also Frits Versteijnen, *The Catholic Mission of Bagamoyo* (Bagamoyo, 1968).
9. The Frenchmen continued the practice into the 1880s. See Oliver, *Missionary Factor*, 21; *BSE*, 5(1886), 500, and 14(1888), 616; Joseph Simon, *Pater Anton Horner* (Lauterbourg, 1934), 12. The practice was as old as the arrival of the first Christians in East Africa: Justus Strandes (trans. Jean F. Wallwork), *The Portuguese Period in East Africa* (Nairobi, 1961), 175.
10. Jablonski to Thouvenel, 20 June 1862, PZ 3; Horner, 29 December 1867, *MC* 4(1871–1872), 57.
11. Rebmann to Krapf, 30 April 1861, in Krapf, 5 September 1861, *UMFCM* 4(1861), 737.
12. Ibid., 5(1862), 399ff.; R. C. Bridges, "A Manuscript Kinika Vocabulary and a Letter of J. L. Krapf," *B. of the Society for African Church History*, 2(1968), 293–298; Eckett to Russell, 14 June 1861, Wodehouse to Eckett, 8 July 1861, E–29, Pelly to Forbes, 10 January 1862, Pelly to Stewart, 8 March 1862, 22 April 1862, Krapf to Pelly, 9 March 1862, E–31, Wakefield to Seward, 13 July 1866,

Seward to Wakefield, 31 August 1866, E–41, Wakefield and New to Seward, 22 February 1867, Wakefield and New to Majid, 22 February 1867, E–44, Wakefield to Kirk, 16 January 1882, P–16, ZA; Wakefield to Barton, 25 July 1864, *UMFCM* 8(1865), 68; J. L. Krapf, "My Late Mission Tour to the East Coast of Africa," *CWTW* 1(1863), 193ff.; New, *Life;* E. S. Wakefield, *Thomas Wakefield* (London, 1904), 16ff.

13. See Norman R. Bennett and Marguerite Ylvisaker, eds., *The Central African Journal of Lovell J. Procter, 1860–1864* (Boston, 1971).

14. Buttersworth to Barton, 5 February 1854 *UMFCM* 7(1864), 478; Tozer to Festing, 1 June 1864, 18 June 1864, Tozer to Bishop of Cape Town, 14 June 1864. Steere, Memorandum on the present state and prospects of the Central African Mission, 18 June 1864, A.1.I, Steere to Mrs. Steere, 1 September 1864, A.1.III, UMCA; Zanzibar Diary, 31 August 1864, UMCA archives, Zanzibar; Tozer to Playfair, 18 June 1864, FO to Playfair, 8 August 1865, E–33, ZA; Miss Tozer, journal, 25 September 1865, *ML* 1(1866), 129; Gertrude Ward, ed., *Letters of Bishop Tozer and His Sister with Some Other Records of the Universities' Mission from 1863–1873* (Westminster, 1902), 43ff.

15. Henry C. Arc Angelo, 29 May 1844, *Colbourn's United Service Magazine* (1845, pt. I), 127–128; Rigby in Lieutenant von Schickh, "Report on the Disasters that have happened to the Expedition of the Baron Charles von der Decken," *PRGS,* 10(1865–1866), 99.

16. Krapf, journal, 10 February 1844, C.A5/M1, CMS; Hamerton to Aberdeen, 13 April 1844, FO 54/6; Browne, *Etchings,* 436; Sheriff, "Zanzibar," 200ff., for this and other ventures.

17. Loarer, Ile de Zanguebar, No. 5, O. I. 5/23, AOM; Belligny to MAE, 17 August 1850, 2 April 1851, CCZ 1 and O. I. 15/65, AOM.

18. Captain Colomb, *Slave-Catching in the Indian Ocean* (London, 1873), 493–494; Hines to SD, 31 March 1864, Bennett and Brooks, *New England Merchants,* 525; Wakefield journal, February 1866, *UMFCM,* 10(1867), 174; Seward to FO, 25 October 1866, Seward to Stanley, 15 March 1867, Fraser to Egerton, 14 August 1867, Articles of Agreement between Majid and Fraser, 25 March 1864, Egerton to Fraser, 19 December 1867, *PP* 1867–1868 (4000–4001), LXIV, 101ff.; Kirk to FO, 22 May 1872, FO 84/1357; Frere to Granville, 12 February 1873, FO 84/1389; Steere, 22 July 1876, *Central African Mission, Occasional Paper,* VI, 4.

19. See Loarer, Ile de Zanguebar, No. 3, O.I. 5/23, AOM; Burton, *Zanzibar,* I, 221–222; Norman R. Bennett, ed., *The Zanzibar Letters of Edward D. Ropes, Jr., 1882–1892* (Boston, 1973), 97–98; O. Kersten, "Ueber Colonisation in Ost-Afrika," *Internationale Revue* 1(1866), 267; Jablonski to MAE, 6 August 1862, CCZ 2.

20. Miles to FO, 1 February 1883, E–78, ZA; Lacau to MAE, 3 May 1888, CCZ 5; Holmwood, The Clove Trade of Zanzibar, 4 February 1888, FO 84/1915.

21. Parker to Hamerton, 9 April 1847, F–7, ZA; Hamerton to Parker, 12 April 1847, ZM; Krapf, *Reisen,* I, 297ff.

22. Hamerton to Malet, 3 June 1853, E–3, ZA; Cochet to MAE, 30 October 1856 (with enclosures), 15 January 1857, CCZ 2; Burton, *Zanzibar,* I, 319–320; Hieke, "Wm. O'Swald & Co.," 69ff.; Bennett, "France and Zanzibar," 42–48.

23. Wakefield journal, February 1866, *UMFCM,* 10(1867), 176; Kirk to Granville, 17 November 1873, *PP* 1874 (c.1064), LXII, 107; Kirk to Sec. Royal Geog. Soc., 23 June 1879, u.v., ZA; Clements R. Markham, *The Fifty Years' Work*

of the Royal Geographical Society (London, 1881), 78; Mackay, Account of a Journey up the Kingani River in East Africa, July 1876, C.A6/016b, CMS.

24. LeRoy, "Rapport," 2 December 1885, *APF*, 58(1886), 188; Wright and Hutchinson to Baxter, 17 October 1878, C.A6/L1, CMS.

25. Cameron, *Across Africa*, I, 24.

26. Hore to Mullens, 10 January 1879, CA 2, LMS; Stanley, *Livingstone*, 193; Cameron to Derby, 4 March 1877, *PP* 1872 (c.657), LIV, 49; Livingstone to Stanley, 15 November 1870, *PP* 1873 (c.598), 1. Hore's life also once was saved by an Arab: Edw. Coode Hore, "Lake Tanganyika," *PRGS* 4(1882), 24.

27. Bridges, "British Exploration of East Africa," 99ff.; Bialloblotzky to Palmerston, 27 August 1849, Ayrton to Bidwell, 5 December 1849, FO 54/13; Burton, *Zanzibar*, I, 58, II, 256–257; C. T. Beke, "Snowy Mountain in Africa," *The Athenaeum* (1849), 357–358.

28. Bennett, "France and Zanzibar," 607ff.; There is a full dossier on Maizan in O. I. 10/43, AOM.

29. Burton, "Lake Regions," 94; Broquant to MAE, 1 January 1847, O. I. 10/43, Zevasco to MAE, 24 May 1847, in Guillain to MAC, 20 October 1847, O. I. 14/55, AOM; Speke, *Journal*, 30; Krapf to King of Prussia, undated, C.A5/M1, CMS.

30. A. Rabaud, "L'Afrique Equatoriale," *BSGM* 5(1881), 79–80.

31. See Krapf statement in Bennett, "France and Zanzibar," 617.

32. Burton, *Zanzibar*, I, 472–474, and "Lake Regions," 12–13.

33. "Dr. A. Roscher's Reise nach Inner-Afrika," and Roscher letter, *PM*, 5(1859), 478–480, 518; "Roscher's Tagebuch," 1–4; O. Hartleb, "Albrecht Roscher, ein Pionier deutscher Afrikaforschung," *Afrika Rundschau*, 2(1936–1937), 209–212; Swinney journal, 1 January 1887, u.v., UMCA; Coupland, *Exploitation*, 109–110; Rigby to Anderson, 18 August 1860, IOE, 144.

34. Decken, 26 October 1860, 20 February 1861, *ZAE*, 10(1861), 135, 467–471; Rigby to BG, 17 April 1861, E–27, Pelly to Stewart, 17 August 1862, E–31, Pelly to Decken, 2 May 1865, E–46, ZA; Decken to Pelly, 1 May 1865, 2 May 1865, ZM; Tozer to Festing, 23 November 1865, A.1.I, UMCA; Jablonski to MAE, 15 April 1866, CCZ 3; Kersten, *Decken's Reisen 1859–61*, especially p. 224; Reichard, *Deutsch-Ostafrika*, 113; J. Simmons, "A Suppressed Passage in Livingstone's Last Journals Relating to the Death of Baron von der Decken," *JRAS* 41(1941), 344; Norman R. Bennett, "Livingstone's Letters to William F. Stearns," *IJAHS* 1(1968), 247.

CHAPTER 4

1. Horner, 5 August 1873, *MC* 5(1873), 388; Bennett, *Zanzibar*, 95ff., for this and the following discussions.

2. R. J. Gavin, "The Bartle Frere Mission to Zanzibar," *Historical J.* 5(1962), 122–148; Norman R. Bennett, "Charles de Vienne and the Frere Mission to Zanzibar," *BUP*, 2(1966), 107–122; Kirk to FO, 3 July 1873, E–63C, ZA.

3. Kirk to FO, 20 June 1871, FO 84/1344; Kirk to FO, 31 May 1873, enc. his memo on the Somali slave trade, E–63B, ZA.

4. Kirk to FO, 3 July 1873, 22 July 1873, 27 August 1873, E–63C, ZA.

5. Elton to Prideaux, 20 December 1873, and succeeding despatches, E–64, ZA; Foot to Adm., 4 February 1874, Ward to Cumming, 25 June 1874, *PP* 1875 (c.657), LIV, 52, 112.

6. H. Greffulhe, "Voyage à Lamoo," *BSGM* 2(1878), 333–335; Guillois to Broglie, 11 December 1873, PZ 4; Prideaux to FO, 2 February 1874, 8 April 1874, Elton to Prideaux, 4 April 1874, E–64, Holmwood to Prideaux, 17 November 1874, E–65, ZA; Prideaux to FO, 7 February 1874, 6 April 1874 (enc. Elton report, 2 April 1874), Elton to Prideaux, 28 January 1874, FO 84/1398; Kirk to Lister, 19 September 1874, FO 84/1400; Frederick Holmwood, "Introductory Chapter on Africa and the Slave Trade," in J. Frederic Elton (ed. by H. B. Cotterill), *Travels and Researches among the Lakes and Mountains of Eastern & Central Africa* (London, 1879), 9–12; Elton, *Travels*, 94ff.; Coupland, *Exploitation*, 221; Prideaux to Aitcheson, 9 March 1875, Holmwood to Kirk, 10 March 1875, E–71, ZA.

7. Sulivan to Cumming, 4 May 1875, *PP* 1875 (c.657), LIV, 241; Prideaux to FO, 27 February 1875, E–71, Euan Smith to FO, 31 July 1875, Kirk to FO, 29 November 1875, E–72, ZA; Mackay to Kirk, 25 February 1875, ZM; Kirk to Derby, 19 January 1875, FO 84/1415.

8. Lister to Kirk, 1 April 1876 (enc. a Ward extract), Q–15, ZA; Kirk to Derby, 20 April 1876 (enc. proclamations), 15 May 1876, FO 84/1453; Coupland, *Exploitation*, 225–226.

9. Kirk to Frere, 18 March 1873, 20 May 1873, E–63B, ZA; Pelly, memo on the Kilwa affair, 13 March 1873, in Frere to Granville, 27 March 1873, FO 84/1390.

10. Edward Steere to A. Steere, 2 June 1876, A.1.III, UMCA; Kirk to Derby, 1 June 1876, 18 May 1876, FO 84/1453; Kirk to Derby, 20 July 1876, 15 August 1876 (enc. Holmwood to Kirk, 2 July 1876), FO 84/1454; Kirk to Mackinnon, 17 October 1876, MP 22; Kirk to Salisbury, 6 March 1880, FO 84/1574.

11. Kirk to FO, 5 February 1877, Q–18, ZA; Kirk to Mackinnon, 5 February 1877, MP 22. In 1875 there was only one British vessel watching the entire coast: Euan Smith to FO, 31 July 1875, E–72, ZA.

12. Allen to Allen, St. Bartholemew's Day 1877, A.1.IV, Steere to Heanley, 6 December 1877, A.1.III, UMCA; Kurt Weiss, *Meine Reise nach dem Kilima-Ndjarogebiet* (Berlin, 1886), 10; Kirk to Wylde, 6 May 1876, FO 84/1453; Kirk to Derby, 17 August 1877, FO 84/1486; Salisbury to Kirk, 12 April 1878, FO 84/1513, 22 June 1878, FO 84/1514; Charles Courret, *A l'Est et à L'Ouest dans l'Océan Indien* (Paris, 1884), 123; Fischer, *Mehr Licht*, 75; Giraud, *Afrique Equatoriale*, 23; Robert Nunez Lyne, *An Apostle of Empire: Being the Life of Sir Lloyd William Mathews* (London, 1936), 47ff.; Etienne Marras, "L'Isle de Zanzibar," *BSGM* 5(1881), 196–197.

13. Marras, "Zanzibar," 196; Burdo, *Zanzibar au Tanganika*, 149–150; Courret, *A l'Est*, 124; Alfred Smith, "From Zanzibar to Nosibe," *The Antananarivo Annual and Madagascar Magazine* 7(1883), 30; *CA* 1(1883); 48.

14. Steere to Heanley, 4 November 1880, A.1.III, Johnson to Steere, December 1881, A.1.IV, Smythies, 26 September 1884, A.1.VI, UMCA; Kirk to Salisbury, 12 November 1878, enc. Maples to *Times*, 14 October 1879, FO 84/1548; C. Smith to Kirk, 5 July 1884, in Kirk to Granville, 25 July 1884, FO 84/1678; W. P. Livingstone, *Laws of Livingstonia* (London, n.d.), 117; Johnson to Steere, 28 May 1881, *CAMOP* 17(1881), 20; *Slave Boy to Priest: The Autobiography of Padre Petro Kilekwa* (trans. K. H. Nixon Smith) (Westminster, 1937), 9–14; Giraud, *Afrique Equatoriale*, 92–94; Maples to Allen, 11 June 1883, *CA* 1(1883), 170–171; Williams, 3 May 1885, *CA* 3(1885), 107; Smith to Kirk, 24 February 1885, E–84, ZA.

15. Steere to West, 22 October 1874, A.1.III, UMCA; Robert Ferguson (ed. Leslie Stair), *Harpooner: A Four Year Voyage on the Barque Kathleen, 1880–1884* (Philadelphia, 1936), 95; F. Flynn, "A Report of Missionary Work at Zanzibar and Elsewhere," *CA* 5(1887); 100; undated Zanzibar letter, *BSAF* (1888–1889), 496–497; Guillemé, 3 August 1884, *BMA,* (1883–1886), 234; Fischer, *Mehr Licht,* 65–66; Weiss, *Reise,* 4.

16. Smythies to Penney, 3 May 1885, SL; Charles S. Smith, "Explorations in the Zanzibar Dominions," *Royal Geographical Soc. Supplementary Papers* 2(1887), 104–105.

17. Kirk to FO, 13 November 1879, Q–22, 23 February 1880, 6 March 1880 (enc. Holmwood to Kirk, 30 January 1880), Q–24, Miles to FO, 1 March 1883 (with a Kirk note), 23 June 1883, Kirk to FO, 24 November 1883, E–78, 9 May 1884, E–83, ZA; Kirk to Salisbury, 22 June 1879 (with note of G. W.), FO 84/1548; Kirk to Mackinnon, 25 May 1879, 11 November 1879, MP 22 and 23; Kirk to Granville, 14 April 1883, FO 84/1644. For Miles's view of the problem with Barghash, Elst to Orban, 14 April 1883, Af–6–B, MAEB.

18. Coupland, *Exploitation,* 231; Bennett, *Zanzibar,* 101.

19. Ellen Maples, *Chauncy Maples* (London, 1897), 56.

20. Sparshott to CMS, 21 August 1874, C.MA/M4, CMS; Cottoni to Decazes, 28 August 1874, 25 September 1874, Gaspary to MAE, 27 January 1875, PZ 4; Sparshott to Prideaux, 16 January 1875, Sulivan to Adm., 25 January 1875, E–69, Prideaux to FO, 13 January 1875, 23 February 1875, Prideaux to Sulivan, 15 January 1875 (two letters), Prideaux to Cumming, 22 January 1875, E–71, ZA; Berg, "Mombasa under the Busaidi," 121–126; Mbarak al Hinawi, *Al-Akida and Fort Jesus, Mombasa* (London, 1950), 17ff.; A. I. Salim, *The Swahili-speaking Peoples of Kenya's Coast, 1895–1965* (Nairobi, 1973), 42–43; Harries, *Swahili Prose Texts,* 129ff.; Jan Knappert, *Four Centuries of Swahili Verse* (London, 1979), 167–180.

21. Cumming to Adm., 13 March 1875, *PP* 1875 (c.1168), LXXI, 212.

22. The following are useful for Mbarak's life up to 1885: T. H. R. Cashmore, "Sheikh Mbaruk bin Rashid bin Salim el Mazrui," in Norman R. Bennett, ed., *Leadership in Eastern Africa: Six Political Biographies* (Boston, 1968), 111–120; Morton, "Slaves, Fugitives, and Freedmen," 138–144; Berg, "Mombasa under the Busaidi," 129–133; William F. McKay, "A Precolonial History of the Southern Kenya Coast," (Ph.D. diss., Boston University, 1975), 201–205; Hinawy, *Al-Akida,* 33ff.; John Gray, "Zanzibar and the Coastal Belt, 1840–1884," in Oliver and Mathew, *History of East Africa,* I, 246; New, undated letter, *UMFCM* 14(1871), 341; Hardinge to Salisbury, 26 August 1895, *PP* 1896 (c.8274), 31–32.

23. Kirk to BG, 19 December 1871, E–61, 26 February 1872, E–62, ZA.

24. Report of a talk between Pelly and Rebmann, in Frere to Granville, 5 April 1873, FO 84/1390; Frere to Granville, 7 May 1873, FO 84/1391; Guillois to Broglie, 4 September 1873, PZ 4.

25. Guillois to Broglie, 4 September 1873, PZ 4; Mbarak to Kirk, 26 August 1873, and Wakefield to Kirk, 26 July 1873, in Kirk to FO, 29 August 1873, FO 84/1375; Kirk to FO, undated, E–63C, ZA.

26. Prideaux to FO, 14 January 1874, 9 February 1874, 9 April 1874, E–64, ZA; Sparshott to CMS, 12 December 1873, C.MA/M4, CMS; Greffuhle, "Voyage," 338ff.; Greffuhle, 24 July 1895, *B. de la Soc. de Géographie Commerciale de Paris* 17 (1895–1896), 795.

27. Mackay, journal, 26 December 1876, C.A6/016b, CMS.

28. Binns to Miles, 6 July 1882, Miles to Luxmore, 19 July 1882, N–14, ZA; During, 4 August 1882, *UMFCM* 26(1883), 55–56; Price, journal, 8 February 1882, G3.A5/01, CMS; Miles to Granville, 10 February 1882, FO 84/1620, 6 April 1882, FO 84/1621; Ledoulx to Freycinet, 7 March 1882, PZ 6; Kitchener to Rosebury, 15 March 1886, FO 84/1798; Lyne, *Mathews*, 132ff.

29. Miles to Granville, 3 May 1882, FO 84/1621; Kouri to Flourens, 6 April 1882, PZ 6.

30. Binns to Lang, 7 July 1882, 10 August 1882, G3.A5/01, CMS; Miles to Granville, 28 September 1882 (enc. Cracknall to Miles, 4 August 1882), 22 July 1882 (enc. Binns to Miles, 6 July 1882 and Mbarak to Miles, 18 Shaaban 1299), FO 84/1622, 17 November 1882, FO 84/1623; Kirk to FO, 3 July 1885, E–87, ZA; Ramshaw, 25 September 1882, *UMFCM* 26(1883), 57.

31. McKay, "Southern Kenya Coast," 205; Morton, "Slaves, Fugitives, and Freedmen," 148.

32. Steere to Festing, 22 October 1879, A.1.III, Central African Mission Diary, Zanzibar, 18 December 1880, A.1.VI, UMCA.

33. Bartle Frere, *Eastern Africa as a Field for Missionary Labour* (London, 1874), 35; Edgar V. Winans, *Shambala* (London, 1962), 25; New, "Journey," 414–417; Fischer, "Massai-Land," 96–97 (with illustration); Farler, 4 September 1876, *ML* 7(1876), 583–584; Kirk to FO, 10 October 1877, 7 January 1881 (with enc.), Q–18 and Q–25, ZA; Kirk to Granville, 11 January 1881 (with enc.), FO 84/1599; Farler to UMCA, 1 December 1881, Symthies to ?, 9 July 1884, A.1.IV, UMCA; Coupland, *Exploitation*, 421.

34. Behr, *Kriegsbilder*, 216–217; Kirk to FO, 8 December 1873, E–55, ZA.

35. Lyne, *Mathews*, 49–51; Kirk to Granville, 26 April 1881, 3 May 1881, FO 84/1599; J. P. Farler, "England and Germany in East Africa," *Fortnightly R.* 266(1889), 159.

36. Bagamoyo District Book, BUM; Burton, "Lake Regions," 45, 96, 99, 145, and *Zanzibar*, II, 267–269, 272, 329.

37. James Christie, *Cholera Epidemics in East Africa* (London, 1875), 425; Annie B. Hore, *To Lake Tanganyika in a Bath Chair* (London, 1889), 14.

38. Clement H. Hill, "Boat Journey up the Wami River," *PRGS* 17 (1872–1873), 338–339; Kitchener to Rosebury, 15 March 1886, FO 84/1798; Stuhlmann, *Emin Pascha*, 34.

39. Edwin W. Smith, "The Earliest Ox-Wagons in Tanganyika—An Experiment which Failed," *TNR* 40(1955), 3.

40. Hockin to Bateman, 28 July 1873, in Kirk to Granville, 8 August 1873, *PP* 1873 (c.867–1), LXI, 63–65; Elton, *Travels*, 62–64; Kirk to FO, 29 March 1875, E–71, ZA.

41. *Private Journal of the Rev. Roger Price* (privately printed), 21; Biddlecomb to Smith, Mackenzie & Co., undated, Smith, Mackenzie & Co. to CMS, 4 October 1880, C.A6/03, CMS.

42. T. O. Beidelman, *The Matrilineal Peoples of Eastern Tanzania (Zaramo, Luguru, Kaguru, Ngulu, etc.)* (London, 1967), 68; Last to Wright, 2 June 1879, C.A6/04, CMS; Holmwood memo on the Zigula, in Miles to Granville, 21 November 1881, FO 84/1601.

43. *PP*. Baur and LeRoy, *A Travers le Zanguebar* (Tours, 1899), 167–169, 200–203; Burton, "Lake Regions," 45, 100, and *Lake Regions*, I, 76; Stanley, *Livingstone*, 116–117; Feierman, *Shambaa Kingdom*, 138; Kirk to FO, 10 December 1873, FO 84/1376.

44. Mackay, journal, 3 January 1878, C.A6/016b, CMS; Elton, *Travels*, 408–

409; Etienne Baur, *Voyage dans l'Oudoé & l'Ouzigoua (Zanguebar)* (Lyon, 1882), 68–69; Baur and LeRoy, *Zanguebar*, 203, 220–223; Ledoulx to MAE, 11 October 1884, 23 October 1884, PZ 6 and CCZ 5; Lucien Heudebert, *Vers les Grands Lacs de l'Afrique Orientale d'après les notes de l'explorateur Géorges Révoil* (Paris, 1900), 153.

45. *A. M. Mackay* (By His Sister) (London, 1890), 51.

46. Woodward in *CA*, 2(1884), 9; Wakefield, 5 October 1883, *UMFCM* 27(1884), 65; Bloyet to ?, 1 January 1884, PZ 6; *BSE*, 13(1883), 95; Frederick Jackson, *Early Days in East Africa* (London, 1930), 130; see also R. P. Picarda, "Autour de Mandéra. Notes sur l'Ouzigoura," *MC* 18(1886), 184.

47. E. Marras, "Bagamoyo," *BSGM* 7(1883), 25; *BSE*, 13(1880), 45. Russell, *Rigby*, 333; Prideaux to FO, 19 September 1874, E–65, ZA; Kirk to FO, 22 August 1879, Q–22, ZA (information from Baxter).

48. V. L. Cameron, "On his Journey across Africa, from Bagamoyo to Benguela," *PRGS* 20(1875–1876), 304; H. M. Stanley, "A Geographical Sketch of the Nile and Livingstone (Congo) Basins," *PRGS* 22(1877–1878), 384; Last to CMS, 18 March 1881, G3.A5/01, CMS; P. LeRoy, "A Travers le Zanguebar," *MC* 16(1884), 30.

49. *BSE* 6(1868), 627–628, 8(1871), 765–767.

50. For this and the following: Brown, "Politics of Business," 639–642; Nimtz, "Sūfī Order," 127–128, 173–175.

51. Baur, *BSE* 10(1875), 724–725; Gaspary to Euan Smith, 9 September 1875, Euan Smith to Senior Naval Officer *London*, 9 September 1875, E–70, Euan Smith to FO, 14 August 1875, E–71, ZA; Baur to Thorax, 8 September 1875, in Gaspary to Decazes, 22 September 1875, PZ 4; Frere to Granville, 7 May 1873, FO 84/1391; Leue, "Bagamoyo," 4–5.

52. See Elton's report, 2 April 1874, in Prideaux to FO, 6 April 1874, FO 84/1398.

53. Gaume, *Horner*, 126; Kirk to Salisbury, 13 November 1878, FO 84/1515; Giraud, *Afrique Equatoriale*, 41; Joseph Thomson, *To the Central African Lakes and Back* (London, 1881), I, 135ff. For relationships with other coastal ports and the interior during Barghash's reign, see below, pp. 119ff.

CHAPTER 5

1. Kirk to Smith, 4 March 1873 (enc. Cameron to Kirk, undated), 10 March 1873, E–63B, ZA.

2. MAE to Ferry, 4 April 1878 (with enc.), Ferry to MAE, 25 July 1878, CCZ 4; Alfred Rabaud, *L'Abbé Debaize et sa Mission Géographique et Scientifique dans l'Afrique Centrale* (Marseille, 1880).

3. See, for example, Dutrieux, *La Question Africaine*, 25; Mullens to Kirk, 4 April 1879, u.v., ZA.

4. Coulbois, *Tanganyka*, 64, claimed Barghash's letters included secret hostile messages.

5. Miles to FO, 2 February 1883, E–78, ZA.

6. Swann to Euan Smith, 6 August 1890, B–10, ZA.

7. Lenz, September 1886, *MGGW*, 30(1887), 97.

8. A crossed-out section of Kirk to FO, 6 November 1873, E–63C, ZA.

9. Price to Kirk, 23 February 1875, E–69, ZA. For the Mombasa mission,

Norman R. Bennett, "The Church Missionary Society at Mombasa, 1873–1894," *BUP* 1(1964), 157–194; Morton, "Slaves, Fugitives, and Freedmen," 201ff.

10. Price to Kirk, 14 December 1875 (with Kirk notes), E–72, ZA; "Journal of Rev. W. S. Price," *CMIR* 1(1876), 210, 213; Kirk to Derby, 25 December 1875, *PP* 1877 (c.1829), LXXVIII, 186–187.

11. Steere to UMCA, 6 April 1867 (addenda of 14 April), Steere diary, 26 November 1867, Tozer to Steere, 19 January 1869, 25 April 1869, A.1.I, Steere to A. Steere, 20 April 1865, Jones to Steere, 4 May 1869, A.1.III, UMCA; Sparshott to CMS, 12 December 1873, Sparshott to Wright, 21 May 1884, C.MA/M4, Price to Wright, 3–11 March 1875, C.A5/M4, Price, Report on the East African Mission, 6 October 1882, G3.A5/01, CMS.

12. Kirk to FO, 19 July 1871, E–61, ZA; Joseph B. Harris, ed., *Recollections of James Juma Mbotela* (Nairobi, 1977), 88–89.

13. Kirk to FO, 29 August 1873, FO 84/1375, 8 December 1873, FO 84/1376; Burton, "Lake Regions," 355; Smith to FO, 26 July 1875, E–77, ZA; Cooper, *Plantation Slavery,* 204–210.

14. Steere to Festing, 2 June 1875, A.1.III, UMCA; Kirk to FO, 25 December 1875, E–72, ZA.

15. Price, journal, 23–24 May 1876, C.A5/023, CMS; Ali bin Nassur to Kirk, 27 May 1876, Price to Kirk, 24 and 25 May 1876, Petition from Mombasans, all in Kirk to Derby, 7 June 1876, FO 84/1453.

16. Price to CMS, 1 March 1876, C.A5/M4, CMS; Hutchinson to Derby, April 1876, in Lister to Kirk, 4 May 1876, Q–15, Price to Euan Smith, 16 July 1875, E–72, ZA; Kirk to Derby, 21 June 1876, FO 84/1453.

17. Russell to Wright, 10 September 1876, C.A5/M4, 21 June 1877, Praeger to Wright, 21 April 1877, C.A5/M5, CMS; Kirk to FO, 30 March 1877, Q–18, ZA; Randolph fragment, 5 April [1877], A.1.IV, UMCA.

18. Streeter to CMS, 30 January 1880, C.A5/M6, CMS.

19. Streeter to Wright, 10 August 1878, 7 November 1878, Jones to Wright, 10 October 1878, C.A5/M5, CMS.

20. Streeter to Hutchinson, 29 January 1879, Binns to Wright, 5 October 1879, 3 February 1880, Streeter to Wright, 1 November 1879, C.A5/M6, CMS; Kirk to FO, 9 January 1880, Q–24, ZA.

21. Streeter to Wright, 17 July 1880, C.A5/M6, CMS.

22. Kirk to FO, 22 September 1880, 19 October 1880, Q–24, ZA; Oliver, *Missionary Factor,* 82; Hutchinson to Menzies, 19 November 1880, C.A5/L2, CMS.

23. Holmwood to Streeter, 21 January 1881, N–27, Lister to Kirk, 31 May 1881, N–24, ZA.

24. Sparshott to CMS, 8 January 1874, C.MA/M4, Russell to Wright, 10 September 1876, C.A5/M4, Russell to Hutchinson, 1 January 1877, Streeter to Wright, 22 May 1878, C.A5/M5, Streeter to Wright, 5 December 1878, C.A5/M6, 1 November 1879, C.A5/027, Binns to CMS, 30 December 1879, C.A5/M6, CMS; Price to Kirk, 9 October 1875, 21 November 1875, Kirk to Price, 18 October 1875, E–70, ZA.

25. Kirk to FO, 1 July 1881, 20 July 1881, 21 July 1881, 25 July 1881 (all with enc.), Q–25, Kirk to Holmwood, 30 June 1881, Kirk to Brownrigg, 11 July 1881, N–27, ZA; Kirk to Derby, 5 May 1876, FO 84/1453; Miles to Granville, 6 April 1882, FO 84/1621; Menzies to Stock, 21 July 1881, 6 December 1881, Streeter to Kirk, 18 June 1881, Streeter to Stock, 12 July 1881, Price to Wigram, 14 December 1881, Lister to CMS, 21 October 1881 (précis book), Price to

Whiting, 24 January 1882, Price to Hutchinson, undated, Price to Miles, 24 January 1882, G3.A5/01, CMS.

26. Muhammad bin Suliman to Barghash, 21 May 1882, N–14, Lane to Miles, 3 January 1882, E–77, Kirk to FO, 31 May 1884, E–83, ZA.

27. Binns to Lang, 17 March 1883, Taylor to Lang, 6 July 1883, Taylor to Stock, 12 July 1887, G3.A5/01, CMS.

28. Frere to Granville, 7 May 1873, enc. appendix B by A. Horner, 3 May 1873, FO 84/1391; Kieran, "Holy Ghost Mission," 25ff., 117, 357–360.

29. Wakefield to Bushell, 21 April 1877, *UMFCM* 20(1877): 637; Wakefield, *T. Wakefield,* 150. For the land regulation, see also Baur, 27 August 1882, *BSE* 13(1883), 55.

30. Robert Brewin, *Memoirs of Rebecca Wakefield* (London, 1876), 125–126; Kirk to FO, 7 January 1881, Q–25, Kirk to Ramshaw, 6 June 1881, During to Kirk, 14 June 1881, two letters of 6 August 1881, Kirk to During, 28 June 1881, N–27, ZA; Ramshaw to Felkin, 25 November 1880, G3.A5/01, CMS.

31. Kirk to FO, 5 September 1871, E–61, ZA.

32. Wilson to Steere, 10 June 1881, A.1.IV, Jones-Bateman to Penney, 17 January 1886, A.1.VI, UMCA; P. L. Jones-Bateman, "Our Work in Zanzibar Town," *CA* 2(1884), 39; *CA* 4(1886), 59.

33. Kirk to BG, 8 August 1872, E–62, ZA; Steere to Festing, 15 November 1872, A.1.III, UMCA; Ward, *Tozer,* 99.

34. Oliver, *Missionary Factor,* 115–116, leaving out Hutley, claims only five Europeans died violent deaths before 1884, none caused by Arabs. His list is incomplete: see, for example, *A l'Assaut des Pays Nègres. Journal des Missionaires d'Alger dans l'Afrique Equatoriale* (Paris, 1884), 218.

35. Zanzibar diary, 29 January 1874, 15 February 1874, UMCA Zanzibar; Steere to A. Steere, 7 March 1874, A.1.III, UMCA; Prideaux to FO, 4 June 1874, FO 84/1398; Derby to Prideaux, 24 July 1874, FO 84/1399; Prideaux to Derby, 8 February 1875, *PP* 1876 (c.1588), LXX, 59.

36. See H. W. Woodward, "A Story of a Woman's Wrongs," *CA* 2(1884), 131–133.

37. Steere to Penney, 4 March 1881, 1 May 1882, Steere to Johnson, Easter Monday 1881, A.1.III, Farler to Steere, 19 November 1881, with Steere note on rear, A.1.IV, UMCA; Zanzibar diary, printed document with Steere to Maples, 5 August 1882, UMCA Zanzibar; Chauncey Maples, "A Village Community in East Africa," *ML* 13(1882), 101–104, 157–162.

38. Farler to Penney, 31 August 1885, A.1.VI, UMCA.

39. Lewis Gann, "The End of the Slave Trade in British Central Africa: 1889–1912," *Human Problems in British Central Africa,* 16(1954), 30; Harry W. Langworthy, "Central Malawi in the 19th Century," in Roderick J. Macdonald, ed., *From Nyasaland to Malawi: Studies in Colonial History* (Nairobi, 1975), 11, 15–16, and "Swahili Influence in the Area between Lake Malawi and the Luangwa River," *IJAHS* 4(1971), 583–585; Owen J. Kalinga, "The Ngonde Kingdom of Northern Malawi, c. 1600–1895," (Ph.D. diss., University of London, 1974), 188–189; Samuel Josia Ntara (ed. Beatrix Heintze; trans. W. S. Kamphandira Jere), *The History of the Chewa (Mbiri Ya Achewa)* (Wiesbaden, 1973), 111–112; George Shepperson, "The Jumbe of Kota Kota and Some Aspects of the History of Islam in British Central Africa," in I. M. Lewis, ed., *Islam in Tropical Africa* (London, 1966), 196.

40. Shepperson, "Jumbe," 196–197; Behr in *AEC,* 14(1893), 37; Kirk to Derby, 4 February 1878 (with Elton (?) notes), FO 84/1514; E. D. Young, *Nyassa*

(London, 1877), 126; Young, 18 February 1876, *PM* 22(1876), 276; Elton, *Travels*, 294–295; H. H. Johnston, "British Central Africa," *PRGS* 12(1890), 723; H. B. Cotterill, "On the Nyassa and a Journey from the North End to Zanzibar," *PRGS* 22(1877–1878), 239.

41. Kirk to Derby, 24 August 1877, FO 84/1486; Derby to Kirk, 2 October 1877, FO 84/1483.

42. C. A. Smythies, *A Journey to Lake Nyassa and Visit to the Magwangwara and the Source of the Rovuma in the Year 1886* (Zanzibar, c. 1886), 35; see also O'Neill to Euan Smith, 23 June 1888, in Euan Smith to Salisbury, 2 July 1888, FO 84/1909.

43. Ian Linden, "The Maseko Ngoni at Domwe: 1870–1900," in Bridglal Pachai, ed., *The Early History of Malawi* (Evanston, 1972), 237ff.; H. Langworthy and J. D. Omer-Cooper, "The Impact of the Ngoni and Yao on the 19th Century History of Malawi," in B. Pachai, G. W. Smith, and R. K. Tangri, eds., *Malawi Past and Present: Studies in Local and Regional History* (n.p., 1971), 15–20.

44. E. D. Young. "On a Recent Sojourn at Lake Nyassa, Central Africa," *PRGS* 21(1876–1877), 229; Goodrich to Granville, 19 March 1885, FO 84/1702; Smythies, *Journey to Lake Nyassa*, 32; Smythies, August 1886, A.1.VI, UMCA; Yohanna B. Addullah (trans. Merith Sanderson), *The Yaos: Chikala Cha Wayao* (London, 1973), 40ff.

45. Maples, 12 August 1886, *CA* 4(1886), 186; see also Hawes to FO, 8 April 1887, FO 84/1829.

46. *HFMRFCS* (1875), 242; John McCracken, *Politics and Christianity in Malawi, 1875–1940: The Impact of the Livingstonia Mission in the Northern Province* (Cambridge, 1977), 17ff., for the mission's history.

47. Steere to Festing, 9 April 1875, A.1.III, UMCA.

48. Robert Laws, *Reminiscences of Livingstonia* (London, 1934), 14ff.; Janson, journal, 19 January ?, u.v., UMCA; Livingstone, *Laws*, 67ff.; Young, *HFMRFCS* (1876), 55; James W. Jack, *Daybreak in Livingstonia: The Story of the Livingstonia Mission, British Central Africa* (New York, n.d.), 37ff.; Young to Wilson, 24 October 1875, Laws, 19 October 1875, *ML* 7(1876), 165, 207–209.

49. Young, 19 February 1876, Young to Waller, 18 February 1876, *ML* 7(1876), 380, 388; Henderson to Macrae, 19 October 1875, *CSHFMR* 9(1874–1876), 605; Kirk to Derby, 10 January 1876, FO 84/1452.

50. The first significant reference to Arabs in their periodical appears in Macdonald, 13 January 1879, *CSHFMR* 11(1878–1879), 340. For the mission, Andrew C. Ross, "Livingstone and the Aftermath: The Origins and Development of the Blantyre Mission," in Bridglal Pachai, ed., *Livingstone, Man of Africa: Memorial Essays* (London, 1973), 191ff.

51. Stewart, *HFMRFCS* (1877), 112; McCracken, *Politics and Christianity*, 42.

52. Laws, 28 November 1877, *HFMRFCS* (1878), 86.

53. Livingstone, *Laws*, 158; Laws, 16 July 1878, 10 August 1878, *HFMRFCS* (1878), 251, (1879), 66–67.

54. Steere to Festing, 9 April 1875, A.1.III, UMCA.

55. H. B. Cotterill, "The Nyassa—With Notes on the Slave Trade, and the Prospects of Commerce and Colonization of that Region," *JSA* 26(1877–1878), 679ff., and "On the Nyassa," 233ff.; Laws, *Reminiscences*, 53–54; Stewart to Dunn, 27 February 1877, *GM* 4(1877), 206; *GJ* 65(1925), 86–87; Cotterill to Derby, 22 March 1876, in Kirk to FO, 8 April 1876, Q–15, Cotterill to Kirk, 25 February 1877, 13 March 1877, in Kirk to FO, 5 May 1877, Q–18, Kirk to

Cotterill, 23 August 1877, E–73, ZA; Derby to Kirk, 8 April 1876, FO 84/1451; Pauncefote to Kirk, 13 July 1877, FO 84/1483; *Scottish Guardian,* 9 November 1877, in *ML* 8(1877), 558–559.

56. John McCracken, "Religion and Politics in Northern Ngoniland, 1881–1904," in Pachai, *Early History of Malawi,* 222; Stuhlmann, *Emin Pascha,* 601.

57. H. W. Macmillan, "Notes on the Origins of the Arab War," in Pachai, *Early History of Malawi,* 268; Moir, *After Livingstone,* 7ff.; McCracken, *Politics and Christianity,* 45.

58. Kalinga, "Ngonde Kingdom," 11ff.; Godfrey Wilson, *The Constitution of Ngonde* (Rhodes-Livingstone Papers, No. 3, 1939); 7ff.; Lugard, "Slave-Traders," 336; H. H. Johnston, "British South-Central Africa," *New R.* 3(1890), 107; McCracken, *Politics and Christianity,* 107–108.

59. Kalinga, "Ngonde Kingdom," 189ff.; Livingstone, *Laws,* 189. In the usual confusion over ethnic identity a missionary described Msalama as "a released slave, a Yao": Swinney journal, 6 September 1886, u.v., UMCA. For the Senga Arabs, Marcia Wright and Peter Lary, "Swahili Settlements in Northern Zambia and Malawi," *IJAHS* 4(1971), 562ff.

60. James Stewart, "Survey of the Eastern Coast of Lake Nyassa, and the Latest News of the 'Lake-Junction Road,'" *PRGS* 5(1883), 689; Foot to Granville, 8 March 1884, FO 84/1662; Moir, *After Livingstone,* 89ff.; Giraud, *Afrique Equatoriale,* 541; Fotheringham, *Adventures,* 12ff.; Macmillan, "Arab War," 263–268.

61. See below, p. 91.

62. Lenz, December 1886, *MGGW* 30(1887), 100; Swinney journal, 31 August 1886, u.v., UMCA; Carson, Journal from Quillamane to Niamkolo, 28 March–4 July 1886, LMS.

63. "The African Lakes Company," *CA* 5(1882), 14; Drummond, *HFMRFCS* (1887), 53; Oliver, "Some Factors," 52.

64. Randolph to Musgrove, 25 September 1875, A.1.IV, Steere, Trip to Masasi (incomplete ms.), A.1.VI, Steere to Penney, 30 August 1878(?), Steere to Farler, 7 January 1879, A.1.III, UMCA; Kirk to Salisbury, 12 November 1878, FO 84/1515; Kirk to Salisbury, 23 November 1879, 6 March 1880, *PP* 1878–1879 (c.2422), LXVI: 279–280, 305, 308; Holmwood to Kirk, 30 January 1880, in Kirk to FO, 6 March 1880, Q–24, ZA; Foot to Kirk, 26 July 1881, in Kirk to Granville, 13 September 1881, Foot to Kirk, 8 August 1881, in Kirk to Granville, 3 September 1881, FO 84/1600; Kitchener to Rosebery, 10 February 1886, FO 84/1797.

65. Steere to Heanley, 13 November 1877, Steere to Roy, 12 January 1881, A.1.III, Johnson to Staffarth, undated, Johnson to Steere, 3 November 1880, Johnson to ?, 21 February ?, A.1.VI, UMCA.

66. Foot to Kirk, 26 July 1881, in Kirk to Granville, 13 September 1881, FO 84/1600; Madan to UMCA, 14 February 1881, A.1.VI, Kirk to Penney, 26 December 1881, A.1.IV, UMCA.

67. Johnson, *African Reminiscences,* 69–73; Johnson to Kirk, 7 November 1881, FO 84/1601; Maples to UMCA, 7 October 1881, Steere to UMCA, 21 November 1881, Steere extract, 21 October 1881, A.1.III, Johnson to Steere, December 1881, A.1.IV, UMCA; Miles to Granville, 12 January 1882, FO 84/1620; Miles to Mataka, undated, Barghash to Mataka, 2 Moharam 1299, Barghash to Gov. Kilwa, undated, all in Zanzibar diary, 20 November 1881, UMCA Zanzibar.

68. Granville to Foot, 1 October 1883, FO 84/1643; A. J. Hanna, *The*

Beginnings of Nyasaland and North-Eastern Rhodesia (Oxford, 1956), 62–67; Ledoulx to MAE, 4 November 1883, CCZ 5; Alan K. Smith, "The Anglo-Portuguese Conflict over the Shire Highlands, 1875–91," in Macdonald, *Nyasaland to Malawi*, 49.

69. Kirk to FO, 18 December 1883, E-78, ZA.
70. Foot to Granville, 7 February 1884, FO to Foot, 5 September 1884, FO 84/1622; Kirk to FO, 25 July 1884, enc. O'Neill to Foot, 16 May 1884, E-83, Lister to Kirk, 11 July 1884, E-81, ZA.
71. Granville to Hawes, 16 January 1885, FO 84/1702; Goodrich to Kirk, 18 December 1884, FO 84/1662; Goodrich to Kirk, 6 September 1884, in Kirk to Granville, 25 October 1884, FO 84/1679; Hanna, *Beginnings of Nyasaland*, 72–75.
72. Kirk to FO, 15 April 1875, E-68, ZA; Steere, *Walk to Nyassa*, 40–41; Euan Smith to Derby, 2 July 1875, FO 84/1417.
73. Porter, Brief summary of history of Masasi as Mission Station, 8 October 1877, A.1.VI, UMCA; Kirk to Salisbury, 15 August 1879, *PP* 1880 (c.2720), LXIV, 255; Holmwood to Kirk, 30 January 1880, in Kirk to FO, 6 March 1880, Q-24, Kirk to FO, 11 May 1885, E-89, ZA; Clark to Steere, 8 October 1878, *CAMOP*, X, 5; Maples, 4 September 1881, *CAMOP* 18(1882), 9–10; Hathorne to Bertram, 16 October 1888, Hathorne Papers, PM; Henry Rowley, *Twenty Years in Central Africa: Being the Story of the Universities' Mission to Central Africa* (London, 1889), 277; Karl Weule (trans. Alice Werner), *Native Life in East Africa* (London, 1909), 140–143; Wilhelm Wolfrum, *Briefe und Tagebuchblätter aus Ostafrika* (München, 1893), 108–109; P. A. Wathen, "News from Newala," *CA* 6(1888), 103.

CHAPTER 6

1. Frere to Granville, 7 May 1873, FO 84/1319.
2. Burton, "Lake Regions," 106; Tippu Tip, *Maisha*, 73; Reichard, "Afrikanische Elfenbein," 165; Norman R. Bennett, ed., *Stanley's Despatches to the New York Herald, 1871–1872, 1874–1877* (Boston, 1970), 31; C. T. Wilson and R. W. Felkin, *Uganda and the Egyptian Sudan* (London, 1882), I, 133; Stanley, *Livingstone*, 220; Jérome Becker, *La Troisième Expédition Belge* (Bruxelles, n.d.), 89; Burdo, *Zanzibar au Tanganika*, 296 (for a poor illustration of the Nasibus).
3. S. Smith to Wright, 13 September 1876, C.A6/M1, Mackay to Wright, 12 December 1876, C.A6/016, CMS.
4. *Mackay*, 66; Kirk to Derby, 4 April 1878, FO 84/1514; Smith to Wright, 1–18 January 1877, C.A6/022, Mackay to Wright, 25 May 1878, C.A6/016, Kirk to Hutchinson, 20 October 1878, C.A6/013, CMS; G. Smith, 8 February 1878, *CMIR* 3(1878), 490; Wilson and Felkin, *Uganda*, I, 132–133; Dodgshun, 8 January 1879, *CLMS* (1879), 94; Gerald W. Hartwig, "Bukerebe, the Church Missionary Society, and East African Politics, 1877–1878," *IJAHS* 1(1968), 226.
5. Dodgshun to Mullens, 23 January 1879, Southon to LMS, 24 December 1879, CA 2, Southon journal, 25 August 1879, LMS; Hutchinson to Kirk, 28 August 1878, C.A5/L2, Stokes to Mackay, 23 December 1878, C.A6/024, Copplestone to Wright, 17 November 1879, C.A6/09, CMS; *MAGD* 1(1878–1879), 163; Southon to Kirk, 9 September 1878, K-1, Kirk to FO, 31 May 1879, 15 October 1879, Q-22, Kirk to Said bin Salim, 2 July 1878, N-25, ZA.
6. J. B. Thomson, *Joseph Thomson: African Explorer* (London, 1896), 69;

Hutley to Whitehouse, 13 November 1881, CA 4, LMS; Mary Yule, *Mackay of Uganda* (London, n.d.), 84.

7. Mackay to Wright, 2 November 1879, C.A6/016, Last to Wright, 5 March 1876, C.A6/014, CMS; Paul Reichard, *Dr. Emin Pascha* (Leipzig, 1891), 76; Guillet to Lavigerie, 12 August 1881, *BMA* (1879–1882), 466. For Segère, see below, p. 110.

8. Reichard, *Deutsch-Ostafrika*, 101; Guillet, 8 September 1881, in *A l'Assaut*, 334, and 8 March 1882, *APF* 55(1883), 65; Blanc, 25 June 1882, *BMA* (1883–1886), 28; Bennett, *Mirambo*, 151–152.

9. Bennett, *Mirambo*, 152; Faure, 16 May 1883, *BMA* (1883–1886), 115–116.

10. The fundamental work for understanding Lake Tanganyika and Ujiji is Beverly Bolser Brown, "Ujiji: the History of a Lakeside Town, c.1800–1914," (Ph.D. diss., Boston University, 1973), 53ff.

11. Coulbois, *Tanganyka*, 63–64; *Missieleven in Afrika. Uit de Brieven van den West-Vlaamschen Missionaris Ameet Vyncke der Witte Paters, 1850–1882* (Leuven, 1927), 122.

12. *Brieven van Vyncke,* 121.

13. Hutley to Whitehouse, 19 October 1879, CA 2, LMS; Stanley, *Dark Continent,* II, 6; Swann, *Slave-Hunters,* 75; Beverly Brown, "Muslim Influence on Trade and Politics in the Lake Tanganyika Region," *IJAHS* 4(1971), 628.

14. For Buganda from the late eighteenth century, M. S. M. Kiwanuka, *A History of Buganda from the Foundation of the Kingdom to 1900* (London, 1971), 127ff. See also Arye Oded, *Islam in Uganda: Islamization through a Centralized State in Pre-Colonial Africa* (New York, 1974), 37ff.

15. John A. Rowe, "The Western Impact and the African Reaction: Buganda 1880–1900," *The J. of Developing Areas* 1 (1966), 58.

16. J. M. Gray, "Mutesa of Buganda," *UJ* 1 (1934), 24–25. For Mutesa, M. S. M. Kiwanuka, *Muteesa of Uganda* (Kampala, 1967), 1ff.; John Allen Rowe, "Revolution in Buganda, 1856–1900. Part One: The Reign of Kabaka Mutesa, 1856–1884," (Ph.D. diss., University of Wisconsin, 1966), 5ff.

17. A. I. Richards, "The Assimilation of Immigrants," in Audrey I. Richards, ed., *Economic Development and Tribal Change: A Study of Immigrant Labour in Buganda* (Cambridge, n.d.), 170–171; Robert W. Felkin, "Notes on the Waganda Tribe of Central Africa," *P. of the Royal Soc. of Edinburgh,* 13(1884–1886), 746; Livinhac, 25 March 1888, *BMA* (1888–1889), 354.

18. Robert W. Felkin, "Uganda," *SGM* 2(1886), 217–218; Peter C. W. Gutkind, *The Royal Capital of Buganda* (The Hague, 1963), 12–13; Speke, *Journal,* 284, 288; John Roscoe, *Twenty-Five Years in East Africa* (Cambridge, 1921), 63, 98, and *Baganda,* 268–269, 412–413, 447; Felkin diary, 17 March 1880, C.A6/010, CMS.

19. Apolo Kagwa and Henry Wright Duta, "How Religion Came to Uganda," *UJ* 11(1947), 110–111; Gray, "Mutesa," 26–27. For this period and the later persecutions, Kiwanuka, *Buganda,* 160ff.; Oded, *Islam in Uganda,* 60ff.; Rowe, "Revolution in Buganda," 60ff.; D. A. Low, *Buganda in Modern History* (Berkeley, 1971), 18–26.

20. Kirk to BG, 13 November 1871, E–61, ZA; Kirk to Derby, 6 April 1877, FO 84/1485; Gray, "Mutesa," 28, "Ahmed bin Ibrahim—The First Arab to Reach Buganda, *UJ* 11(1947), 96–97, and "Sir John Kirk and Mutesa," *UJ* 15(1951), 1–2; Geoffrey Mansfield, "Livingstone and the Baganda," *UJ* 10(1946), 81; J. A. Rowe, "Mika Sematimba," *UJ* 28(1964), 183.

21. Apolo Kagwa (trans. Mary M. Edel), *The Customs of the Baganda* (New York, 1934), 79.

22. Richard Gray, *A History of the Southern Sudan, 1839–1889* (London, 1961), 86ff.; Oded, *Islam in Uganda,* 167ff.

23. J. M. Gray, "The Diaries of Emin Pasha," *UJ* 27(1963), 9; Ahmed Katumba and F. B. Welbourn, "Muslim Martyrs of Buganda," *UJ* 28(1964), 151–163; Rowe, "Sematimba," 181, and "The Purge of Christians at Mwanga's Court," *JAH* (1964), 68.

24. Quoted in Wright to Mackay, 5 April 1878, C.A6/L1, CMS.

25. Mackay to Wright, 24 May 1878, C.A6/016, Edmonds to Lang, 22 January 1883, G3.A6/01, CMS; Becker, *Troisième Expédition,* 130, 141, 223; Giraud, *Afrique Equatoriale,* 450; Journal de la Station de Mpala, 7 March 1885, SP; A. Leue, "Udjiji," *BKK* 2(1900–1901), 325–327.

26. For details, Norman R. Bennett, "Dodgshun, the London Missionary Society, and the Effort to Solve the Transportation Problems of Nineteenth-Century East Africa," in Norman R. Bennett, ed., *From Zanzibar to Ujiji: The Journal of Arthur W. Dodgshun, 1877–1879* (Boston, 1969), viii ff.

27. Wright to Smith, 19 October 1877, C.A6/L1, CMS; Israel K. Katoke, "Karagwe (Kafuro) and the Founding of the Nyanza Mission (C. M. S.)," *TNR* 66(1966), 155–162.

28. Hutchinson to Smith, 22 September 1876, C.A6/L1, Smith to Dickeson, 31 August 1876, C.A6/M1, CMS.

29. *Report of the Rev. R. Price of His Visit to Zanzibar and the Coast of Eastern Africa* (London, 1876), 37; R. P. Levesque, "Dans l'Afrique Orientale," *B. de la Soc. de Géographie de Lille,* 4(1885), 321; Clark to Wright, 3 September 1876, 27 September 1876, Smith to Wright, 22 October 1876, C.A6/07, Smith to Kirk, 7 November 1876, in Kirk to CMS, 12 December 1876, C.A6/013, CMS.

30. Wright to Mackay, 9 February 1877, C.A6/L1, CMS; Bennett, "Dodgshun," xix–xx.

31. Instructions to Last and Henry, 6 November 1877, C.A6/L1, Baxter to Wright, 6 February 1878, 13 June 1878, C.A6/05, Copplestone to Wright, 16 May 1878, C.A6/09, CMS.

32. Last to Wright, 20 January 1879, 3 March 1879, 6 June 1879, 24 December 1879, C.A6/04, Baxter to Wright, 8 May 1879, C.A6/05, CMS.

33. Last to Wright, 20 January 1879, C.A6/014, CMS.

34. Baxter to Wright, 18 April 1879, 21 March 1880, 15 April 1880, 13 June 1879, C.A6/05, Fenn and Hutchinson to Baxter, 19 November 1880, C.A6/L1, CMS; Burdo, *Zanzibar au Tanganika,* 203–204, 212–215; J. Dutreuil de Rhins, "Notes sur les Voyages et les Travaux de M. Bloyet," *BSG* 3(1882), 356; P. L. Jones-Bateman, *The Autobiography of an African Slave-Boy* (Westminster, 1899), 23; Kirk to FO, 1 May 1879, 22 August 1879, Q–22, ZA; Kirk to Granville, 18 October 1880, FO 84/1575. For the International African Association, Bloyet, and Matthews, see below, p. 97.

35. Baxter to Hutchinson, 18 March 1881, Price to Wright, 11 June 1881, Baxter to Grey, 11 August 1881, G3.A5/01, Baxter to Whiting, 29 November 1881, G3.A6/01, CMS.

36. Cole to Lang, 15 May 1882, 3 July 1883, Baxter to Lang, 18 March 1883, G3.A6/01, CMS.

37. Edmunds to Lang, 8 September 1882, G3.A6/01, CMS.

38. Hore to LMS, 26 May 1880, CA 3, LMS.

39. For the Europeans at Ujiji, Brown, "Ujiji," 141 ff. See also Hore to LMS,

17 September 1878, CA 1, LMS; Hore to Kirk, 15 April 1878, Q–22, ZA.

40. Hore to Whitehouse, 7 December 1880, CA 3, LMS; Hore, 16 April 1879, *CLMS* (1880), 9; Bennett, *Dodgshun,* 119; Barghash to Mwenyi Akida et al., 17 June 1880, Kirk to Hore, 21 June 1880, N–7, Kirk to FO, 25 June 1880, Q–24, Hore to Kirk, 20 July 1880, P–16, ZA.

41. Hore to LMS, 10 January 1879, CA 2, Hutley to LMS, 11 February 1881, CA 4, LMS; Hore to Kirk, 26 December 1879, in Kirk to FO, 27 February 1880, Kirk to FO, 6 March 1880, Q–24, Hore to Kirk, 25 February 1880, N–7, Hore to Kirk, 20 July 1880, P–16, Lister to Kirk, 21 May 1880, Q-23, ZA; Oliver, *Missionary Factor,* 88.

42. Per Hassing and Norman R. Bennett, "A Journey across Tanganyika in 1886," *TNR* 58 & 59(1962), 131.

43. J. Perraudin, "Le Cardinal Lavigerie et Leópold II," *Zaire* 11(1958), 903ff.; M.-B. Stoorme, *Rapports du Père Planque, de Mgr Lavigerie et de Mgr Comboni sur l'Association Internationale Africaine* (Bruxelles, 1957), 5ff.

44. François Renault, *Lavigerie, l'Esclavage Africaine et l'Europe, 1868–1892* (Paris, 1971), I, 179; Livinhac to Lavigerie, 18 February 1878, Deniaud to Lavigerie, 26 April 1880, Guillet to Lavigerie, 12 August 1881, 20 August 1881, *BMA* (1879–1882), 80, 255, 466–469; Faure, 16 May 1883, *BMA* (1883–1886), 115; Guillet, 8 March 1882, *APF* 55(1883), 56–77.

45. Deniaud to Lavigerie, 12 April 1878, *BMA* (1879–1882), 174.

46. Deniaud to Lavigerie, 10 June 1879, 26 February 1880, Dromaux, 12 September 1881, *BMA* (1879–1882), 176–177, 251–252, 479–480; Renault, *Lavigerie,* I, 185–193; Roger Heremans, *Les Etablissements de l'Association Internationale Africaine au Lac Tanganika et les Pères Blancs: Mpala et Karéma, 1877–1885* (Tervuren, 1966), 87–88; Lavigerie to Deniaud's parents, in *l'Univers,* 23 October 1881, clipping in PZ 5; Ledoulx to MAE, 21 September 1881, CCZ 4bis.

47. Deniaud, 24 November 1879, *CTSMA* (1ᵉ trim. 1880), 127–128; Mgr. Charbonnier, "Près des Grands Lacs: Le Tanganyka," *MC* 17(1885), 309; Guillet, 12 January 1883, *BMA* (1883–1886), 77–82; Renault, *Lavigerie,* I, 412; Heremans, *L'A. I. A. au Tanganika,* 39, 91, 100–104; Josset to Lavigerie, 9 January 1891, *BSAF* (1891–1892), 81.

48. Mwinyi Kheri to Barghash, 28 Cherral 1299, in Ledoulx to MAE, 10 December 1881, CCZ 4 bis; Griffiths to LMS, 29 May 1881, Hutley to LMS, 21 June 1881, CA 4, LMS.

49. For this period of Ganda history, Rowe, "Revolution in Buganda," 114ff.; Oded, *Islam in Uganda,* 221ff.

50. Wilson and Felkin, *Uganda,* I, 210–211; Wilson, 4 July 1887, with addenda of 26 July, *CMIR* 3(1878), 155; *Mackay,* 104.

51. Wilson and Felkin, *Uganda,* I, 111; Wilson to Wright, 8 February 1878, C.A6/025, CMS; Schweitzer, *Emin,* I, 55; Emin Bey, "Reisen zwischen dem Victoria- und Albert-Nyanza," *PM* 26(1880), 26.

52. Wilson to Wright, 23 September 1878, with addenda of 18 November, C.A6/025, Mackay to Wright, 17 November 1878, C.A6/016, CMS.

53. Mackay to Wright, 26 December 1878, C.A6/016, CMS; E. Linant de Bellefonds, "Itinéraire et Notes . . . ," *B. trim. de la. Soc. Khédivale de Géographie du Caire* 1(1875–1876), 78.

54. Pearson to Wright, 14 February 1879, 10 March 1879, C.A6/019, Wright and Hutchinson to Buganda missionaries, 31 October 1879, C.A6/L1,

CMS; Kirk to Mutesa, 25 September 1878, in Kirk to Salisbury, 15 October 1879, FO 84/1548.

55. Litchfield to Wright, 3 July 1879, 23 June 1879, C.A6/015, Mackay to Wright, 14 March 1879, with addenda of 17 April, C.A6/016, Felkin to Wright, 4 March 1879, C.A6/010, CMS.

56. Lourdel to his brother, 22 July 1879, *MC* 12(1880), 221; Norman R. Bennett, "Some Notes on French Policy in Buganda and East Africa, 1879–1890," *Makerere J.* 6(1962), 2–4; Lourdel to Lavigerie, 12 June 1879, *BMA* (1879–1882), 171.

57. Felkin diary, 6–22 March 1880, C.A6/010, CMS. Kirk earlier had written a similar letter to the Tabora Arabs: Kirk to Derby, 4 April 1878, 28 June 1878 (enc. Kirk to Gov. Tabora, 18 June 1878), FO 84/1514.

58. J. Cussac, *L'Apotre de l'Ouganda: Le Père Lourdel* (Paris and Toulouse, 1944), 91; Pearson to Mackay, 1 July 1880, 29 July 1880, G3.A6/01, CMS.

59. Wright and Hutchinson to O'Flaherty, 30 June 1880, C.A6/L1, CMS; *CMIR* 5(1880), 516.

60. Pearson to Mackay, 19 June 1880, Pearson to Wright, 8 January 1881, G3.A6/01, CMS; Pearson to Kirk, 25 January 1881, in Kirk to Granville, 27 July 1881, FO 84/1600.

61. O'Flaherty to Hutchinson, 31 March 1881, 15, 18, and 24 April 1881, Mackay, Log of the Maiden Trip of CMS Eleanor, 5 January [1884?], G3.A6/01, CMS; *Mackay,* 188.

62. O'Flaherty to Hutchinson, 12 July 1881, 25 December 1881, G3.A6/01, CMS; Cussac, *Lourdel,* 108–118; Livinhac, 24 October 1881, *BMA* (1878–1882), 536–537.

63. Renault, *Lavigerie,* I, 176–178; Rowe, "Revolution in Buganda," 179.

64. O'Flaherty to Wright, January 1883, 28 February 1883, 19 June 1883, G3.A6/01, CMS.

65. O'Flaherty to Wright, July 1884, G3.A6/01, CMS.

66. Ibid. O'Flaherty reported he declined Mutesa's offer.

67. Horner, 15 October 1877, *MC* 9(1877), 604; Kieran, "Holy Ghost Mission," 366ff.

68. Ledoulx to St. Hilaire, 16 March 1881, 23 April 1881, PZ 5, 3 June 1881, CCZ 4bis; Baur, *Voyage,* 56; J. A. Kieran, "Christian Villages in North-Eastern Tanzania," *Transafrican J. of History* 1(1971), 29–30.

69. See P. A. Roeykens, *Léopold II et l'Afrique 1855–1880* (Bruxelles, 1958); Roger Anstey, *Britain and the Congo in the Nineteenth Century* (Oxford, 1962), 73–79.

70. A. Roeykens, *Les Débuts de l'Oeuvre Africaine de Léopold II (1875–1879)* (Bruxelles, 1955), 208; J. Stengers, "Rapport sur une étude du R. P. M. Stoorme, intitulée: 'Rapports du Père Planque, de Mgr Lavigerie et de Mgr Comboni sur l'Association Internationale Africaine," *BSARSC* 2(1956), 1012–1015.

71. Leopold to Barghash, undated, and 9 February 1879, Sultan's Correspondence, ZA; Flourens to MAE, 31 January 1878, CCZ 4; Heremans, *L'A. I. A. au Tanganyka,* 1ff.

72. Henry M. Stanley, *The Congo and the Founding of Its Free State* (London, 1885), I, 39–44; M. Luwel, "Le Mexique et l'Afrique Centrale ou la Carrière Aventureuse du Lieutenant Jean-Baptiste Wautier (1844–1878)," *A-T* 20(1975), 75ff.

73. R. P. Avon, "Vie Sociale des Wabende au Tanganika," *Anthropos,* 10–

11(1915–1916), 109; Burdo, *Zanzibar au Tanganika*, 54, 59; Jêrome Becker, *La Vie en Afrique* (Bruxelles, 1887), I, 269; Paul Reichard, "Karema," *DKZ* 2(1889), 13–14; E. C. Hore, "A Voyage on Lake Tanganyika," *CLMS* (1884), 360.

74. Barghash to Abdullah bin Nasibu, June 1880, N–7, ZA. The quotation given here was crossed out on the draft, probably to avoid recriminations if seen by outsiders; doubtlessly the spirit of the message remained the same.

75. Van den Heuvel, 25 January 1880, in Association Internationale Africaine, *N° 3. Extraits des Rapports des Voyageurs de l'Association Internationale Africaine* (Bruxelles, 1880), 117; Becker, *La Vie en Afrique*, I, 210–228, 388–389, II, 28, 68; Burdo, *Zanzibar au Tanganika*, 496.

76. Bennett, *Studies*, 78.

77. Ramaeckers to Strauch, 18 January 1882, 31 January 1882, SP; Heremans, *L'A. I. A. au Tanganika*, 25–27.

78. Heremans, *L'A. I. A. au Tanganika*, 28ff.; Capitaine Storms, "Establissement de la Station de Mompara," *MG* 1(1884), 22–23; Norman R. Bennett, "Captain Storms in Tanganyika, 1882–1885," *TNR* 54(1960), 56–60.

79. Becker to Strauch, 8 September 1881, Storms, carnet, May 1882 ff., Strauch to Storms, 8 December 1882, 19 January 1883, SP; M. Luwel, "Kapitein Ernest Cambier Te Zanzibar, 1882–1885," *A–T* 8(1962), 91–93; Ceulemans, *La Question Arabe*, 63–64, 190–192; Becker, *Troisième Expédition*, 173–174, 196; René J. Cornet, *Maniema* (Bruxelles, 1955), 81; Mrs. James S. Jameson, ed., *The Story of the Rear Column of the Emin Pasha Relief Expedition by the Late James S. Jameson* (London, 1890), 239; Tippu Tip, *Maisha*, 139.

80. Roeykens, *Léopold II et l'Afrique*, 328ff.; R. C. Bridges, "The R. G. S. and the African Exploration Fund, 1876–80," *GJ* 129(1963), 25–35; Grahame to Kirk, 6 March 1877, u.v., Elton to Derby, 1 March 1877, Q–21, ZA.

81. Association Internationale Africaine. Comité Français à Paris, *Rapport au Ministre de l'Instruction Publique* (Paris, n.d.), 1–3; Henri Brunschwig, *Mythes et Réalités de l'Imperialisme Colonial Français* (Paris, 1960), 43, and *L'Avènement de l'Afrique Noire de XIX' Siècle à nos Jours* (Paris, 1963), 135; Robert Stanley Thomson, *Fondation de l'Etat Indépendant du Congo* (Bruxelles, 1933), 49–50, 81; *BSG* 18(1879), 578; *BSGM* 1(1877), and succeeding volumes, for full reports.

82. Baumann, *Massailand*, 110–113; Stuhlmann, *Emin Pascha*, 803–807; "Dr. Stuhlmann's Rückreise vom Victoria-Nyansa nach Bagamoyo," *MFGDS* 5(1892), 186–187; Mgr de Courmont, "Seconde Tournée dans le Vicariat Apostolique du Zanguebar," *MC* 18(1886), 604.

83. Ledoulx to MAE, 8 March 1881, CCZ 4bis; Becker, *Troisième Expédition*, 52; Burdo, *Zanzibar au Tanganika*, 448, 452–453; Dutreuil de Rhins, "Bloyet," 353–361; Bloyet, 28 January 1882, *BSBG* 6(1882), 232; Baur et LeRoy, *Zanguebar*, 264; Capt. Bloyet, "L'Oussagara, Cofaranhi, Mcondoa, Mbourni," *BSGM* 5(1881), 203.

84. Dutreuil de Rhins, "Bloyet," 359–361; *BSGM* 6(1882), 155; Ledoulx to MAE, 7 September 1883, *BSBG* 7(1883), 897; Bloyet report, 1 January 1884, PZ 6; Baxter to Lang, 15 April 1882, G3.A6/01, CMS; Elst to Frère-Orban, 2 July 1882, Correspondance et Documents, Afrique, A. I. A., MAEB; Ledoulx to MAE, 8 February 1882, CCZ 4bis; Joaquim Graf v. Pfeil, *Die Erwerbung von Deutsch-Ostafrika* (Berlin, n.d.), 100, 103.

85. See below, p. 129.

86. Bloyet, 24 April 1881, *BSGM* 6(1882), 264; Courmont, "Seconde Tournée," 596–597; Baur and LeRoy, *Zanguebar*, 263; A. LeRoy, "A la Découverte!," *MC* 19(1887), 365; Courmont, 8 June 1888, *APF* 61(1889), 60;

M. Bloyet, "Sur les Travaux de la Station de Kondôa, établi par le Section Française de la Société Internationale Africaine," *Comtes Rendus Hebdomaires des Séances de l'Académie des Sciences* 100(1885), 1021; Courmont, 8 October 1885, *BSE* 13(1886), 1130–1132; *BSGM* 10(1886), 170.

87. *MAGD* 1(1878–1879), and succeeding volumes; Thomson, *Fondation du Congo*, 50–51; *BSGM* 4(1880), 120; "Einige Worte über den augenblicklichen Stand der Slaverei in Ostafrika. Brieflich an Dr. Reichenow von Dr. med. G. Fischer in Zanzibar," *ZGEB* 17(1882), 71; Burdo, *Zanzibar au Tanganika*, 318; Richard Böhm, *Von Sansibar zum Tanganjika* (Leipzig, 1888), 4ff.; Paul Reichard, "Bericht über seine Reisen in Ostafrika und dem Quellgebiet des Kongo," *VGEB* 13(1886), 107–125, and "Meine Erwerbung des Landes Ugunda," *DKZ* 3(1890), 77–79.

88. Norman R. Bennett, "Philippe Broyon: Pioneer Trader in East Africa," *AA* 62(1963), 156–164; Broyon to Rabaud, 8 October 1877, *BSGM* 2(1878), 43; M. Bonzon, "Broyon l'Africain," copy of an unpublished *causerie* kindly sent to me by the author.

89. Little is known of Segère apart from his three-year connection with the firm of Roux de Fraissenet. Paul Masson, *Marseille et la Colonisation Française* (Marseille, 1906), 453–456; Arnold Maes, *Reis naar Midden-Afrika* (Leuven, 1879), 134; A.-J. Wauters, *Voyages en Afrique* (Bruxelles, n.d.), 47; A. T. Matson, "Sewa Haji: A Note," *TNR* 65(1966), 91–94.

90. Stokes to Wright, 2 June 1880, C.A6/024, CMS; Southon to Kirk, 1 January 1881, in Kirk to FO, 8 March 1881, Q–25, ZA.

91. Hutchinson to Stokes, 7 May 1880, C.A6/L1, Copplestone journal, 26–28 February 1881, 19–20, and 28 March 1881, Stokes to Wigram, 14 June 1881, G3.A6/01, CMS; Kirk to FO, 5 May 1881, Q–25, ZA; Association Internationale Africaine, Comité Nationale Belge, *Séance Publique du 1ᵉʳ Mars 1880* (Bruxelles, 1880), 18; Notes on Segère, SP; Becker, *Troisième Expédition*, 54–55, 95–96, 152–153; Heudebert, *Révoil*, 379–380; *L'Exploration* 9(1879), 531; Reichard, *Deutsch-Ostafrika*, 100–101.

CHAPTER 7

1. For the general setting of this era: Jan Vansina, "L'Afrique Centrale vers 1875," in Académie Royale des Sciences d'Outre-Mer, *La Conférence de Géographique de 1876: Receuil d'Etudes* (Bruxelles, 1976), 1–31, and *Kingdoms of the Savanna* (Madison, 1966), 227ff.; Anne Wilson, "Long Distance Trade and the Luba Lomami Empire," *JAH* 13(1972), 575–589; Ceulemans, *La Question Arabe*, passim; Thomas O. Reefe, *The Rainbow and the Kings: A History of the Luba Empire to 1891* (Berkeley, 1981).

2. The basic source for Tippu Tip's life is his autobiography, *Maisha ya Tippu Tip*. For its extensive textual notes see also the French edition, François Bontinck, trans. and ed., with the aid of Koen Janssen, *La Autobiographie de Hamed ben Mohammed el-Murjebi Tippo Tip (ca. 1840–1905)* (Bruxelles, 1974).

3. Vansina, *Kingdoms*, 235–236; Andrew D. Roberts, *A History of the Bemba: Political Growth and Change in North-eastern Zambia before 1900* (Madison, 1973), 136, 149, 153–156, and "The History of Abdullah ibn Suliman," *African Social Research*, 4(1967), 241ff.

4. Burton, "Lake Regions," 255–256; Said bin Salim to L. Damji, 25 March 1858, in Rigby to Anderson, 20 August 1858, IOE 136.

5. R. Foskett, ed., *The Zambesi Doctors: David Livingstone's Letters to John Kirk, 1858:1872* (Edinburgh, 1964), 142; Stanley, *Dark Continent*, II, 86–87; Richard Stanley and Alan Neame, eds., *The Exploration Diaries of H. M. Stanley* (London, 1961), 134.

6. Waller, *Livingstone's Journals*, II, 24; Stanley, *Dark Continent*, I, 44, 114, II, 117–118, 120; Cameron, *Across Africa*, II, 1–3.

7. Stanley, *Dark Continent*, II, 116, 118; Cameron, *Across Africa*, I, 378, II, 1–3; Hermann Wissmann, *Unter deutscher Flagge quer durch Afrika* (Berlin, 1889), 177–179; Albert Chapaux, *Le Congo* (Bruxelles, 1894), 290.

8. Cornet, *Maniema*, 21; Le Clément de Saint-Marcq, "A Kassongo," *MG*, 7(1890), 40; Stuhlmann, *Emin Pascha*, 599; Wissmann, *Durch Afrika*, 177; Lippens report, from *Le Belge* (29 September ?), press clippings, DP.

9. Notes on "Munie Moharra," DP; Waller, *Livingstone's Journals*, II, 133–138; Stanley, *Dark Continent*, II, 119–120; George Grenfell, "Exploration of the Tributaries of the Congo, between Leopoldville and Stanley Falls," *PRGS* 8(1886), 631–632; E. Hinck, "Des Stanley-Falls à Riba-Riba," *MA* 4(1891–1892), 302; Bennett, *Stanley's Despatches*, 117–118.

10. For Said, see Norman R. Bennett, "Said bin Habib: Arab Trader and Explorer," forthcoming.

11. Cameron, *Across Africa*, I, 251, 299, II, 54–56; Stanley, *Dark Continent*, I, 44; Wissmann, *Durch Afrika*, 179–183; Hermann Wissmann et al., *Im Innern Afrikas* (Leipzig, 1888), 280ff.

12. Cornet, *Maniema*, 20–21; Jameson, *Rear Column*, 298; Lippens report, *Le Belge* (29 September ?), press clippings, DP.

13. Kirk to Murchison, 25 September 1871, *PRGS* 16(1871–1872), 103; Kirk to BG, 9 February 1872, E–62, ZA.

14. Coupland, *Livingstone's Last Journey*, 116; Waller, *Livingstone's Journals*, II, 120; Cameron, "Journey," 324.

15. Waller, *Livingstone's Journals*, II, 24, 73, 128; Coupland, *Livingstone's Last Journey*, 167; "Dr. Livingstone's Letters to Sir Thomas Maclear," *PRGS* 17(1872–1873), 70.

16. "Letters of the Late Dr. Livingstone," *PRGS* 18(1873–1874), 276; Hore to Kirk, 17 September 1878, K–1, 20 July 1880, P–16, ZA; Bennett, *Dodgshun*, 69.

17. Vansina, *Kingdoms*, 137; Cameron, *Across Africa*, II, 11–13.

18. Jameson, *Rear Column*, 127.

19. Edouard Janssens and Albert Cateaux, *Les Belges au Congo* (Anvers, 1908), 70; Trivier, *Voyage*, 91, 139, 194; Vansina, *Kingdoms*, 238–239; Sidney L. Hinde, *The Fall of the Congo Arabs* (London, 1897), 86–87; *Maisha ya Tippu Tip*, 143, 147.

20. Hore to Kirk, 25 February 1880, N–7, ZA.

21. Stanley, *Dark Continent*, II, 95–96; Thos. Heazle Parke, *My Personal Experiences in Equatorial Africa* (London, 1891), 18; [A. van Gele], "Tipo–Tip," *MG* 2(1885), 53.

22. Becker, news clippings, DP; [A. Hodister], "Les Arabes sur le Haut Congo," *MG* 8(1891), 84; Stanley, *Dark Continent*, II, 95; *Maisha ya Tippu Tip*, 55. There are other versions: Waller explained that Livingstone's companion Susi reported that Tippu Tip, after the Nsama affair, said the name meant "the gatherer together of wealth"; LeRoy suggested it came from the Kinyamwezi verb *kutipula*, to devastate. *Livingstone's Journals*, I, 230; P. LeRoy, "L'Expedition Stanley," *MC* 22(1890), 157.

23. Luwel, "Cambier," 92; *CLMS* (1887), 45.

24. Joseph A. Moloney, *With Captain Stairs to Katanga* (London, 1893), 35; Griffith to LMS, 24 January 1881, CA 4, LMS; E. J. Glave, *Six Years of Adventure in Congo-Land* (London, 1893), 209.

25. Swann, *Slave Hunters,* 86–87; "Tippo Tib (From a Correspondent)," *The Times* (31 December 1889), 4; Herbert Ward, *A Voice from the Congo* (New York, 1910), 67.

26. Ceulemans, *La Question Arabe,* 57; Slade, *Leopold's Congo,* 24ff.; Albert Maurice, *H. M. Stanley: Unpublished Letters* (London, 1957), 52–55.

27. *Maisha ya Tippu Tip,* 119ff.; Thomson, *Central African Lakes,* II, 73–74.

28. Hore to LMS, 29 March 1883, 22 April 1884, CA 5, LMS.

29. *BSE* 13(1883), 45; Giraud, *Afrique Equatoriale,* 34; Dorothy Middleton, ed., *The Diary of A. J. Mounteny Jephson: Emin Pasha Relief Expedition, 1887–1889* (Cambridge, 1969), 79.

30. *Maisha ya Tippu Tip,* 139–143; Jameson, *Rear Column,* 293; Kirk to FO, 27 October 1883, E–78, ZA; Giraud, *Afrique Equatoriale,* 34.

CHAPTER 8

1. Bennett, *Zanzibar,* 107, and *Ropes,* 20.

2. Waller, *Livingstone's Journals,* II, 194; Kirk to BG, 30 November 1872, E–62, ZA; Frere to Granville, 7 May 1873, FO 84/1391; Sulimani bin Abedi to Barghash, 14 el Kaada 1294, in Kirk to Derby, 6 February 1878, FO 84/1514; Ledoulx to MAE, 7 May 1884, CCZ 5; Last to Wright, 20 January 1879, 24 November 1879, C.A6/014, CMS; Aylward Shorter, *The Kimbu,* 281–288, and "The Rise and Decline of Bungu Power," *TNR* 73(1973), 1–18; Cotterill, "On the Nyassa," 244; Marcia Wright, "Chief Merere and the Germans," *TNR* 69(1968), 41–49; Missionar Heese, "Sitte and Brauch der Sango," *Archiv für Anthropologie* 12(1913), 141–142; Brode, *Tippoo Tib,* 29.

3. Burton, *Lake Regions,* I, 220; Peter Rigby, *Cattle and Kinship among the Gogo* (Ithaca, 1969), 6ff.; Reichard, "Afrikanische Elfenbein," 163; Cameron, *Across Africa,* I, 93–94, 125; Lieutenant Herrmann, "Ugogo, das Land und seine Bewohner," *MFGDS* 5(1892), 191ff.; Heinrich Claus, *Die Wagogo* (Leipzig and Berlin, 1911), 4–5; Burdo, *Zanzibar au Tanganika,* 232; "Bericht von Leiutenant Wissmann," *MAGD* 4(1883–1885), 54; Christie, *Cholera Epidemics,* 429; Bennett, *Studies,* 76–80.

4. See above, p. 106.

5. Levesque, "Afrique Orientale," 325; Toeppen, "Handel," 233; Carl Peters, *Das Deutsch-Ostafrikanische Schutzgebiet* (München and Leipzig, 1895), 242; Ménard, 28 June 1881, *BMA* (1879–1882), 431; Reichard, *Deutsch-Ostafrika,* 328–330; Kirk to FO, 10 March 1881, 4 April 1881, Q–25, ZA; Böhm, *Sansibar,* 27–28; Becker, *Troisième Expédition,* 69–70, 75; Adolphe Burdo, *Les Arabes dans l'Afrique Centrale* (Bruxelles, 1885), 43–46; Bennett, *Dodgshun,* 117; Association Internationale Africaine, "Rapport succinct sur la route suivie par l'expédition Burdo, depuis Mpwapwa jusqu'à Kouihara (Ounyanyembe)," *BSBG,* 510; Shorter, *The Kimbu,* 267ff.

6. Toeppen, "Handel," 233; Wissmann, *Durch Afrika,* 277; Père Schynse, *A Travers l'Afrique avec Stanley & Emin-Pacha: Journal de Voyage* (Paris, 1890), 177–178; Heudebert, *Révoil,* 294–304; P. Reichard, "Unser letzter Kamp auf meine Rückreise," *Deutsche Revue über das gesamte nationale Leben der Gegenwart*

12(1887), 318ff.; Kapitän Spring, *Selbsterlebtes in Ostafrika* (Dresden and Leipzig, n.d.), 156–165; "Bericht des Lieutenants Prince über den Rückmarsch der Tabora-Expedition vom 5. Februar bis 18. April d. Js.," *DKB* 4(1893), 266–269; "Einem Berichte des Chefs der Station Tabora Sigl vom 30. September 1893," *DKB* 5(1894), 7.

7. Kirk to Salisbury, 27 June 1878, *PP* 1878–1879 (c.2422), 230; Kirk to FO, 24 August 1880, 18 October 1880, 13 November 1880, Q–24, ZA; Ledoulx to MAE, 7 September 1880, 11 November 1880, PZ 5; Burdo, *Les Arabes*, 19–20; *L'Exploration* 10(1880), 923–924; Last to CMS, 18 March 1881, G3.A5/01, CMS; J. T. Last, "A Visit to the Wa-itumba Iron-Workers and the Managheri, near Mamboia, in East Central Africa," *PRGS* 5(1883), 582; A. Hore, *Tanganyika*, 26; "Voyage dans l'Oukami, par les PP. Horner, Duparquet et Baur, du 11 Aôut au 22 Septembre 1870," *BSE* 8(1872), 778.

8. Akinola, "Zanzibar," ii–x, 31, 41ff., 304; Coupland, *Exploitation*, 5–6; Oliver, "Some Factors," 52.

9. Sheriff, "Zanzibar," 3, 17, 412; Paul Bohannan and Philip Curtin, *Africa and Africans* (Garden City, 1971), 293, 314.

10. Johnston quoted in Oliver, *Missionary Factor*, 98.

11. Kirk to FO, 8 March 1881, Q–24, Lister to Kirk, 18 April 1881, N–24, ZA; Roland Oliver, *Sir Harry Johnston & the Scramble for Africa* (New York, 1958), 57; and see above, p. 79.

12. Kirk to FO, 23 September 1884, E–83, ZA.

13. Quoted in Hourani, *Arabic Thought*, 296.

14. F. J. Berg, "The Swahili Community of Mombasa, 1500–1900," *JAH* 9(1968), 39, 54.

15. C. R. Whittaker, "Carthaginian Imperialism in the Fifth and Fourth Centuries," in P. D. A. Garnsey and C. R. Whittaker, eds., *Imperialism in the Ancient World* (Cambridge, 1978), 85.

16. Claude Cahen, "Economy, Society, Institutions," in P. M. Holt et al., eds., *The Cambridge History of Islam* (Cambridge, 1970), II, 532.

17. Coupland, *Exploitation*, 304–318; Marie de Kiewiet, "History of the Imperial British East African Company, 1876–1895" (Ph.D. diss., University of London, 1955), 20–53.

18. Bennett, *Zanzibar*, 121–122.

19. Rabaud to Barghash, 21 July 1880, in Kirk to FO, 27 July 1880, Q–24, ZA; Kirk to Granville, 3 March 1881, 8 March 1881, FO 84/1599; Coupland, *Exploitation*, 343–344.

20. Kirk to FO, 7 June 1884, E–83, ZA; Farler reports, *CA* 2(1884), 136, 147–149.

21. Cooper, *Plantation Slavery*, xi; Kirk to Derby, 12 December 1877, Kirk to Salisbury, 13 November 1878, *PP* 1878–1879 (c.2422), 163, 253.

CHAPTER 9

1. The best sources for Germans in East Africa are Fritz Ferdinand Müller, *Deutschland-Zanzibar-Ostafrika: Geschichte einer Kolonialeroberung, 1884–1890* (Berlin, 1959), 97ff., and Hans-Ulrich Wehler, *Bismarck und der Imperialismus* (Köln-Berlin, 1969), 333–367.

2. Kirk to Granville, 18 December 1884, Kirk to Anderson, 24 November 1884, FO 84/1679; Piat to MAE, 18 December 1884, 17 January 1885, CCZ 5.

3. Salim bin Hamid and Peters, treaty of 26 November 1884, plus other

agreements, *PP,* 1886 (c. 4609), 6–8; Kirk to Salisbury, 19 November 1885, FO 84/1729; LeRoy, "Zanguebar," 149.

4. Carl Peters, *Die Gründung von Deutsch-Ostafrika* (Berlin, 1906), 76.
5. Stokes to Lang, 6 October 1884, G3.A6/02, CMS.
6. Peters, *Die Gründung,* 61ff.; Pfeil, *Die Erwerbung,* 60ff.
7. Norman R. Bennett, "The British on Kilimanjaro: 1884–1892," *TNR* 63(1964), 1–3.
8. Konrad Guenther, *Gerhard Rholfs* (Freiburg i. Br., 1912), 217ff.; Müller, *Deutschland-Zanzibar,* 192ff.
9. Müller, *Deutschland-Zanzibar,* 73; Kirk to Granville, 14 February 1885, 17 February 1885, FO 84/1724; Piat to Freycinet, 10 May 1885, Ledoulx to Freycinet, 8 March 1885, PZ 7.
10. Kitchener to Rosebery, 4 June 1886, in Coupland, *Exploitation,* 471.
11. Kirk to Granville, 8 December 1884, FO 84/1679; Billot to Ledoulx, 5 December 1884, PZ 6; Lister to Kirk, 31 December 1884, E–81, 3 January 1885, E–85, Kirk to FO, 8 January 1885, 30 January 1885, E–89, ZA; Ledoulx to MAE, 15 January 1885, PZ 7.
12. Quoted in Coupland, *Exploitation,* 405; Müller, *Deutschland-Zanzibar,* 134ff., for the following paragraphs.
13. For the 1862 declaration, Bennett, "France and Zanzibar," 53; J. A. Kieran, "Origins of the Zanzibar Guarantee Treaty of 1862," *Canadian J. of African Studies* 2(1968), 147–166.
14. Kirk to FO, 28 April 1885, E–89, ZA.
15. Barghash to Wilhelm, 27 April 1885, in Kirk to Granville, 28 April 1885, FO 84/1725; Barghash to Bismarck, 8 May 1885, in Kirk to Granville, 9 May 1885, E–89, ZA.
16. Münster, aide-mémoire, 5 May 1885, FO 84/1712.
17. Müller, *Deutschland-Zanzibar,* 287ff.; Ylvisaker, *Lamu,* 215ff.
18. Kirk to Granville, 9 May 1885, FO 84/1725.
19. H. Bismarck to O. Bismarck, 7 March 1885, in E. T. S. Dugdale, ed., *German Diplomatic Documents, 1871–1914* (New York, 1928), I, 192; Lister to Kirk, two dispatches of 20 May 1885, E–85, ZA; Bennett, *Ropes,* 68, for Kirk's reaction.
20. Peters, *Die Gründung,* 99ff.
21. Boeufré to Freycinet, 2 September 1885, AD 9; Carl Peters, *Deutsch-National. Kolonialpolitische Aufsätze* (Berlin, 1887), 75–76.
22. Piat to MAE, 27 April 1885, PZ 7; Kurt Toeppen, "Einige Beobachtungen und Erkundigung in der Deutschen Schutzgebieten Ostafrikas," *DKZ* 3(1886), 518–523. For the Germans at Tabora, see below, p. 211.
23. Müller, *Deutschland-Zanzibar,* 155–159; Avricourt to Freycinet, 31 July 1885, 17 September 1885, AH 11, 6 May 1886, AH 12; Kirk to Mackinnon, 15 September 1886, MP 24.
24. Piat to MAE, 10 April 1885, 1 June 1885, PZ 7.
25. For Kimameta, see Jackson, *Early Days,* 193–196; Thomson, *Masai Land,* 224; Adolf von Tiedemann, *Tana-Baringo-Nil* (Berlin, 1907), 151; Höhnel, *Rudolf and Stephanie,* I, 7–9.
26. Mathews correspondence, FO 84/1726; Mathews to Smith, 25 May 1885, in Smith to FO, 10 June 1885, FO 84/1730; Lyne, *Mathews,* 66ff.; Karl Jülkhe, "Meine Wanderung nach dem Kilima-Ndscharo," microfilm from the *Köln Zeitung,* BUM; Weiss, *Kilima-Ndjargobiet,* 16ff.; Plessen, 28 August 1885, with Jülkhe documents, FO 84/1718.
27. Pfeil, *Die Erwerbung,* 118–121; Kirk to Granville, 5 June 1885, FO 84/

1726; Bruno Kurtze, *Die Deutsch-Ostafrikanische Gesellschaft* (Jena, 1913), 63; Heudebert, *Révoil,* 201.

28. Rholfs to Barghash, 8 May 1885, in Kirk to Granville, 9 May 1885, FO 84/1725; Kirk to Granville, 5 June 1885, FO 84/1726; Piat to MAE, 27 May 1885, PZ 7; Anderson on Kirk to Granville, 18 May 1885, FO 84/1730.

29. Malet to Granville, 24 May 1885, 30 May 1885, FO 84/1714; Lister to Kirk, 27 May 1885, E–85, ZA; Moritz Busch, *Bismarck,* (New York, 1898), 391.

30. Taylor to Lang, 17 March 1885, G3.A5/02, CMS; Smith to Kirk, 18 May 1885, in Kirk to FO, 30 May 1885, E–87, Lister to Kirk, 10 July 1885, E–86, ZA.

31. Müller, *Deutschland-Zanzibar,* 214–216; Paschen to Barghash, 13 August 1885, in Cheney to SD, 31 August 1885, CDZ 10; Scott to Granville, 11 August 1885, 12 August 1885, FO 84/1715; Kirk to Granville, 11 August 1885, 14 August 1885 (with enc.), FO 84/1727; Salisbury to Kirk, 12 August 1885, FO 84/1730; Piat to MAE, 11 August 1885, PZ 7.

32. Kirk to Salisbury, 9 November 1885, E–88, ZA; Farler to Penney, 8 November 1885, A.1.VI, UMCA; Roscoe to Lang, 11 November 1886, G3.A6/02, CMS; Raffray to MAE, 16 November 1885, PZ 7; Schmidt, *Deutschlands Kolonien,* 32–38; Schmidt was known for a violent temper: see Raffray to MAE, 17 November 1886, PZ 8.

33. Müller, *Deutschland-Zanzibar,* 254; Kitchener to FO, 10 February 1886 (enc. commission proceedings), FO 84/1797; Rosebery to Malet, 22 May 1886, FO 84/1798; Raffray to MAE, 12 February 1886, PZ 8.

34. Kirk to FO, 7 June 1884, E–83, Gissing to Kirk, 2 March 1884, u.v., Kirk to FO, 3 July 1885 (enc.: Smith to Kirk, 4 May 1885, Mbarak to Kirk, 30 April 1885, Hannington to Kirk, 4 May 1885), E–87, 16 February 1885, E–89, 27 June 1885, 2 July 1885, 7 July 1885, E–87, ZA; Kitchener to Rosebery, 15 March 1886, FO 84/1789; Gissing to Kirk, 14 September 1884, in Kirk to Granville, 8 October 1884, FO 84/1679; Hannington to CMS, February 1884, March 1884, Hannington to Lang, 16 April 1884, 4 May 1884, 17 May 1884, G3.A5/01, 18 February 1885, 7 May 1885, 30 June 1885, July 1885, Taylor to Lang, 28 November 1885, G3.A5/02, CMS; Smith to Rosebery, 22 March 1885, FO 84/1778; Piat to MAE, 1 July 1885, PZ 7.

35. Kirk to FO, 8 February 1886, 11 February 1886, 12 February 1886, E–93, ZA; Raffray to MAE, 13 February 1886, 14 February 1886, PZ 8; Kirk to Kitchener, 26 [January] 1886, PRO 30/57–8; Kirk to Anderson, 22 January 1886, FO 84/1772; Rosebery to Scott, 10 February 1886, Scott to Rosebery, 11 February 1886, Kitchener to FO, 13 February 1886, 14 February 1886, FO 84/1797; Scott to Rosebery, 13 February 1886, FO 84/1759; Müller, *Deutschland-Zanzibar,* 254–255; Otto Ulrich, "Mitteilungen und Gedanken eines alten Seefahrers über Ostafrika," *DKZ* 3(1886), 772–773.

36. Rosebery to Malet, 25 March 1886, FO 84/1757; Hatzfeld notes, 17 March 1886, 10 August 1886, FO 84/1753.

37. Buchanan to Macdonald, 26 October 1887, E–98, ZA, reported a few Germans landing at Takaungu to intrigue with Mbarak and other Arabs.

38. Kirk to FO, 23 March 1886, 7 June 1886, E–93, Drummond to Holmwood, 23 January 1887, P–5, ZA; Baumann, *Usambara,* 189–191; Taylor to CMS, [mid-1886], G3.A5/03, Parker to Lang, 8 July 1887, G3.A5/04, CMS.

39. Müller, *Deutschland-Zanzibar,* 255–258; Kitchener to Rosebery, 15 March 1886 (enc. commission proceedings), 9 April 1886, 30 April 1886 (enc. commission proceedings), FO 84/1798, 5 June 1886 (with enc.), 8 June 1886, 30

June 1886 (with enc.), FO 84/1799; Raffray to MAE, 11 March 1886, 9 April 1886, PZ 8.

40. Lyne, *Mathews*, 96.

41. Bennett, *Ropes*, 60–61.

42. Cazenave to Chimay, 5 July 1886, Af 6 B, 5 June 1886, CPC 18, MAEB; Heudebert, *Révoil*, 82; Karl Wilhelm Schmidt, *Sansibar: Ein ostafrikanisches Culturbild* (Leipzig, 1888), 41–45; Kirk to FO, 8 March 1886, 11 March 1886, E–93, ZA; Raffray to MAE, 21 March 1886, PZ 8; Muxworthy to Price, 13 August 1888, G3.A5/05, CMS.

43. Farler to Kirk, 22 March 1886, in Kirk to FO, 5 April 1886, FO 84/1773.

44. Albrecht Freiherr von Bülow, "Aus dem Kolonistenleben in Deutsch-Ostafrika," *Daheim* 23(1887), 166–168; *GWE* 4(1892), 154, 175–179; Kirk to FO, 5 June 1886 (enc. document of 1 June 1886 from Dunda area Africans), E–93, ZA; Kitchener to Rosebery, 5 June 1886, FO 84/1799; Arendt to Barghash, 8 June 1886, in Kirk to FO, 1 July 1886, FO 84/1773; Raffray to MAE, 3 May 1886, PZ 8; Krenzler, *Ostafrika*, 73ff.

45. Oskar Karstedt, *Der Weisse Kampf um Afrika* (Berlin, 1938), II, 84; Avricourt to Flourens, 25 February 1887, AH 12; Raffray to MAE, 12 July 1886, PZ 8.

46. Raffray to MAE, 21 September 1886, 3 November 1886, PZ 8; "Der Stand der Stationen, Facktorien und Depots der Deutsch Ostafrikanischen Gesellschaft am 1 November 1886," *DKZ* 4(1887), 75–76; Karstedt, *Der Weisse Kampf*, II, 84–87; Müller, *Deutschland-Zanzibar*, 178.

47. Bennett, *Zanzibar*, 131–132; Müller, *Deutschland-Zanzibar*, 217–218, 258–262.

48. Müller, *Deutschland-Zanzibar*, 161–162; Carl Peters, *Wie Deutsch-Ostafrika entstand!* (Leipzig, 1940), 125, 129; Avricourt to Freycinet, 23 October 1886, 11 December 1886, Avricourt to Flourens, 28 January 1887, 25 February 1887, AH 12.

49. See below, p. 177.

50. Müller, *Deutschland-Zanzibar*, 267–286; Emile DeGroot, "Great Britain and Germany in Zanzibar: Consul Holmwood's Papers, 1886–1887," *The J. of Modern History* 25(1953), 127; Peters, *Die Gründung*, 56ff.; Holmwood to FO, 25 May 1887, FO 84/1852, 6 June 1887, 5 July 1887, E–99, ZA; Holmwood (?) to Anderson, 5 July 1887, FO 84/1863; Barghash to Bismarck, 5 July 1887, FO 97/602.

51. Scott to Salisbury, 28 July 1887, FO 84/1837; Wylde note, 3 August 1887, FO 84/1855; Günther Jantzen, *Ostafrika in der deutsch-englischen Politik, 1884–1890* (Hamburg, 1934), 61.

52. Peters, *Deutsche-Ostafrikanische Schutzgebiet*, 71, 73; Peters, 19 September 1887, *DKZ* 1(1888), 7; Müller, *Deutschland-Zanzibar*, 242–243; Albrecht von Bülow, "Die Landwirtschaft in Deutsch-Ostafrika," *Daheim* 24(1888), 580; Hans Meyer. *Across East African Glaciers* (London, 1891), ix; Fritz Bley, *Deutsche Pionierarbeit in Ostafrika* (Berlin, 1891), 111ff.

53. *NOM* 1(1888), 23ff.; lease of 10 December 1887, *NOM* 2(1888), 74–75; Ehlers, "Ein Besuch," 320; S. von Sicard, *The Lutheran Church on the Coast of Tanzania, 1887–1914* (Uppsala, 1970), 52ff.

54. Peters to Holmwood, 14 July 1887, 15 July 1887, in Holmwood to FO, 6 July 1887, E–99, ZA.

55. Freida Freiin von Bülow, "Eine unblutige Eroberungfahrt an der osta-

frikanischen Küste," *Daheim* 24(1888), 22–24, 38–40; Edm. Elson, "Kustenfahrten in Ostafrika," *DKZ* 4(1887), 623–624; Peters, 12 December 1887, *DKZ* 1(1888), 19.

56. Piat to MAE, 8 August 1887, PZ 9; Peters, *Die Gründung,* 188–189; Zanzibar journal, 30 July 1887, *CTSM* (4me trim. 1887), 122.

57. Arendt to Holmwood, 1 March 1887, Buchanan to Macdonald, 26 October 1887, E–98, ZA; Price, Diary of an itineration in Giriama, 8 October–8 December 1887, G3.A5/05, CMS; Macdonald to FO, 21 November 1887, FO 84/1854.

58. Peters, *Die Gründung,* 191–195; Müller, *Deutschland-Zanzibar,* 282; Avricourt to Flourens, 19 June 1888, AH 12; Euan Smith to Salisbury, 8 April 1888, FO 84/1906; *DKZ* 2(1889), 128.

CHAPTER 10

1. Pruen to Lang, 2 January 1888, Price to Lang, 2 January 1888, Mrs. Pruen to Lang, 5 March 1888, G3.A5/05, CMS; Hutchinson to Salisbury, 27 February 1888, in Lister to Euan Smith, 22 March 1888, E–102, ZA.

2. Edward Vizetelly, *From Cyprus to Zanzibar by the Egyptian Delta* (London, 1901), 399.

3. Euan Smith to Salisbury, 10 April 1888, 13 April 1888, 14 April 1888, 8 April 1888, FO 84/1906, 7 May 1888, FO 84/1907; Müller, *Deutschland-Zanzibar,* 286.

4. Euan Smith to Salisbury, 25 April 1888, FO 84/1906; Lacau to MAE, 25 May 1888, CCZ 5.

5. Euan Smith to Salisbury, 1 June 1888, FO 84/1907; Lacau to MAE, 25 May 1888, CCZ 5; Kurtze, *Deutsch-Ostafrikanische Gesellschaft,* 105ff.

6. Farler to Penney, 7 May 1888, Trinity Sunday 1888, A.1.VI, UMCA; J. A. Kieran, "Abushiri and the Germans," *Hadith* 2(1970), 165–166.

7. Euan Smith to Salisbury, 21 June 1888, 23 June 1888, FO 84/1907, 26 July 1888, 30 July 1888, FO 84/1908; Kurtze, *Deutsch-Ostafrikanische Gesellschaft,* 73, 106–109; Lacau to MAE, 10 August 1888, CCZ 6; Ehlers, "Ein Besuch," 314, 321.

8. *DKZ* 1(1888), 318, 336; Euan Smith to Salisbury, 18 August 1888, 21 August 1888, 22 August 1888, 25 August 1888 (with enc.), FO 84/1908; Leue, "Bagamoyo," 17; Franz Stuhlmann, "Bericht über eine Reise durch Usegua and Ungúu," *MGGH* 8(1887–1888), 145; J. Sturtz and J. Wangemann, *Land und Leute in Deutsch-Ost-Afrika* (Berlin, 1894), 31, 69; Michahelles to Euan Smith, 26 August 1888, E–105, ZA; Zanzibar letter, 28 August 1888, *The Times* (28 September 1888), 6. For full accounts of the Arab-German war: Müller, *Deutschland-Zanzibar,* 357ff., and Akinola, "Zanzibar," 308ff.

9. Euan Smith to Salisbury, 18 August 1888, 22 August 1888, 25 August 1888, FO 84/1908; T. L. Marunji et al. to Euan Smith, 18 August 1888, 0–1–16, ZA; Statement of the people of Pangani submitted to Dr. Michahelles, 13 September 1888, in Euan Smith to Salisbury, 21 September 1888, FO 84/1909; Albert F. Calvert, *German East Africa* (London, 1917), 5; "Misdoings of the Germans," A.1.IV, UMCA; C. Falkenhorst, *Deutsch-Ostafrika* (Berlin, 1890), 78–79; statement of a Pangani man in Stevens, 24 February 1889, in *The World* (14 April 1889), 23; Schmidt, *Deutschlands Kolonien,* 45–46; Sturtz and Wangemann, *Land und Leute,* 69–70; Brix Förster, *Deutsch-Ostafrika* (Leipzig, 1890), 38; *DKZ* 1(1888), 333–334.

10. For the southern stations, see below, p. 150.

11. Euan Smith to Salisbury, 22 August 1888, FO 84/1908; Scott to Salisbury, 25 August 1888, FO 84/1892; Scott to Salisbury, 28 August 1888, in Lister to Euan Smith, 6 September 1888, E–106, ZA.

12. *DKZ* 1(1888), 331–334, 338; Euan Smith to Salisbury, 3 September 1888, 6 September 1888, 7 September 1888, FO 84/1909; Berkeley to Euan Smith, 8 September 1888, E–105, ZA.

13. Michahelles to Euan Smith, two of 6 September 1888, E–108, ZA; Euan Smith to Salisbury, 15 September 1888, 21 September 1888, FO 84/1909; *DKZ* 1(1888), 331–332; Lyne, *Mathews,* 101.

14. Euan Smith to Salisbury, 12 September 1888, 14 September 1888, 17 September 1888, 21 September 1888 (with statement of Pangani delegation), FO 84/1909; Lister to Euan Smith, 20 September 1888, E–106, ZA.

15. Michahelles, 24 September 1888, *DKZ* 1(1888), 349; Euan Smith to Salisbury, 23 September 1888, 25 September 1888, FO 84/1909; Lacau to MAE, 25 September 1888, CCZ 6; J. P. Farler, "The Bondei Missions, and Magila," *CA* 6(1888), 150; Hemedi bin Abdullah el Buhriy, *Utenzi wa Vita vya Wadachi Kutamalaki Mrima 1307 A. H. (The German Conquest of the Swahili Coast 1891 A.D.)* (Dar es Salaam, 1960), 41–43.

16. Reichard, *Deutsch-Ostafrika,* 121–122; Oscar Baumann, *In Deutsch-Ostafrika Während des Aufstandes* (Wien and Olmütz, 1890), 137–139, and *Usambara,* 64, 111–112; Behr, *Kriegsbilder,* 8; Schmidt, *Deutschlands Kolonien,* 54; K. Johnston in *PRGS* 1(1879), 329; Euan Smith to FO, 4 March 1889, E–110, ZA; Stuhlmann, 19 October 1888, *DKZ* 1(1888), 389; Hans Meyer, "Über seine letzte Expedition in Deutsch-Ostafrika," *VGEB* 16(1889), 88–89; G. Richelmann, "Die Besiegung der Feinde vom Rufiji bis zum Umba," in A. Becker et al., *Hermann von Wissmann* (Berlin, 1914), 205–206; Euan Smith to Salisbury, 18 August 1888, FO 84/1908.

17. Churchill to Euan Smith, 25 September 1888, E–105, ZA; Schmidt, *Deutschlands Kolonien,* 52; Euan Smith to Salisbury, 23 September 1888, 25 September 1888 (enc. Arbuthnot to Freemantle, 25 September 1888), 28 September 1888, FO 84/1909; Courmont, 4 October 1888, *BSE* 14(1888), 724; *DKZ* 1(1888), 359; Sturtz and Wangemann, *Land und Leute,* 35–38; Leue, "Bagamoyo," 17; *BSE* 15(1890), 676; John Anderson Dougherty, *The East Indies Station; or the Cruise of the "Garnet" 1887–90* (Malta, 1892), 42.

18. Chr. Pfrank, "Die Flaggenhissung in Ostafrika 1888: Persönliche Erinnerungen," unlabeled clipping inserted in BUM copy of Paul Burg, *Forscher, Kaufherrn und Soldaten: Deutschlands Bahnbrecher in Afrika* (Leipzig, 1936); Michahelles, 24 September 1888, *DKZ* 1(1888), 350, 359–360.

19. DK2, 1(1888) 334, 350, 361; Euan Smith to Salisbury, 6 September 1888, FO 84/1909; Freemantle to Euan Smith, 29 September 1888, in Euan Smith to FO, 1 October 1888, u.v., ZA.

20. Krieger, 18 September 1888, Michahelles, 24 September 1888, 25 September 1888, "Die Vorgänge in Deutsch-Ostafrika," *DKZ* 1(1888), 357, 337, 361; Reichard, *Deutsch-Ostafrika,* 134–137; Michahelles, 3 October 1888, in Raindre to Goblet, 8 November 1888, AD 85; Euan Smith to Salisbury, 24 July 1888, 25 September 1888, 28 September 1888, 4 October 1888, 8 October 1888 (enc. Hall to Freemantle, 27 September 1888), 9 October 1888, FO) 84/1909; Heinrich Hessel, *Deutsch Kolonisation in Ostafrika* (Bonn, 1889), 69ff.

21. Lacau to MAE, 25 September 1888, addenda of 30 September, CCZ 6.

22. Kurt Blümcke, *Der Aufstand in Deutsch-Ostafrika und seine Niederwerfung im nördlichen Theil* (Berlin, 1890), 12; A. Leue, "Dar-es-Salaam," *DKZ* 2(1889),

206–207, 210; Daniel v. Cölln, *Bilder aus Ostafrika* (Berlin, 1891), 93–95; Kurtze, *Deutsch-Ostafrikanische Gesellschaft*, 120.

23. Stuhlmann, 19 October 1888, *DKZ* 1(1888), 387–389; "Die Rettung der Beamten von Lewa," ibid., 386–387, 393; Behr, *Kriegsbilder*, 9; Baumann, *In Deutsch-Ostafrika*, 123.

24. Malet to Salisbury, 26 September 1888, Leyden to FO, 8 October 1888, both in Currie to Euan Smith, 1 November 1888, E–106, ZA; Malet to Salisbury, 8 October 1888, FO 84/1894; Beauclerk to Salisbury, 12 October 1888, FO 84/1893; H. Nirrnheim, "Hamburg als Träger der deutschen Kolonialverwaltung. Ein Plan des Fürsten Bismarck," *Z. des Vereins für Hamburgische Geschichte* 34(1934), 186.

25. Lyne, *Mathews*, 102–103; Bismarck to Khalifa, 30 September 1888, Khalifa to Bismarck, 3 October 1888, both in Euan Smith to FO, 3 October 1888, u.v., ZA; Euan Smith to Salisbury, 4 October 1888, FO 84/1909; Khalifa to Euan Smith, 8 November 1888, 0-1-16, ZA.

26. Leyden note, 8 October 1888, FO 84/1894; Salisbury to Euan Smith, 11 October 1888, FO 84/1912; Salisbury to Malet, 5 November 1888, FO 84/1891; MAE to Lacau, 10 November 1888, PZ 10; Goblet to Herbette, 2 November 1888, AD 85; Euan Smith to Khalifa, 6 November 1888, Khalifa to Euan Smith, 18 November 1888, 0-1-16, ZA; Negocios Externos, *Documentos Apresentados ás Côrtes na Sessão Legislativa de 1889 pelo Ministro e Secretário d'Estado dos Negócios Estrangeiros. Bloquoio na Costa Oriental da Africa* (Lisboa, 1889), 11–13.

27. Gravenreuth, 29 October 1888, *DKZ* 1(1888), 409; Euan Smith to Salisbury, 22 October 1888, 14 November 1888, 20 November 1888, FO 84/1910.

28. Gravenreuth, 1 November 1888, *DKZ* 1(1888), 410; Euan Smith to Salisbury, 20 November 1888, FO 84/1910.

29. Farler to Allchin, 23 February 1877, A.1.VI, UMCA; Farler to Churchill, 4 July 1885, in Lister to Kirk, 15 August 1885, E–86, ZA; Maples to Sowerbutts, 27 July 1885, *JMGS* 1(1885), 227; C. A. Smythies, "The Mountain Towns of the Bondei Country," *CA* 4(1886), 78.

30. Lister to CMS, 10 April 1886, G3.A5/03, Parker to Lang, 18 January 1887, G3. A5/04, CMS.

31. Bennett, "French Policy in Buganda," 11–12.

32. Euan Smith to Salisbury, 1 June 1888 (with Anderson note), 23 June 1888 (with Salisbury note), FO 84/1907.

33. Farler, "Bondei Missions," 149–150; "Die Antisklaverei-Bewegnung und Deutsch-Ostafrika," *DKZ* 1(1888), 349.

34. Farler to Penney, 15 January 1888, A.1.VI. UMCA.

35. Euan Smith to Smythies, 5 November 1888, A.1.V, UMCA; Smythies to Penney, 25 September 1888, SL.

36. Euan Smith to Salisbury, 25 September 1888, 28 September 1888 (enc. Abushiri to Euan Smith, 26 September 1888), FO 84/1909; Smythies to Penney, 10 November 1888, 13 November 1888, 19 November 1888, SL; Euan Smith to Salisbury, 10 November 1888, FO 84/1913, 19 November 1888 (enc. Smythies to Euan Smith, 15 November 1888), FO 84/1910; Goodyear, 2 October 1888, Smythies, 19 November 1888, *CA* 7(1889), 12, 17–20; Euan Smith to Khalifa, 25 January 1889, u.v., ZA. For Meyer and Baumann, see below, p. 158.

37. Hutchinson to Lister, 2 August 1888, in Lister to Euan Smith, 9 August 1888, E–106, ZA; Euan Smith to Price, 27 August 1888, G3.A5/05, CMS.

38. Ashe to Lang, 6 October 1888, Roscoe to Lang, 7 November 1888,

Pruen to Muxworthy, 16 November 1888, Muxworthy to Lang, 19 November 1888, Boustead, Ridley & Co. to CMS, 23 October 1888 (précis book), G3.A5/05, CMS; Pruen to Euan Smith, 24 November 1888, in Euan Smith to Salisbury, 1 December 1888, FO 84/1911; Ashe, *Two Kings*, 278, and *Chronicles of Uganda* (London, 1894), 432–433; Pruen, *Arab and African*, 95–97; Mrs. Pruen, "Through German East Africa," *CMIR* 14(1889), 98–107.

39. Euan Smith to Salisbury, 3 December 1888, FO 84/1910, 14 December 1888, FO 84/1911; Euan Smith to FO, 4 March 1889, E–110, ZA; *CA* 7(1889), 27; Zoller in *DKZ* 2(1889), 168.

40. Michahelles, 17 December 1888, 2 January 1889, *DKZ* 1(1889), 35; Lacau to MAE, 30 December 1888, CCZ 6; Sturtz and Wangemann, *Land und Leute*, 41; letter of A. F., 4 January 1889, *BSAF* (1888–1889), 269; Nimtz, "Sūfī Order," 157; Robert N. Lyne, *Zanzibar in Contemporary Times* (London, 1905), 153–154.

41. Reichard, *Deutsch-Ostafrika*, 138–140; Förster, *Deutsch-Ostafrika*, 36, 41; Leue, 28 December 1888, *DKZ* 2(1889), 36; Sturtz and Wangemann, *Land und Leute*, 57; Leue, "Dar-es-Salaam," 211; Müller, *Deutschland-Zanzibar*, 391.

42. Eberstein, "Ostafrika," 60–61; Oscar Baumann, "Reise in Deutsch-Ostafrika," *MGGW* 32(1889), 32, and *In Deutsch-Ostafrika*, 36; Meyer, *East African Glaciers*, ix–xi; Dougherty, *Cruise of the Garnet*, 50–51; Smythies, 19 November 1888, SL; Meyer and Baumann, 28 September 1888, 23 October 1888, *PM* 34(1888), 372; "Dr. Hans Meyer's Usambara-Expedition," *MFGDS* 1(1888), 199–205; O'Swald to Euan Smith, 20 December 1888 (enc. Baumann statement), E–105, ZA; Smythies, 29 January 1889, *CA* 7(1889), 51.

43. Euan Smith to FO, 9 February 1889 (enc. Euan Smith to Smythies, 9 February 1889), 11 February 1889, 14 June 1889, Smythies to Euan Smith, 12 February 1889, E–120, Euan Smith to FO, 4 March 1889, 18 March 1889, E–110, ZA; Jones-Bateman to Penney, 15 January 1889, A.1.VI, UMCA; Smythies to Penney, 28 January 1889, 25 February 1889, SL; Salisbury to Euan Smith, 18 January 1889, FO 84/1973; Edward Francis Russell (ed. G[ertrude]. W[ard].), *The Life of Charles Allen Smythies* (London, 1898), 131.

44. Brooks to Brit. Consul, 26 December 1888, Amani wad Mabruki statement, 24 January 1889, E–118, Euan Smith to Khalifa, 24 January 1889, u.v., Euan Smith to FO, 1 February 1889, E–120, ZA; Euan Smith to Salisbury, 13 February 1889, FO 84/1984; Roscoe, *Twenty Five Years*, 36; Swann, *Slave Hunters*, 165–166; Alexandre LeRoy, "Au Zanguebar Anglais," *MC* 22(1890), 620, 628; Brooks to Thompson, 24 December 1888, Muxworthy to Thompson, 14 January 1889, CA 7, LMS.

45. See below, p. 164.

46. Euan Smith to Salisbury, 24 January 1889, 29 January 1889, 13 February 1889 (with Pauncefote note), FO 84/1984; Lister to Euan Smith, 25 January 1889, 27 January 1889, 31 January 1889, E–114, Euan Smith to FO, 1 February 1889, 2 February 1889, E–120, 27 February 1889, E–110, ZA; Baur to Euan Smith, 19 February 1889, in Euan Smith to Salisbury, 26 February 1889, FO 84/1976.

47. Boustead, Ridley & Co. to CMS, 18 December 1888 (précis book), G3.A5/05, CMS; Zanzibar letter, 29 March 1889, *BSAF* (1888–1889), 435–436.

48. Salisbury to Beauclerk, 9 March 1889, FO 84/1953.

49. See below, p. 161.

50. Lacau to MAE, 23 February 1889, CCZ 6; Smythies to Euan Smith, 2 February 1889, Euan Smith to Smythies, 4 February 1889, A.1.V, 17 January

1889 (enc. Euan Smith to Khalifa, 17 January 1889), C. Smith to Smythies, 18 April 1889 (enc. Suliman bin Nassir to Khalifa, 14 April 1889), D 3, UMCA; Euan Smith to FO, 8 February 1889, E–120, 12 March 1889 (enc. Smythies to Euan Smith, 3 March 1889), 1 April 1889 (enc. Jones-Bateman to Euan Smith, 26 March 1889), E–110, ZA; Anderson note on Portal to Salisbury, 6 May 1889, FO 84/1978.

51. Euan Smith to FO, 4 March 1889, 12 March 1889, E–110, ZA; *BSE* 15(1889), 712; Zöller in *DKZ* 2(1889), 168.

52. Price to Lang, 17 January 1889, 13 February 1889, G3.A5/06, Lang and Gray to Price, 20 February 1889, G3.A5/L5, CMS.

53. Lister to Euan Smith, 1 February 1889, E–114, Euan Smith to FO, 18 March 1889, Hawes to FO, 8 April 1889, 21 April 1889, E–110, Euan Smith to Khalifa, 25 January 1889, 26 January 1889, u.v., Euan Smith to FO, 11 January 1889, 14 January 1889, 11 February 1889, E–120, Sanderson to Hawes, 17 April 1889, E–114, ZA; Euan Smith to Price, 15 January 1889, Price to Lang, 3 March 1889, Cole to Lang, 6 March 1889, Edwards to CMS, 20 April 1889, Roscoe to Lang, 28 April 1889, 8 May 1889, Boustead, Ridley & Co. to CMS, 3 May 1889, 6 May 1889 (both in précis book), G3.A5/06, CMS; Euan Smith to Mpwapwa-Mamboya missionaries, 2 February 1889, in Euan Smith to Salisbury, 2 February 1889, FO 84/1976; Roscoe, *Twenty Five Years*, 36–41; Hooper in *CMIR* 14(1889), 572–573; Smythies to Penney, 27 April 1889, SL; Khalifa to Hawes, 19 April 1889, *PP* 1889 (c.5822), 90; Hawes to Salisbury, 29 April 1889, Portal to Salisbury, 6 May 1889, FO 84/1978; Portal to Salisbury, 1 June 1889, FO 84/1984; E. R. Freemantle, *The Navy as I Have Known It, 1849–1899* (London, 1904), 350–351; Wissmann report, 1 May 1889, *MG* 6(1889), 46.

The Meyer ransom affair, after long and complex negotiations, finally was settled in September 1890.

54. W. Salter Price, *My Third Campaign in East Africa* (London, 1890), 282–283; Kurtze, *Deutsch-Ostafrikanische Gesellschaft*, 127; Lacau to MAE, 29 January 1889, CCZ 6; Vohsen in *DKZ* 2(1889), 116–117.

55. Herbette to Goblet, 17 December 1888, AD 85; Malet to Salisbury, 14 December 1888, FO 84/1893; Avricourt to Flourens, 16 November 1888, 16 December 1888, HD 12. For Lavigerie's crusade, see below, p. 249.

56. Hermann von Wissmann, *My Second Journey through Equatorial Africa* (London, 1891), 185; Scott, 24 April 1888, *CSHFMR* 18(1891–1892), 508.

57. Lister to Malet, 1 January 1889, FO 84/1953; Wissmann's orders, 8 February 1889, *DKZ* 2(1889), 70; Rochus Schmidt, *Hermann von Wissmann und Deutschlands Koloniales Wirken* (Berlin, 1925), 75–79; G. Richelmann, "Wissmann wird Kaiserlicher Reichskommissar," in Becker et al., *Wissmann*, 179–180.

58. G. Richelmann, "Schaffung der Wissmanntruppe," in Becker et al., *Wissmann*, 184–201; Salisbury-Baring correspondence in Lister to Euan Smith, 21 February 1889, E–114, Portal to Salisbury, 11 March 1889, E–110, ZA; Rochus Schmidt, *Geschichte des Araberaufstandes in Ost-Afrika* (Frankfurt a. Oder, 1892), 44; Behr, *Kriegsbilder,* 12ff.; Georg Maercker, *Unsere Schutztruppe in Ostafrika* (Berlin, 1893), passim.

59. Euan Smith to Salisbury, 19 November 1888 (citing the opinions of Nassir bin Suliman), FO 84/1910; Euan Smith to FO, 1 February 1889, E–120, 4 March 1889, E–110, ZA; Avricourt to Spuller, 16 March 1889, HD 15; Stevens's letters of 24 February 1889, 14 March 1889 (citing Khalifa's opinions), in *The World* (14 April 1889), 22–23, (28 April 1889), 23.

60. Greiner diary, 14 October 1888 on, *NOM* 3(1889), 4, 17–23, 25–32; Euan Smith to FO, 1 February 1889, E–120, ZA; Lacau to MAE, 29 January 1889, CCZ 6; A. Leue, *Dar-es-Salaam: Bilder aus dem Kolonialleben* (Berlin, 1903), 25ff., and "Dar-es-Salaam," 211–213; Courmont in *APF* 61(1889), 304–306; Cölln, *Bilder,* 93ff. For the Pugu ransom, see above, p. 160.
61. Euan Smith to Salisbury, 2 January 1889, 14 January 1889, E–120, Hawes to FO, 8 April 1889, E–110, ZA; Euan Smith to Pauncefote, 15 January 1889, FO 84/1975; Euan Smith to Salisbury, 6 February 1889, FO 84/1984; Zanzibar letter, 27 January 1889, *CA* 7(1889), 62; Lacau to MAE, 15 February 1889, CCZ 6; Pauncefote to Euan Smith, 15 February 1889, FO 84/1973.
62. Euan Smith to Salisbury, 9 March 1889, E–110, ZA.
63. Salisbury to Euan Smith, 13 March 1889, E–114, Euan Smith to Salisbury, 20 March 1889, 1 April 1889, E–110, ZA.
64. Euan Smith to FO, 3 April 1889, E–110, C. Smith note, c. December 1889, E–118, ZA; Portal to Salisbury, 24 June 1889, FO 84/1979; Smythies to Travers, 3 December 1890, SL; *The Times* (6 March 1889), 5; Taylor to Hawes, 28 April 1889, in Hawes to Salisbury, 29 April 1889, FO 84/1978; Richelmann, "Die Beseigung," 204–205; Rust report, *DKZ* 2(1889), 179; Zanzibar letter, 29 March 1889, *BSAF* (1888–1889), 345; Lacau to MAE, 29 May 1889, CCZ 6.
65. Wissmann to Bismarck, 1 May 1889, *DKZ* 2(1889), 171; Richelmann, "Die Beseigung," 205; Hawes to FO, 25 April 1889, E–110, ZA; Smith to Penney, 9 May 1889, SL; Kieran, "Abushiri and the Germans," 175; Lacau to MAE, 29 May 1889, CCZ 6.
66. Wissmann to Bismarck, 1 May 1889, and "Bericht des Reichskommissars Wissmann über die Erstürmung des Lagers von Bushiri," *DKZ* 2(1889), 171–172, 222–223; Reichard notes, DKZ 2(1889), 165; Michahelles to Portal, 9 May 1889, in Portal to Salisbury, 16 May 1889, FO 84/1978; Behr, *Kriegsbilder,* 55ff.; G. Richelmann, *Meine Erlebnisse in der Wissmann-Truppe* (Madgeburg, 1892), 20ff., and "Die Beseigung," 208ff.
67. Wissmann, "Ersturmung," 223–224, and Reichard note, *DKZ* 2(1889), 253; Portal to Salisbury, 24 June 1889, FO 84/1979; Greiner note, *NOM* 3(1889), 85; Richelmann, *Meine Erlebnisse,* 153, and "Die Beseigung," 224–225; Behr, *Kriegsbilder,* 71ff.; Schmidt, *Araberaufstandes,* 66–70.
68. See, for example, Schmidt, *Araberaufstandes,* 73–74.
69. Richelmann, "Die Beseigung," 229–243; Reichard note, *DKZ* 2(1889), 253; Baumann, *Usambara,* 91–92, 112; Behr, *Kriegsbilder,* 15ff.; Schmidt, *Araberaufstandes,* 74–77; Blümkhe, *Der Aufstand,* 29; Portal to Salisbury, 16 May 1889, 28 May 1889, FO 84/1978, 24 June 1889, 17 July 1889, FO 84/1979; Lacau to MAE, 24 June 1889, CCZ 6, 25 August 1889, CCZ 7; Korvetten-Kapitän Hirschberg, *Neunzehn Monate kommandant S. M. Kreuzer "Schwalbe" während der militarischen Aktion 1889/90 in Deutsch-Ostafrika* (Kiel, 1895), 106–113, 117–121, 153.
70. Portal to Salisbury, 6 July 1889, 28 July 1889, FO 84/1979; Lacau to MAE, 24 June 1889, CCZ 6; G. Richelmann, "Die erste Durchquerung Äquatorial-Afrikas von West nach Ost," and A. Becker, "Die endgültige Niederwerfung Bana Heris," both in Becker et al., *Wissmann,* 53, 292–300; Richelmann, "Die Beseigung," 226–227; Portal to FO, 2 September 1889, 8 September 1889, E–112, ZA.
71. See below, p. 169.
72. Kieran, "Abushiri and the Germans," 180–181, and "Holy Ghost

Fathers," 293–297; Courmont, 2 July 1889, and other mission reports, *BSE* 15(1889–1890), 284, 424, 678–679, 722; Ladonne, 1 February 1894, *GWE* 6(1894), 207–208.

73. See above, p. 144.

74. Price to Lang, 4 April 1889, 25 July 1889, Wood journal, 19 June–17 July 1889, Boustead, Ridley & Co. to CMS, 2 August 1889, 3 September 1889 (précis book), Cole to Lang, 28 August 1889, G3.A5/06, CMS.

75. Rochus Schmidt, "Die Mpapua-Expedition: Wissmann, Emin und Stanley," in Becker et al., *Wissmann*, 252–264; Capitän-Lieutenant a. D. Rust, *Die Deutsche Emin Pascha-Expedition* (Berlin, 1890), 24; Behr, *Kriegsbilder*, 192–205; Blümkhe, *Der Aufstand*, 36–50; Schmidt, *Araberaufstandes*, 99–121; Giese in *DKZ* 2(1889), 368, 351–353; *AEC* 10(1889), 197; Wood to Lang, 13 October 1889, 25 October 1889, Price to Lang, 18 October 1889, Cole to Lang, 2 November 1889, G3.A5/06, CMS; Portal to Salisbury, 28 July 1889, FO 84/1979; Portal to FO, 9 September 1889, E–112, ZA; Lacau to MAE, 25 August 1889, 27 September 1889, CCZ 7; Kieran, "Abushiri and the Germans," 184–185.

76. Elzear Ebner, *History of the Wangoni* (N.p., 1959), 85; L. E. Larson, "A History of the Mbunga Confederacy ca. 1860–1907," *TNR* 81–82(1977), 35–39.

77. Schynse, *Stanley et Emin*, 275–279; Reichard, *Deutsch-Ostafrika*, 202–211; A. Becker, *Aus Deutsch-Ostafrikas Sturm- und Drangperiode* (Halle a. S., 1911), 4–5; Wilhelm Langheld, *Zwanzig Jahre in deutschen Kolonien* (Berlin, 1909), 5–6; Behr, *Kriegsbilder*, 259ff.; Greiner, 16–22 October 1889, *NOM* 3(1889), 86.

78. Malet to Salisbury, 14 December 1888, in Lister to Euan Smith, 22 December 1888, E–106, Portal to FO, 19 August 1889, E–112, ZA; Sturtz and Wangemann, *Land und Leute*, 66; Euan Smith to Salisbury, 25 December 1888, FO 84/1911, 4 January 1889, 23 January 1889, 27 January 1889, FO 84/1984; Dougherty, *Cruise of the Garnet*, 60–63; Hirschberg, *Neunzehn Monate*, 17ff.; Freemantle, *The Navy*, 333ff.; Maercker, *Unsere Schutztruppe*, 12–16; Zanzibar letters, 4 January 1889, 2 July 1889, undated, *BSAF* (1888–1889), 269, 431–432, 497; Price to Lang, 28 December 1888, G3.A5/06, CMS; Freemantle to Adm., 10 April 1889, *PP* 1889 (c.5822), 78; *The Times* (4 February 1889), 5.

79. Kieran, "Abushiri and the Germans," 186–188.

80. The other men captured with Abushiri were hanged in Bagamoyo on December 18.

81. Becker, *Aus Deutsch-Ostafrika*, 5–21; A. LeRoy, *Au Kilima-Ndjaro* (Paris, n.d.), 449–450; Salisbury to Malet, 18 December 1889, FO 84/1955; Malet to Salisbury, 19 December 1889, FO 84/1958; Currie to Euan Smith, 21 December 1889, E–116, Euan Smith to FO, 23 December 1889, 26 December 1889, E–113, 13 February 1890, u.v., ZA; Salisbury to Portal, 21 December 1889, FO 84/1983; Salisbury to Euan Smith, 18 February 1889, FO 84/2067; Behr, *Kriegsbilder*, 329–334; Schmidt, *Araberaufstandes*, 158–163; Zanzibar news, 16 December 1889, *CTSM* (1er trim. 1890), 342; D. R. Gillard, "Salisbury's African Policy and the Heligoland Offer of 1890," *English Historical R.* 75(1960), 647.

82. Behr, *Kriegsbilder*, 219–235; Schmidt, *Araberaufstandes*, 175; Baumann, *Usambara*, 194, and "Über das nördliche Deutsch-Ostafrika," *VGEB* 18(1891), 80; Hermann v. Wissmann (with notes by D. H.), "Afrikanische Diplomatie," *KJ* 4(1891), 1–5; LeRoy, *Kilima-Ndjaro*, 436–437.

83. See below, p. 173.

84. Wolfrum, *Briefe aus Ostafrika,* 17–19, 61–62; Schmidt, *Araberaufstandes,* 161–183, 318; Euan Smith to FO, 7 January 1890, 21 March 1890, 15 April 1890 (enc. Bwana Heri to Khalifa, 14 April 1890), u.v., 3 April 1890, 13 April 1890, Salisbury to Euan Smith, 6 April 1890, E–125, ZA; Smythies to Travers, 7 January 1890, SL; Becker, "Die endgültige Niederwerfung," 300–315; Leue, *Dar-es-Salaam,* 58–67; Tom v. Prince, *Gegen Araber und Wahehe* (Berlin, 1914), 6–15; Euan Smith to Salisbury, 24 March 1890, FO 84/2060; Piat to MAE, 15 March 1890, 17 April 1890, CCZ 7bis; Schmidt, *Wissmann,* 263; Hooper in *CMIR* 14(1889) 572; Schynse, *Stanley et Emin,* 257; Journal de voyage de Pères Achte et Schynse, *CTSM* (4me trim. 1890), 85; Hirschberg, *Neunzehn Monate,* 153ff.; Langheld, *Zwanzig Jahre,* 13–17.

85. Euan Smith to FO, 17 April 1890, 1 July 1890, Euan Smith to Wissmann, 20 December 1890, u.v., Lenc to Euan Smith, 14 January 1891, Muxworthy to Smith, 17 July 1891, E–131, ZA; JHS (sic) to Euan Smith, 10 June 1890, FO 84/2068.

86. ? to Smith, Mackenzie & Co., 8 March 1889, in Euan Smith to Salisbury, 9 March 1889, FO 84/1977; Porter to Heanley, 14 July 1890, A.1.VI, UMCA.

87. A. Becker, "Die Niederwerfung des Aufstandes in Süden," in Becker et al., *Wissmann,* 316–334; Schmidt, *Araberaufstandes,* 210–216; 223; Leue, *Dar-es-Salaam,* 68–87; Euan Smith to FO, 24 February 1890, 13 March 1890, u.v., 7 May 1890, E–125, ZA; Salisbury to Euan Smith, 21 February 1890, FO 84/2058; Euan Smith to Salisbury, 1 May 1890 (enc. Sultans of Mkindani region to Khalifa, 22 March 1890), 21 May 1890, FO 84/2061.

88. For contemporary slave trade proponents: Vohsen in *DKZ* 2(1889), 116; Zöller letter in Avricourt to Spuller, 17 June 1889, HD 15. For recent slave trade assertions: Kimambo, *Pare,* 199; William H. Friedland, "The Evolution of Tanganyika's Political System," in Stanley Diamond and Fred G. Burke, eds., *The Transformation of East Africa* (New York, 1966), 253; R. W. Beachey, *The Slave Trade of Eastern Africa* (London, 1976), 200. For contemporary balanced views: August Boshart, "Die Zustände im deutschen Schutzgebiete von Ostafrika, deren Ursache und Wirkungen," *DRGS* 12(1890), 391ff.; Euan Smith to Salisbury, 23 September 1888, FO 84/1909.

89. Walter Rodney, "European Activity and African Reaction in Angola," in T. O. Ranger, ed., *Aspects of Central African History* (London, 1968), 70; Zöller in *DKZ* 2(1889), 168.

90. Robert D. Jackson, "Resistance to the German Invasion of the Tanganyikan Coast, 1888–1891," in Robert I. Rotberg and Ali M. Mazrui, eds., *Protest and Power in Black Africa* (New York, 1970), 58.

91. John Iliffe, *A Modern History of Tanganyika* (Cambridge, 1979), 91, 94, and *Tanganyika under German Rule, 1905–1912* (Cambridge, 1969), 13; Müller, *Deutschland-Zanzibar,* 375, 384, also labels Khalifa a collaborator.

92. Bennett, *Zanzibar,* 156.

93. William Hichens, "Khabar al-Lamu: A Chronicle of Lamu by Shaihu Faraji Bin Hamed al-Bakiry al-Lamuy," *BS* 12(1938), 31. Akinola, "Zanzibar," 320–321, 348–350, 382–384, also fairly treats Khalifa.

94. Portal to FO, two of 21 October 1889, E–112, E–113, Euan Smith to FO, 4 January 1890, 11 January 1890, E–126, Euan Smith to Salisbury, 16 January 1890, u.v., ZA; Euan Smith to Salisbury, 23 December 1889, FO 84/1982; Portal to FO, 17 August 1889, FO 84/1985.

95. Piat to MAE, 20 January 1890, 19 February 1890, CCZ 7; Euan Smith to Salisbury, 10 January 1890, FO 84/2059.

96. Euan Smith to FO, 20 February 1890, E–126, ZA; Ottavi to Ribot, 12 June 1890, PZ 12; Euan Smith to Salisbury, 19 June 1890, FO 84/2062.

97. Ali to German Consul, 28 June 1890, in Euan Smith to Salisbury, 1 July 1890, u.v., ZA; Bennett, *Zanzibar*, 163–164.

98. Lytton to Salisbury, 28 June 1890, FO 84/2027.

99. Ottavi to Ribot, 26 June 1890, PZ 12; Avricourt to Spuller, 3 July 1890, HD 17; Herbette to Ribot, 26 June 1890, AD 97; Becker, "Die Niederwerfung in Süden," 336–337; A. C. Yate, "British and German East Africa," *The Nineteenth Century and After*, 80(1916), 338–339; Manfred Sell, *Das deutsch-englische Abkommen von 1890 über Helgoland und die afrikanischen Kolonien im Licht der deutschen Presse* (Berlin-Bonn, 1961), 125–130; Euan Smith to FO, 11 February 1890, 4 April 1890, 19 April 1890, u.v., 28 June 1890, E–125, ZA; Avricourt to Casimir-Périer, 19 January 1894, HD 22.

100. For the British company, de Kiewiet, "History of the IBEA," especially 92ff.

101. Taylor to Lang, 9 June 1885, G3.A5/02, CMS.

102. Shaw to Lang, 11 February 1886, Jones to Lang, October [1886], G3.A5/03, Statistics of the Eastern Equatorial African Mission, Price to Euan Smith, 15 September 1888, Price to Lang, 5 September 1888, 28 November 1888, G3.A5/05, CMS; Berkeley to Holmwood, 24 June 1887, in Holmwood to FO, 10 July 1887, E–99, Churchill to Euan Smith, 25 May 1888, E–104, Macdonald to FO, 13 February 1888, E–107, ZA; Price, *Third Campaign*, 153–154.

103. Drummond to Holmwood, 23 January 1887, P–5, ZA; Höhnel, *Rudolf and Stephanie*, I, 171; Berkeley-Mbarak agreement, 9 June 1887, FO 84/2264; Euan Smith to Salisbury, 7 May 1888, FO 84/1907.

104. Euan Smith to Salisbury, 26 July 1888, FO 84/1908; Piat to MAE, 10 July 1887, PZ 9.

105. Euan Smith to Salisbury, 17 October 1888, FO 84/1910; IBEA, *Report of the Court of Directors . . . 6th June, 1889*, 6; Price, *Third Campaign*, 230–231; Mackenzie to IBEA, 1 December 1888, in Euan Smith to FO, 2 September 1890, u.v., Mackenzie to Euan Smith, 28 February 1889, in Euan Smith to FO, 5 March 1889, E–110, Mackenzie to Euan Smith, 13 March 1889, N–6, ZA; Mathews, 6 March 1891, FO 84/2153; Zélie Colvile, *Round the Black Man's Garden* (Edinburgh and London, 1893), 69; Berg, "Mombasa under the Busaidi," 296ff.

106. Price to Euan Smith, 16 October 1888, Euan Smith to Price, 17 October 1888, G3.A5/05, CMS; Mackenzie to Euan Smith, 18 October 1888, 20 October 1888, both in Euan Smith to Salisbury, 22 October 1888, FO 84/1910; Price journal, 23 October 1888, *CMIR* 13(1888), 786–787; *SGM* 4(1888), 558.

107. Price to Lang, 6–24 October 1888, Binns to Lang, 15 November 1888, G3.A5/05, CMS.

108. Mackenzie to Euan Smith, 26 October 1888, N–6, Lister to Hawes, 10 April 1889, E–114, Sanderson to Portal, 20 August 1889, E–115, Euan Smith to FO, 11 January 1889, E–120, ZA; Euan Smith to Salisbury, 20 November 1888 (enc. Price, 3 November 1888 and other documents), FO 84/1910; Price, Memorandum No. 2 on the Runaway Slave Question at Rabai, 29 January 1889, G3.A5/06, CMS. For Fuladoyo, Mackenzie to Euan Smith, 12 February 1890, in Euan Smith to Salisbury, 24 February 1890, FO 84/2059; Lugard to Euan Smith, 9 June 1890, in Euan Smith to Salisbury, 14 June 1890, FO 84/2062.

109. Mackenzie to Euan Smith, 15 November 1888, in Euan Smith to Salisbury, 20 November 1888, FO 84/1910.

110. Euan Smith to Salisbury, 3 December 1888, 27 December 1888, FO

84/1911, 31 December 1888, FO 84/1913, 8 February 1889, FO 84/1976.

111. Euan Smith to Salisbury, 19 July 1889, FO 84/1979; Beauclerk to Salisbury, 18 July 1889, FO 84/1958; Salisbury to Beauclerk, 20 August 1889, FO 84/1954; Hatzfeldt, 21 August 1889 (enc. Bismarck, 15 August 1889), FO 84/1961; Currie, 15 August 1889, FO 84/1890.

112. Salisbury to Portal, 22 August 1889, 30 August 1889, 5 September 1889, 9 September 1889, FO 84/1974; Portal to Salisbury, 23 August 1889, 7 September 1889, 13 September 1889, FO 84/1984, 23 September 1889, FO 84/1980; Salisbury to Beauclerk, 9 September 1889, FO 84/1955; proclamation in Euan Smith to Salisbury, 23 December 1889, FO 84/1982; Portal to Salisbury, 29 October 1889, FO 84/1981.

113. Euan Smith to Salisbury, 9 January 1890, 16 January 1890, 27 January 1890, FO 84/2059; Euan Smith to Salisbury, 10 January 1889, E–126, ZA.

114. Lacau to MAE, 3 August 1890, 15 August 1890, CCZ 7bis; Euan Smith to Mackinnon, 3 August 1890, MP 4; Smith to Purday, 13 August 1890, G3.A5/06, CMS; Euan Smith to Salisbury, 2 August 1890, E–126, ZA; Euan Smith to Salisbury, 3 August 1890, 14 August 1890, 17 August 1890, FO 84/2063; C. Smith to Salisbury, 5 August 1891, FO 84/2149; Pratt to SD, 6 August 1890, CDZ 9.

115. Euan Smith to Mackinnon, 19 August 1890, MP 4; Mathews to Portal, 12 September 1891, in Portal to Salisbury, 14 September 1891, FO 84/2149.

116. Bennett, *Zanzibar*, 176–184; G. H. Mungeam, *British Rule in Kenya, 1895–1912* (Oxford, 1966), 60; Iliffe, *Modern Tanganyika*, 131–132, 263.

117. Dougherty, *Cruise of the Garnet*, 54; Behr, *Kriegsbilder*, 218.

118. Kirk to Mackinnon, 27 December 1888, MP; Euan Smith to FO, 4 March 1889, 11 March 1889, E–110, Portal to FO, 11 September 1889, E–112, ZA; Mackenzie to Euan Smith, 13 March 1889, in Euan Smith to Salisbury, 20 March 1889, 29 March 1889, FO 84/1977; Portal to Salisbury, 22 June 1889, FO 84/1979; Euan Smith to Salisbury, 24 February 1890, FO 84/2059, 26 March 1890, FO 84/2060. The Tabora venture failed.

119. Euan Smith to Salisbury, 11 January 1890 (enc. Mackenzie to Euan Smith, 8 January 1890), FO 84/2059, 12 March 1890 (enc. Mackenzie to Euan Smith, 7 March 1890), FO 84/2060, 2 September 1890, FO 84/2064, 8 October 1890 (enc. de Winton to Euan Smith, 26 September 1890), FO 84/2065, 8 November 1890 (enc. Mbarak to Fumo Bakari, 17 April 1890), 24 November 1890 (enc. de Winton to Euan Smith, 18 November 1890), FO 84/2066; Berkeley to Con. Zanzibar, 9 May 1892, u.v., ZA; Hardinge to Salisbury, 12 April 1896, *PP* 1896 (c. 8274), 87; Stuhlmann, *Emin Pascha*, 34; Perham, *Lugard Diaries*, I, 44, 55–56; C. W. Hobley, *Kenya: From Chartered Company to Crown Colony* (London, 1929), 29; LeRoy, *Kilima–Ndjaro*, 54.

120. Hardinge to Salisbury, 12 April 1896, *PP* 1896 (c.8274), 87; McKay, "Southern Kenya Coast," 208–210.

121. For the crisis: Mungeam, *Kenya*, 21–24; Hardinge to Kimberley, 13 February 1895, FO 107/34, 1 May 1895, 7 June 1895, 25 June 1895, 6 July 1895, and ff., FO 107/36; Hardinge to Salisbury, 31 July 1895, 26 August 1895, 12 April 1896, and ff. in *PP* 1896 (c.8274); Hardinge report, 20 July 1897, *PP* 1897 (c.8638), 65–66. See also: Cashmore, "Mbaruk bin Rashid," 127ff.; Morton, "Slaves, Fugitives, and Freedmen," 347ff.; McKay, "Southern Kenya Coast," 212ff.; Cynthia B. Smith, "The Giriama Rising, 1914: Focus for Political Development in the Kenya Hinterland, 1850–1963," (Ph.D. diss., University of California, Los Angeles, 1973), 116ff.

122. Mohun to SD, 9 April 1896, CDZ 10; "Dar-es-Salaam to Bagamoyo (& Mbaruk's Town)," *ZG* (14 April 1897), 2.
123. The causes of decline are brilliantly analyzed in Frederick Cooper, *From Slaves to Squatters: Plantation Labor and Agriculture in Zanzibar and Coastal Kenya, 1890–1925* (New Haven, 1980). See also Mungeam, *Kenya*, 25–28, 59–60, 241.

CHAPTER 11

1. See Oliver, "Some Factors," 55, 63; Stuhlmann, *Emin Pascha*, 67, 403.
2. O'Neill quoted in Oliver, *Missionary Factor*, 115; Euan Smith to Salisbury, 28 June 1888, *PP* 1888 (c.5603), 25; Euan Smith to FO, 18 March 1888, 20 March 1888, E–110, ZA.
3. Michahelles, 5 October 1888, in Hessel, *Kolonisation*, 79; Leyden memo, 18 October 1888, FO 84/1894, and his note in *The Times* (14 November 1888), in Waddington to Goblet, 14 November 1888, AngD 835; Laws, 18 December 1887, *The Scotsman* (25 February 1888), 10.
4. Oliver, *Missionary Factor*, 101–103; Kenneth Ingham, *The Making of Modern Uganda* (London, 1958), 37–38; Ruth M. Slade, *English-Speaking Missions in the Congo Independent State (1878–1908)* (Bruxelles, 1959), 85–86; Ceulemans, *La Question Arabe*, 162–165. B. G. Martin, *Muslim Brotherhoods in Nineteenth-Century Africa* (Cambridge, 1976), 167, offers, without adequate supporting evidence, interesting speculation upholding a concerted Arab movement.
5. Among others rejecting the conspiracy theory are Renault, *Lavigerie*, I, 345; Brown, "Ujiji," 186–187.

CHAPTER 12

1. Macmillan, "Arab War," 270–276; this study is the basic source for the war.
2. Fotheringham, *Adventures*, 33; Fred L. M. Moir, "Englishmen and Arabs in East Africa," *Murray's Magazine* 4(1888), 629; Lugard, "Slave-Traders," 336; Hanna, *Beginnings of Nyasaland*, 81, 83. Hanna's study, although grounded in impressive research, must be used with caution since he accepts European views without critical reserve.
3. For the following account: Fotheringham, *Adventures*, 34ff.; Hawes to FO, 11 November 1887 (enc. Fotheringham to Hawes, 10 October 1887), 10 December 1887, FO 84/1829; Fotheringham and Bains to Hawes, 17 October–17 December 1887, and Tomory to Hawes, 14 January 1888, in Buchanan to FO, 16 January 1888, FO 84/1883; letter from Karonga, 21 October [1887], *SGM* 4(1888), 163; O'Neill to Salisbury, 20 January 1888, FO 84/1901; Moir, *After Livingstone*, 135ff. The most useful secondary accounts are: Macmillan, "Arab War," 271–273; Kalinga, "Ngonde Kingdom," 223 ff.; Wright and Lary, "Swahili Settlements," 565–569; P. T. Terry, "The Arab War on Lake Nyassa, 1887–1895," *NJ* 18(1965), 55–77; McCracken, *Politics and Christianity*, 103–104.
4. T. Cullen Young, *Notes on the History of the Tumbuka-Kamanga Peoples in the Northern Province of Nyasaland* (London, 1932), 70–71, 134–135; Nkonjera, "History of the Kamanga Tribe of Lake Nyassa: A Native Account," *JAS* 11(1911–1912), 231–234; Macmillan, "Arab War," 266–267; Kalinga, "Ngonde Kingdom," 14, 177–184, 250–258.

5. O'Neill to FO, 31 October 1887, FO 84/1846. Hawes later instructed the company agents to remain uninvolved: Hawes to FO, 16 November 1887, FO 84/1829.

6. Bains to Laws, 13 October 1887, quoted in McCracken, *Politics and Christianity*, 103–104; Hanna, *Beginnings of Nyasaland*, 83.

7. Kalinga, "Ngonde Kingdom," 237–259; Macmillan, "Arab War," 270.

8. McCracken, *Politics and Christianity*, 103–104.

9. Hawes to FO, 10 December 1887, FO 84/1829; Laws, 18 December 1887, Cross, 18 December 1887, *The Scotsman* (25 February 1888), 10; Karonga news, 7 December 1887, *The Times* (23 April 1888), 15; Moir to Penney, 27 April 1888, with O'Neill excerpt of 24 February 1888, A.1.VI, UMCA; Alfred Sharpe, *The Backbone of Africa* (London, 1921), 42; Cross information, *JMGS* 4(1888), 154; Buchanan to FO, 11 January 1888, 16 January 1888, FO 84/1883; Moir, *After Livingstone*, 140; O'Neill to FO, 10 February 1888, FO 84/1901.

10. O'Neill to Salisbury, 20 January 1888, FO 84/1901; O'Neill to Euan Smith, 15 January 1888, E–104, ZA; Henry E. O'Neill, "Notes on the Nyassa Region of East Africa," *JMGS* 4(1888), 98; Livingstone, *Laws*, 238–239.

11. See above, p. 79.

12. Laws, 22 August 1888, *HFMRFCS* (1889), 13–14; Johnson to Penney, 26 December 1887, A.1.VI, UMCA; Maples, *Maples*, 289; Lugard to Cross, 25 May 1888, Moir to Cross, 25 May 1888, *HFMRFCS* (1888), 307–308; Tomory to Thompson, 31 October 1887, 14 December 1887, CA 7, LMS.

13. Hawes to FO, 28 January 1888, FO 84/1883.

14. Buchanan to FO, 15 February 1888 (enc. Moir to Hawes, two of 8 February 1888, 11 February 1888), Buchanan to Hawes, 18 February 1888, FO 84/1883; Hawes to O'Neill, 8 February 1888, in O'Neill to Salisbury, 10 February 1888, FO 84/1901; Åke Holmberg, *African Tribes and European Agencies: Colonialism and Humanitarianism in British South and East Africa, 1870–1895* (N.p., 1966), 250–253; Livingstone, *Laws*, 240.

15. Fotheringham, *Adventures*, 147–155; Johnson, 30 April 1888, *CA* 6(1888), 94–97; Johnson to Frere, 11 April [1888], A.1.VI, UMCA; Buchanan to FO, 12 April 1888 (enc. Mlozi letters), FO 84/1883.

16. Buchanan to FO, 16 January 1888, FO 84/1883; O'Neill to Salisbury, 3 February 1888, FO 84/1901; Euan Smith to Salisbury, 2 July 1888, 11 August 1888 (with enc.), FO 84/1908; Lister to Euan Smith, 18 May 1888, E–102, O'Neill to Euan Smith, 23 June 1888, E–104, 14 July 1888, E–105, Khalifa to L. Nyasa Arabs, 7 July 1888, Khalifa to Jumbe et al., 10 August 1888, Khalifa to Euan Smith, 26 June 1888, O–1–16, ZA; Johnson, *African Reminiscences*, 150; Maples to Buchanan, 28 October 1888, *PP* 1888 (c.5601), 110.

17. Fotheringham notes, 21 and 26 January [1888], Fotheringham to African Lakes Company, undated, Johnson to Penney, c.1 May 1888, A.1.VI, UMCA; Buchanan to Hawes, 8 May 1888, J. Moir to Buchanan, 10 May 1888, FO 84/1883; Fotheringham, *Adventures*, 156ff.; F. D. Lugard, *The Rise of Our East African Empire* (Edinburgh and London, 1893), I, 60–61; Cross in *HFMRFCS* (1889), 239; Moir, *After Livingstone*, 143–144; Quelimane correspondent, 9 July 1888, *The Times* (31 August 1888), 8.

18. War Office board medical report, February 1888, in Thomson to FO, 23 August 1888, FO 84/1926; Perham, *Lugard Diaries*, I, 11.

19. See Dorothy Hammond and Alta Jablow, *The Africa that Never Was* (New York, 1970), 107–109.

20. Lugard, *East African Empire*, I, 21; Buchanan to Hawes, 24 April 1888,

FO 84/1883; Johnson to Penney, 21 February 1888, A.1.VI, UMCA.

21. Buchanan to FO, 20 May 1888, 13 July 1888, Lugard to Buchanan, 16 May 1888, 10 September 1888, Buchanan to Hawes, 16 June 1888, FO 84/1883; Fotheringham, *Adventures,* 177ff.; Lugard, *East African Empire,* I, 65ff.; Cross, 29 May 1888, 14 June 1888, 22 June 1888, *HFMRFCS* (1888), 308–309; Cross to Smith, 27 January 1888, *The Times* (17 May 1888), 6; J. Moir journal, 18 May 1888ff., ibid. (7 September 1888), 9, (11 October 1888), 13; "Extracts from the Diary and Letters of Peter Moore, 1888," *NJ* 11(1958), 33.

22. Cross to Smith, 20 August 1888, *HFMRFCS* (1889), 14.

23. Lugard to Buchanan, 4 December 1888, FO 84/1942; Fotheringham, *Adventures,* 194–218.

24. FO to Buchanan, 26 May 1888, FO 84/1883; Salisbury to Buchanan, 9 August 1888, Anderson note on O'Neill to Salisbury, 30 May 1888, FO 84/1901.

25. Jameson, *Rear Column,* 253; Trivier, *Voyage,* 283–286; Carson to Thompson, 27 June 1889, CA 7, LMS.

26. Lugard, *East African Empire,* I, 133–144; Fotheringham, *Adventures,* 219; Zanzibar news, *The Times* (11 February 1888), 5; Ewing, 12 February 1888, ibid. (14 February 1888), 10; Lugard, 15 January 1889, ibid., (18 April 1889), 10; Khalifa to Kopa Kopa, Mlozi, Msalama, 10 August 1888, O–1–16, ZA; Laws, 24 December 1888, *HFMRFCS* (1889), 111–112. For Lugard's opinions of Afro-Arabs, see above, p. 8.

27. Cross, 13 December 1888, *HFMRFCS* (1889), 112.

28. Johnston, *British Central Africa,* 76; Mlozi to Fotheringham, 15 November 1888, Lugard to Buchanan, 18 January 1889, FO 84/1942, 19 January 1889, in Hawes to FO, 8 April 1889, E–110, Euan Smith to FO, 3 January 1889, 14 January 1889, E–120, ZA.

29. Fotheringham, *Adventures,* 226–237; Lugard, *East African Empire,* I, 143–151; Buchanan to FO, 27 March 1889, Lugard to Buchanan, 1 March 1889, 5 April 1889, Laws to Buchanan, 30 May 1889, FO 84/1942; Hawes to Salisbury, 8 April 1889 (enc. Lugard to Euan Smith, 8 January 1889, Moir to Euan Smith, 7 February 1889), FO 84/1978.

30. Buchanan to FO, 8 April 1889, FO 84/1942; Portal to Salisbury, 2 June 1889, FO 84/1979; Fotheringham, *Adventures,* 237–238; Lugard, *East African Empire,* I, 159; Cross, 20 April 1889, 27 May 1889, 1 August 1889, *HFMRFCS* (1889), 239, 301, 364–365; Hawes to FO, 8 April 1889, E–110, ZA.

31. Portal to Salisbury, 4 May 1889, FO 84/1978, 6 July 1889, FO 84/1979.

32. Buchanan to FO, 29 August 1889, FO 84/1942; Hawes to Anderson, 7 May 1889, FO 84/1969. See also Rankin, 26 April 1889, *The Times* (30 April 1889), 10.

33. Anderson note, 13 June 1889, and other notes, on Lugard to Buchanan, 5 April 1889, Hawes to Salisbury, 8 April 1889, Portal to Salisbury, 4 May 1889, FO 84/1978. One official described Lugard as "a lunatic aiming at being a second Gordon." Robert Rhodes James, *Rosebery* (London, 1963), 264, 266.

34. Hanna, *Beginnings of Nyasaland,* 103; Cameron reports, *The Times* (23 April 1889), 9, (11 May 1889), 18.

35. Waller to Penney, 10 July 1888, A.1.VI, UMCA; Ewing to Salisbury, 10 March 1888, FO 84/1917.

36. For the following paragraphs: Johnston to Salisbury, 26 August 1889, 16 October 1889 (enc. treaty with Jumbe, 22 September 1889), FO 84/1969; Johnston to Br. Con. Zanzibar, 26 October 1889 (enc. treaty with Mlozi, 22 October 1889), B–5, ZA; Johnston report, 17 March 1890, FO 403/127; John-

ston to Salisbury, 1 February 1890, FO 84/2051; Fotheringham, *Adventures,*
272–279; Johnston, "British Central Africa," 713, 723–727, and *British Central
Africa,* 91–94; Moir, *After Livingstone,* 149–150; Oliver, *Johnston,* 161–164; Euan
Smith to FO, 4 March 1890 (enc. Khalifa letter), 4 April 1890, u.v., ZA; Murray
to Smith, 5 October 1889, *HFMRFCS* (1890), 107.

37. Fotheringham, *Adventures,* 295.

38. Lugard, in *The Times* (31 August 1889), 11, and *East African Empire,* I,
165–166; Oliver, *Johnston,* 166.

39. Hanna, *Beginnings of Nyasaland,* 154; Salisbury to Johnston, 24 March
1891, FO 84/2113.

40. Johnston, *British Central Africa,* 101ff.; Johnston report, 17 March 1890,
FO 403/127; Johnston to Salisbury, 18 July 1891, 24 July 1891, 24 November–
29 December 1891, FO 84/2114, and succeeding files; Heurtebise, 29 October
1891, *BMA* (1891–1892), 297–299; Eric Stokes, "Malawi Political Systems and
the Introduction of Colonial Rule, 1891–1896," in Eric Stokes and Richard
Brown, eds., *The Zambesian Past: Studies in Central African History* (Manchester,
1966), 360; Robin H. Palmer, "Johnston and Jameson: A Comparative Study in
the Imposition of Colonial Rule," in Pachai, *Early History of Malawi,* 301, 318.

41. Descamps journal, 12–13 August 1893, *MA* 6(1893–1894), 9; Moore,
"Diaries and Letters," 64, 66.

42. Merensky note, *AEC* 14(1893), 48–49; Richard, 27 November 1893, 7
December 1893, *MBB* 58(1894), 115; Buchanan to Salisbury, two of 29 March
1891, FO 84/2115.

43. Johnston to Salisbury, 20 February 1892, FO 84/2197; Johnston to
Rosebery, 8 April 1893, FO 2/54; Johnston to Br. Con. Zanzibar, 27 August
1893 (a note accompanying two Arabs returned to Zanzibar by Johnston), B–25,
ZA.

44. Sharpe to Johnston, 17 December 1892, FO 2/54; Shepperson, "The
Jumbe," 199–201; Moloney, *With Stairs,* 269; Horace Waller, "Looking Lake-
wards," *CA* 10(1892), 128; Langworthy, "Swahili Influence," 598–602, and
"Central Malawi," 38–39; Johnston report, 31 March 1894, *PP* 1894 (c.7504),
29; Johnston to Salisbury, 20 February 1892, FO 84/2197; Sim, 19 November
1894, 1 December 1894, Glossop, 4 January 1895, *CA* 13(1895), 37, 52–53, 71;
Hardinge to Kimberly, 21 March 1895, 25 April 1895, FO 107/35.

45. Richard report, 1891, *MBB* 56(1892), 76.

46. Johnston, *British Central Africa,* 135–143; Reuters agent, Blantyre, 20
December 1895, *CA* 14(1896), 66–68.

CHAPTER 13

1. For previous Buganda events, see above, pp. 91, 100.

2. O'Flaherty to Lang, 26 July 1885, Mackay to Lang, May 1885, 29 September 1885, O'Flaherty to Wright, October 1885, G3.A6/02, CMS; Gray,
"Diaries of Emin [3]," 151.

3. Mackay to CMS, 10–20 December 1885, G3.A5/03, CMS; Robert P.
Ashe, *Two Kings of Uganda* (London, 1889), 224.

4. Mackay to Kirk, 30 January 1886, in Kirk to FO, 10 May 1886, FO 84/
1773. For the German trader, see below, p. 211.

5. Holmwood to FO, 30 September 1886, FO 84/1775.

6. J. F. Faupel, *African Holocaust: The Story of the Uganda Martyrs* (New York,

1962), 82ff.; Cussac, *Lourdel,* 192–193; Rowe, "Purge of Christians," 57ff., and "Sematimba," 185–187.

7. Mackay to Holmwood, 19 April 1887, in Macdonald to FO, 27 August 1887, FO 84/1853; Mackay to Holmwood, 29 May 1887, in Macdonald to FO, 25 October 1887, FO 84/1854; Mackay journal, 6 June 1887 on, G3.A5 /04, CMS.

8. Mackay to Br. Con. Zanzibar, 28 February 1888, in Euan Smith to Salisbury, 6 May 1888, FO 84/1907; Mackay to Euan Smith, 18 April 1888, in Lacau to Goblet, 8 July 1888, PZ 10; Euan Smith to Salisbury, 27 August 1888, FO 84/1908.

9. Rubaga journal, 1 August 1886, *CTSM* (3me trim. 1887), 580–581; Gordon to Parker, 6 March 1888, Gordon to Mackay, 24 April 1888, G3.A5/05, CMS; Mackay to Ashe, 8 March 1887, *CMIR* 12(1887), 629; Cussac, *Lourdel,* 209–212; Abbé Nicq, *Le Père Siméon Lourdel* (Alger, 1922), 439–444; Lourdel, 25 June 1886, *BMA* (1887), 21; Livinhac, 6 November 1888, *BMA* (1888–1889), 505–506; Rowe, "Purge of Christians," 70–71; Kiwanuka, *Buganda,* 204–209; David Kavulu, "The Islamic-Christian Civil Wars in Buganda, 1888–90," in Social Science Council, University of East Africa, *War and Society in Africa,* vol. I, *History, Religious Studies* (Nairobi, 1969), 274–280; James Miti, "History of Buganda," in David Robinson and Douglas Smith, *Sources of the African Past: Case Studies of Five Nineteenth-Century African Societies* (New York, 1979), 101ff.; Michael Twaddle, "The Muslim Revolution in Buganda," *JAS* 71(1972), 57–64; John Gray, "The Year of the Three Kings of Buganda," *UJ* 14(1950), 21–24.

10. Nicq, *Lourdel,* 443ff.; Gordon to Lang, 7 November 1888, Mackay to Lang, 27 November 1888, G3.A5/06, CMS; Ashe, *Two Kings,* 262ff., and *Chronicles,* 114–121; Gray, "Three Kings," 24–28; Kalema to Khalifa, 6 December 1888, in Euan Smith to Salisbury, 29 April 1890, FO 84/2061; Kiwanuka, *Buganda,* 210–218; Kavulu, "Civil Wars," 282–285.

11. Mackay to Euan Smith, 19 March 1889, in Euan Smith to Salisbury, 26 November 1889, FO 84/1891; Euan Smith to FO, 11 January 1889, E–120, 27 February 1889 (enc. Khalifa to Euan Smith, 20 January 1889, 15 February 1889), u.v., ZA. The priests, however, praised Said bin Sayf for assistance during this troubled time: Cussac, *Lourdel,* 213.

12. Hooper to Lang, 12 October 1888, Mackay to Lang, 23 October 1888, 6 June 1889, Deekes to Lang, 7 November 1888, Walker to Mackay, 27 September 1889, Gordon to Lang, 24 July 1889, G3.A5/06, CMS; Mackay to Euan Smith, 10 June 1889, in Euan Smith to Salisbury, 26 November 1889, FO 84/ 1981; Juma bin Salim to Hashir bin Swellam, undated, in Euan Smith to Salisbury, 14 February 1889, FO 84/2059; Stokes to Euan Smith, 11 January 1890, B–5, ZA; Denoit, 30 September 1889, *CTSM* (1er trim. 1890), 358–359; Cussac, *Lourdel,* 222–231; Nicq, *Lourdel,* 464ff.; Livinhac, 3 November 1889, *BMA* (1890), 663–666; Gray, "Three Kings," 28ff.; Kavulu, "Civil Wars," 284–291.

13. Schynse, *Stanley et Emin,* 50–51; Gordon to Mackay, 27 September 1889, 3 October 1889, 19 October 1889, Walker to Mackay, 21 October 1889, Walker to Lang, 19 December 1889, Gordon to Lang, 18 March 1890, G3.A5/ 06, CMS; Denoit, 30 September 1889, 10 October 1889, 13 October 1889, Zanzibar journal, 15 February 1890, *CTSM* (1er trim. 1890), 373–374, 378–379, 347; Lourdel journal, *BMA* (1891), 49–55; Perham, *Lugard Diaries,* II, 16; Walker to father, 24 October 1889, 4 January 1890, *CMIR* 15(1890), 367, 621; J. W. Nyakatura (trans. Teopista Muganwa; ed. Godfrey N. Uzoigwe), *Anatomy of an African Kingdom: A History of Bunyoro-Kitara* (Garden City, 1973), 143–146.

14. P. L. McDermott, *British East Africa, or IBEA* (London, 1895), 111ff.;

Stokes to Euan Smith, 26 February 1890, Mwanga to Jackson, 15 June 1889, both in Euan Smith to Salisbury, 15 April 1890, FO 84/2061; Gordon to Lang, 8 May 1890, G3.A5/06, CMS; Henry M. Stanley, *In Darkest Africa* (London, 1890), II, 349–352; Mwanga to Euan Smith, 28 October 1889, B–12, ZA.

15. Gordon to Lang, 15 August 1890, G3.A5/06, 2 October 1890, Walker to J. Walker, 1 November 1890, G3.A5/07, CMS; Hirth, 4 October 1890, *BMA* (1891–1892), 57.

16. Oliver, *Missionary Factor,* 148; Kiwanuka, *Buganda,* 220ff.

17. Perham, *Lugard Diaries,* II, 158ff., III, 65ff.; Hirth, 22 May 1891, Rubaga diary, 28 March 1892, *BMA* (1891–1892), 201, 454; Lugard to IBEA, March–August 1892, *PP* 1893 (c.6848), 71–74; Lugard to IBEA, 24 December 1890–7 January 1891, *PP* 1892 (c.6555), 102–105; Baskerville journal, 6 May 1892 on, Baskerville to Stock, 10 May 1892, G3.A5/08, CMS; Stuhlmann, *Emin Pascha,* 197; Kiwanuka, *Buganda,* 236–239.

18. Euan Smith to Salisbury, 18 April 1890, 21 June 1890, u.v., Currie to Euan Smith, 29 July 1890, E–124, ZA; Ali bin Sultan escaped major punishment; see *Mackay,* 391.

19. For the future of the Muslims in Buganda: Kiwanuka, *Buganda,* 236–239; Oded, *Islam in Uganda,* 309ff.

CHAPTER 14

1. Heudebert, *Révoil,* 364, 376; Taylor to Lang, 14 December 1886, Mackay journal, 6 June–1 August 1887, G3.A5/04, CMS; Kirk to FO, 3 June 1886, E–93, Stokes to Holmwood, 16 July 1886, E–90, Holmwood to FO, 10 July 1887, E–99, ZA; Hassing and Bennett, "Trip across Tanganyika," 137; Muxworthy to Thompson, 15 February 1886, CA 6, LMS; Stuhlmann, *Emin Pascha,* 59–63; Lake Tanganyika White Fathers journal, undated, *BMA* (1887), 125–127; Stanley, *Dark Continent,* I, 44; Waller, *Livingstone's Journals,* II, 177–178, 222; Becker, *Troisième Expédition,* 171–172; Barghash to Said bin Juma and others, 30 September 1884, in Ledoulx to MAE, 22 October 1884, PZ 6.

2. Ledoulx to MAE, 27 April 1885, PZ 7; Blackburn to Lang, 24 September 1885, G3.A6/02, CMS; Brode, *Tippo Tib,* 172–175; "Deutsche Handelspioniere in Afrika," *DKZ* 3(1886), 473–479; "Die Meyer'sche Handelsexpedition ins Innere Afrikas," ibid., 810; Kirk to FO, 11 March 1886, E–93, ZA; Mackay to Kirk, 24 August 1886, in Holmwood to FO, 18 October 1886, FO 84/1775; Raffray to MAE, 17 November 1886, PZ 8; Hassing and Bennett, "Trip across Tanganyika," 138; Kipalpala journal, 11 September 1885–17 May 1886, *CTSM* (4me trim. 1886), 98ff., (1er trim. 1887), 248–259.

3. "Die Meyer'sche Handelsexpedition," 816; Heudebert, *Révoil,* 359–360, 380–389; "Die deutsche Handel in Ost-Afrika und die Araber," *DKB* 1(1890), 182–183; Stokes to Holmwood, 5 November 1886, Stokes to Kirk, 11 February 1887, E–90, Holmwood to Anderson, 23 November 1886, E–95, ZA; Hooper to Lang, 24 October 1886, G3.A5/03, CMS; Raffray to MAE, 17 November 1886, PZ 8; Mackay to Kirk, 30 January 1886, in Kirk to FO, 10 May 1886, FO 84/1773; Brooks, 30 September 1886, in Ashe, *Two Kings,* 245–246; Brode, *Tippo Tib,* 175–180; Wilhelm Junker, *Travels in Africa during the Years 1882–1886* (London, 1892), 559–562; Kipalapala journal, 5 May–24 July 1886, 24 September–3 November 1886, *CTSM* (1er trim. 1887), 257–271, (2me trim. 1887), 435–442; Wissmann, *Second Journey,* 269–270.

4. Michahelles to Macdonald, 20 September 1887, Macdonald to Micha-

helles, 30 September 1887, E–98, Stokes to Euan Smith, 12 May 1890, B–8, Euan Smith to FO, 21 May 1890, u.v., ZA; Mackay to Ashe, 17 April 1887, G3.A5/05, CMS; "Die deutsche Handel," 183; Wissmann, *Second Journey*, 232, 238; Schmidt, *Araberaufstandes*, 184, 217–219; Stuhlmann, *Emin Pascha*, 807; Zanzibar journal, 12–14 November 1886, *CTSM* (1er trim. 1887), 320–321; Ottavi to MAE, 30 June 1890, CCZ 7bis; Jameson, *Rear Column*, 285; Renault, *Lavigerie*, I, 317–318.

5. Muxworthy to Holmwood, 7 April 1887, Stokes to Kirk, 11 February 1887, E–97, ZA. For some account of his life: Anne Luck, *Charles Stokes in Africa* (Nairobi, 1972).

6. Iain R. Smith, *The Emin Pasha Relief Expedition, 1886–1890* (Oxford, 1972), offers the best account.

7. Euan Smith to FO, 18 March 1890, E–126, 3 April 1890, u.v., 19 May 1890, E–125, ZA; Euan Smith to Salisbury, 21 May 1890, FO 84/2061; Schweitzer, *Emin*, II, 41; Schmidt, "Die Mpapua-Expedition," 275–280.

8. Schweitzer, *Emin*, II, 55–56; Stuhlmann, *Emin Pascha*, 30; Carl Peters (trans. H. W. Dulcken), *New Light on Dark Africa* (London, 1891), 517–518.

9. Emin to Peters, 10 October 1890, *MGGW* 34(1891), 48; Euan Smith to Salisbury, 25 April 1890, E–125, ZA; Stuhlmann, *Emin Pascha*, 2ff.; Langheld, *Zwanzig Jahre*, 22ff.; Peters, *New Light*, 541–542; Schweitzer, *Emin*, II, 76–77.

10. Schweitzer, *Emin*, II, 78–79; Emin letter, *AEC* 12(1891), 4–5; Euan Smith to Salisbury, 3 April 1890, 22 September 1890, u.v., ZA; Karl Hespers, ed., *P. Schynse's letzte Reisen: Briefe und Tagebuchblätter* (Köln, 1892), 6; Langheld, *Zwanzig Jahre*, 46–48 (with text of the treaty); G. Leblond, *La Père Auguste Achte* (Alger, 1928), 71–72; Stuhlmann, *Emin Pascha*, 66–68; Schmidt, *Araberaufstandes*, 342–343; "Emin Pascha und Wissmann," *KJ* 5(1892), 17–19; Dr. Latrille, "Eine Unteredung mit dem Reichskommissar Major v. Wissmann," *NOM* 4(1890), 162; Bennett, "Isike," 62.

11. H. Hermann von Schweinitz, *Deutsch-Ost-Afrika in Krieg und Frieden* (Berlin, 1894), 55–56, 89, 91; Langheld, *Zwanzig Jahre*, 54; Stuhlmann, *Emin Pascha*, 61–64; Schynse, *Emin et Stanley*, 46; Lionel Decle, *Three Years in Savage Africa* (London, 1898), 352.

12. Schweinitz, *Deutsch-Ost-Afrika*, 43ff.; Spring, *Selbsterlebtes*, 67ff.; Prince, *Gegen Araber*, 194–212, and "Bericht," 204; Jacques journal, September 1891, *MA* 4(1891–1892), 96–97; Long journal, 20 August–19 September 1892, *MA* 5(1892–1893), 145–151; H. Schwesinger, "Vörgange in Tabora," *DKB* 3(1892), 444–446; Baumann, *Masailand*, 105; Moloney, *With Stairs*, 68–71; Schmidt, *Deutschlands Kolonien*, 214–215; "Bericht des Leutnants Meyer," *DKZ* 5(1892), 155–156; "Die Expedition des Antisklaverei-Komitees," *KJ* 5(1892), 163–169; Bennett, "Isike," 63–67; Andrew Roberts, "The Nyamwezi," in Roberts, *Tanzania*, 140–144.

13. Langheld, *Zwanzig Jahre*, 55; Hespers, *P. Schynse*, 8; Schweitzer, *Emin*, II, 80–81; Stuhlmann, *Emin Pascha*, 71.

14. For the Magu Arabs: Mackay to Euan Smith, 1 January 1890, B–5, ZA; Mackay to Lang, 28 December 1889, Walker to Lang, 17 July 1890, 4 September 1890, 17 September 1890, G3.A5/06, CMS; Peters, *Deutsch-Ostafrikanische Schutzgebiet*, 182, and *New Light*, 486–487; Schynse, 4 October 1890, *MGGW* 34(1891), 47; Stuhlmann, *Emin Pascha*, 234; Bresson, 31 January 1891, *MA* 3(1890–1891), 110; Hirth, 18 December 1889, 28 October 1890, *CTSM* (1er trim. 1890), 356, and *MC* 23(1891), 133–134.

15. Bresson, 31 January 1891, *MA* 3(1890–1891), 111; Hirth, 28 October 1890, *MC* 23(1891), 134–135; Swann interview, *ZG* (18 October 1893), 3;

Schmidt, *Deutschlands Kolonien*, 215–216, and *"Die Mpapua-Expedition,"* 278; Stuhlmann, *Emin Pascha*, 107–113, 832; Schweitzer, *Emin*, II, 96, 106; Ottavi to MAE, 20 January 1891, CCZ 8; Perham, *Lugard Diaries*, II, 35; Lugard, *East African Empire*, II, 55; Leblond, *Achte*, 80–81.

    16. Iliffe, *Modern Tanganyika*, 215, 543. See also August H. Nimtz, Jr., *Islam and Politics in East Africa: The Sufi Order in Tanzania* (Minneapolis, 1980).

CHAPTER 15

    1. Stanley, *Congo*, I, 120ff.; Camille Coquilhat, *Sur le Haut-Congo* (Paris, 1888), 166–167, 178; Abed bin Salim to Tippu Tip, 20 Rajeb 1301, Tippu Tip to Topan, undated, Tippu Tip to Barghash, undated excerpt, all in Kirk to Granville, 23 October 1884, E–83, Abed bin Salim to Barghash, 2 Rajab 1301 (16 May 1884), in Kirk to Salisbury, 31 July 1885, E–87, ZA; Ledoulx to MAE, 4 July 1884, CCZ 5, 22 October 1884, PZ 6; Cambier to Storms, 25 February 1884, SP.

    2. Kirk to FO, 23 September 1884, E–83, ZA.

    3. Ledoulx to MAE, 15 January 1885, PZ 7; Giraud to Strauch, 16 June 1884, Strauch to Becker, 18 October 1884, SP; Elst to Caraman, 14 April 1885, CPC 18.

    4. Storms to AIA, 16 April 1884, SP; *AEC* 5(1884), 282; Giraud, *Afrique Equatoriale*, 508; Brooks to LMS, 6 August 1884, CA 5, LMS. See also M. Luwel, "Cambier," 91, and *H. H. Johnston et H. M. Stanley sur le Congo* (Bruxelles, 1978), 27–28.

    5. Kirk to Granville, 6 July 1885, Kirk to Salisbury, 31 July 1885, E–87, ZA.

    6. Ceulemans, *La Question Arabe*, 66.

    7. See references in fn. 1, above. For ivory sales from 1884 to 1887, Ceulemans, *La Question Arabe*, 194.

    8. Coquilhat, *Haut-Congo*, 227, 400–406 (with text of treaty); J.-P. Cuypers, *Alphonse Vangele (1848–1939), d'après des Documents Inédits* (Bruxelles, 1960), 25–26; J. R. Werner, *A Visit to Stanley's Rear-Guard* (Edinburgh and London, 1889), 88–91; F. Bontinck, "La Station des Stanley Falls (10 Déc. 1883–5 Juillet 1884)," *BSARSDM* 4(1979), 615–630; E. H. Taunt report, in U.S., 49th Congress, 2d Session, Senate-Ex. Doc. No. 77, pp. 38–39; Hore to Thompson, 24 July 1886, CA 6, LMS.

    9. Coquilhat, *Haut-Congo*, 317, 407–411; Cuypers, *Vangele*, 26–32; George Hawker, *The Life of George Grenfell, Congo Missionary and Explorer* (London, 1909), 215; Grenfell, "Tributaries of the Congo," 611, 632; Vivian to Granville, 1 May 1885, in Lister to Kirk, 8 June 1885, E–85, ZA.

    10. Jean Stengers, *Belgique et Congo: l'Elaboration de la Charte Coloniale* (Bruxelles, 1963), 32; Renault, *Lavigerie*, I, 319–320; Eduard Van der Smissen, *Léopold II et Beernaert d'après leur Correspondence Inédit* (Bruxelles, 1920), I, 413–417; Vivian to Salisbury, 2 July 1886, FO 123/221.

    11. Cuypers, *Vangele*, 33–35; Ceulemans, *La Question Arabe*, 68–73; Marcel Luwel, *Sir Francis de Winton: Administrateur General du Congo, 1884–1886* (Tervuren, 1964), 108–121, 258; Oskar Lenz, *Wanderungen in Afrika* (Wien, 1895), 65; Lenz, 19 February 1886, *MGGW* 29(1886), 264–265; Oscar Baumann, "Die Station der Stanley-Fälle," ibid., 506–507, 650–656; Coquilhat, *Haut-Congo*, 412–425; Lenz to de Winton, 20 February 1886, in Francis de Winton, "The Congo Free State," *PRGS* 8(1886), 616.

    12. Holmwood to FO, 8 January 1887, E–99, ZA; Cazenave to Chimay, 16

January 1887, 27 January 1887 (enc. Muhammad bin Said to Tippu Tip, 14 Shawal 1303 [1 September 1886]), CPC 18; Wissmann, *Second Journey,* 231–232 (with information from Juma Merikani); F. M. De Thier, *Singhitini, la Stanleyville Musulmane* (Bruxelles, 1963), 26–29; *Le Moniteur Belge* (11 December 1887); *IB* (21 December 1887); Coquilhat, *Haut-Congo,* 429–462; Hawker, *Grenfell,* 232–234, 238; Ward, *Five Years,* 196–213; Werner, *Rear-Guard,* 91ff.; Schynse, *Stanley et Emin,* 55; Ceulemans, *La Question Arabe,* 73–78.

13. Moinet to Storms, 10 February 1886, SP.

14. Dorothy Stanley, ed., *The Autobiography of Sir Henry Morton Stanley* (London, 1909), 345–346; Gosselin to Iddesleigh, 25 November 1886, in Lister to Holmwood, 14 December 1886, E–92, ZA; Gosselin to Stanley, 19 December 1886, FO 123/221.

15. Wissmann, *Second Journey,* 220ff.; Makay to Holmwood, 19 April 1887, in Macdonald to FO, 27 August 1887, FO 84/1853 (for a reaction from Buganda to the news).

16. Hore, *Tanganyika,* 274.

17. L. Joubert, "De Kibanga à Bagamoyo," *MA* 1(1888), 37.

18. Junker, *Travels,* 565–566; Pruen, *Arab and African,* 213–214.

19. Raffray to MAE, 17 November 1886, PZ 8.

20. Cazenave to Chimay, 16 January 1887, 14 February 1887, CPC 18; Lenz interview, *JB* (29 April 1887).

21. Tippu Tip, *Maisha,* 151; Holmwood to Iddesleigh, 24 December 1886, E–95, Holmwood to FO, 8 January 1887, E–99, ZA; Wylde note on the preceding dispatch, FO 84/1777.

22. A.-J. W[auters], "La Huitième Traversée de l'Afrique Centrale de Banana à Zanzibar par le Lieutenant Gleerup," *MG* 3(1886), 74–75; Lenz, 20 April 1886, 19 May 1886, 1 June 1886, *MGGW* 29(1886), 577–592; Wissmann, *Second Journey,* 183ff.; Ludwig Wolf, "Reisen in Central Afrika," *VGEB* 14(1887), 93.

23. Stanley, *Darkest Africa,* I, 63–71, 117–119; J. Scott Keltie, *The Story of Emin's Rescue as Told in Stanley's Letters* (Boston, 1890), 163; Werner, *Rear-Guard,* 308–309; Holmwood to FO, 3 March 1887, E–99, Stanley to Euan Smith, 17 December 1889, in Euan Smith to FO, 28 December 1889, E–113, ZA; Stanley to de Winton, 31 August 1889, *The Times* (21 December 1889), 8; Jameson, *Rear Column,* 7; Ward, *Five Years,* 215–216; Ceulemans, *La Question Arabe,* 98–103; Smith, *Emin Pasha,* 83ff.

24. Tippu Tip interview in *MG* 4(1887), 49.

25. Swann to Thompson, 20 June 1890, CA 8, LMS; *Mackay,* 368; Horace Waller, "The Mutual Relations of Commerce and the Church's Missions," *ML* 8(1890), 377.

26. Vivian to Stanley, 9 April 1897, FO 123/232; Werner, *Rear-Guard,* 244; Charles Warlomont, *Correspondance d'Afrique* (Bruxelles, 1888), 29–30; Baert in Herbert Ward, *My Life in Stanley's Rear Guard* (London, 1891), 109–110; Ceulemans, *La Question Arabe,* 104–107.

27. Becker, Le Consulat de Zanzibar, Af–6–B–A, MAEB. Others also made the claim.

28. See below, p. 226.

29. Tippu Tip, *Maisha,* 153. See also Renault, *Lavigerie,* I, 338.

30. Werner, *Rear-Guard,* 244, 308; Ward, *Five Years,* 217.

31. Tippu Tip to Holmwood, 21 July 1887, ZM; Stanley to Mackinnon, 23 June 1887, MP 55; Jameson, *Rear Column,* 74.

32. Ward, *Five Years,* 167; George Walter Barttelot, *The Life of Edmund*

Musgrave Barttelot (London, 1890), 230; Jameson, *Rear Column,* 293–294.

33. A. J. Wauters, "Les Derniers Evénements du Haut Congo," *MG* 5(1888), 81–83; J. R. Werner, "The Congo, and the Ngala and Aruwimi Tributaries," *PRGS* 11(1889), 349–350; Barttelot, *Life,* 240–246; Jameson, *Rear Column,* 301–305; Ceulemans, *La Question Arabe,* 117–121; Troup, *With Stanley,* 253–263; Pierre Salomon, *Le Voyage de Van Kerckhoven aux Stanley Falls et au Camp de Yambuya (1888)* (Bruxelles, 1978), 15ff.

34. Vivian to Salisbury, 25 August 1888, 25 September 1888, FO 123/244.

35. Glave, *Six Years,* 209; Tippu Tip to Muhammad bin Massud and Saif bin Ahmed, undated, in Euan Smith to FO, 2 January 1889, E–120, ZA. Copies of most letters relating to Congo matters from Tippu Tip and other Arabs were passed on by the British to the Belgians. For examples, Ceulemans, *La Question Arab,* 115–117.

36. Tippu Tip to Portal, 19 March 1889, in Portal to Salisbury, 31 July 1889, FO 84/1979; Ward, *Stanley's Rear Guard,* 141; Vivian to Salisbury, 12 September 1889, FO 123/259; Tippu Tip to Br. Con. Zanzibar, 20 October 1888, in Portal to Salisbury, 15 June 1889, FO 84/1970.

37. Thys to Leopold, 25 October 1886, in P. Daye, *Léopold II* (Paris, 1934), 303.

38. "La Tribu des Bazoko," *CI* 1(1892), 67; "Le Capitaine Roget," ibid., 105; Chapaux, *Le Congo,* 170–174; Louis Chaltin, *Léopold II et l'Etat Indépendent du Congo* (Anvers, 1926), 9; Dhanis journal, 24 October–12 March 1889, DP; Ceulemans, *La Question Arabe,* 153–161.

39. Parminter letter, *BSAF* (1888–1889), 481–482; Van Kerckhoven to Dhanis, 23 February 1889, fragment of a letter (? January 1893), DP; Ceulemans, *La Question Arabe,* 166.

40. "Le Lieutenant le Clément de Saint-Marcq," *CI* 2(1893), 169; Trivier, *Voyage,* 41; *MG* 6(1889), 32, 43, 60, 75, 100; Tobback, 4 March 1889, 9 April 1889, ibid., 66–67; Baert interview, *IB* (23 February 1889).

41. Van Kerckhoven report, 5 July 1889, in Ceulemans, *La Question Arabe,* 170.

42. Sarita Ward, *A Valiant Gentleman: Being the Biography of Herbert Ward, Artist and Man of Action* (London, 1927), 107–108. See also Trivier, *Voyage,* 85–86.

43. Ward, *Stanley's Rear Guard,* 65.

44. Middleton, *Jephson Diary,* 73; Ward, *Voice from the Congo,* 73.

45. Ward, *Stanley's Rear Guard,* 65; Trivier, 10 April 1889, *MG* 7(1890), 7–8. Trivier's letter also offers a useful picture of a day in the Kasongo life of Muhammad bin Said.

46. M. van Ronslé, "De Bangala aux Stanley-Falls," *MG* 7(1890), 94; Troup, *With Stanley,* 236; Jameson, *Rear Column,* 278; Trivier, *Voyage,* 104ff.; "Les Arabes sur le Haut Congo," *MG* 8(1891), 84 (information from Hodister); Aleksander Lopasic, *Commissaire General Dragutin Lerman, 1863–1918: A Contribution to the History of Central Africa* (Tervuren, 1971), 145–147.

47. Trivier, *Voyage,* 148ff.; Zanzibar correspondent, 2 November 1890, *The Times* (3 November 1890), 5.

48. G. A. von Götzen, *Durch Afrika von Ost nach West* (Berlin, 1895), 314; Slade, *Missions,* 84.

49. Stengers, "Congo before 1914," 267, 276.

50. Lysle E. Meyer, "Henry S. Sanford and the Congo: A Reassessment," *IJAHS* 4(1971), 37; Ceulemans, *La Question Arabe,* 224–235.

51. *MG* 7(1890), 50.

52. Swann, *Slave Hunters,* 173; Stanley, *Darkest Africa,* II, 428–429; Brode, *Tippoo Tib,* 216–217; Euan Smith to Mackinnon, 30 December 1889, MP 4; Portal to Salisbury, 27 June 1889, 6 July 1889, FO 84/1979; Euan Smith to FO, 28 January 1890, 3 April 1890, u.v., 26 December 1889, E–113, Mathews to Euan Smith, 23 December 1889, E–118, Currie to Euan Smith, 4 March 1890, E–123, Baring to Euan Smith, 3 April 1890, 4 April 1890 (passing on information from Stanley), Euan Smith to Baring, 3 April 1890, E–125, Johnston to Euan Smith, 17 February 1890, Euan Smith to Baring, 17 February 1890, Baring to Euan Smith, 17 February 1890, Euan Smith to Johnston, 18 February 1890, E–126, ZA.

53. De Thier, *Singhitini,* 53; Bridoux, 6 September 1890, *APF,* 62(1890), 278; Sharpe to Johnston, 8 September 1890, in Johnston to Salisbury, 3 May 1891, FO 84/2114.

54. Leopold to Euan Smith, 8 April 1890, FO 123/272.

55. Euan Smith to Leopold, 3 May 1890, B–7, ZA; Ceulemans, *La Question Arabe,* 176, 179–184.

56. Tobback to Tippu Tip and Rashid bin Muhammad, 2 April 1891, in Portal to Salisbury, 27 August 1891, FO 84/2149; S. J. S. Cookey, *Britain and the Congo Question, 1885–1913* (New York, 1968), 9–10; A. J. Wauters, *Histoire Politique du Congo Belge* (Bruxelles, 1911), 92–94, 122, 127, 184; *MG* 3 (1886), 63.

57. Vivian to Salisbury, 17 October 1891, FO 123/291; Eetvelde to Vivian, 24 October 1891, in Sanderson to Portal, 5 November 1891, E–133, ZA; Lister to Vivian, 31 October 1891, FO 123/290; Renault, *Lavigerie,* I, 425.

58. A. Roeykens, "Le Baron Léon de Béthune et la Politique Religieuse de Léopold en Afrique," *Zaïre* 10(1956), 244–245; "La Force Publique de l'Etat du Congo," *CI* 1(1892), 58–59.

59. Chapaux, *Le Congo,* 232ff.; Milz to Gov. Gen. Congo, 30 November 1890, 17 January 1891, Vangele, 12 January 1891, *IB* (9 July 1891); Ponthier to Gov. Gen. Congo, 22 October 1891, *IB* (25 March 1892); Ponthier interview, *EB* (18 October 1892), and report, *EB* (5 February 1894); Cuypers, *Vangele,* 65–67; Bannister to FO, 24 December 1893, FO 629/3; Ponthier, 29 October 1891, *BSAF* (1891–1892), 291–294; R. Dorsey Mohun, "The Death of Emin Pasha," *Century Magazine* 27(1894–1895), 591; A. J. Wauters, "L'Expedition Hodister," *MG* 9(1892), 99; Van der Smissen, *Léopold et Beernaert,* II, 221.

60. Sefu to Tippu Tip, 3 February 1892, in Portal to FO, 24 August 1892, E–140, ZA.

61. Hinck, 15 October 1891, *MA* 3(1891–1892), 110–112. For Jacques, see below, p. 251.

62. A. Hodister, "De Bangala à Nyangoué," *MG* 7(1890), 120; Lenz, 22 November 1885, *MGGW* 29(1886), 147; Renault, *Lavigerie,* II, 418; M. Coosemans, "Arthur Hodister," *BCB,* I, 514–516; "Arthur Hodister," *CI* 1(1892), 129; "Les Arabes du Haut Congo," 131.

63. Margery, 23 March 1892, Hodister excerpts, 23 March 1892, 6 April 1892, *MG* 9(1892), 59, 69; Tobback report, 14 March 1892, M. no. 3(561), MCB.

64. Reports from various private and official sources, *MG* 9(1892), 81–83, 92–103; Chapaux, *Le Congo,* 252–259; Hinck interview, press clippings, DP; *ZG* (16 November 1892).

65. Tobback report, *EB* (20 August 1892); Chaltin, 29 June 1892, *MG* 9(1892), 93; Ceulemans, *La Question Arabe,* 306–311.

66. Monson to Rosebery, 17 October 1892, 18 August 1892, FO 123/306; *EB* (17 October 1892); *JB* (29 July 1892); [M. Pauwels], *Aux Belges! Vérités sur le Congo par un Echappé au Massacre de l'Expedition Hodister* (Anvers, n.d.).

67. Edgard Verdick, *Les Premiers Jours au Katanga (1890–1903)* (Bruxelles, 1952), 18–19; Chapaux, *Le Congo*, 186–187; Oscar Michaux, *Au Congo: Carnet de Campagne: Episodes & Impressions de 1889 à 1897* (Namur, 1913), 94–100; "L'Expedition Le Marinel de Lousambo à Bena Kamba," *MG* 8(1891), 39; M. Parminter, "Sur le Kassai et de Sankuru," *MG* 10(1893), 80; Constant de Decken, *Deux Ans au Congo* (Anvers, 1900), 183, 207–208.

68. Ceulemans, *La Question Arabe*, 346.

69. Alex. Delcommune, *Vingt Années de Vie Africaine* (Bruxelles, 1922), II, 59–60; Dr. Briart, "Sur le Lomami," *MG* 8(1891), 124.

70. Hinde, *Congo Arabs*, 71–72, 85–92, and "Three Years' Travel in the Congo Free State," *GJ* 5(1895), 429–432; Janssens and Cateaux, *Les Belges au Congo*, I, 76–82; "La Campagne du Baron Dhanis Racontée par lui-même," *MA* 6(1893–1894), 380; Comeliau, *Dhanis*, 65, 73–81, Wahis to Dhanis, 29 July 1892, Scheerlinck to Dhanis, 23 August 1892, DP; Michaux, *Au Congo*, 162–167.

71. Lippens and De Bruyne to Dhanis, 6 October 1892, DP.

72. Hinde, *Congo Arabs*, 96–117; Dhanis, "Campagne," 380; Comeliau, *Dhanis*, 82–93; Louis Chaltin, "La Question Arab au Congo," *B. de la Soc. d'Etudes Coloniales* 5(1894), 184–185; Scheerlinck to Dhanis, 21 October 1892, 22 October 1892, 4 November 1892, 14 November 1892, 15 November 1892, 19 November 1892, De Bruyne to Dhanis, 18 October 1892, Duchesne to Dhanis, 10 October 1892, 16 November 1892, De Bruyne to Scheerlinck, 27 October 1892, Michaux interview, press clippings, DP; Michaux, *Au Congo*, 168–179; Janssens and Cateaux, *Les Belges au Congo*, 83–92.

73. Rashid to Tippu Tip, 3 December 1892, in Rodd to FO, 17 April 1893, E–144, ZA; Rashid to Tippu Tip, 23 December 1892, in Rodd to Rosebery, 11 May 1893, FO 123/317.

74. Tippu Tip to Becker, 13 April 1893, *IB* (27 May 1893); Labosse to Develle, 26 April 1893, PZ 17.

75. Wahis to Dhanis, 24 December 1892, undated fragment of a letter, Dhanis to Delcommune, 28 December 1892, DP; Comeliau, *Dhanis*, 104–106; Ceulemans, *La Question Arabe*, 345–347.

76. Rapport [June 1893], Meurtre de Lippens et De Bruyne, DP.

77. Schweitzer, *Emin*, II, 286–295; *MG* 10(1893), 92; Mohun interview, *ZG* (7 November 1894), and "Emin Pasha," 591–598; Stuhlmann, *Emin Pascha*, 829–830. See above, p. 216.

78. "Les Arabes sur le Haut Congo," 84 (Hodister information).

79. Janssens and Cateaux, *Les Belges au Congo*, I, 93–100; Hinde, *Congo Arabs*, 117ff.; Michaux, 19 January 1893, *MA* 5(1892–1893), 268; Wouters and Cassart to Dhanis, 11 January 1893, DP; Sims to Johnston, 6 October 1893, in Anderson to Plunkett, 17 May 1894, FO 123/326.

80. Hinde, *Congo Arabs*, 153–179, and "Three Years' Travel," 434; *EB* (29 August 1893); Nyangwe letter, 3 February 1893, *ZG* (11 October 1893); de Wouters d'Oplinter, 20 February 1892, 5 March 1892, *MA* 5(1892–1893), 368–369; Michaux, *Au Congo*, 217–218; Fivé to Dhanis, 3 April 1893, DP; Janssens and Cateaux, *Les Belges au Congo*, I, 101–106; Comeliau, *Dhanis*, 91–97.

81. Scheerlinck in *EB* (12 April 1893); *IB* (17 November 1893); Hinde, *Congo Arabs*, 181–203, and "Three Years' Travel," 435; "Kassongo," *MA* 6(1893–1894), 89–94 (information from C. Gillain); Janssens and Cateaux, *Les Belges au Congo*, I, 107–112.

82. Chaltin report, *MG* 10(1893), 70–72; *IB* (10 December and 13 December 1893); Agenda 1893 de Ponthier, DP; Janssens and Cateaux, *Les Belges au Congo*, I, 112–113.

83. Tobback report, 21 January 1892 on, MCB; Chaltin and Tobback in *EB* (17 August 1893); Tobback interview, *EB* (25 September 1893); *MG* 10(1893), 77; De Thier, *Singhitini,* 44–50; Chapaux, *Le Congo,* 304–309.

84. Marie to Dhanis, 24 August 1893, ? to Dhanis, 1 September 1893, 7 January 1894, Wouters to Dhanis, 29 October 1893, 13 November 1893, Dhanis to Wouters, 29–30 October 1893, 9 January 1894, Dhanis to Commander Stanley Falls, undated, 7 November 1893, and other correspondence, DP; Mubaha Shihaibi to Tippu Tip, 13 February 1894, Sayf bin Khamis bin Said to Tippu Tip, 7 March 1894, B–27, ZA; A. Verbecken, "La Campagne contra le Chef Arabe Rumaliza: Textes Inédits," *BSARSC* 4(1958), 813–842; Mohun interview, *EB* (21 September 1894); Josué Henri, *De Kiroundou au Tanganika* (Bruxelles, 1896), 5–18; *ZG* extracts in Blauchon to MAE, 14 May 1894, PZ 19; Janssens and Cateaux, *Les Belges au Congo*, I, 114–134; M. Coosemans, "Fernand Hambursin," *BCB,* I, 475–477; Comeliau, *Dhanis,* 118–128.

85. Tippu Tip to Euan Smith, 6 December 1890, E–131, ZA; Euan Smith to Salisbury, 31 December 1890, with FO note on Johnston's views, FO 84/2066; Tippu Tip, *Maisha,* 163, 165; C. Smith to Salisbury, 20 July 1891, FO 84/2148; Ottavi to Ribot, 18 August 1891, in MAE to Etienne, 6 October 1891, OI 18/100, AOM; Portal to Salisbury, 9 October 1891 (enc. Tippu Tip's version of the case), FO 84/2149; Boustead, Ridley and Co. to Thompson, 21 May 1892, CA 8, LMS; Smith, *Emin Pasha,* 295; Zanzibar correspondent, 20 July 1891, *The Times* (21 July 1891), 5; Luwel, *Johnston,* 89; Norman R. Bennett, "Introduction to the Second Edition," in Swann, *Slave-Hunters,* lv–lvi, n. 117.

86. Rodd to Rosebery, 5 March 1893, FO 107/3; Jacques journal, 25 March 1893, *MA* 5(1892–1893), 411; Jacques interview, press clippings, DP; Anderson to Plunkett, 19 April 1894 (enc. Cracknall to FO, 18 April 1894), Hardinge to FO, 6 June 1894, FO 123/326; Blauchon to MAE, 29 May 1894, PZ 19.

87. Cracknall to Kimberley, 25 April 1894, FO 107/19.

88. Hinde, *Congo Arabs,* 23–24; Agenda de Ponthier, 1893, DP; Sims to Johnston, 6 October 1893, in Anderson to Plunkett, 17 May 1894, FO 123/326.

89. Blauchon to MAE, 29 May 1894, PZ 19; Hardinge to FO, 6 June 1894, FO 123/326; Hamed bin Muhammad bin Sinan el Barwani to Tippu Tip, 8 September 1894, Rashid bin Muhammad to Tippu Tip, 9 September 1894, in Hardinge to Kimberley, 30 November 1894, in Kimberley to Plunkett, 2 January 1895, FO 123/337.

90. Schweitzer, *Emin,* II, 298–300; Léo Lejeune, *Lothaire* (Bruxelles, 1935), 93–94; *MG* 11(1894), 321–322; M. Coosemans, "Rachid Ben Mahomed," *BCB,* II, 793–796; Michaux, *Au Congo,* 257.

91. Pickersgill to Rosebery, 18 September 1893 (information from Bannister), FO 63/1252; Francken to Dhanis, 10 February 1894, DP; Slade, *Leopold's Congo,* 117.

92. De Thier, *Singhitini,* 57ff.; H. Sutton Smith, *"Yakusu": The Very Heart of Africa* (London, n.d.), 145; Armand Abel, *Les Musulmans Noirs du Maniema* (Bruxelles, 1960).

93. Lopasic, *Lerman,* 66; summary of Stanley speech, 24 April 1890, Correspondance et Documents, Afrique, Conférence Anti-Esclavagiste de Bruxelles, 3, MAEB; Brode, *Tippoo Tib,* 253; Lyne, *Mathews,* 214–215; E. D. Moore, *Ivory, Scourge of Africa* (New York, 1931), 143; *B. des Amis des Esclaves,* 11(1896), 112;

Cooper, *Plantation Slavery*, 68–69; Frank Vincent, *Actual Africa, or, the Coming Continent* (New York, 1895), 282; Roy Devereux, *Side Lights on South Africa* (London, 1899), 229–230; *ZG* (19 November 1897), 5, (21 December 1898), 3–6, (14 June 1905), 3.

CHAPTER 16

1. Storms, Description de Zanzibar, and Notes, SP; Foot to Granville, 7 February 1884 (Pulley information), FO 84/1662; Johnston, "British Central Africa," 738–739; Frederick L. Maitland Moir, "Eastern Route to Central Africa," *SGM* 1(1885), 110, *After Livingstone*, 82–85, and "Englishmen and Arabs," 628; Giraud, *Afrique Equatoriale*, 376, 429–430; Trivier, *Voyage*, 275, 283–286; Thomson, *Central African Lakes*, II, 16–17; Wissmann, *Second Journey*, 268–270; Hore, *Tanganyika*, 235–237; Hore to Thompson, 25 November 1885, CA 6; Carson to Thompson, 27 June 1889, CA 7, LMS; Wright and Lary, "Swahili Settlements," 554–558; Roberts, "Abdullah ibn Suliman," 244.

2. Trivier, *Voyage*, 215, 231; Prouvot, 15 October 1891, *GWE* 4(1892), 204; Renault, *Lavigerie*, I, 323–324; Brown, "Ujiji," 113–116, 166–167; Swann, *Slave-Hunters*, 87; W. S. Palmer, "Lake Tanganyika: A Voyage from Ujiji to Uguha," *The Juvenile Missionary Magazine and Annual* 15(1881), 123.

3. Jane F. Moir, *A Lady's Letters from Central Africa* (Glasgow, 1891), 43; Hore, *Tanganyika*, 86–87, and "An Arab Friend in Central Africa," *CLMS* (1891), 235–238; Swann, *Slave-Hunters*, 87; Jameson, *Rear Column*, 284.

4. Dromaux, 10 July 1884, Coulbois, 2 September 1884, *CTSM* (1er trim. 1885), 286–287, 292–293; Kibanga journal, 12 November 1884, *CTSM* (2me trim. 1885), 419; Jones to Thompson, 2 December 1884, CA 5, Hore to Thompson, 21 March 1885, CA 6, LMS; Guillet, undated, Coulbois, 3 December 1885, *BMA* (1883–1886), 298–299, 455; Joubert to Lavigerie, 8 June 1889, 8 October 1890, *BSAF* (1890), 90, (1891–1892), 82–88; Brown, "Ujiji," 172–174.

5. Kitchener to Rosebery, 30 June 1886, FO 84/1799; Jacques, 10 August 1892, *MA* 5(1892–1893), 44; Brown, "Ujiji," 176–177, 189.

6. Thomson, *Fondation du Congo*, 178ff.; M. L. Stiers, "La Frontière Orientale du Congo Belge," *BSIRCB* 8(1937), 307–329; Wm. Roger Louis, *Ruanda-Urundi* (Oxford, 1963), 4–29.

7. Bennett, "Introduction," x–xvii; Brown, "Ujiji," 179ff.

8. Moinet to Lavigerie, 20 June 1883, *APF* 56(1884), 166–185; Guillet to Lavigerie, 19 October 1883, *BMA* (1883–1886), 175–176; Notice sur Storms, and Journal de la Station de Mpala, 6 September 1884 on, SP; Moinet, 15 September 1884, *CTSM* (1er trim. 1885), 294, 302; Hore to Thompson, 7 September 1885, CA 6, LMS; Renault, *Lavigerie*, I, 268–273; Heremans, *L'A. I. A. au Tanganika*, 51, 106–110.

9. Journal de la Station de Mpala, 30 January 1885, SP; Kibanga journal, 1–2 May 1886, 22 July 1886, 13–14 August 1886, 6 September 1886, *CTSM* (1er trim. 1887), 306–308, (2me trim. 1887), 454, 459–460, 467; Coulbois, *Tanganyka*, 78ff.

10. Moinet to Storms, 26 August 1885, 15 September 1885, 30 September 1885, 4 November 1885, 14 January 1886, 10 February 1886, May 1886, SP; Moinet, 12 January 1886, *CTSM* (1er trim. 1886), 193–194; Mpala journal, March–April 1886, *CTSM* (2me trim. 1886), 476; Heremans, *L'A. I. A. au Tanganika*, 108–117.

11. Rumaliza quoted in Brown, "Ujiji," 172; Moinet journal, Kibanga, December 1887, Coulbois, 2 January 1889, *BMA* (1888–1889), 300–305, 545–546; Kibanga journal, 13 November 1888, 23 November 1888, 16 December 1888, *CTSM* (4me trim. 1889), 155–158.

12. Wright to Thompson, 26 July 1888, Swann to Thompson, 30 January 1889, CA 7, LMS; Bresson, 1 January 1890, *BMA* (1890), 684–685.

13. Playfair to Lister, 3 September 1886 (enc. Lavigerie's note, with Kirk memo., 8 September 1886), E–95, ZA; Courcel to MAE, 9 July 1886, AD 71; Freycinet to Herbette, 3 January 1887, AD 74; Note pour l'Ambassadeur d'Allemagne à Paris, AD 75; Mgr. Baunard, *Le Cardinal Lavigerie* (Paris, 1912), II, 348–351.

14. Vivian to Salisbury, 16 August 1888, FO 123/244; Bennett, "Introduction," xxiv; Cardinal Lavigerie, *Documents sur la Fondation de l'Oeuvre Antiesclavagiste* (St. Cloud, 1889) (for all Lavigerie's speeches); Renault, *Lavigerie,* II, 73ff.

15. Waddington to Goblet, 31 July 1888, AngD 832, 7 August 1888, AngD 833, 3 November 1888, 28 November 1888, AngD 835; Cameron to Kirk, 24 August 1888, Kirk to Hill, 27 August 1888, notes of Ferguson, Lister, Salisbury, and Hill on Vivian's account of Lavigerie's planned crusade, August–September 1888, *Correspondence . . . Relative to the Slave Trade* (printed for the private use of the Foreign Office), ZA; Waller, "Slave-Stick," 533–537; Stanley, 19 October 1890, *The Times* (21 October 1890), 8.

16. Jean Bruhat, "Léopold II," in Ch.-André Julien, ed., *Les Politiques d'Expansion Impérialiste* (Paris, 1949), 97; Roeykens, "Béthune," 1ff., 227ff.

17. Joubert, undated report, Moinet to Storms, September 1888, *MA* 1(1888), 57–59, 130; Mpala journal, 5 November 1888, *CTSM* (4 trim. 1889), 164–165; Moinet, 20 March 1889, *BMA* (1888–1889), 643–644; Joubert to his brother, 23 January 1889, *BSAF* (1888–1889), 640.

18. Carson to Euan Smith, 7 January 1889, in Euan Smith to FO, 4 March 1889, E–110, Carson to Euan Smith, 10 September 1889, in Euan Smith to FO, 2 February 1890, u.v., statement of Ali Shangwe, 29 December 1890, B–10, Johnston to Euan Smith, 29 January 1891, E–137, ZA; Kibanga journal, 11 January 1889, Mpala journal, 23 January 1889, *CTSM* (4me trim. 1889), 162, 169.

19. Guillemé, n.d., *BMA* (1891–1892), 18–23; Joubert to Keller, 12 April 1890, Joubert to Charette, 27 June 1890, *MA* 3(1890–1891), 17–24; Joubert to his brother, 3 May 1891, 2 June 1891, *MA* 4(1891–1892), 69–72.

20. Bridoux, 6 September 1890, *APF,* 62(1890), 277–278; Josset, 17 October 1890, *BMA* (1891–1892), 118.

21. Moinet, January 1891, van Oost, 10 November 1891, *BMA* (1891–1892), 175, 384; Jacques, 21 April 1891, Joubert to his brother, 8 May 1891, *MA* 4(1891–1892), XXVII, 70; Bennett, "Introduction," xxviii; Brown, "Ujiji," 197.

22. Jacques, 17 October 1891, and subsequent letters, *MA* 4(1891–1892), 83ff., 233ff.; Jacques, 5 January 1893, *MA* 5(1892–1893), 325; van Oost, [November 1891], *BMA* (1891–1892), 387; Marquis de Bonchamps in Joseph Ch. M. Verhoeven, *Jacques de Dixmude l'Africain: Contribution à l'Histoire de la Société Antiesclavagiste Belge, 1888–1894* (Bruxelles, n.d.), 87; Labosse to Develle, 30 January 1893, PZ 17.

23. Swann information, in Sharpe to Rosebery, 16 May 1892, FO 2/56; Jacques, 5 and 11 June 1892, in Verhoeven, *Jacques,* 99, 102; Jacques to State Kasongo resident, 17 June 1893, DP; Jacques, 10 August 1892, *MA* 5(1892–1893), 42–44; Portal to FO, 14 May 1892, E–140, Rumaliza to Tippu Tip, 4

Shaban 1309, B–15, Rumaliza to Holmwood, 21 February 1893, B–24, ZA; Renault, *Lavigerie*, II, 429.

24. Bonchamps information, in A. J. W[auters], "La Révolte Arabe," *MG* 9(1892), 72; Decle, *Savage Africa*, 307; Ottavi to Ribot, 5 July 1892, PZ 16; Labosse to Develle, 30 January 1893, PZ 17; Jacques, 21 April 1892, *MA* 4(1891–1892), XXVIII–XXIX; A.-M. de Saint-Berthuin, *Alexis Vrithoff* (Lille, 1893), 151ff.

25. Jacques, 10 August 1892, 8 September 1892, Delcommune, undated, Joubert, 27 September 1892, A. Duchesne, "Notre Interview avec M. Diderrich," *MA* 5(1892–1893), 45–58, 194; Labosse to Ribot, 23 November 1893, PZ 16; Delcommune, *Vingt Anées*, II, 474–476; Renault, *Lavigerie*, II, 431.

26. Joubert, 17 October 1892, Jacques, 5 January 1893, 10 February 1893, Long, 7 January 1893, *MA* 5(1892–1893), 139, 314–318, 326, 347–348, 350; Renault, *Lavigerie*, II, 433–437.

27. Jacques, 10 February 1893, 25 March 1893, *MA* 5(1892–1893), 350, 410–418; Doquier, 11 June 1893, M. de Tiège, "Nouvelles du Tanganika," *MA* 6(1893–1894), 7, 147; Note (no. 610), DP; Swann to Thompson, 17 May 1893, 21 June 1893, Shaw to Thompson, 7 June 1894, CA 9, LMS; Decle, *Savage Africa*, 285, 331–332; Sigl, "Berichte," 6–7.

28. Reports of the operations are in *MA* 6(1893–1894) and 7(1895).

29. Elliot, *Mid-Africa*, 285; Sone (?) to Dhanis, 11 October 1893, Report of meeting Sef bin Rashid in October 1893 (15 June 1896), DP; Shaw to Thompson, 7 June 1894, CA 9, LMS; *JB* (7 September 1894); Prince, *Gegen Araber*, 293; Renault, *Lavigerie*, II, 443–444; Tippu Tip, *Maisha*, 169; Kandt, *Caput Nili*, I, 29; German Consul to Sultan of Zanzibar, 25 October 1899, F–2, ZA; Moore, *Ivory*, 142; Swann, *Slave-Hunters*, 87; Bontinck, *Tippo Tib*, 294.

30. Leue, "Udjiji," 321–328; Ramsay, 1 August 1896, *DKB* 7(1896), 770–773; Sigl, "Berichte," 7–11; Draper to Thompson, 11 April 1896, 6 June 1896, 12 September 1896, CA 9, LMS; Brown, "Ujiji," 280ff.

Index

Abd al Gawi bin Abdullah, 146, 147
Abdullah bin Nasibu. *See* Kisessa
Abed bin Salum al Khaduri, 113, 114
Abed bin Salim al Khetiri, 217, 218,
    224, 311n.
Abushiri (Arab leader), 149, 150, 151,
    155–59, 161, 164, 165, 166–67,
    168, 169, 170, 171, 172, 174,
    175, 202, 298n.
African Christians. *See* Bombay
    Christians
African Lakes Co., 82–83, 84, 87,
    187, 193, 199
Agriculture, 234
    cattle herds, 83
    cloves, 45
    sesame plant, 45
    sugar cane, 45
Ahmad bin Fuomo Loti. *See* Simba
Akinola, G. K., 121
Ali bin Sultan, 203, 204, 211, 214
Ali bin Surur, 193, 196, 197, 199
Amir bin Suliman al Lemki, 146, 147
Apostasy, 5
Arabs
    and African-Arab relations, 79, 91,
        122
    in the Congo, 113–14
    conspiracy theory about, 185–86,
        192, 302n.
    defined, 9, 261n.

ethnic composition of, 9, 10
and European expansion into East
    Africa, 68, 78–79, 95–111
European views about, 7–9, 8–11,
    12–13, 14, 80, 90, 94, 113
expansion by, 7, 93, 121, 122
important, 112–14
mistreatment by Europeans of, 27,
    147, 171
and Scots, 81
and slave trade, 13–14, 180
working for Europeans, 94–95

Bagamoyo, 32, 42, 56, 66, 146, 150,
    153, 157, 165, 242, 298n.
Barghash (Arab Sultan), 5, 25, 27, 38
    in the Congo, 118, 218, 22–23
    and the Germans, 130–35, 141,
        142, 143
    in Lake Tanganyika region, 246
    political influence of, 60, 87–88,
        123, 124
    and the Sultanate, 53–67
Basoko, 233, 241
Baumann, Oscar, 31, 158
Baxter, E. J., 95, 96, 97, 98
Becker, Jerôme, 12, 106, 107, 218
Berlin (Germany), 147, 148
Berlin Conference, 131
Bismarck, 138, 149, 162, 181
Blood brotherhood, 110

Speke, John, 6, 36, 37, 48, 49, 93
Stanley, Henry M., 36, 47, 69, 89, 91,
   94, 95, 100, 106, 107, 113, 117,
   129, 208, 214, 217, 225, 226
Stanley, Henry M. *How I Found
   Livingstone,* 129
Stanley Falls, 115, 217, 219, 223,
   232, 234, 235, 238, 241, 243
Steere, Edward, 7, 34, 43, 44, 55, 57,
   76, 78, 80, 82, 85
Stewart, James, 81
Stokes, Charles, 173, 206, 207, 213,
   214, 308n.
Storms, Emile, 107, 109, 247
Streeter, J., 72, 74
Sulayman bin Hamid, 65
Suliman bin Nassir, 151, 167
Suliman bin Sayf, 164, 167
Suliman bin Zahayr, 204, 206, 209
Sulimani bin Abedi, 119
Sultan, defined, 22–23
Syphilis, 6

Tabora, 35, 36, 46, 48, 89, 90, 106,
   107, 109, 211
Tanzania, 34, 110, 149, 174
Taylor, Isaac, 12
Taylor, W., 134
Thetis (ship)
Toeppen, Kurt, 31, 133, 211–12
Tippu Tip, 5, 11, 12, 14, 35, 69, 89,
   90, 91, 107, 112, 113, 114, 115,
   118, 123, 196, 212, 217, 218,
   219, 220, 223, 236, 245, 247,
   251, 285n.
  and Arabs, 226, 238, 239
  and Europeans, 222–26, 228–30,
   232, 242–44
  as a personality, 116–17
  and Rumaliza, 246
  and Stanley, 224–26, 227, 230–31
Tongwe, 30
Tozer, Bishop William, 27, 43, 44, 76
Trade, 4, 31–32, 35, 36, 110–11, 114,
   116, 205

Trade routes, 32, 37, 83, 89, 91, 95,
   96, 131
Tumbatu, 23

Ugogo, 32, 35, 120, 130
Ujiji, 48, 81, 98, 100, 116, 246, 252,
   253
Uman, 3, 21, 22, 33
United States, 4, 11, 39
Universities' Mission, 6, 43, 57, 72,
   76, 77, 78, 80, 86, 88, 124
Unyanyembe, 35, 36, 37, 38, 47, 48,
   49, 89, 91, 133
Urban II (pope), 15

Vangele, Alphonse, 219–20
Vohsen, Ernst, 146, 147, 148, 153,
   162, 176

Wakefield, Thomas, 43, 76
West, Arthur, 4, 12
White Fathers (mission), 78, 99, 100,
   102, 104, 105, 212, 247, 248,
   250
White Nile, 47
Wilson, George, 100, 101
Wissmann, Hermann von, 12, 69,
   120, 162–63, 169, 171, 172,
   173, 174, 177, 181, 183, 202,
   214, 215, 222, 231, 252, 253

Yao (tribe), 34, 56, 79, 80, 85–86, 88,
   150–51, 200
Young, E. D., 79, 80

Zanzibar
  African-German struggle in, 150–
   51, 163
  Arab-British relations in, 21–23,
   25–27, 131, 137, 141, 145, 155–
   56, 179–83
  Arab-German relations in, 129–43,
   144, 146–52, 153, 158, 162–74,
   176
  Arab-German war in, 162, 165–76

and neighboring coastal regions,
  28–35
and neighboring inland regions, 35–
  38

political influence of, 119, 121
state revenues in, 12, 119
and Treaty of 1886, 140–41
Zaramo (tribe), 32, 47, 66, 125